The Ultimate
FRENCH
Review and Practice

The *Ultimate* FRENCH

Review and Practice

Second Edition

MASTERING FRENCH GRAMMAR
FOR CONFIDENT COMMUNICATION

DAVID M. STILLMAN, PH.D.,
AND RONNI L. GORDON, PH.D.

New York Chicago San Francisco Lisbon London Madrid Mexico City
Milan New Delhi San Juan Seoul Singapore Sydney Toronto

Copyright © 2011 by The McGraw-Hill Companies, Inc. All rights reserved. Printed in the United States of America. Except as permitted under the United States Copyright Act of 1976, no part of this publication may be reproduced or distributed in any form or by any means, or stored in a database or retrieval system, without the prior written permission of the publisher.

Printed in the United States of America.

9 10 11 12 13 14 15   QVS/QVS   1 9 8 7 6 5

ISBN   978-0-07-174414-0 (book and CD set)
MHID   0-07-174414-2

ISBN   978-0-07-174415-7 (book alone)
MHID   0-07-174415-0

Library of Congress Control Number   2010925184

By the same authors

The Ultimate French Verb Review and Practice: Mastering Verbs and Sentence Building for Confident Communication
The Big Blue Book of French Verbs
The Blue Pocket Book of French Verbs

The Ultimate Spanish Verb Review and Practice: Mastering Verbs and Sentence Building for Confident Communication
The Big Red Book of Spanish Verbs
The Red Pocket Book of Spanish Verbs

Interior design by Village Bookworks, Inc.

CD-ROM for Windows
To install: Insert the CD-ROM into your CD-ROM drive. The CD-ROM will start automatically. If it does not, double-click on MY COMPUTER; find and open your CD-ROM disk drive, then double-click on the install.exe icon.

CD-ROM for Mac
To install: Insert the CD-ROM into your CD-ROM drive. A window will open with the contents of the CD. Drag the program icon to your Applications folder. For easy access, create an alias of the program on your desktop or your dock.

Minimum System Requirements
Computer: Windows 2000, XP, Vista, 7 / Mac OS X 10.3.x, 10.4.x, 10.5.x
Pentium II, AMD K6-2, or better / Power PC (G3 recommended) or better; any Intel processor
256 MB RAM
14″ color monitor
8× or better CD-ROM
Sound card
Installation: Necessary free hard-drive space: 300 MB
Settings: 800 × 600 screen resolution
256 (8-bit) colors (minimum)
Thousands (24- or 32-bit) of colors (preferred)

For additional audio practice
Further audio practice is available online at www.audiostudyplayer.com. To access the recordings within the Audio Study Player application:
> French > For Study and Review > The Ultimate French Review and Practice

McGraw-Hill books are available at special quantity discounts to use as premiums and sales promotions or for use in corporate training programs. To contact a representative, please e-mail us at bulksales@mcgraw-hill.com.

This book is printed on acid-free paper.

Pour Alex, Mimi, Kathleen, Juliana et Moriah,
les étoiles de notre firmament

Preface

He who does not know foreign languages does not know anything about his own.
    —Johann Wolfgang von Goethe

The Ultimate French Review and Practice, Second Edition, is a uniquely comprehensive, integrated, and engaging review book that will provide learners with the solid knowledge needed to increase their confidence in using French to express their own thoughts, to comprehend those of French speakers, and to communicate in both speaking and writing in a wide variety of situations.

Designed to provide advanced beginners, intermediate students, and advanced learners of French with a powerful tool for review and progress in the language, this book presents clear, concise, and well-organized grammar explanations with examples that reflect everyday usage, most often in the form of conversational exchanges. The presentations of structure are easy to understand, and the examples will encourage learners to see the study of grammar as a stepping stone to communication.

We have expanded and enhanced the exercises to give you even more practice. The exercises provide extensive practice for all the grammar topics that learners of French at this level should know. These engaging exercises are contextualized, and the instructions in French help set the scene and prepare you for the task at hand. Vocabulary lists provide a review of the vocabulary common to most first- and second-year French textbooks, as well as new words and phrases essential for particular exercises, thus increasing your vocabulary and enhancing your ability to express yourself on a variety of topics. Vocabulary presentations are grouped by topic and are integrated with the exercises. Exercises reflect authentic, everyday language usage and touch on all areas of modern life, including business and technology.

Many self-expression exercises are included to encourage you to use the target grammar and vocabulary presented to express your own ideas. The **Activité orale** at the end of each chapter is a culminating exercise in which you and a friend or colleague can practice the grammatical structures and topics presented in the chapter by exchanging information with each other.

The Ultimate French Review and Practice, Second Edition, has 28 chapters divided into five parts.

I   Verbs—Basic Forms and Uses
II   Nouns and Their Modifiers; Pronouns
III Other Elements of the Sentence
IV   Verbs in Two-Clause Sentences
V   Idiomatic Usage

Notes culturelles are featured throughout the book. These cultural notes enhance the effectiveness of the grammar exercises by providing an authentic French context in which to practice. To further your progress, we have also included a chapter of important idioms and proverbs (Chapter 28).

New to this edition are seven sections called **Speak Real French**. Placed strategically in the book, they explain key differences between spoken and written French, thus enhancing students' abilities to speak correctly and understand French as spoken by native speakers.

For convenient learner reference, the appendices of *The Ultimate French Review and Practice*, Second Edition, include easy-to-read verb charts. Also included in the appendices is a section on written conventions, which explains French rules of spelling and punctuation. The Answer Key provided at the end of the book allows you to check your work.

The CD-ROM component of *The Ultimate French Review and Practice*, Second Edition, contains hundreds of multiple-choice exercises that allow you to practice the tenses, grammatical structures, and idiomatic usage included in the five parts of the book. The **Diagnostic Test** and **Review Test** provide you with an excellent tool to assess your progress. To aid you in your comprehension and pronunciation, **Listening for Key Contrasts** drills help you distinguish verb endings that may sound similar to English speakers but are very different in meaning. This section targets some of the most important sound contrasts in the French verb system. The **Audio Modules**, recorded by native speakers of French, present dialogues and narratives designed to improve your listening comprehension and pronunciation. Preceding each audio passage is a list of **Ten Key Words and Expressions** for listening and repeating that helps you prepare for listening to the passage. After listening to and repeating the audio passage, you will do exercises to test your comprehension. You can read a **Transcription** of the audio passage as you listen to the passage a second time. A **Glossary** of words and expressions can be activated to check meaning, and you can highlight words in the audio passage to view definitions in English.

The **Audio Modules** present delightful, authentic scenes with real people who talk about their families, work, travels, and life goals in settings and with stories that reflect our daily lives—buying a house, business and the office, remodeling a home, love, problems at the airport, owning a restaurant, family problems, career changes, conversing on the telephone, shopping, and others. The passages contain useful, authentic vocabulary that will serve you well in your communication with native speakers of French. You will be amazed at how much you will understand and be able to say after you have worked through the CD-ROM!

The Ultimate French Review and Practice, Second Edition, retains the highly effective pedagogy and most important features that made the first edition so popular and successful with users. It is ideal for learners working on their own and as an ancillary for students using a textbook in a classroom setting. Chapters may be covered in any order, allowing learners and teachers to individualize grammar practice.

David M. Stillman, Ph.D.
Ronni L. Gordon, Ph.D.

Contents

II Nouns and Their Modifiers; Pronouns

III   Other Elements of the Sentence

IV Verbs in Two-Clause Sentences

V Idiomatic Usage

The Ultimate
FRENCH
Review and Practice

Verbs—Basic Forms and Uses

Present Tense

Verbs are presented in conjugation paradigms that summarize the forms that the verbs have in each tense. French verbs change their form for person and number. Verbs are said to have three persons: the speaker, the person spoken to, and a third person, referring neither to the speaker nor the person spoken to. French, like English, has two numbers: singular and plural.

The persons of the verb and their corresponding pronouns in English are as follows.

	SINGULAR	PLURAL
FIRST PERSON	I	we
SECOND PERSON	you	you
THIRD PERSON	he/she/it	they

The persons of the verb and their corresponding pronouns in French are as follows.

	SINGULAR	PLURAL
FIRST PERSON	je	nous
SECOND PERSON	tu	vous
THIRD PERSON	il/elle/on	ils/elles

Note these differences between the two languages:

1 · English has only one form for *you*; French has two. **Tu** is a singular form and is informal; it is used to address one person with whom you have an informal relationship: a family member, a close friend, a fellow student, etc. **Vous** is both the plural of **tu** and a formal singular form. It is used to address one person with whom you have a formal relationship: a stranger, a customer, a colleague at work, etc.

2 · French has no word for *it*. All nouns, whether animate or inanimate, are referred to as either **il** or **elle**. Thus, masculine nouns such as **le jeune homme** and **le crayon** are referred to as **il**, while feminine nouns such as **la femme** and **la ville** are referred to as **elle**.

3 · French makes a gender distinction in the third person plural. **Ils** refers to masculine plural nouns, while **elles** refers to feminine plural nouns. **Ils** also refers to groups of males and females, while **elles** refers to groups consisting of females only.

—Où sont Martin et Élisabeth?   *Where are Martin and Elizabeth?*
—**Ils** sont là.   *They're here.*

—Où sont Caroline et Anne?   *Where are Caroline and Anne?*
—**Elles** sont là.   *They're here.*

4 · The pronoun **on** has two main uses in French.

- **On** is used as a general subject similar to English *one, people, you, they,* or the passive voice.

    On mange bien à Paris.   ***People eat*** *well in Paris.*
    Ici **on parle** français.   *French* ***is spoken*** *here.*

- In contemporary French, **on** replaces **nous** in everyday speech and writing. Note that even when **on** is used to mean *we,* it takes a third person singular verb form.

    —Toi et ta famille, vous restez   *Are you and your family staying in town?*
    en ville?
    —Non, **on part** en vacances.   *No,* ***we're leaving*** *on vacation.*

The Present Tense of Regular -er, -ir, and -re Verbs

The present tense of a regular verb is formed by dropping the infinitive ending (-**er**, -**ir**, or -**re**) and adding the appropriate present tense ending.

Verbs of the first conjugation (-**er** verbs) are conjugated like **parler** (*to speak*).

	SINGULAR		PLURAL	
FIRST PERSON	je	parl**e**	nous	parl**ons**
SECOND PERSON	tu	parl**es**	vous	parl**ez**
THIRD PERSON	il/elle	parl**e**	ils/elles	parl**ent**
	on	parl**e**		

Some Common -er Verbs

accepter *to accept*
accompagner *to accompany*
actualiser *to bring up to date*
adorer *to adore, love*
afficher *to post; to display* (computer)
aider *to help*
aimer *to like, love*
allumer *to light, turn on (an appliance)*
apporter *to bring*
apprécier *to appreciate (value, rate highly)*
arriver *to arrive*
bavarder *to chat*
casser *to break*
cesser *to stop*
chanter *to sing*

chercher *to look for*
cliquer *to click* (computer)
coller *to paste* (computer)
continuer *to continue*
copier *to copy*
couper *to cut*
créer *to create*
danser *to dance*
déboguer *to debug*
décider *to decide*
déjeuner *to have lunch*
demander *to ask, ask for*
dépenser *to spend (money)*
désirer *to desire, want*
dessiner *to draw*

détester *to hate*
dîner *to have dinner*
discuter *to discuss*
donner *to give*
écouter *to listen to*
éditer *to edit*
emporter *to carry/take away, carry off*
emprunter *to borrow*
enseigner *to teach*
entrer *to go/come in, enter*
étudier *to study*
exporter *to export*
fermer *to close; to turn off (an appliance)*
fonder *to found*
formater *to format*
frapper *to strike, hit*
gagner *to earn, win*
garder *to keep*
habiter *to live (reside)*
hésiter *to hesitate*
importer *to import*
imprimer *to print*
installer *to install*
inviter *to invite*
jouer *to play*
laisser *to leave, let*
laver *to wash*
marcher *to walk*
monter *to go up(stairs)*
montrer *to show*
naviguer (sur Internet) *to surf the Web*
organiser *to organize*
oublier *to forget*

parler *to speak*
passer *to pass; to spend (time)*
penser *to think*
photocopier *to photocopy, xerox*
porter *to carry, wear*
pousser *to push*
pratiquer *to practice*
préparer *to prepare*
présenter *to present*
prêter *to lend*
quitter *to leave (a person/place)*
raconter *to tell, tell about, relate*
refuser *to refuse*
regarder *to look at*
remercier *to thank*
rencontrer *to meet (by chance)*
rentrer *to return, go back*
retourner *to return, come/go back*
retrouver *to meet (by appointment)*
rouler *to move, travel (of a vehicle)*
saluer *to greet*
sauvegarder *to save (a computer file)*
supporter *to bear, stand*
supprimer *to delete (a computer file); to cancel*
surfer (sur) le Web *to surf the Web*
téléphoner *to phone*
texter *to send a text message to*
tourner *to turn*
travailler *to work*
traverser *to cross*
trouver *to find*
voler *to fly*

Verbs of the second conjugation (-**ir** verbs) are conjugated like **finir** (*to finish*).

	SINGULAR		PLURAL	
FIRST PERSON	je	fin**is**	nous	fin**issons**
SECOND PERSON	tu	fin**is**	vous	fin**issez**
THIRD PERSON	il/elle	fin**it**	ils/elles	fin**issent**
	on	fin**it**		

Some Common -ir Verbs

agir *to act*	**guérir** *to cure, make better*
applaudir *to applaud*	**maigrir** *to get thin*
atterrir *to land*	**mincir** *to get thin*
avertir *to warn*	**obéir** *to obey*
bâtir *to build*	**périr** *to perish*
choisir *to choose*	**réfléchir** *to think, reflect*
définir *to define*	**remplir** *to fill*
désobéir *to disobey*	**réunir** *to bring together, collect, gather*
établir *to establish*	**réussir** *to succeed*
finir *to finish*	**rougir** *to blush*
gémir *to moan*	**salir** *to make dirty*
grossir *to get fat*	

Verbs of the third conjugation (-**re** verbs) are conjugated like **rendre** (*to give back*).

	SINGULAR		PLURAL	
FIRST PERSON	je	rends	nous	rend**ons**
SECOND PERSON	tu	rends	vous	rend**ez**
THIRD PERSON	il/elle	rend	ils/elles	rend**ent**
	on	rend		

Some Common -re Verbs

attendre *to wait for*	**prétendre** *to claim*
confondre *to confuse*	**rendre** *to give back*
défendre *to forbid*	**répondre** *to answer*
descendre *to go down(stairs)*	**rompre** *to break, break off* (especially figuratively)
entendre *to hear*	
interrompre *to interrupt*	**tendre** *to stretch out, offer; to tend to*
mordre *to bite*	**tordre** *to twist*
perdre *to lose*	**vendre** *to sell*

NOTES

1 · If the verb begins with a vowel or mute **h**, then **je** becomes **j'**.

j'arrive
j'entends
j'habite

2 · The subject pronoun **on** refers to people in general or to a nonspecific subject. It is often equivalent to the passive voice in English.

Ici **on parle** français.	*French **is spoken** here.*
On cherche un secrétaire.	*Secretary **wanted**.*

In everyday French, **on** + third person singular verb means *we* and replaces the **nous** form of the verb.

Aujourd'hui **on dîne** au restaurant.	*Today **we're having dinner** at a restaurant.*
On habite à Paris maintenant.	***We live** in Paris now.*

3 · Most verbs of the third conjugation (**-re** verbs) have a stem ending in **-d** like **vendre**. Those few whose stems don't end in **-d**, such as **rompre** (*to break*) and **interrompre** (*to interrupt*), add a **t** in the third person singular.

il/elle romp**t**
il/elle interromp**t**

 A *Une soirée en famille.* *Hélène Poiret décrit une soirée passée en famille. Formez des phrases pour savoir ce qu'elle dit. Suivez le modèle.*

> MODÈLE   aujourd'hui / nous / passer la soirée / à la maison
> → Aujourd'hui nous passons la soirée à la maison.

1. maman / préparer / un bon dîner

2. papa / finir / son livre

3. ma sœur Lise / attendre / un coup de téléphone

4. moi, je / écouter / mon nouveau cédé

5. maman / inviter nos cousins / à prendre le dessert avec nous

6. ils / accepter

7. mon cousin Philippe / jouer de la guitare

8. nous / chanter / ensemble

9. nous / applaudir

10. après, nous / bavarder / jusqu'à une heure du matin

B *Des invités.* *Les Trichard ont invité l'oncle Charles à dîner. Complétez les phrases de Robert Trichard avec les verbes entre parenthèses pour savoir ce qui s'est passé.*

1. (attendre)   Nous _____ l'arrivée de l'oncle Charles et sa famille.

2. (dîner)   Ils _____ chez nous.

3. (arriver)   Ils _____ à sept heures.

4. (saluer)   Je _____ nos invités.

5. (apporter)   L'oncle Charles _____ des fleurs et des bonbons.

6. (remercier)   Ma mère _____ son frère.

7. (passer)   Tout le monde _____ à la salle à manger.

8. (remplir)   Mon père _____ les verres.

C *À la faculté.* *C'est comment la classe d'informatique de Raoul? Pour savoir, complétez les phrases avec les verbes entre parenthèses.*

1. (entrer)   Le professeur _____ dans la salle de classe.

2. (choisir)   Nous _____ un programme pour analyser.

3. (regarder)   Les étudiants _____ leurs écrans.

4. (chercher)   Moi, je _____ mon cahier.

5. (écouter)   Tout le monde _____ l'explication du professeur.

6. (réussir)   Je demande à mon amie Gisèle, «Tu _____ à comprendre ce programme?»

7. (répondre)   Elle _____ que oui.

8. (finir)   La classe _____ à dix heures et quart.

9. (fermer)   Nous _____ nos ordinateurs.

10. (descendre)   Les étudiants _____ au cours suivant.

Spelling Changes in the Present Tense of Regular -er Verbs

First-conjugation verbs whose stems end in **-c**, **-g**, or **-y** have spelling changes in the present tense. These changes are required by the rules of French spelling.

The letter **c** represents two sounds in the French writing system. It stands for the sound /s/ before **e** and **i**, but before **a**, **o**, and **u** it represents the sound /k/. Compare the pronunciation of the initial **c** in **casser** and **cesser**. For the letter **c** to represent the sound /s/ before **a**, **o**, and **u**, a cedilla is added under the **c**. Therefore, verbs whose stems end in -**c**, such as **commencer** (*to begin*), add a cedilla under the **c** (**c** > **ç**) before the **o** of the ending of the **nous** form: **commençons**.

	SINGULAR		PLURAL	
FIRST PERSON	je	commence	nous	commençons
SECOND PERSON	tu	commences	vous	commencez
THIRD PERSON	il/elle	commence	ils/elles	commencent
	on	commence		

Some Common Verbs like commencer

amorcer *to boot (a computer)*   **placer** *to place, invest*
annoncer *to announce*   **prononcer** *to pronounce*
avancer *to advance*   **réamorcer** *to reboot (a computer)*
divorcer *to divorce*   **relancer** *to restart*
effacer *to erase*   **remplacer** *to replace*
lancer *to launch*   **renoncer** *to resign, quit*
menacer *to threaten*

The letter **g** represents two sounds in the French writing system. It stands for the sound /zh/ (like English *s* in *pleasure*) before **e** and **i**, but before **a**, **o**, and **u** it represents the sound /g/ as in English *go*. Compare the pronunciation of the initial **g** in **garder** and **geler**. For the letter **g** to represent the sound /zh/ before **a**, **o**, and **u**, an **e** is added after the **g**. Therefore, verbs whose stems end in -**g**, such as **manger** (*to eat*), are written with **ge** before the **o** of the ending of the **nous** form: **mangeons**.

	SINGULAR		PLURAL	
FIRST PERSON	je	mange	nous	mangeons
SECOND PERSON	tu	manges	vous	mangez
THIRD PERSON	il/elle	mange	ils/elles	mangent
	on	mange		

Some Common Verbs like **manger**

aménager *to fix up, convert (a room, etc.)*
arranger *to arrange*
changer *to change*
corriger *to correct*
décourager *to discourage*
déménager *to move (change residence)*
déranger *to bother*
diriger *to direct*

encourager *to encourage*
nager *to swim*
partager *to share*
plonger *to dive*
ranger *to put away*
rédiger *to draft, write*
télécharger *to download*
voyager *to travel*

Verbs whose stems end in -**y**, such as **nettoyer** (*to clean*), change the **y** to **i** before a silent **e** (in all the singular forms and the third person plural).

	SINGULAR		PLURAL	
FIRST PERSON	je	nettoie	nous	nettoyons
SECOND PERSON	tu	nettoies	vous	nettoyez
THIRD PERSON	il/elle	nettoie	ils/elles	nettoient
	on	nettoie		

NOTE Verbs ending in -**ayer** may either make the above change or keep the **y** in all forms: **je paie** or **je paye**. Verbs ending in -**oyer** and -**uyer** must change **y** to **i** before a silent **e**.

Some Common Verbs Ending in -yer

aboyer *to bark*
appuyer *to support; to press (a button)*
balayer *to sweep*
broyer *to grind, make into powder*
effrayer *to frighten*
employer *to use*
ennuyer *to bore*
envoyer *to send*
essayer *to try, try on*
essuyer *to wipe*

nettoyer *to clean*
noyer *to drown*
payer *to pay*
rayer *to cross out*
renvoyer *to send back, dismiss, fire*
tutoyer *to use the* tu *form to address someone*
vouvoyer *to use the* vous *form to address someone*

D *On fait le ménage. Complétez les phrases suivantes avec les verbes entre parenthèses pour savoir ce que Claudette Legrand et sa famille font pour mettre la maison en ordre pour la visite de leurs cousins.*

1. (ranger)   Ma sœur et moi, nous _____ nos affaires.

2. (balayer)   Ma mère _____ le salon.

3. (nettoyer)   Mon père _____ la cuisine.

4. (commencer)   Mon frère et moi, nous _____ à travailler dans le jardin.

5. (essuyer)   Mes grands-parents _____ les assiettes.

6. (essayer)   J'_____ d'aider tout le monde.

E *Est-ce que c'est comme ça dans votre classe de français? Répondez à ces questions sur votre classe de français. Utilisez **nous** comme sujet dans chaque réponse.*

1. Est-ce que vous commencez à lire des livres en français?

2. Est-ce que vous corrigez vos copies en classe?

3. Est-ce que vous effacez les mots mal écrits?

4. Est-ce que vous employez le français dans vos conversations?

5. Est-ce que vous dérangez les autres étudiants?

6. Est-ce que vous tutoyez le professeur?

7. Est-ce que vous prononcez correctement?

8. Est-ce que vous téléchargez des documents en français?

First-Conjugation (-er) Verbs with Mute e as the Stem Vowel

First-conjugation verbs that have mute **e** as their stem vowel, such as **acheter** (*to buy*), change the mute **e** to **è** in those forms where the ending has a mute **e**.

	SINGULAR		PLURAL	
FIRST PERSON	j'	achète	nous	achetons
SECOND PERSON	tu	achètes	vous	achetez
THIRD PERSON	il/elle	achète	ils/elles	achètent
	on	achète		

This spelling change reflects an important pronunciation change. The stem vowel **e** in **nous achetons**, in **vous achetez**, and in the infinitive **acheter** is a mute **e** and is usually not pronounced in these forms: /ashtõ/, /ashté/. The vowel **è** represents the sound /ɛ/, as in **tête** and **lettre**, and is a full-fledged vowel that is always pronounced.

Some Common Verbs like **acheter**

amener *to bring (someone)*	**lever** *to pick up, raise*
emmener *to take (someone)*	**mener** *to lead*
enlever *to remove, take off*	**peser** *to weigh*
geler *to freeze*	**promener** *to walk*

Verbs like **appeler** (*to call*) double the consonant after the mute **e** instead of changing **e** to **è**. The **e** before the single consonant represents a mute /e/ that often drops in spoken French: **nous appelons** /nu za plõ/, **vous jetez** /vu zhté/.

	SINGULAR		PLURAL	
FIRST PERSON	j'	appelle	nous	appelons
SECOND PERSON	tu	appelles	vous	appelez
THIRD PERSON	il/elle	appelle	ils/elles	appellent
	on	appelle		

Some Common Verbs like **appeler**

épeler *to spell*	**rappeler** *to call back*
feuilleter *to leaf through*	**rejeter** *to reject*
jeter *to throw*	**renouveler** *to renew*
projeter *to plan*	

First-Conjugation (-er) Verbs with é as the Stem Vowel

Verbs that have **é** as the stem vowel, such as **espérer** (*to hope*), change **é** to **è** when the ending has a mute **e**. This change represents a pronunciation change. The vowel **é** represents French closed **e** (somewhat similar to the *a* of English *date*). The vowel **è** represents the sound /ɛ/ (French open **e**), as in **tête** and **lettre**.

	SINGULAR		PLURAL	
FIRST PERSON	j'	espère	nous	espérons
SECOND PERSON	tu	espères	vous	espérez
THIRD PERSON	il/elle	espère	ils/elles	espèrent
	on	espère		

In verbs such as **préférer** (*to prefer*), only the **é** before the infinitive ending changes to **è**.

	SINGULAR		PLURAL	
FIRST PERSON	je	préfère	nous	préférons
SECOND PERSON	tu	préfères	vous	préférez
THIRD PERSON	il/elle	préfère	ils/elles	préfèrent
	on	préfère		

Some Common Verbs like **espérer** and **préférer**

céder *to yield*
célébrer *to celebrate*
compléter *to complete*
protéger *to protect*

refléter *to reflect*
répéter *to repeat*
révéler *to reveal*

F *Entre amis. Refaites les questions suivantes en remplaçant le pronom **vous** par le pronom familier **tu**.*

1. Est-ce que vous préférez travailler en été?

2. Qu'est-ce que vous espérez faire après l'université?

3. Combien est-ce que vous pesez?

4. Comment est-ce que vous épelez votre nom?

5. Est-ce que vous rejetez les idées extrémistes?

6. Où est-ce que vous achetez les livres pour les cours?

G *Portrait de Jean-Claude. Jean-Claude est un jeune homme dynamique. Formez les phrases indiquées pour savoir quels sont ses projets.*

1. Jean-Claude / espérer devenir interprète

2. il / préférer les langues

3. il / projeter un voyage aux États-Unis

4. il / feuilleter des brochures de l'agence de voyages

5. il / renouveler son passeport

6. il / compléter un cours intensif d'anglais

7. ses idées / refléter l'influence de sa mère

8. elle / lui répéter toujours l'importance d'une orientation internationale

Uses of the Present Tense

1 · The French present tense has several equivalents in English.

En général **nous nageons** dans une piscine, mais aujourd'hui **nous nageons** dans la mer.

*We generally **swim** in a pool, but today we are swimming in the ocean.*

2 · French has no equivalent for the English auxiliary *do/does* in questions or negative sentences.

—Quelle langue étudiez-vous? Le chinois?
—Non, je n'étudie pas le chinois. J'apprends le japonais.

What language do you study? Chinese?

No, I don't study Chinese. I'm learning Japanese.

3 · The French present tense can express the future, especially if an expression in the sentence refers to future time.

—**Je t'emmène** en ville demain.   *I'll take you downtown tomorrow.*
—Merci, tu es gentil. Mais demain **je**   *Thanks, that's nice of you. But **I'm***
   travaille.   ***working** tomorrow.*

4 · French uses the present tense to refer to actions that began in the past but continue into the present. English uses a construction containing *have/has been doing something* for this function. The French construction consists of the following elements.

- To ask how long something has been going on

Depuis combien de temps + Verb in Present Tense?

Depuis combien de temps est-ce que   *How long have you been looking for an*
   vous cherchez un appartement?   *apartment?*

There are informal versions of this question.

Il y a combien de temps que vous cherchez un appartement?
Ça fait combien que vous cherchez un appartement?

- To tell how long something has been going on

Verb in Present Tense + depuis + Time Expression

Je cherche un appartement **depuis**   *I've been looking for an apartment **for***
   un an.   ***a year**.*

There are informal versions of this response pattern.

Il y a un an que je cherche un appartement.
Voilà un an que je cherche un appartement.
Ça fait un an que je cherche un appartement.

The word **déjà** may be added to the above sentences as the equivalent of English *now*.

Il y a **déjà** un an que je cherche   *I've been looking for an apartment for*
   un appartement.   *a year **now**.*

- To specify the starting point of an action that began in the past and continues into the present

Depuis quand is used in the question, and **depuis** in the answer.

—**Depuis quand** est-ce que vous   ***Since when** have you been waiting for*
   attendez l'avion?   *the plane?*
—J'attends **depuis** midi.   *I've been waiting **since** noon.*

H **Problèmes de bureau.** *Françoise n'aime pas son travail. Pour savoir ce qui se passe dans son bureau, complétez les phrases avec les verbes entre parenthèses et traduisez les phrases en anglais.*

1. (changer) Demain je _____ de travail.

2. (travailler) Il y a deux ans que je _____ dans le même bureau.

3. (gagner) Je _____ le même salaire depuis dix-huit mois.

4. (demander) Il y a dix mois que je _____ une augmentation.

5. (répéter) Et il y a dix mois que mon chef _____ la même réponse: Non.

6. (chercher) Tous mes collègues _____ de nouveaux emplois.

7. (désirer) Il y a longtemps qu'ils _____ renoncer à leur travail ici.

8. (annoncer) La semaine prochaine ils _____ leur décision au chef.

I **Un professeur dynamique.** *Formez des phrases pour connaître les efforts de Madame Ferron, professeur de langues, pour envoyer ses étudiants faire des études à l'étranger. Employez* **il y a**, **voilà** *ou* **depuis** *et variez les constructions. Suivez le modèle.*

MODÈLE   Madame Ferron / huit ans / envoyer des étudiants à l'étranger
→ Il y a (Voilà) huit ans que Madame Ferron envoie des étudiants à l'étranger.
OU Madame Ferron envoie des étudiants à l'étranger depuis huit ans.

1. Madame Ferron / dix ans / enseigner dans notre lycée

2. elle / huit ans / encourager les étudiants à étudier à l'étranger

3. elle / sept ans / organiser des voyages pour les étudiants

4. trois étudiants / quatre ans / passer un semestre au Québec chaque année

5. mon ami Charles / trois ans / étudier l'allemand

6. il / deux mois / projeter un voyage d'études en Allemagne

7. Charles / six semaines / feuilleter des brochures

8. Madame Ferron / un mois / chercher le programme idéal pour Charles

J **Comment est-ce que ça se dit?** *Traduisez les phrases suivantes en français. Faites attention aux formes verbales.*

1. *He takes off his shoes and puts on his slippers (pantoufles).*

2. *At the office, we draft and correct articles.*

3. *I'm cleaning the kitchen. I wipe the table and sweep the floor.*

4. *He leafs through the magazine, but he buys the newspaper.*

5. *Are you (tu) completing the work today? Or do you prefer to finish tomorrow?*

6. *We send text messages (le texto (text message)) to our friends.*

K *Activité orale.* Parlez avec un compagnon pour découvrir trois choses que cette personne aime faire et depuis combien de temps elle les fait. Racontez ce que vous apprenez à un autre ami.

Pour parler un français authentique | **Speak Real French**

The Prefix re-

French shares with English the prefix **re-** (**r-** or **ré-** before a vowel).

FRENCH	ENGLISH
écrire	*to write*
réécrire	*to rewrite*
faire	*to do*
refaire	*to redo*
lire	*to read*
relire	*to reread*

Si je ne suis pas satisfait du travail, je le refais.	*If I'm not satisfied with the work, I redo it.*
Il faut relire ce poème pour le comprendre.	*You have to reread this poem to understand it.*

However, the use of the prefix **re-** is much more widespread in French. It is often added to verbs where English would use the adverb *again*.

allumer *to turn on (a light, etc.)*
rallumer *to turn on (a light, etc.) again*

fonctionner *to work, be working* (of a machine)
refonctionner *to be working again*

s'habiller *to get dressed*
se rhabiller *to get dressed again*

Si j'éteins et rallume mon ordinateur, il va refonctionner.	*If I shut down my computer and turn it on again, it will start working again.*
Les enfants se rhabillent après la piscine.	*The children get dressed again after the pool.*

With verbs of motion, the prefix **re-** often means *back,* as in **revenir** (*to come back*).

—Je n'ai pas mes lunettes.	*I don't have my glasses.*
—Remonte les chercher.	*Go back upstairs to look for them.*
Elle descend faire les courses.	*She went down to do the shopping.*
Elle redescendra acheter du pain avant le dîner.	*She'll go back down to buy bread before dinner.*
—Les enfants ne sont pas là?	*The children aren't here?*
—Non, ils sont ressortis.	*No, they went back out.*

The English equivalent of a verb with the prefix **re-** may not be immediately apparent.

—J'aime bien ces épinards.	*I really like this spinach.*
—Allez-y. Vous pouvez en reprendre.	*Go ahead. You may have some more.*

Note also the verb **ravoir** (*to get something again, get something back, get something clean*). This verb is used only in its infinitive form.

Si tu perds ce cédé, tu ne vas jamais le ravoir.	*If you lose this CD, you'll never get another one.*
Je ne sais pas si je peux ravoir ce pantalon.	*I don't know if I can get this pair of pants clean again.*

L *Vocabulaire. Trouvez l'équivalent anglais de ces verbes au préfixe **re-**. Les équivalents anglais sont tous des mots apparentés (cognates).*

1. réabsorber

2. réadmettre

3. remplacer

4. rénover

5. représenter

6. reproduire

M *Enrichissez votre vocabulaire. En partant de ce vocabulaire, complétez les phrases suivantes avec des verbes au préfixe **re-**. Suivez le modèle.*

> MODÈLE   *I added some salt to the soup. You should try it again.*
> J'ai ajouté du sel à la soupe. Tu dois la ___*réessayer*___.

avoir un rhume *to have a cold*
donner un médicament à qqn *to give someone medicine*
essayer *to try; to taste; to try on*
formuler *to phrase*
grimper sur qqch *to climb up something*
mettre *to put*
partir *to leave*
verser *to pour*
voir *to see*

1. *He has just arrived, but I think he's going to leave again.*

   Il vient d'arriver, mais je crois qu'il va _____.

2. *You like this wine? I'll pour you another glass.*

   Tu aimes ce vin? Je vais te _____ un verre.

3. *We shouldn't leave all these books on the table. We should put them back.*

   Nous ne devons pas laisser tous ces livres sur la table. Nous devons les _____.

4. *He left for Australia. Who knows when we will see him again?*

   Il est parti en Australie. Qui sait quand on va le _____?

5. *I don't understand what you want. Can you rephrase your question?*

   Je ne comprends pas ce que vous voulez. Est-ce que vous pouvez _____ votre question?

6. *If you go out without a coat, you are going to catch a cold again.*

   Si tu sors sans manteau, tu vas _____ ton rhume.

7. *If he doesn't get better, you must give him more of his medicine.*

   S'il ne guérit pas, il faut lui _____ son médicament.

8. *I'm sure the children will climb back up the tree.*

   Je suis sûr que les enfants vont _____ sur l'arbre.

N   ***Approfondissons!*** *Traduisez ces expressions en anglais. Employez des mots* up, back *et* again *dans vos traductions.*

1. ramener un malade à l'hôpital

2. rappeler qqn demain

3. rapporter les documents

4. rattacher le chien

5. réapprendre à parler après son accident

6. retomber amoureux

7. retoucher une peinture

8. rouvrir les négociations

Present Tense of Irregular Verbs

Common Irregular Verbs

French verbs not conjugated like **parler**, **finir**, or **rendre** are called irregular verbs. The two most important and most frequent irregular verbs are **avoir** (*to have*) and **être** (*to be*).

avoir

	SINGULAR		PLURAL	
FIRST PERSON	j'	**ai**	nous	**avons**
SECOND PERSON	tu	**as**	vous	**avez**
THIRD PERSON	il/elle	**a**	ils/elles	**ont**

être

	SINGULAR		PLURAL	
FIRST PERSON	je	**suis**	nous	**sommes**
SECOND PERSON	tu	**es**	vous	**êtes**
THIRD PERSON	il/elle	**est**	ils/elles	**sont**

Also irregular are the verbs **aller** (*to go*) and **faire** (*to make, do*).

aller

	SINGULAR		PLURAL	
FIRST PERSON	je	**vais**	nous	**allons**
SECOND PERSON	tu	**vas**	vous	**allez**
THIRD PERSON	il/elle	**va**	ils/elles	**vont**

faire

	SINGULAR		PLURAL	
FIRST PERSON	je	**fais**	nous	**faisons**
SECOND PERSON	tu	**fais**	vous	**faites**
THIRD PERSON	il/elle	**fait**	ils/elles	**font**

Compounds of irregular verbs, such as **refaire** (*to redo*) and **défaire** (*to undo*), are conjugated like the simple verb.

The irregular verb **prendre** (*to take*) has the following forms.

	SINGULAR		PLURAL	
FIRST PERSON	je	**prends**	nous	**prenons**
SECOND PERSON	tu	**prends**	vous	**prenez**
THIRD PERSON	il/elle	**prend**	ils/elles	**prennent**

Note that the singular forms of **prendre** and **venir** (see below) end in a nasal vowel. The third person plural has the vowel /è/ + the nasal consonant /n/, and the **nous** and **vous** forms have a mute **e**.

Conjugated like **prendre**: **apprendre** (*to learn*), **comprendre** (*to understand*), **reprendre** (*to start again*), **surprendre** (*to surprise*).

Verbs like **venir** (*to come*) and **tenir** (*to hold*) have the following forms.

venir

	SINGULAR		PLURAL	
FIRST PERSON	je	**viens**	nous	**venons**
SECOND PERSON	tu	**viens**	vous	**venez**
THIRD PERSON	il/elle	**vient**	ils/elles	**viennent**

tenir

	SINGULAR		PLURAL	
FIRST PERSON	je	**tiens**	nous	**tenons**
SECOND PERSON	tu	**tiens**	vous	**tenez**
THIRD PERSON	il/elle	**tient**	ils/elles	**tiennent**

Conjugated like **venir** and **tenir**: **devenir** (*to become*), **revenir** (*to return*), **appartenir** (*to belong*), **maintenir** (*to maintain, support (financially)*), **obtenir** (*to obtain*), **retenir** (*to retain, hold back*), **soutenir** (*to support, hold up*).

The irregular verbs **devoir** (*should, ought, must; to owe*), **pouvoir** (*to be able to*), and **vouloir** (*to want*) often occur before an infinitive.

devoir

	SINGULAR		PLURAL	
FIRST PERSON	je	**dois**	nous	**devons**
SECOND PERSON	tu	**dois**	vous	**devez**
THIRD PERSON	il/elle	**doit**	ils/elles	**doivent**

pouvoir

	SINGULAR		PLURAL	
FIRST PERSON	je	**peux**	nous	**pouvons**
SECOND PERSON	tu	**peux**	vous	**pouvez**
THIRD PERSON	il/elle	**peut**	ils/elles	**peuvent**

vouloir

	SINGULAR		PLURAL	
FIRST PERSON	je	**veux**	nous	**voulons**
SECOND PERSON	tu	**veux**	vous	**voulez**
THIRD PERSON	il/elle	**veut**	ils/elles	**veulent**

 A **Devoir *n'est pas toujours* vouloir.** *Ces gens doivent faire certaines choses, mais ils ne veulent pas. Répondez aux questions selon le modèle avec **devoir** et **vouloir**.*

MODÈLE   Martine travaille?
→ Elle doit travailler, mais elle ne veut pas.

1. Tu passes la journée à la bibliothèque?

2. Catherine reste à la maison aujourd'hui?

3. Jean-Claude et Philippe vont chez le médecin?

4. Tes amis et toi, vous rentrez tôt?

5. Moi, je prépare le dîner?

6. Solange et moi, nous prenons un taxi?

B ***Qui fait quoi chez Hélène?*** *Hélène parle de sa famille, qui est assez grande. Chacun fait une partie des travaux du ménage. Utilisez les éléments proposés pour savoir ce qu'elle dit.*

Vocabulaire utile
faire du bricolage *to do odd jobs, putter around*
faire les carreaux *to do the windows*
faire les courses *to do the shopping/marketing*
faire la cuisine *to do the cooking*
faire le jardin *to do the gardening*
faire le linge, faire la lessive *to do the laundry*
faire le(s) lit(s) *to make the bed(s)*
faire le ménage *to do the housework*
faire la vaisselle *to do the dishes*

1. moi / la vaisselle

2. mon grand-père / du bricolage

3. mes frères / le jardin

4. ma sœur et moi / les courses

5. ma grand-mère / le linge

6. mon père / les carreaux

7. moi / les lits

8. ma mère, ma grand-mère et moi / la cuisine

Expressions with **avoir**, **être**, **faire**, and **prendre**

Expressions with **avoir**

Physical Sensations

avoir faim	*to be hungry*
avoir soif	*to be thirsty*
avoir sommeil	*to be sleepy*
avoir chaud	*to be warm*
avoir froid	*to be cold*
avoir mal à la tête	*to have a headache*
avoir mal à l'estomac	*to a stomachache*
avoir mal aux yeux	*to have sore eyes*
avoir mal au cœur	*to be sick to one's stomach*

Other Expressions

avoir de la chance	*to be lucky*
avoir besoin de qqch	*to need something*
avoir envie de qqch	*to feel like (having) something*
avoir envie de faire qqch	*to feel like doing something*
avoir honte	*to be ashamed*
avoir l'intention de faire qqch	*to intend to do something*
avoir peur	*to be afraid*
avoir raison	*to be right*
avoir tort	*to be wrong*
avoir _____ ans	*to be _____ years old*

—Quel âge avez-vous? *How old are you?*
—J'ai dix-huit ans. *I'm eighteen years old.*

avoir l'air + *adjective* *to look*

Il a l'air triste/intelligent/distrait. *He looks sad/intelligent/absent-minded.*

avoir l'air de + *noun* *to look like a*

Elle a l'air d'une artiste/ *She looks like an artist/a teacher.*
d'un professeur.

Expressions with **être**

être au régime	*to be on a diet*
être en vacances	*to be on vacation*
être en colère	*to be angry*
être bien	*to be nice looking; to be comfortable*
être de bonne/mauvaise humeur	*to be in a good/bad mood*
être sur le point de faire qqch	*to be about to do something*

être à l'heure	*to be on time*
être en avance	*to be early*
être en retard	*to be late*
être de retour	*to be back*
être d'accord avec qqn	*to agree with someone*
être en train de faire qqch	*to be busy doing something*
être à qqn	*to belong to someone*

À qui est ce stylo?	*Who(m) does this pen belong to?*
C'est (Il est) à Yvette.	*It's Yvette's. It belongs to Yvette.*

être à qqn de faire qqch	*to be someone's turn/responsibility to do something*

C'est à qui de jouer?	*Whose turn is it to play?*
C'est à vous d'en parler au professeur.	*It's up to you to talk to the teacher about it.*

Expressions with faire

Weather Expressions

Il fait beau/mauvais.	*The weather's good/bad.*
Il fait chaud/froid.	*It's hot/cold (outside).*
Il fait du soleil/vent.	*It's sunny/windy.*
Il fait jour/nuit.	*It's daytime/dark.*
Il fait un sale temps.	*The weather is lousy.*
Il fait 30 degrés.	*It's 30 degrees.*
Quel temps fait-il?	*What's the weather?*
Quelle température fait-il?	*What's the temperature?*

Other Expressions

faire attention	*to pay attention*
faire un voyage	*to take a trip*
faire des projets	*to make plans*
faire une promenade à pied	*to go for a walk*
faire une promenade en voiture	*to go for a ride*
faire du sport	*to play sports*
faire du jogging	*to jog*
faire du vélo	*to bike ride*
faire 10 kilomètres	*to travel/cover 10 kilometers*
faire sa toilette	*to wash up and get dressed* (especially in the morning)

Expressions with prendre

Food Expressions

prendre	*to have (a meal, food, drink)*
prendre le petit déjeuner	*to have breakfast*
prendre un café	*to have coffee*
prendre un thé	*to have tea*
prendre un Coca	*to have a Coke/soft drink*
prendre un sandwich	*to have a sandwich*
prendre une glace	*to have an ice cream*

Other Expressions

prendre froid	*to catch cold*
prendre un rhume	*to catch cold*
prendre de l'essence	*to get/buy gasoline*
prendre du poids	*to put on weight*
prendre qqn pour un autre	*to mistake someone for someone else*
passer prendre qqn	*to go by to pick someone up*

NOTE CULTURELLE

La France est un pays très varié. Sur une superficie un peu plus petite que celle du Texas se trouvent quatre types de climat très différents.

- **Le climat continental**: Ce climat se trouve dans le centre et dans l'est du pays. C'est le climat de Paris et aussi de Nancy, de Metz et de Strasbourg. Dans cette région de la France, l'été est chaud, mais moins chaud que dans la plupart des États-Unis. L'hiver est froid et pluvieux, mais Paris ne connaît pas en général les températures basses et les grandes neiges de l'est des États-Unis, par exemple.
- **Le climat atlantique**: Ce climat est caractéristique de l'ouest de la France et de la côte nord qui se trouve face à l'Angleterre. Ce climat est plus modéré que le climat continental. L'hiver est assez doux et en été il ne fait pas très chaud. Mais il pleut beaucoup pendant toute l'année. Les spécialistes calculent que dans la région du climat atlantique il y a 240 jours de pluie par an.
- **Le climat montagnard**: Comme l'indique son nom, c'est le climat des régions de montagne—les Alpes, les Pyrénées, le Massif central. À cause de l'élévation, l'été est court et l'hiver est long et il neige beaucoup.
- **Le climat méditerranéen**: C'est le climat typique du Midi, région qui se trouve sur la côte de la Méditerranée. Avec un hiver court et très doux (il ne gèle que rarement) et un été long, chaud et presque sans pluie, cette région est un grand centre touristique.

C   *Synonymes.*   *Transformez chaque phrase en une autre phrase formée avec une des expressions avec le verbe **avoir** qui a le même sens ou qui explique pourquoi le sujet a réalisé l'action.*

1. Il veut dormir.
2. Je veux manger.
3. Nous voulons boire.
4. Elles ouvrent la climatisation.
5. Tu mets un pull-over.
6. Il entend des pas dans son appartement.
7. Vous donnez la réponse correcte.
8. On rougit.
9. Tu dis quelque chose qui n'est pas correct.
10. Elle a gagné deux fois à la loterie.

D *Après l'accident.* *Un groupe d'amis a eu un accident de route. L'un d'eux raconte où chacun a mal. Suivez le modèle.*

MODÈLE   Marthe / tête
→ Marthe a mal à la tête.

1. Pierre et Michèle / jambes
2. Frédéric / bras
3. Rachelle / dos

4. toi / épaule droite
5. moi / genoux
6. Alfred et moi / pieds

E *Un voyage dans le Midi.* *Complétez les phrases suivantes avec la forme correcte de **faire**, **avoir**, **être** ou **prendre** pour savoir comment les Duverger et leurs enfants passent leurs vacances.*

1. Les Duverger et leurs deux enfants _____ en vacances.

2. Ils _____ envie de connaître Marseille.

3. «On _____ un voyage dans le Midi!» disent les enfants.

4. Ils voyagent en TGV. Le train _____ 800 kilomètres en moins de quatre heures.

5. Les Duverger _____ soif quand ils arrivent à Marseille.

6. Ils _____ une limonade dans le café de la gare.

7. Ils cherchent un guide. Le guide _____ des projets.

8. Les Duverger _____ attention quand le guide parle.

9. Le guide propose, «Aujourd'hui on _____ une promenade en voiture pour connaître la ville.»

10. Les Duverger trouvent que c'est une excellente idée. Ils _____ de l'essence et ils partent à la découverte de Marseille.

NOTE CULTURELLE

Le Midi est le nom donné au sud de la France. La région la plus connue du Midi est sans doute la Provence. Douée d'un climat très doux, la Provence est un grand centre touristique. Les plages de la Côte d'Azur attirent des milliers de Français et d'étrangers. Ici on trouve Marseille, le premier port français; Grasse, centre de l'industrie du parfum; Aix-en-Provence, ville universitaire; Cannes, site du festival de cinéma le plus prestigieux du monde; Nice, connu pour ses plages et son carnaval et Monte-Carlo, lieu fréquenté pour ses casinos de renommée internationale.

Cette région était une province très appréciée de l'Empire romain et offre au visiteur des ruines romaines spectaculaires. En fait, le nom Provence dérive du mot latin «Provincia». Les arènes d'Arles sont un amphithéâtre très bien conservé où ont lieu même de nos jours des courses aux taureaux. La Maison carrée de Nîmes est un petit temple romain presque intact qui se trouve au centre de la ville.

F **Et toi?** *Demandez à des camarades s'ils font les mêmes choses que vous. Suivez le modèle.*

MODÈLE   Moi, j'ai envie de sortir.
→ Toi aussi, tu as envie de sortir?

1. Moi, je prends un café.

2. Moi, j'ai faim.

3. Moi, je fais les courses maintenant.

4. Moi, j'ai vingt ans.

5. Moi, je suis en vacances.

6. Moi, j'ai mal à la tête.

7. Moi, je comprends l'italien.

8. Moi, je suis sur le point de sortir.

G **Où ça?** *Utilisez le verbe* **être** *pour décrire où se trouvent les personnes ou les établissements par rapport aux endroits indiqués dans chaque cas. Suivez le modèle.*

MODÈLE   le magasin / à côté de / cinéma
→ Le magasin est à côté du cinéma.

Les prépositions

à *to, at*	**près de** *near*
dans *in*	**loin de** *far from*
sur *on*	**à côté de** *next to*
sous *under*	**en face de** *across from*
devant *in front of*	**entre** *between*
derrière *in back of*	**parmi** *among*

Note the following contractions:

à + le → au   de + le → du
à + les → aux   de + les → des

1. le journal / sous / le banc

2. moi / à côté de / le banc

3. mes amis / assis sur / le banc

4. les arbres / derrière / le banc

5. toi et moi / près de / le lac

6. nous / en face de / le café

7. le lac / entre / la forêt et le pré (*meadow*)

8. vous / devant / le café

H **C'est une belle journée qui commence!** *Chantal ne travaille pas aujourd'hui. Elle est très contente. Complétez ces phrases avec la forme correcte de* **faire, avoir, être** *ou* **prendre** *pour savoir comment elle se prépare pour sortir.*

1. Il est 7 heures. Il _____ très beau aujourd'hui.

2. Il _____ chaud.

3. Je ne travaille pas aujourd'hui et je _____ de très bonne humeur.

4. J'_____ envie de sortir.

5. Je _____ ma toilette.

6. Je _____ le petit déjeuner.

7. Je _____ des projets pour la journée.

8. Mon ami François va passer la journée avec moi. Le matin, nous _____ du jogging.

9. L'après-midi nous _____ une promenade en voiture.

10. Le soir nous _____ une glace ensemble dans un café.

Irregular Verbs Resembling Regular Verbs

A small number of -**ir** verbs have the endings of -**er** verbs in the present tense. Study the conjugation of **ouvrir** (*to open*).

j'	ouvre	nous	ouvrons
tu	ouvres	vous	ouvrez
il/elle	ouvre	ils/elles	ouvrent

Conjugated like **ouvrir**: **accueillir** (*to welcome*), **couvrir** (*to cover*), **cueillir** (*to gather, pick (flowers)*), **découvrir** (*to discover*), **rouvrir** (*to reopen*), **souffrir** (*to suffer*).

Another group of -**ir** verbs is conjugated like -**re** verbs. Study the conjugation of **partir** (*to leave, set out (for a destination)*).

je	pars	nous	partons
tu	pars	vous	partez
il/elle	part	ils/elles	partent

Conjugated like **partir**: **dormir** (*to sleep*), **mentir** (*to lie*), **repartir** (*to leave again*), **sentir** (*to feel*), **servir** (*to serve*), **sortir** (*to go out*).

The verbs **mettre** (*to put*) and **battre** (*to beat*) are conjugated like an -**re** verb, but they have only one **t** in the singular.

mettre

je	mets	nous	mettons
tu	mets	vous	mettez
il/elle	met	ils/elles	mettent

battre

je	bats	nous	battons
tu	bats	vous	battez
il/elle	bat	ils/elles	battent

Conjugated like **mettre** and **battre**: **combattre** (*to fight, combat*), **débattre** (*to debate*), **omettre** (*to omit*), **permettre** (*to permit*), **promettre** (*to promise*).

The verbs **convaincre** (*to convince*) and **vaincre** (*to conquer*) have two stems. The singular stem ends in -**c**, and the plural stem ends in -**qu**.

je	convaincs	nous	convainquons
tu	convaincs	vous	convainquez
il/elle	convainc	ils/elles	convainquent

Infinitives ending in -**aindre**, -**eindre**, and -**oindre** have two stems. The singular stem ends in -**n**, and the plural stem ends in -**gn**. They follow the pattern of the verb **craindre** (*to fear*).

je	crains	nous	craignons
tu	crains	vous	craignez
il/elle	craint	ils/elles	craignent

Conjugated like **craindre**: **atteindre** (*to reach, attain*), **éteindre** (*to put out, extinguish*), **joindre** (*to join*), **peindre** (*to paint*), **plaindre** (*to pity*), **rejoindre** (*to rejoin*).

Verbs like **connaître** (*to know*) have a singular stem ending in **-ai**. In the third person singular form, the **-i** changes to **-î**. The plural stem ends in **-ss**.

je	connais	nous	connaissons
tu	connais	vous	connaissez
il/elle	connaît	ils/elles	connaissent

Conjugated like **connaître**: **apparaître** (*to appear*), **disparaître** (*to disappear*), **paraître** (*to seem, appear*), **reconnaître** (*to recognize*).

Verbs with infinitives ending in **-uire** like **construire** (*to build*) have two stems. The singular stem ends in **-i** and the plural stem ends in **-s**.

je	construis	nous	construisons
tu	construis	vous	construisez
il/elle	construit	ils/elles	construisent

Conjugated like **construire**: **conduire** (*to drive*), **détruire** (*to destroy*), **introduire** (*to introduce*), **produire** (*to produce*), **traduire** (*to translate*).

The verb **recevoir** (*to receive*) is conjugated similarly to **devoir**. Note the change of **c** to **ç** before **o**.

je	reçois	nous	recevons
tu	reçois	vous	recevez
il/elle	reçoit	ils/elles	reçoivent

Conjugated like **recevoir**: **décevoir** (*to disappoint*), **apercevoir** (*to notice*).

I *Rien!* *Jean-Baptiste a une attitude très négative aujourd'hui, comme vous pouvez le voir par ses réponses. Suivez le modèle.*

MODÈLE   Vous servez quelque chose?
→ Non, je ne sers rien.

1. Vous craignez quelque chose?

2. Vous recevez quelque chose?

3. Vous devez quelque chose?

4. Vous construisez quelque chose?

5. Vous reconnaissez quelque chose?

6. Vous peignez quelque chose?

7. Vous traduisez quelque chose?

8. Vous découvrez quelque chose?

J *Un peintre qui réussit.* *L'art de Nicole évolue avec beaucoup de succès. Formez les phrases indiquées pour savoir comment.*

1. Nicole / peindre / tous les jours

2. la nature / apparaître / dans ses tableaux

3. nous / apercevoir / son talent

4. nous / découvrir / de nouveaux thèmes

5. maintenant / Nicole / introduire / la vie de la ville dans son art

6. ses nouveaux tableaux / ne pas décevoir

7. le public / accueillir / son art avec enthousiasme

K *Nous aussi.* *Dans une conversation avec Lise Dulac, Monsieur et Madame Sauvignon découvrent qu'ils ont beaucoup en commun avec elle. Suivez le modèle.*

MODÈLE   Madame Dulac: Je sors le week-end.
           → Monsieur et Madame Sauvignon: Nous aussi, nous sortons le week-end.

1. En été j'ouvre toutes les fenêtres.

2. J'accueille souvent des étudiants étrangers à la maison.

3. Je reçois beaucoup de lettres des étudiants étrangers.

4. Je conduis avec prudence.

5. Je connais beaucoup de monde dans le quartier.

6. Je pars en vacances au mois de juillet.

7. Je cueille des fleurs dans mon jardin.

8. Je peins en été.

L *Des vacances dans le désert.* *Refaites cette petite histoire pour qu'elle raconte les aventures (et mésaventures!) de Josette. Suivez le modèle.*

MODÈLE   Alain et Marc ne travaillent pas cette semaine.
           → Josette ne travaille pas cette semaine.

1. Alain et Marc partent en vacances. (Josette)

2. Ils rejoignent des amis. (Elle)

3. Ils conduisent une vieille voiture. (Elle)

4. Ils dorment dans des hôtels très modestes. (Elle)

5. Ils arrivent dans le désert. (Elle)

6. Ils sentent la chaleur. (Elle)

7. Ils souffrent d'allergies. (Elle)

8. Ils repartent à la maison. (Elle)

Other Irregular Verbs

Écrire, savoir, vivre, boire, and suivre

écrire *to write*			
j'	écris	nous	écrivons
tu	écris	vous	écrivez
il/elle	écrit	ils/elles	écrivent

savoir *to know*			
je	sais	nous	savons
tu	sais	vous	savez
il/elle	sait	ils/elles	savent

vivre *to live*			
je	vis	nous	vivons
tu	vis	vous	vivez
il/elle	vit	ils/elles	vivent

boire *to drink*			
je	bois	nous	buvons
tu	bois	vous	buvez
il/elle	boit	ils/elles	boivent

suivre *to follow*			
je	suis	nous	suivons
tu	suis	vous	suivez
il/elle	suit	ils/elles	suivent

Expressions with **suivre**: **suivre un cours** (*to take a course*), **suivre un régime** (*to be on a diet*), **suivre l'actualité** (*to keep up with the news*).

Dire, lire, courir, and mourir

dire *to say, tell*			
je	dis	nous	disons
tu	dis	vous	dites
il/elle	dit	ils/elles	disent

lire *to read*			
je	lis	nous	lisons
tu	lis	vous	lisez
il/elle	lit	ils/elles	lisent

courir *to run*			
je	cours	nous	courons
tu	cours	vous	courez
il/elle	court	ils/elles	courent

mourir *to die*			
je	meurs	nous	mourons
tu	meurs	vous	mourez
il/elle	meurt	ils/elles	meurent

Expressions with **mourir**: **mourir de faim** (*to be starving, be very hungry*), **mourir de soif** (*to be very thirsty*), **mourir d'ennui** (*to be bored to death*).

Voir and croire

voir *to see*			
je	vois	nous	voyons
tu	vois	vous	voyez
il/elle	voit	ils/elles	voient

croire *to believe*			
je	crois	nous	croyons
tu	crois	vous	croyez
il/elle	croit	ils/elles	croient

M *Maintenant il s'agit de vacances à la plage.* Raconte l'expérience de Josette.

1. Les cousins de Josette veulent aller au bord de la mer. (Josette)

2. Ils croient que ça va être amusant. (Elle)

3. Ils écrivent aux copains pour les inviter. (Elle)

4. Ils savent arriver à la plage. (Elle)

5. Ils boivent de l'eau parce qu'il fait chaud. (Elle)

6. Ils meurent de soif. (Elle)

7. Ils courent sur la plage pour faire de l'exercice. (Elle)

8. Ils voient le coucher du soleil (*sunset*) sur la mer. (Elle)

9. Ils disent que c'est très joli. (Elle)

10. Le soir, ils lisent des romans. (Le soir, elle)

11. Ils suivent l'actualité en écoutant la radio. (Elle)

12. Ils vivent des jours heureux au bord de la mer. (Elle)

Verbal Constructions

The verbs **vouloir** and **pouvoir** are followed directly by an infinitive.

—Tu **veux jouer** au football avec nous?   *Do you **want to play** soccer with us?*
—Je **ne peux pas sortir** aujourd'hui.   *I **can't go out** today.*

When **aller** is followed by an infinitive, it expresses future time, like English *to be going to*.

—À quelle heure est-ce que vous **allez prendre** un café avec nos amis?   *What time **are you going to have** a cup of coffee with our friends?*
—Aujourd'hui je **vais étudier**. Pas de café jusqu'à demain!   *Today I**'m going to study**. No coffee till tomorrow!*

Verbs of motion, such as **venir**, **sortir**, **monter**, and **descendre**, can also be followed directly by an infinitive.

—Je **descends faire** les courses.   *I**'m going down to do** the shopping.*
—Et moi, je **sors prendre** les billets pour le concert de demain soir.   *And I**'m going out to buy** the tickets for tomorrow night's concert.*
—Marc **vient chercher** son livre.   *Marc **is coming to get** his book.*
—Il est dans ma chambre. Il **peut monter le chercher**, s'il veut.   *It's in my room. He **can go upstairs to get it**, if he wants to.*

The present tense of **venir** + **de** + infinitive expresses an action that has just taken place.

—Je **viens de voir** Élise.   *I **just saw** Élise.*
—Elle **vient de recevoir** un texto de son frère.   *She **just received** a text message from her brother.*

When **savoir** is followed by an infinitive, it means *to know how to do something.*

—Tu **sais nager**?   ***Do** you **know how to swim**?*
—Oui, mais je **ne sais pas plonger**.   *Yes, but I **don't know how to dive**.*

—Elle **ne sait pas monter** à bicyclette.   *She **doesn't know how to ride** a bike.*
—Mais elle **sait conduire** sa Ferrari.   *But she **knows how to drive** her Ferrari.*

Apprendre is followed by **à** before an infinitive.

—Tu **apprends à jouer** de la flûte?   ***Are** you **learning to play** the flute?*
—Non, je joue déjà de la flûte.   *No, I already play the flute. **I'm learning***
   J'**apprends à jouer** du piano.   *to play the piano.*

N   *Moi aussi.* Dites dans chaque cas que vous voulez faire la chose que votre ami(e) apprend à faire. Suivez le modèle.

   MODÈLE   parler russe
            → —J'apprends à parler russe.
              —Moi aussi, je veux parler russe.

1. danser   4. conduire

2. jouer aux échecs   5. faire la cuisine

3. chanter   6. programmer l'ordinateur

O   *C'est déjà fait.* Formez des échanges avec **aller** et **venir de** selon le modèle.

   MODÈLE   Baudouin / prendre un café
            → —Est-ce que Baudouin va prendre un café?
              —Mais il vient de prendre un café.

1. toi / faire le linge   4. Christine / messager

2. les étudiants / déjeuner   5. nous / visiter les monuments

3. vous deux / faire les courses   6. moi / voir un film

P   *Même pas pour la santé.* Ces gens savent ce qu'ils doivent faire pour être en forme, mais ils ne le font pas. Exprimez leur refus en suivant le modèle.

   MODÈLE   Jean-Pierre doit courir tous les jours.
            → Il sait qu'il doit courir, mais il dit qu'il ne peut pas et qu'il ne veut pas.

1. Mes parents doivent marcher tous les jours.

2. Mes amis, vous devez faire de l'exercice.

3. Je dois nager une heure tous les jours.

4. Tu dois faire du sport.

5. Catherine doit suivre un régime pour maigrir.

6. Ma sœur et moi, nous devons faire du vélo.

Q *Comment est-ce que ça se dit?* *Traduisez les phrases suivantes en français.*

1. *When are you (vous) leaving?*

2. *We're leaving tomorrow.*

3. *And when are you coming back (revenir)?*

4. *I'm coming back on Friday. My wife and the children are coming back next week.*

5. *What are you (tu) doing today?*

6. *My wife and I are painting the house.*

7. *You (vous) know how to paint the house?*

8. *My brother is going to help us. **He** knows how to paint.*

9. *I'm coming to watch (regarder).*

10. *If you're coming, you're going to paint.*

R *Activité orale. Ma journée.* *Avec un(e) ami(e), parlez de votre journée—quand vous avez faim et soif, ce que vous prenez, quand vous sortez et quand vous êtes de retour, combien d'heures vous dormez, etc.*

| **Pour parler un français authentique** | **Speak Real French** |

The Verb System in Spoken French

Written French and spoken French have different rules for determining the forms of the verb. For instance, for **-er** verbs such as **parler**, the written conjugation of the present tense has five forms.

je	parle	nous	parlons
tu	parles	vous	parlez
il/elle	parle	ils/elles	parlent

In spoken French, however, all the singular forms and the third person plural are pronounced alike: /parl/. The **nous** and the **vous** forms are distinct in both written and spoken French. Thus, the present tense of **-er** verbs in spoken French has three, not five, forms.

The characteristic feature of **-er** verbs like **parler** in spoken French is the uniformity of the stem in all forms of the present. The stem **parl-** is pronounced /parl/ in all forms of the present tense. This means that the third person singular and third person plural forms are pronounced alike: **il parle** and **ils parlent** are both pronounced /il parl/.*

---

*Note that the third person singular and third person plural forms are distinct in spoken French if the verb begins with a vowel. In this case, the final **s** of **ils**, **elles** is pronounced as /z/: **il arrive** /i la riv/ vs. **ils arrivent** /il za riv/. Pronouncing a final consonant before a following vowel is called *liaison.*

S *Écrivez et prononcez les formes* **il** *et* **ils** *des verbes suivants. Ne manquez pas de faire la liaison du* **-s** *final du pronom* **ils** *si le verbe commence par une voyelle.*

1. casser (*to break*)
2. couper (*to cut*)
3. pousser (*to push*)
4. recommander (*to recommend*)
5. travailler (*to work*)
6. visiter (*to visit*)
7. aider (*to help*)
8. allumer (*to turn on* (*lights, appliances*))
9. apporter (*to bring*)
10. écouter (*to listen to*)
11. imiter (*to imitate*)
12. oser (*to dare*)

French verbs other than **-er** verbs follow a different pattern. Most of these, whether regular or irregular, form the singular in written French with the endings **-s, -s, -t**.

finir

je	finis	nous	finissons
tu	finis	vous	finissez
il/elle	finit	ils/elles	finissent

descendre

je	descends	nous	descendons
tu	descends	vous	descendez
il/elle	descend	ils/elles	descendent

Note that the **-t** of the third person singular is not written after **d**.

écrire

j'	écris	nous	écrivons
tu	écris	vous	écrivez
il/elle	écrit	ils/elles	écrivent

The three verbs above share a key feature: the final consonant of the stem is not pronounced in the singular. This may or may not be indicated in the writing system, but it is the central feature of verbs other than **-er** verbs in spoken French. In these verbs, the three singular forms are pronounced alike, but the third person plural form (**ils**) is distinct in speech from the third person singular form (**il**).

Examine the pronunciation of the stems and the singular forms.

	STEM	SINGULAR
finir	/finis/	/fini/
descendre	/desãd/	/desã/
écrire	/ekriv/	/ekri/

Thus, although all the forms of **descendre** are spelled with a **d**, that **d** is not pronounced in the singular forms. The singular forms end in the nasal vowel /ã/.

T *Écrivez et prononcez les formes **il** et **ils** des verbes suivants. Identifiez la consonne finale de la racine. Faites attention à la prononciation de la consonne finale de la racine au pluriel et à son absence au singulier.*

INFINITIF	CONSONNE FINALE ORALE	CONSONNE FINALE ÉCRITE	**il**	**ils**
1. connaître	/____/	_____	_____	_____
2. dormir	/____/	_____	_____	_____
3. réfléchir	/____/	_____	_____	_____
4. vendre	/____/	_____	_____	_____
5. partir	/____/	_____	_____	_____
6. mettre	/____/	_____	_____	_____
7. réussir	/____/	_____	_____	_____
8. construire	/____/	_____	_____	_____
9. rompre	/____/	_____	_____	_____
10. entendre	/____/	_____	_____	_____
11. devoir	/____/	_____	_____	_____
12. recevoir	/____/	_____	_____	_____
13. vivre	/____/	_____	_____	_____
14. dire	/____/	_____	_____	_____

Negative Sentences

Basic Negative Structures

Verbs are made negative by placing **ne** before the verb and **pas** after it.

—Je **ne** dîne **pas** au restaurant ce soir.   *I'm **not** having dinner out this evening.*
    Et toi?   *How about you?*
—Moi, je **ne** travaille **pas**. Donc, je sors.   *I'm **not** working. So, I'm going out.*

Ne becomes **n'** before a vowel or mute **h**.

Je **n'**aime pas écouter cette musique.   *I **don't** like listening to this music.*

Note the similar negative constructions **ne** + verb + **jamais** meaning *never* and **ne** + verb + **plus** meaning *not anymore, no more*.

—Tu **n'**invites **plus** Jeanine.   *You **don't** ask Jeanine out **anymore**.*
—Ce n'est pas la peine. Elle **n'**accepte   *It's not worth it. She **never** accepts.*
  jamais.

Ne + verb + **personne** means *no one,* and **ne** + verb + **rien** means *nothing*.

—Vous cherchez quelqu'un,   *Are you looking for someone, sir?*
  monsieur?
—Non, madame. Je **ne** cherche   *No, ma'am. I'm **not** looking for **anyone**.*
  personne.

—J'entends un bruit.   *I hear a noise.*
—Moi, je **n'**entends **rien**.   *I **don't** hear **anything**.*

Personne and **rien** may be used as subjects. Then they precede the verb and are followed by **ne**.

—**Rien ne** change ici.   ***Nothing** changes here.*
—C'est vrai. **Personne ne** déménage.   *It's true. **No one** moves out. Everything*
  Tout reste comme avant.   *remains just as it was before.*

SPOKEN VS. WRITTEN FRENCH

In spoken French, the negative word **ne** is often omitted, thus creating sentences that seem quite far from the written standard.

Je ne sais pas.	(three syllables)	/zhən sé pa/
Je sais pas.	(two syllables)	/shsé pa/

The **ne** should not be omitted in writing.

Positive and Corresponding Negative Words

encore, toujours *still*	**plus** *no more*
encore, davantage *more*	**plus** *no more, not anymore*
quelquefois *sometimes*	**jamais** *never*
toujours *always*	**jamais** *never*
souvent *often*	**jamais** *never*
quelqu'un *someone, somebody*	**personne** *no one, nobody*
quelque chose *something*	**rien** *nothing*
quelque part *somewhere*	**nulle part** *nowhere*

A   *Comme c'est triste.* *Pierrot n'est pas tout à fait content pendant ses premiers jours à l'université. Écrivez ses réponses négatives aux questions, en employant le mot négatif correspondant. Suivez le modèle.*

MODÈLE   Est-ce que tu connais beaucoup de monde?
            → Non, je ne connais personne.

1. Est-ce que ta petite amie téléphone tous les jours?

2. Est-ce que tu manges avec quelqu'un?

3. Est-ce que tu regardes souvent la télé?

4. Est-ce que tu travailles encore?

5. Est-ce que quelqu'un organise des activités pour les nouveaux étudiants?

6. Est-ce que tu aimes quelque chose ici?

B   *Ça va mieux.* *Pierrot est content à l'université maintenant. Écrivez ses réponses négatives aux questions, en employant le mot négatif correspondant.*

1. Est-ce que tu es encore seul?

2. Est-ce que tu es triste quelquefois?

3. Est-ce que tu désires encore rentrer chez toi?

4. Est-ce que quelqu'un dérange les étudiants quand ils travaillent?

5. Est-ce que tu trouves quelque chose à critiquer?

6. Est-ce que quelque chose t'effraie maintenant?

C *Jamais!* *Les étudiants racontent ce qu'ils ne font jamais à l'école. Écrivez ce qu'ils disent avec* **jamais.** *Suivez le modèle.*

MODÈLE   fumer en classe
→ Nous ne fumons jamais en classe.

1. arriver en retard

2. interrompre le professeur

3. oublier nos devoirs

4. perdre nos livres

5. applaudir après la classe

6. jeter nos stylos en l'air

7. confondre les rois de France dans la classe d'histoire

8. texter nos amis pendant le cours

D *Tout change.* *Josette retourne à son quartier après plusieurs années d'absence. Son amie Valérie lui raconte comment les choses ont changé. Écrivez ce qu'elle dit à Josette en employant* **ne... plus.** *Suivez le modèle.*

MODÈLE   mon frère / travailler à la bibliothèque
→ Mon frère ne travaille plus à la bibliothèque.

1. les Dulac / habiter l'immeuble en face

2. M. Beauchamp / vendre sa poterie aux voisins

3. nous / acheter le journal au kiosque du coin

4. ma mère / descendre faire les courses tous les jours

5. moi / jouer du piano

6. Mme Duverger / enseigner au lycée du quartier

7. nos amis / passer beaucoup de temps dans le quartier

E *Quelle école!* *Dans cette école on ne s'occupe pas des étudiants. Écrivez des phrases avec le mot* **personne** *comme sujet pour expliquer tout ce qu'on ne fait pas. Suivez le modèle.*

MODÈLE   aider les étudiants
→ Personne n'aide les étudiants.

1. avertir les étudiants

2. parler avec les étudiants

3. écouter les étudiants

4. saluer les étudiants

5. encourager les étudiants

6. donner des conseils aux étudiants

F   *Et vous?* *Écrivez si vous faites ces activités souvent, quelquefois, jamais, ou si vous ne les faites plus.*

1. jouer au volley-ball

2. étudier toute la nuit

3. parler au téléphone

4. regarder la télé

5. assister aux concerts de musique classique

6. dîner au restaurant avec tes amis

7. descendre à la rue en pyjama à 4 heures du matin

8. arriver en retard à l'école

Other Negative Structures

Aucun(e) with the meaning *no, not any* precedes a noun. **Ne** precedes the verb.

—Tu crois qu'il va rentrer?	*Do you think he's coming back?*
—Je **n'**ai **aucune idée**.	*I have **no idea**.*
—Ce cours est très difficile.	*This course is very difficult.*
—C'est que le professeur **ne** nous donne **aucun exemple**.	*That's because the teacher **doesn't** give us **any examples**.*

Note that **aucun(e)** is always used in the singular.

Aucun(e) + noun or **aucun(e) des** + plural noun may function as the subject of a sentence. **Ne** precedes the verb.

Aucun ami n'accepte son invitation.	***No friend** accepts his invitation.*
Aucun de ses amis n'accepte son invitation.	***None of his friends** accepts his invitation.*

Ni... ni... means *neither . . . nor . . .* Like **aucun(e)**, **personne**, and **rien**, it may either follow or precede the verb. **Ne** precedes the verb in both cases. When **ni... ni...** refers to the subject of the sentence, a plural verb is used.

—Je **ne** vois **ni Charles ni Hélène**.	*I don't see **either Charles or Hélène**.*
—**Ni Charles ni Hélène ne** sont là.	***Neither Charles nor Hélène** is here.*

(Ni)... non plus means *neither* or *not either* in a sentence where the French equivalent of *nor* does not appear.

—Charles n'est pas là.	*Charles isn't here.*
—**(Ni) Hélène non plus.**	***Neither is Hélène**. (**Hélène either**.)*
—Je n'aime pas le professeur d'informatique.	*I don't like the computer science teacher.*
—**Moi non plus.**	***Neither do I**.*

Ne + verb + **guère** means *hardly*.

    Il **n'**est **guère** content.   *He's **hardly** happy.*

 G   ***Un étudiant en difficulté.*** *Jean-Marc a beaucoup de problèmes au lycée. Décrivez-les en employant* ***ni... ni...*** *dans chaque cas, selon le modèle.*

       MODÈLE   arriver / en avance / à l'heure
                   → Il n'arrive ni en avance ni à l'heure.

1. aimer / la physique / la littérature

2. finir / ses devoirs / ses compositions

3. étudier / à la bibliothèque / à la maison

4. réfléchir / à son travail / à son avenir

5. demander des conseils / à ses amis / à ses professeurs

6. écouter / les conférences / les discussions

H   ***Un professeur paresseux.*** *Utilisez le mot* ***aucun*** *pour savoir pourquoi les étudiants ne sont pas contents dans la classe du professeur Malherbe. Suivez le modèle.*

       MODÈLE   donner / devoir
                   → Il ne donne aucun devoir.

1. expliquer / texte

2. corriger / composition

3. recommander / livre

4. proposer / thème de discussion

5. présenter / idée

6. analyser / problème

Ne... que

Ne... que means *only*. **Ne** precedes the verb and **que** precedes the word or words emphasized.

—Paulette aime la musique classique?	*Does Paulette like classical music?*
—Non, elle **n'**écoute **que** des chansons populaires.*	*No, she listens **only** to popular songs.*
—Tu veux aller à Avignon par le train?	*Do you want to go by train to Avignon?*
—Je **ne** voyage **qu'**en voiture.	*I travel **only** by car.*

Ne... pas que means *not only*.

Il **n'**y a **pas que** le travail. Il faut vivre aussi.	*Work is**n't all there is**. You have to live too.*
Il **n'**aime **pas que** la physique. Il adore la géographie aussi.	*He does**n't only** like physics. He loves geography too.*

****Ne... que** is not considered a negative, so the partitive article following it is not reduced to **de**.

I *Il n'y en a pas d'autre.* *Refaites les phrases suivantes avec* **ne... que**, *selon le modèle.*

> MODÈLE   La chimie est la seule classe que j'aime.
> → Je n'aime que la chimie.

1. Philippe est la seule personne que je respecte ici.

2. Ma chambre est la seule que je nettoie.

3. Alice est la seule personne que j'invite.

4. La littérature française est la seule qu'elle apprécie.

5. L'avenir est la seule chose à laquelle ils réfléchissent.

6. Odile est la seule personne à qui je téléphone.

7. Le football est le seul sport auquel je joue.

8. Le dîner est le seul repas qu'elle prépare à la maison.

J *Comment est-ce que ça se dit?* *Traduisez en français.*

1. *We're not making any (de) plans because we're not taking a (de) trip.*

2. *No one feels like leaving on vacation.*

3. *So (donc), we're not going anywhere.*

4. *We're not going either to the beach or to the mountains. Or to Paris either.*

5. *And we don't want to go abroad anymore.*

K *Activité orale.* *Avec un(e) ami(e) de classe, discutez des choses que vous ne faites pas chez vous. Comparez les règles.*

Pour parler un français authentique | **Speak Real French**

Further Uses of **ne... que** *only*

The idiom **n'avoir qu'à faire qqch** means *all someone has to do is . . .*

Tu **n'as qu'à lui téléphoner.**	*All you **have to do is call him**.*
Ils **n'ont qu'à essayer.**	*All they **have to do is try**.*
Nous **n'avons qu'à patienter.**	*All we **can do is be patient**.*
Je **n'ai qu'à réamorcer.**	*All I **have to do is reboot**.*
Vous **n'avez qu'à prendre vos billets.**	*All you **have to do is buy your tickets**.*

Rien qu'à + infinitive means *merely by doing something.*

Rien qu'à le voir, on comprend qu'il est malade.	*Merely by seeing him, you understand he's sick.*
Rien qu'à lire son article, on voit que c'est un homme tolérant.	*Merely by reading his article, you see that he's a tolerant man.*

Rien qu'à followed by a noun or a prepositional phrase means *merely, only.*

Rien qu'à l'affiche, le concert est formidable.	*Merely (judging) by the poster, the concert is terrific.*

Rien que means *only, nothing but.*

Rien que la vérité.	*Nothing but the truth.*
Rien que pour toi.	*Just for you. Only for you.*

Que often has the meaning *only* at the beginning of a phrase.

Que ça!	*That's all there is! Just that!*
Que de la bière?	*(There's) only beer?*

The idiom **ne faire que** + infinitive means *to do nothing but . . .* , or sometimes *to be merely doing . . .*

Cet enfant **ne fait que pleurer.**	*This child **cries all the time.***
Je **ne fais que manger.**	*I **do nothing but eat.***
Tu **ne fais que me mentir.**	*All you **do is lie to me.***
Je **ne fais que passer.**	*I'm **just stopping by.***
Je **ne fais que regarder.**	*I'm **just looking.***
Je **ne fais que partager ma joie.**	*All I'm **doing is sharing my joy.***

L   *Traduisez ces phrases en anglais.*

1. Ils ne nous ont pas servi de vin. Que de l'eau.

2. —Qu'est-ce qu'il a dit?
   —Rien que des bêtises.

3. Depuis son divorce il ne fait que boire.

4. Si tu veux prendre rendez-vous avec elle, tu n'as qu'à lui envoyer un courriel.

5. Rien qu'à l'écouter, on soupçonne qu'il n'est pas tout à fait normal.

6. Pourquoi me critiquer? Je ne fais que répéter tes paroles.

7. Il dit qu'il gagne de l'argent rien qu'en surfant sur le Web.

8. Elle écrit un livre rien que sur ce petit village.

Interrogative Sentences

Question Formation

We distinguish two types of questions: yes/no questions and information questions. A yes/no question, as the name implies, asks for either *yes* or *no* as an answer.

> *Is John working today?*
> *Yes, he is.*

An information question begins with a question word and asks for a piece of information as an answer.

> **Where** *is John going?*
> *He's going downtown.*

> **When** *will he be back?*
> *This afternoon.*

Yes/No Questions

There are three ways to change a statement into a yes/no question.

1 · In spoken French, statements are turned into questions by raising the pitch of the voice at the end of the sentence. The word order is the same as that of a statement.

—Tu descends avec moi?	*Are you coming downstairs with me?*
—Non, je reste ici. Tu retournes avant le dîner?	*No, I'm staying here. Are you coming back before dinner?*
—Non. Je dîne en ville.	*No, I'm having dinner in town.*

2 · In both spoken and formal French, **est-ce que** may be placed at the beginning of a statement to turn it into a question.

—**Est-ce que** vous écoutez souvent les concerts à la radio?	*Do you often listen to the concerts on the radio?*
—Oui, toujours. Et vous? **Est-ce que** vous aimez la musique classique aussi?	*Yes, all the time. And what about you? Do you like classical music too?*

3 · In formal French, especially in writing, statements are turned into questions by placing the subject pronoun after the verb and joining the two with a hyphen. This is called *inversion* of the subject and verb.

—**Travaillez-vous** ici, madame?	*Do you work here, ma'am?*
—Oui, monsieur. **Cherchez-vous** un emploi?	*Yes, sir. Are you looking for a job?*

NOTE The pronoun **je** cannot be inverted.

If the third person singular form of a verb ends in a vowel, **-t-** is added between the verb form and the inverted subject pronoun **il**, **elle**, or **on**.

Parle-**t**-il français?	*Does he speak French?*
A-**t**-elle envie de sortir?	*Does she feel like going out?*
Salue-**t**-on le professeur en anglais?	*Does one greet the teacher in English?*

In an inverted question, a noun subject remains before the verb and the corresponding pronoun is added after the verb.

—**Les étudiants** tutoient-**ils** leur professeur?	*Do the students use the tu form to their teacher?*
—Jamais. Ils vouvoient le professeur.	*Never. They use the vous form to the teacher.*
—**Le professeur** tutoie-**t**-il les étudiants?	*Does the teacher use the tu form to the students?*
—Quelquefois.	*Sometimes.*

Negative questions with inversion are used only in formal style. The **ne** and **pas** surround the inverted pronoun and verb. These questions imply that the speaker expects the answer *yes*.

—**N'**appuie-**t**-il **pas** notre candidat?	*Doesn't he support our candidate?*
—Si, bien sûr. **Ne** partage-**t**-il **pas** nos idées?	*Yes, of course he does. Doesn't he share our ideas?*

If the subject of a negative question is a noun, it remains in its position before **ne** and the corresponding pronoun is added after the verb.

—**Les musiciens** de cet orchestre **ne** jouent-**ils pas** merveilleusement?	*Don't the musicians in this orchestra play wonderfully?*
—Si. Et regardez. **Le public** **n'**écoute-**t**-il **pas** avec beaucoup de plaisir?	*Yes. And look. Isn't the public listening with great delight?*

NOTE **Si**, not **oui**, is used to answer *yes* to a negative question.

N'est-ce pas can be added to the end of any statement to ask a question to which the speaker expects the answer *yes*. The meaning is similar to that of negative questions.

Les musiciens jouent bien, **n'est-ce pas?**	*The musicians play well, **don't they?***

Negative questions formed with rising intonation and without inversion expect the answer *no*.

—Tu ne regardes pas la télé?	*You're not watching TV?*
—Non, je téléphone.	*No, I'm making a phone call.*

 Pour faire connaissance. *Vous faites la connaissance d'un vieux monsieur. Vous lui posez des questions en employant l'inversion. Après, vous posez les mêmes questions à une nouvelle étudiante. Formez-les avec* **est-ce que**. *Suivez le modèle.*

> MODÈLE   parler français
> → Parlez-vous français?
>   Est-ce que tu parles français?

1. inviter souvent vos amis à dîner

2. apprécier la musique classique

3. habiter un beau quartier

4. chercher une maison à la campagne

5. travailler près de votre appartement

6. dîner généralement au restaurant

B **L'amoureux.** *Robert s'est entiché de (has fallen for) Chantal. Il se pose toutes sortes de questions à son sujet. Formez ses questions en employant l'inversion. Suivez le modèle.*

> MODÈLE   jouer au tennis
> → Joue-t-elle au tennis?

1. aimer les maths comme moi

2. étudier les mêmes matières que moi

3. habiter près du lycée

4. penser à moi de temps en temps

5. travailler à la bibliothèque

6. déjeuner à la cantine du lycée

C *L'ami de l'amoureux.* *Robert confie son amour à son ami Philippe. Philippe lui pose des questions sur Chantal. Formez ses questions avec* **est-ce que**. *Suivez le modèle.*

MODÈLE   tu / penser constamment à Chantal
→ Est-ce que tu penses constamment à Chantal?

1. Chantal / habiter près de chez toi

2. tu / arriver au lycée à la même heure que Chantal

3. tu / saluer Chantal

4. Chantal / aimer les mêmes activités que toi

5. tu / déjeuner avec elle

6. Chantal / bavarder avec toi de temps en temps

D *La section française.* *Marie-Claire pose des questions à son conseiller sur la section française de son lycée. Elle emploie l'inversion. Que dit-elle? Suivez le modèle.*

MODÈLE   M. Leclerc / apprécier la littérature française
→ M. Leclerc apprécie-t-il la littérature française?

1. Mme Savignac / prononcer parfaitement l'anglais

2. M. Paul / enseigner l'espagnol aussi

3. Mlle Moreau / répondre toujours aux questions des étudiants

4. M. Michelet / arriver au lycée à 7 heures du matin

5. M. et Mme Lamoureux / enseigner dans le même lycée

6. Mme Leboucher / choisir des textes intéressants pour sa classe

7. les professeurs / organiser des activités pour les étudiants

8. les étudiants / aimer les cours de français

E *Des explications.* *Le conseiller du lycée explique à ses collègues ses idées sur les difficultés scolaires de certains étudiants en employant des questions négatives, formées avec inversion du sujet. Suivez le modèle pour écrire ses paroles.*

MODÈLE   regarder trop la télé
→ Ne regardent-ils pas trop la télé?

1. déranger tout le monde

2. désobéir au professeur

3. perdre souvent leurs cahiers

4. bavarder trop en classe

5. confondre les dates

6. travailler sans intérêt

Un succès sûr. *Dans une réunion d'affaires M. Bertin explique à ses collègues pourquoi il croit que leur nouvelle affaire va réussir. Écrivez ce qu'il leur dit en employant des questions négatives formées avec inversion du sujet. Le sujet est* **nous** *dans chaque cas. Suivez le modèle.*

MODÈLE   placer notre argent dans une excellente affaire
           → Ne plaçons-nous pas notre argent dans une excellente affaire?

1. lancer une bonne affaire

2. diriger la compagnie d'une façon intelligente

3. engager de bons travailleurs

4. aménager les bureaux

5. changer nos stratégies selon chaque situation

6. commencer à gagner de l'argent

 Après la réunion. *Nous retrouvons M. Bertin avec un ami. Il lui explique les raisons pour lesquelles il croit que sa nouvelle affaire va réussir. Il utilise des questions négatives avec* **on** *au lieu de* **nous**. *Écrivez les questions deux fois, avec et sans inversion. Suivez le modèle.*

MODÈLE   placer notre argent dans une excellente affaire
           → Ne place-t-on pas notre argent dans une excellente affaire?
             On ne place pas notre argent dans une excellente affaire?

1. lancer une bonne affaire

2. diriger la compagnie d'une façon intelligente

3. engager de bons travailleurs

4. aménager les bureaux

5. changer nos stratégies selon chaque situation

6. commencer à gagner de l'argent

 Au contraire. *Quelle confusion! Alain pose des questions, mais dans chaque cas, c'est le contraire qui est vrai. Écrivez des échanges composés d'une question négative et de la réponse qui indique l'inverse. Suivez le modèle.*

MODÈLE   les employés / être en retard / être en avance
           → —Les employés ne sont pas en retard?
             —Non, ils sont en avance.

1. Claire / arriver ce matin / arriver ce soir

2. Marc et Geneviève / être au bureau / être malades

3. toi / avoir sommeil / avoir envie de sortir

4. moi / avoir raison / avoir tort

5. ton frère et toi / prendre le petit déjeuner à la maison / prendre un café au bureau

6. Lise / suivre un régime / prendre du poids

7. vous et vos parents / être en colère / être de bonne humeur

8. toi / sortir / rester à la maison

I   *Et en plus.* *Écrivez des petits échanges composés d'une question négative et d'une réponse affirmative. Ajoutez à la réponse l'élément proposé. Suivez le modèle.*

     MODÈLE   toi / avoir faim / avoir soif
           →   —Tu n'as pas faim?
               —Si, et j'ai soif aussi.

1. il / avoir mal au dos / avoir mal aux jambes

2. faire du vent / faire froid

3. toi / faire les lits chez toi / faire le linge

4. Marianne / jouer du violon / chanter

5. ta sœur et toi / apprendre à parler chinois / apprendre à écrire

6. moi / pouvoir assister à la conférence / pouvoir aller au concert

J   *Comment est-ce que ça se dit?* *Traduisez les questions suivantes en français.*
        Employez l'inversion.

1. *Is ecology important?*

2. *Do animals play an important role in our lives* [singular in French]?

3. *Do people* (les gens) *suffer because of pollution?*

4. *Are vegetables good for one's* (= the) *health?*

5. *Are cigarettes harmful* (faire mal)?

Information Questions

Information questions begin with a question word. The most common question words in French are the following.

Qui?	*Who? Whom?*
Que?	*What?*
Combien?	*How much? How many?*
Comment?	*How?*
Depuis combien de temps?	*(For) how long?*
Depuis quand?	*Since when?*
Lequel? Laquelle? Lesquels? Lesquelles?	*Which one(s)?*
Où?	*Where?*
D'où?	*From where?*
Pourquoi?	*Why?*
Quand?	*When?*
Quel/Quelle/Quels/Quelles + noun?	*Which?*

Qui? and Que?

The French equivalents of *who(m)* and *what* vary, according to whether the question word is the subject or object of the verb.

When *who* is the subject of the sentence, its French equivalent is **qui**. Since **qui** is the subject, no inversion of subject and verb takes place.

Qui travaille dans ce bureau?	*Who works in this office?*
Qui cherche un appartement?	*Who's looking for an apartment?*
Qui connaît le nouveau conseiller?	*Who knows the new consultant?*

Qui may be replaced by **qui est-ce qui**, especially in speech.

Qui est-ce qui chante si faux?	*Who's singing so off-key?*

When *who(m)* is the direct object of the verb, its French equivalent is **qui**, followed by the inversion of the verb and the subject pronoun. This construction is characteristic of formal style.

Qui recommandez-vous?	*Who(m) do you recommend?*
Qui appelle-t-il?	*Who(m) is he calling?*

In all styles, **qui est-ce que** (**qui est-ce qu'** before a vowel) can be used for *who(m)*.

Qui est-ce que vous recommandez?	*Who(m) do you recommend?*
Qui est-ce qu'il appelle?	*Who(m) is he calling?*

When *what* is the subject of a sentence, its French equivalent is **qu'est-ce qui**.

Qu'est-ce qui vous intéresse?	*What interests you?*
Qu'est-ce qui attire l'attention des clients?	*What attracts the customers' attention?*

When *what* is the direct object of the verb, its French equivalent is **qu'est-ce que** (**qu'est-ce qu'** before a vowel).

Qu'est-ce que vous avez fait?	*What did you do?*
Qu'est-ce qu'elles ont acheté?	*What did they buy?*
Qu'est-ce que j'ai dit?	*What did I say?*

In formal style, **qu'est-ce que** may be replaced by **que**, and the subject pronoun and verb are inverted.

Que choisissez-vous?	*What are you selecting?*
Que devons-nous faire maintenant?	*What should we do now?*

If the subject is a noun, **qu'est-ce que** is more common.*

Qu'est-ce que la secrétaire a envoyé?	*What did the secretary send?*
Qu'est-ce que le chef a décidé de faire?	*What did the boss decide to do?*

---

*Sometimes **que** is used with a noun subject, forcing the noun to a position after the verb: **Qu'ont vu les témoins?** *What did the witnesses see?*

Qui may be used after prepositions, but **que** must be replaced by **quoi** when it is the object of a preposition.

À qui est-ce que vous avez prêté le livre? **À qui** avez-vous prêté le livre?	*Who(m) did you lend the book **to**?*
De qui est-ce que vous parlez? **De qui** parlez-vous?	*Who(m) are you talking **about**?*
Avec qui est-ce que notre équipe va travailler? **Avec qui** notre équipe va-t-elle travailler?	*Who(m) is our team going to work **with**?*
À quoi ressemble le business-plan parfait?	*What does the perfect business plan look like?*
De quoi est-ce que les enfants ont peur? **De quoi** les enfants ont-ils peur?	*What are the children afraid **of**?*
Sur quoi est-ce que les syndicats insistent? **Sur quoi** les syndicats insistent-ils?	*What do the unions insist **on**?*

Here is a summary chart of the French equivalents of *who(m)* and *what*.

	SUBJECT	OBJECT	AFTER A PREPOSITION
Who(m)?	**Qui? / Qui est-ce qui?**	**Qui? / Qui est-ce que?**	**qui**
What?	**Qu'est-ce qui?**	**Que? / Qu'est-ce que?**	**quoi**

Other Question Words

Other question words can be used with **est-ce que** in all styles or with inversion of the verb and subject pronoun in very formal style.

Pourquoi est-ce que vous ne travaillez pas? **Pourquoi** ne travaillez-vous pas?	*Why aren't you working?*
Quand est-ce qu'il prend ses vacances? **Quand** prend-il ses vacances?	*When is he taking his vacation?*
Quand est-ce qu'elles arrivent? **Quand** arrivent-elles?	*When are they arriving?*
Où est-ce que nous pouvons attendre? **Où** pouvons-nous attendre?	*Where can we wait?*
Comment est-ce qu'ils ont gagné cet argent? **Comment** ont-ils gagné cet argent?	*How did they make this money?*

French also allows inversion of the verb and a noun subject if the verb is in a simple tense (with no auxiliary verb) and is not followed by a direct or indirect object.

Quand **arrive le train**?	*When **is the train arriving**?*
Comment **va votre père**?	*How **is your father**?*
Quelle langue **parlent ces gens**?	*What language **do these people speak**?*
Combien **paieront les tourists**?	*How much **will the tourists pay**?*

K **Activité orale.** *Quelles questions poseriez-vous à un(e) nouvel(le) voisin(e) pour parvenir à (get to) le/la connaître? Avec un(e) ami(e) jouez cette conversation entre deux voisins qui font connaissance.*

Imperative

The imperative is used to give a command or make a request. For most verbs, the imperative is formed by using the **tu**, **vous**, or **nous** form of the present tense without the subject pronoun. This is true of both positive and negative commands.

Finis tes devoirs. **Ne perds pas** ton temps.	**Finish** your homework. **Don't waste** your time.
Attendez un moment. **Ne partez pas.**	**Wait** a moment. **Don't leave.**
Rentrons maintenant. **Ne passons plus** de temps ici.	**Let's go back home** now. **Let's not spend any more** time here.

In the imperative **tu** form of regular **-er** verbs, the final **-s** of the present tense form is
dropped. The **-s** is also dropped in the imperative **tu** forms of **aller** and **-ir** verbs conjugated like **-er** verbs, such as **ouvrir** and **souffrir**.

Téléphone à tes parents. **N'oublie pas.**	**Call** your parents. **Don't forget.**
On sonne. **Va. Ouvre** la porte.	The doorbell is ringing. **Go open** the door.

The following verbs have irregular imperative forms.

être	**sois, soyons, soyez**
avoir	**aie, ayons, ayez**
savoir	**sache, sachons, sachez**

 Comment être un bon élève. *Écrivez les conseils d'un professeur à ses élèves.*
Employez le négatif de l'impératif. Suivez le modèle.

> MODÈLE   perdre / vos devoirs
>   → Ne perdez pas vos devoirs.

Vocabulaire utile

Verbes	*Substantifs*
déchirer *to tear*	**les bandes dessinées** *comics*
laisser *to leave*	**la calculette** *calculator*
mâcher *to chew*	**la copie** *composition, exercises*
salir *to dirty*	**le pupitre** *student's desk at school*

1. déchirer / vos copies

2. laisser / vos crayons sur la table

3. manger / dans la salle de classe

4. mâcher / de chewing-gum en classe

5. salir / la salle de classe

6. faire / de bruit

7. jeter / de papiers par terre

8. interrompre / le professeur

9. lire / de bandes dessinées en classe

10. oublier / vos calculettes

 B   ***Projets de vacances.*** *Jean-Claude et Arlette parlent de leurs vacances. À chaque idée de Jean-Claude, Arlette propose une autre possibilité. Employez l'impératif de la première personne du pluriel pour reproduire leur conversation. Suivez le modèle.*

MODÈLE   On reste à Paris? (aller en Italie)
→ Non, ne restons pas à Paris. Allons en Italie.

1. On part la semaine prochaine? (attendre la fin du mois)

2. On prend l'avion? (prendre le train)

3. On descend dans un hôtel de luxe? (choisir une auberge)

4. On visite les monuments en taxi? (louer une voiture)

5. On assiste aux concerts? (aller voir les pièces de théâtre)

6. On mange dans le restaurant de l'hôtel? (dîner dans les restaurants de la ville)

C   ***Des conseils à une amie qui part.*** *Michèle dit à son amie Ghislaine ce qu'il faut faire pour passer une semaine en Suisse. Refaites les phrases suivantes à l'impératif familier. Suivez le modèle.*

MODÈLE   Il faut faire des projets précis.
→ Fais des projets précis.

1. D'abord, il faut descendre dans la rue.

2. Ensuite, il faut chercher une librairie.

3. Là-bas, il faut demander un livre sur la Suisse.

4. Il faut rentrer tout de suite à ton appartement.

5. Après, il faut lire le livre.

6. Il faut choisir ton itinéraire.

7. Après, il faut téléphoner à l'agent de voyages.

8. Finalement, il faut faire les valises.

D *De mère en fille.* Mme Élouard explique à sa fille ce qu'il faut faire pour acheter une nouvelle robe. Écrivez ses conseils en employant l'impératif familier des verbes indiqués. Suivez le modèle.

MODÈLE   prendre le journal
→ Prends le journal.

1. lire les annonces

2. regarder les rabais

3. aller aux grands magasins

4. essayer les vêtements qui te plaisent

5. choisir une robe

6. payer avec la carte de crédit

7. revenir à la maison

8. mettre ta nouvelle robe

E *On fait des projets.* Richard et Zoë vont passer la journée ensemble. Ils expriment leurs idées en employant l'impératif. Suivez le modèle.

MODÈLE   passer la journée ensemble
→ Passons la journée ensemble.

1. aller en ville

2. prendre le train de 9 heures

3. descendre à la gare centrale

4. faire une promenade

5. regarder les vitrines des magasins

6. déjeuner dans un bon restaurant

7. chercher un bon film

8. après le film, flâner dans le jardin public

9. acheter des livres dans une librairie

10. rentrer par le train de 5 heures

F *Ce qu'on doit faire.* Véronique donne des conseils à son amie Geneviève. À chaque question de son amie elle répond par un impératif négatif suivi de l'impératif affirmatif du verbe entre parenthèses. Écrivez les réponses en suivant le modèle.

MODÈLE   Je dois attendre? (partir tout de suite)
→ Non, n'attends pas. Pars tout de suite.

1. Je dois mentir? (dire la vérité)

2. Je dois descendre? (rester en haut)

3. Je dois lire le texte? (écrire la composition)

4. Je dois suivre ce régime? (faire du sport)

5. Je dois mincir? (prendre du corps)

6. Je dois préparer le déjeuner? (faire la vaisselle)

7. Je dois nettoyer la cuisine? (balayer l'escalier)

8. Je dois jeter cette robe? (offrir les vieux vêtements aux voisins)

G *Quel enfant!* Le fils de Mme Bouvier est toujours en train de faire quelque chose de catastrophique. Employez le négatif de l'impératif familier pour écrire ce qu'elle lui défend de faire. Suivez le modèle.

MODÈLE   jouer avec les allumettes
→ Ne joue pas avec les allumettes!

Vocabulaire utile

Verbes	*Substantifs*
cacher *to hide*	**le frigo** *refrigerator*
débrancher *to unplug*	**l'ordinateur** [masc.] *computer*
grimper *to climb*	**le portefeuille** *wallet*
renverser *to knock over*	**la poubelle** *trash can*

1. renverser la bouteille

2. écrire sur les murs

3. débrancher l'ordinateur

4. jeter mon portefeuille à la poubelle

5. dessiner sur mon cahier

6. grimper sur la table

7. laisser le frigo ouvert

8. cacher les clés de la voiture

H *On a des invités ce soir.* Les Lary ont invité leurs amis à dîner ce soir. Employez la deuxième personne du pluriel de l'impératif pour écrire ce que Mme Lary demande à ses fils de faire. Suivez le modèle.

MODÈLE   être prêts de bonne heure
→ Soyez prêts de bonne heure.

1. descendre à 7 heures et demie

2. aller à la boulangerie

3. acheter du pain

4. traverser la rue

5. entrer chez le marchand de légumes

6. prendre un kilo d'asperges et de la salade

7. passer à la boucherie

8. chercher le poulet que j'ai commandé hier

9. rentrer tout de suite

10. commencer à préparer le dîner

I ***Comment est-ce que ça se dit?*** *Quels conseils donneriez-vous à un ami ou à deux amis pour réussir dans leur nouveau travail? Employez l'impératif.*

1. *Arrive on time.*

2. *Listen to the boss* (le patron).

3. *Don't sleep in the office.*

4. *Never forget the documents.*

5. *Answer your e-mails.*

6. *Be nice* (gentil(le)(s)) *to everyone.*

7. *Try to understand your colleagues.*

8. *Don't bother the other employees.*

J ***Activité orale.*** *Avec un(e) ami(e), jouez une des scènes suivantes.*

1. Une mère donne des conseils à son fils quand il commence ses études à l'université.

2. Un épicier dit à son commis (*clerk*) ce qu'il doit faire avant l'ouverture du magasin.

3. Deux amis se proposent des activités pour la semaine de vacances en décembre.

Passé Composé

Passé Composé with **avoir**

The passé composé is used to express an action completed in the past. The passé composé of most verbs consists of a present tense form of the auxiliary verb **avoir** followed by a past participle. Here is the conjugation of **parler** in the passé composé.

parler *to speak*

FIRST PERSON	j'	**ai parlé**	nous	**avons parlé**
SECOND PERSON	tu	**as parlé**	vous	**avez parlé**
THIRD PERSON	il/elle	**a parlé**	ils/elles	**ont parlé**

The past participle of a regular verb is formed by replacing the infinitive ending by the appropriate participle ending: **-é** for **-er** verbs, **-i** for **-ir** verbs, and **-u** for **-re** verbs.

parl**er**	parl**é**
fin**ir**	fin**i**
vend**re**	vend**u**

Many common verbs have irregular past participles.

apprendre	**appris**	devoir	**dû**	prendre	**pris**
atteindre	**atteint**	dire	**dit**	produire	**produit**
avoir	**eu**	écrire	**écrit**	recevoir	**reçu**
boire	**bu**	être	**été**	savoir	**su**
comprendre	**compris**	faire	**fait**	souffrir	**souffert**
conduire	**conduit**	instruire	**instruit**	suivre	**suivi**
connaître	**connu**	joindre	**joint**	tenir	**tenu**
construire	**construit**	lire	**lu**	venir	**venu**
courir	**couru**	mettre	**mis**	vivre	**vécu**
couvrir	**couvert**	ouvrir	**ouvert**	voir	**vu**
craindre	**craint**	paraître	**paru**	vouloir	**voulu**
croire	**cru**	peindre	**peint**		
découvrir	**découvert**	pouvoir	**pu**		

The negative of the passé composé is formed by placing **ne** before the conjugated form of **avoir** and **pas** (or most other negative words) after it.

—Tu **n'as pas** encore fini ton compte rendu? | *Haven't you finished your report yet?*

—Non, je **n'ai rien** écrit. Je n'ai **jamais** eu tant de difficulté. | *No, I haven't written **anything**. I've **never** had so much trouble.*

Personne and **nulle part**, however, follow the past participle.

—Tu **n'as** vu **personne** hier soir? | *Didn't you see **anyone** last night?*

—Non. J'ai cherché mes amis partout, mais je **n'ai** rencontré **personne nulle part**. | *No. I looked for my friends everywhere, but I **didn't** run into **anyone anywhere**.*

When inversion is used to ask a question in the passé composé, the subject pronoun and the auxiliary verb are inverted. In negative questions, the **ne** and **pas** (or most other negative words) are placed around the inverted auxiliary verb and pronoun. Negative questions with inversion in the passé composé are limited to formal language.

—**Les Durand ont-ils décidé** de vendre leur appartement? | *Have the Durands decided to sell their apartment?*

—Oui. **N'avez-vous pas vu** l'annonce dans le journal? | *Yes. **Didn't you see** the advertisement in the newspaper?*

A **C'était hier.** *Vous faites la même réponse à toutes les questions de votre ami(e). Employez le passé composé pour lui dire que tout s'est passé hier. Suivez le modèle.*

MODÈLE   Vous travaillez aujourd'hui?
→ Non. Mais j'ai travaillé hier.

1. Jean nage aujourd'hui?

2. Christine et toi, vous déjeunez en ville aujourd'hui?

3. Marc prend de l'essence aujourd'hui?

4. Toi et moi, nous nettoyons notre chambre aujourd'hui?

5. Les conseillers rédigent un compte rendu aujourd'hui?

6. Tu apprends le vocabulaire aujourd'hui?

7. Jacquot fait le linge aujourd'hui?

8. Vous finissez aujourd'hui, vous deux?

9. Tu attends tes amis aujourd'hui?

10. Alice répond en classe aujourd'hui?

11. Les étudiants obtiennent les résultats de l'examen aujourd'hui?

12. Le film reprend aujourd'hui?

13. Tu as mal à l'estomac aujourd'hui?

14. Je suis en avance aujourd'hui?

15. Il fait beau aujourd'hui?

B *Une aventure routière.* Jean-Pierre a pris la voiture hier, mais il a eu des difficultés. Refaites son histoire au passé composé pour savoir ce qui lui est arrivé.

L'automobile

au bord de la rue *at the side of the street*	**garer la voiture** *to park the car*
avoir un pneu crevé *to have a flat tire*	**le pneu** *tire*
faire le plein *to fill up with gas*	**pousser la voiture** *to push the car*
faire une promenade en voiture *to go for a ride*	**la station-service** *gas station*

1. J'invite mon copain Serge à faire une promenade en voiture avec moi.

2. Nous décidons d'aller à la campagne.

3. Nous faisons le plein avant de partir.

4. Tout d'un coup, nous entendons un bruit.

5. Nous avons un pneu crevé.

6. Nous poussons la voiture au bord du boulevard.

7. Nous achetons un nouveau pneu à la station-service.

8. Nous dépensons tout notre argent.

9. Nous ne pouvons pas aller à la campagne.

10. Je remonte le boulevard.

11. Je gare la voiture devant mon immeuble.

12. Serge et moi, nous passons la journée devant la télé.

C *Un nouvel ordinateur.* Colette raconte comment elle a acheté un nouvel ordinateur. Refaites son histoire au passé composé.

1. Je décide d'acheter un nouvel ordinateur.

2. Mon père et moi, nous lisons une brochure ensemble.

3. Nous demandons d'autres brochures.

4. Mon père trouve un revendeur (*dealer*) bien informé.

5. Nous posons beaucoup de questions au revendeur.

6. Il répond patiemment à nos questions.

7. Nous choisissons un ordinateur multimédia.

8. J'achète des logiciels (*software packages*).

9. Mon père trouve des CD-ROM intéressants.

10. Je mets mon nouvel ordinateur dans ma chambre.

D   ***Une lettre de son cousin.*** *Marie reçoit une lettre de son cousin François. Pour savoir de quoi il s'agit, formez des phrases au passé composé avec les éléments proposés.*

1. Marie / recevoir une lettre

2. elle / ouvrir l'enveloppe

3. elle / lire la lettre

4. son cousin François / écrire la lettre

5. il / être malade

6. il / passer deux semaines à l'hôpital

7. Marie / montrer la lettre à ses parents

8. ils / dire à Marie de téléphoner à François

9. elle / inviter François à passer les vacances chez elle

10. François / accepter

11. il / être très content

12. il / promettre d'arriver au début du mois de juillet

Passé Composé with être

A small number of French verbs form the passé composé with **être** rather than **avoir**. Most of these verbs express motion or describe a change in state. When the passé composé is formed with **être**, the past participle agrees in gender and number with the subject. Study the passé composé of **aller** (*to go*).

je	**suis** allé(e)	nous	**sommes** allé(e)s
tu	**es** allé(e)	vous	**êtes** allé(e)(s)
il	**est** allé	ils	**sont** allés
elle	**est** allée	elles	**sont** allées

The following verbs are conjugated with **être** as the auxiliary in the passé composé.

arriver	je **suis arrivé(e)**	partir	je **suis parti(e)**
descendre	je **suis descendu(e)**	rentrer	je **suis rentré(e)**
devenir	je **suis devenu(e)**	rester	je **suis resté(e)**
entrer	je **suis entré(e)**	retourner	je **suis retourné(e)**
monter	je **suis monté(e)**	sortir	je **suis sorti(e)**
mourir	il/elle **est mort(e)**	tomber	je **suis tombé(e)**
naître	je **suis né(e)**	venir	je **suis venu(e)**

Such verbs are also conjugated with **être** when a prefix is added.

redescendre	je **suis redescendu(e)**	*I went back down*
remonter	je **suis remonté(e)**	*I went back up*
repartir	je **suis reparti(e)**	*I left again*
revenir	je **suis revenu(e)**	*I came back*

E ***Ma soirée.*** *Marguerite raconte ce qu'elle a fait hier soir. Pour savoir ce qu'elle dit, formez des phrases au passé composé avec les éléments proposés.*

1. je / arriver chez moi vers 5 heures et demie

2. je / poser mes affaires sur le lit

3. je / redescendre

4. je / aller au supermarché pour acheter quelque chose à manger

5. je / rentrer tout de suite

6. je / préparer mon dîner

7. Lise et Solange / passer vers 7 heures

8. elles / rester une heure

9. elles / partir à 8 heures

10. je / faire mes devoirs

11. je / regarder les informations à la télé

12. je / fermer le poste vers 11 heures pour me coucher

F ***Pas cette fois.*** *Hélène est sortie avec Robert et Richard, les jumeaux. Elle explique à son amie Elvire que cette fois tout a été différent. Utilisez le passé composé pour écrire ses réponses à Elvire. Suivez le modèle.*

MODÈLE   Robert et Richard mangent rarement au restaurant.
          → Cette fois ils ont mangé au restaurant.

1. Robert et Richard arrivent toujours en retard.

2. Robert et Richard parlent toujours du football.

3. Ils commandent toujours un sandwich.

4. Ils boivent beaucoup de Coca avec le repas.

5. Ils sortent toujours la calculette pour vérifier l'addition.

6. Ils ne paient jamais.

7. Ils ne laissent jamais de pourboire.

8. Ils rentrent tout de suite après le repas.

G *Dormir à la belle étoile.* *Nicolas et ses amis sont allés faire du camping. Ils ont eu une surprise pas très agréable dans le bois à côté de la Seine, en amont (upstream) de Paris. Pour savoir ce qui s'est passé, formez des phrases au passé composé avec les éléments proposés.*

À la campagne

affreux *horrible*
coucher/dormir à la belle étoile *to sleep outdoors*
dresser la tente *to set up the tent*
épuisé *exhausted*
être pris de panique *to be overcome by panic*

ne pas fermer l'œil de la nuit *not to sleep a wink all night*
hurler *to scream, shriek*
plier la tente *to fold up the tent*
ramper *to creep*
le sac de couchage *sleeping bag*

1. trois de mes amis et moi, nous / vouloir coucher à la belle étoile

2. nous / aller à la campagne

3. nous / camper à côté du fleuve

4. Claude et moi, nous / faire un feu

5. Marc et Philippe / dresser les tentes

6. nous / manger autour du feu

7. vers 9 heures, nous / entrer sous nos tentes

8. chacun / entrer dans son sac de couchage

9. soudain, je / entendre un cri affreux

10. Marc / remarquer un serpent sous la tente

11. Philippe et lui / sortir de la tente en courant

12. nous / être pris de panique

13. le serpent / partir en rampant

14. je crois que le pauvre serpent / avoir peur

15. nous / arrêter de hurler

16. chacun / rentrer sous sa tente

17. personne / fermer l'œil de la nuit

18. le matin nous / plier les tentes

19. nous / retourner chez nous

20. tout le monde / être épuisé

Special Cases

Several verbs usually conjugated with **être** in the passé composé are conjugated with **avoir** when they have direct objects. Their English equivalents are different.

monter, descendre

Le chasseur **a monté nos bagages**.
Mais nous **avons descendu nos valises** tout seuls.

*The bellhop **took up our luggage**.*
*But we **brought our suitcases down** by ourselves.*

entrer, rentrer, sortir

Je **n'ai pas encore entré les données**.
Qui **a rentré le lait**?
Elle **a sorti son mouchoir**.

*I **haven't yet entered the data**.*
*Who **brought in the milk**?*
*She **took out her handkerchief**.*

passer

The verb **passer** is conjugated with **être** in the passé composé when it means *to come by, stop by to see, visit, be over.*

Le facteur **est** déjà **passé**.
Hier ma cousine **est passée** me voir.
Le pire **est passé**.

*The mail carrier **has** already **come by**.*
*My cousin **stopped by** to see me yesterday.*
*The worst **is over**.*

In most other cases, **passer** is conjugated with **avoir**.

Elle **a passé** son permis de conduire.
Ils **ont passé** une année en Suisse.

*She **took** her driving test.*
*They **spent** a year in Switzerland.*

H ***Quelle journée!*** *Les Vaillancourt ont eu une journée très compliquée hier. Complétez les phrases suivantes avec le passé composé des verbes entre parenthèses pour savoir tout ce qui s'est passé.*

Vocabulaire utile
l'aîné(e) *the older child*
le cadet/la cadette *the younger child*
étendre le linge sur le fil *to hang the clothes on the line*

M. Vaillancourt _____ (1. sortir) la voiture du garage à 5 heures du matin.

Il _____ (2. partir) au travail. Il _____ (3. monter) la rue de la République, comme toujours.

Mais aujourd'hui il _____ (4. voir) qu'il y avait des travaux. Il _____ (5. devoir) changer

de route. Il _____ (6. arriver) en retard. Mme Vaillancourt _____ (7. demander) à ses filles

de l'aider. Elle _____ (8. sortir) au bureau. L'aînée _____ (9. faire) le linge. La cadette

_____ (10. étendre) le linge sur le fil. Ensuite, les deux sœurs _____ (11. descendre) faire

les courses. Elles _____ (12. descendre) l'escalier de l'immeuble. Elles _____ (13. rentrer)

dans une demi-heure. Elles _____ (14. monter) les paquets. Quand elles _____ (15. entrer) dans l'appartement, il _____ (16. commencer) à pleuvoir. «Le linge!» _____ (17. dire) l'aînée.

Les deux _____ (18. rentrer) le linge à toute vitesse.

Agreement of the Past Participle

The past participle of a verb conjugated with **avoir** agrees in gender and number with a preceding direct object. The preceding direct object may be a noun, an object pronoun, or a relative pronoun.

Quelle **pièce** avez-vous vu**e?**	*Which **play** did you see?*
Combien de **sandwichs** a-t-il mangé**s?**	*How many **sandwiches** did he eat?*
Elle a acheté une nouvelle robe. Elle **l'**a mis**e** aujourd'hui.	*She bought a new dress. She wore **it** today.*
Les fenêtres sont fermées. Personne ne **les** a ouvert**es** aujourd'hui.	*The windows are closed. No one opened **them** today.*
Il m'a montré **les articles qu'**il a lu**s**.	*He showed me **the articles that** he read.*
On va publier **les histoires qu'**elle a écrit**es**.	*They're going to publish **the stories that** she wrote.*

The past participle does not agree with a preceding indirect object.

Marthe? Je **lui** ai téléphoné.	*Marthe? I called **her** up.*
Et tes parents? Tu **leur** as écrit?	*What about your parents? Did you write **to them?***

I   *Élisabeth s'installe à Paris.*   *Complétez l'histoire suivante avec le participe passé des verbes entre parenthèses. Faites les accords nécessaires.*

Élisabeth a _____ (1. quitter) le Québec pour la France. On lui a _____ (2. offrir)

un bon emploi et elle l'a _____ (3. accepter). Elle a _____ (4. faire) ses valises et elle a

_____ (5. prendre) l'avion. Elle est _____ (6. arriver) à Paris il y a un mois. Elle a tout de suite

_____ (7. commencer) à chercher un appartement. Les annonces qu'elle a _____ (8. lire)

sur le journal promettaient beaucoup, mais les appartements qu'elle a _____ (9. voir)

n'étaient pas très jolis et étaient très chers. Quelqu'un lui a _____ (10. donner) l'adresse

d'une agence immobilière. Elle l'a _____ (11. chercher). Elle est _____ (12. entrer)

et a _____ (13. demander) à l'employé de l'aider. Les appartements qu'on lui

a _____ (14. montrer) n'étaient pas mal. L'appartement qu'elle a _____ (15. choisir) n'était

pas loin de son travail. Il se trouvait dans une petite rue qu'elle a _____ (16. trouver)

très agréable. Après, elle a _____ (17. commencer) à travailler. Au bureau, on l'a

_____ (18. présenter) à tout le monde, et on l'a _____ (19. accueillir) très amicalement.

Elle est très contente à Paris maintenant.

J   **Lequel?** *Votre ami(e) s'intéresse à plusieurs de vos affaires. Dans chaque cas demandez-lui s'il s'agit de la chose que vous aviez hier. Employez le verbe entre parenthèses dans votre réponse et faites attention à l'accord du participe passé. Suivez le modèle.*

MODÈLE   Fais voir ta calculatrice. (acheter)
→ La calculatrice que j'ai achetée hier?

1. Montre-moi tes devoirs. (faire)

2. Je peux lire la lettre de Michèle? (recevoir)

3. Où est ta composition? (rédiger)

4. Tu as un nouveau sac à dos? (acheter)

5. Fais voir ton appareil photo. (employer)

6. Montre-moi ton nouveau DVD. (regarder)

7. Je peux écouter tes nouveaux disques compacts? (écouter)

8. Fais voir tes nouvelles chaussures. (mettre)

9. Je veux voir tes lunettes de soleil. (porter)

10. Tu me prêtes les revues? (lire)

K   **Au cinéma.** *Racontez en français cette histoire de Sébastien et Berthe.*

1. *Yesterday I called Berthe.*

2. *I asked her, "Do you want to go the movies?"*

3. *She answered, "Yes."*

4. *I went by to pick her up at 7 o'clock.*

5. *She came downstairs and we took the bus.*

6. *We got to (= arrived at) the movie theater at 7:30.*

7. *I bought the tickets right away.*

8. *Berthe and I looked for a café.*

9. *We had a cup of coffee and a pastry.*

10. *I looked at my watch.*

11. *I said, "It's 7:55."*

12. *We quickly went back to the movie theater and went in.*

L   **Activité orale.** *Avec un(e) ami(e) parlez des choses que vous avez faites hier. Après, racontez à un(e) autre ami(e) les choses que vous avez faites tous les deux. Employez le passé composé dans votre conversation.*

Imperfect; Imperfect Versus Passé Composé

The Imperfect Tense

The imperfect tense is used to describe an ongoing condition or a repeated or incompleted action in the past. It is formed by adding the imperfect endings to the imperfect stem. The stem is found by dropping the **-ons** ending from the present tense **nous** form. The imperfect-tense endings are **-ais, -ais, -ait, -ions, -iez, -aient.**

parler

je	parl**ais**	nous	parl**ions**
tu	parl**ais**	vous	parl**iez**
il/elle	parl**ait**	ils/elles	parl**aient**

finir

je	finiss**ais**	nous	finiss**ions**
tu	finiss**ais**	vous	finiss**iez**
il/elle	finiss**ait**	ils/elles	finiss**aient**

rendre

je	rend**ais**	nous	rend**ions**
tu	rend**ais**	vous	rend**iez**
il/elle	rend**ait**	ils/elles	rend**aient**

Verbs with a spelling change in the **nous** form of the present tense, such as **manger** and **commencer,** have the same spelling change before imperfect endings that begin with **-a.**

manger

je	mangeais	nous	mangions
tu	mangeais	vous	mangiez
il/elle	mangeait	ils/elles	mangeaient

commencer

je	commençais	nous	commencions
tu	commençais	vous	commenciez
il/elle	commençait	ils/elles	commençaient

Verbs whose stem ends in **-i** have a double **i** in the **nous** and **vous** forms of the imperfect.

nous étudiions
vous étudiiez

All verbs are regular in the imperfect except **être**.

être

j'	étais	nous	étions
tu	étais	vous	étiez
il/elle	était	ils/elles	étaient

 A   *Avant c'était différent.*   *Avec le présent et l'imparfait construisez des phrases qui expliquent que tout a changé. Suivez le modèle.*

> MODÈLE   je / travailler tous les jours
> → Je ne travaille plus tous les jours. Avant je travaillais tous les jours.

1. vous / croire à cette histoire

2. il / lire en allemand

3. elles / faire les carreaux

4. tu / habiter en ville

5. ils / vivre bien

6. mon chien / obéir

7. elle / rougir

8. je / répondre en classe

9. tu / voyager

10. elle / prononcer correctement

11. vous / apprécier la musique classique

12. ils / ranger leurs affaires

B   *Ma jeunesse.*   *Caroline parle de son enfance. Formez des phrases à l'imparfait pour savoir comment elle vivait à l'époque.*

1. nous / avoir une maison dans un quartier tranquille

2. elle / être grande

3. la maison / avoir dix pièces

4. mes parents / travailler en ville

5. ils / aller au bureau en autobus

6. l'arrêt / être au coin de la rue

7. beaucoup d'autres jeunes filles / habiter dans notre rue

8. je / jouer avec elles

9. nous / aller à l'école ensemble

10. je / garder souvent ma petite sœur Marguerite

11. je / l'emmener au parc

12. nous / être tous très contents

C *Grand-mère évoque son enfance.* La grand-mère de Nicolas raconte ses souvenirs. Formez des phrases à l'imparfait pour savoir ce qu'elle dit.

1. nous / vivre à la campagne

2. je / partager une chambre avec ma sœur

3. nous / ne pas avoir beaucoup d'argent

4. mais on / être heureux

5. je / nager dans le lac

6. les enfants / courir dans les champs

7. mes parents / élever des vaches

8. nous / vendre le lait

9. ton grand-père / commencer à venir me voir

10. je / avoir 18 ans

D *Nos vacances à l'époque.* Un groupe d'amis évoque les souvenirs de leurs vacances quand ils étaient jeunes. Formez des phrases à l'imparfait pour savoir comment ils ont passé leurs vacances. Faites attention aux adverbes de temps utilisés dans les phrases. Suivez le modèle.

> MODÈLE   Alfred: tous les ans / nous / aller / à la campagne
> → Nous allions tous les ans à la campagne.

1. Lise: souvent / je / passer les vacances / chez ma tante

2. Michel: toujours / je / vouloir / aller au bord de la mer

3. Christine: chaque été / ma famille et moi, nous / visiter / une région de France

4. Paul: tous les ans / mes cousins / m'inviter / chez eux

5. Marianne: le plus souvent / nous, on / prendre les vacances en hiver

6. Robert: en général / ma cousine Élisabeth / venir / chez nous à Paris

7. Françoise: d'habitude / nous / partir / en Suisse

8. Guy: tous les étés / mon père / louer / un appartement à Nice

Uses of the Imperfect Tense:
The Imperfect Contrasted with the Passé Composé

The imperfect tense focuses on past actions or conditions as processes rather than as completed events. It emphasizes the action or condition itself rather than its beginning or end. One use of the imperfect is to express repeated or ongoing actions in the past.

—Qu'est-ce que tu **faisais** quand tu **habitais** à Cannes?	What **did** you **use to do** when you **lived** in Cannes?
—J'**allais** tous les jours à la plage.	I **would go** to the beach every day.
—Est-ce que tu **avais** des cours l'après-midi?	**Did** you **use to have** classes in the afternoon?
—Non, j'**étais** à la faculté le matin. L'après-midi j'**allais** au travail.	No, I **used to be** at the university in the morning. In the afternoon, I **used to go** to work.

The imperfect is also used to describe things and people in the past.

Mes amis **étaient** tous diligents. Ils **étudiaient** sérieusement et **s'intéressaient** à leur travail. Mais ils **savaient** s'amuser aussi. Ils **étaient** tous très gentils et les professeurs du lycée les **trouvaient** sympathiques et intelligents.	My friends **were** all diligent. They **studied** seriously and **took an interest** in their work. But they **knew how** to have a good time too. They **were** all very nice and the high school teachers **found** them pleasant and intelligent.

The passé composé, in contrast to the imperfect, expresses specific actions and events that were started and completed at a specific moment in the past.

J'**ai pris** le petit déjeuner, j'**ai mis** mon manteau et je **suis sorti**.	I **had** breakfast, **put on** my coat, and **left the house**.

The imperfect and the passé composé may appear in the same sentence. The imperfect provides the background for the event stated in the passé composé. In such instances, the imperfect may describe time, weather, or an action that was going on when another event happened.

Il **était** 7 heures et demie quand elle **est rentrée**.	It **was** 7:30 when she **returned home**.
Quand on **est sortis** du restaurant, il **pleuvait**.	When we **left** the restaurant, it **was raining**.
Je **lisais** quand Jacques **a frappé** à la porte.	I **was reading** when Jacques **knocked** at the door.

E *Un temps trop variable.* *Jeanine a vu pas mal de changements atmosphériques pendant sa journée. Formez des phrases avec les éléments proposés en employant un imparfait et un passé composé pour savoir ce qui lui est arrivé. Suivez le modèle.*

MODÈLE   faire du soleil / je / descendre prendre l'autobus
            → Il faisait du soleil quand je suis descendue prendre l'autobus.

1. faire du vent / je / arriver à l'arrêt

2. bruiner (*to drizzle*) / l'autobus / venir

3. pleuvoir / je / monter dans l'autobus

4. faire froid / je / arriver à la faculté

5. geler / je / retrouver mon amie Hélène

6. neiger / nous / entrer dans l'amphithéâtre

7. tonner (*to thunder*) / le professeur / commencer sa conférence

8. grêler (*to hail*) / nous / sortir de l'amphithéâtre

F **Quand ça?** *Jean-Marc donne un aperçu de sa journée par ordre chronologique. Formez des phrases avec les éléments proposés en employant un imparfait et un passé composé pour savoir ce qu'il a fait et quand. Suivez le modèle.*

> MODÈLE   être tôt / je / sortir
> → Il était tôt quand je suis sorti.

1. 8 heures et demie / mon train / venir

2. 9 heures pile / je / arriver en ville

3. un peu tard / je / entrer dans le bureau

4. midi / mon collègue / m'inviter à déjeuner

5. une heure et demie / nous / finir de manger

6. tard dans l'après-midi / je / quitter le bureau

7. déjà 7 heures / je / retrouver ma fiancée pour dîner

8. presque minuit / je / rentrer chez moi

G **Comment faire le ménage?** *M. Fournier a profité de quelques moments de solitude pour faire le ménage. Suivez le modèle pour savoir ce que faisaient les autres membres de la famille pendant qu'il faisait le ménage. Chaque phrase aura un imparfait et un passé composé.*

> MODÈLE   laver le plancher / sa femme / dormir
> → Il a lavé le plancher pendant que sa femme dormait.

1. nettoyer la cuisine / les enfants / jouer dans le jardin

2. faire le linge / sa mère / promener le chien

3. préparer le dîner / sa sœur / faire les courses

4. mettre la table / son fils aîné / réparer la voiture

5. ranger les livres / son père / bricoler (*to fix things, tinker*) dans le **sous-sol** (*basement*)

6. cirer (*to polish*) les meubles / son frère / lire le journal

H *Des explications.* *Pourquoi est-ce que ces amis n'ont pas fait les choses qu'ils devaient faire? Formez des phrases pour expliquer leur manque d'action en écrivant ce qu'ils n'ont pas fait au passé composé et la raison à l'imparfait. Suivez le modèle.*

MODÈLE **Qui?**   **Quoi?**   **Pourquoi?**
        vous   prendre l'avion   avoir peur de voler
        → Vous n'avez pas pris l'avion parce que vous aviez peur de voler.

	Qui?	**Quoi?**	**Pourquoi?**
1.	je	aller au restaurant	ne pas avoir envie de sortir
2.	nous	faire une promenade	ne pas avoir le temps
3.	je	lire le chapitre	avoir mal à la tête
4.	Albert	prendre le petit déjeuner	être trop occupé
5.	Chantal	venir à la réunion	travailler
6.	nos copains	aller au concert	ne pas avoir d'argent
7.	les voisins	sortir	leur voiture être en panne
8.	tu	répondre au professeur	ne pas faire attention à sa question

I *On se souvient de Josette.* *Un groupe d'amis parle du moment où chacun a fait la connaissance de Josette. Écrivez ce qu'ils disent en suivant le modèle.*

MODÈLE   avoir dix-huit ans
            → Quand j'ai connu Josette, elle avait dix-huit ans.

1. être étudiante

2. travailler déjà

3. être institutrice

4. sortir avec Frédéric

5. être mariée

6. avoir deux enfants

J *Dormir (mal) à la campagne.* *Alain et Guy ont passé une mauvaise nuit sous leur tente à cause du sale temps qu'il faisait. Formez des phrases pour raconter leur mésaventure. Les deux propositions seront à l'imparfait. Suivez le modèle.*

MODÈLE   faire du soleil / ils / voyager en voiture
            → Il faisait du soleil pendant qu'ils voyageaient en voiture.

1. le ciel / être couvert / ils / chercher un endroit pour camper

2. bruiner / les deux garçons / dresser leur tente

3. pleuvoir / Guy / faire un feu

4. faire du vent / Alain / cuisiner

5. la température / baisser / ils / manger

6. des éclairs / illuminer le ciel / ils / ouvrir les sacs de couchage

7. tonner / les deux garçons / essayer de dormir

8. mais le matin / faire beau / ils / plier leur tente

Other Uses of the Imperfect Tense

The imperfect is used with time expressions to describe an action that began in the past and was still going on when another past action occurred. The English translations of these sentences usually have the structure *had been doing something for a certain amount of time when something else happened*. The event that happened is in the passé composé.

Combien de temps y avait-il que **vous habitiez** à Paris quand on vous **a offert** le poste à Perpignan?
Depuis combien de temps **habitiez-vous** à Paris quand on vous **a offert** le poste à Perpignan?

*How long **had you been living** in Paris when you **were offered** the position in Perpignan?*

Il y avait dix ans que **j'étais** à Paris quand **je suis parti** pour Perpignan.
J'étais à Paris depuis dix ans quand **je suis parti** pour Perpignan.

*I **had been** in Paris for ten years when **I left** for Perpignan.*

Note that the phrases used before the time expressions are also in the imperfect: **combien de temps y avait-il que**, **il y avait dix ans que**.

In more informal styles, the inverted interrogative may be replaced by **est-ce que** or the interrogative phrase may be placed after the verb.

Combien de temps est-ce qu'il y avait que vous habitiez à Paris?
Il y avait combien de temps que vous habitiez à Paris?

Depuis combien de temps est-ce que vous habitiez à Paris?
Vous habitiez à Paris **depuis combien de temps?**

*How long **had you been living** in Paris?*

Si plus the imperfect tense makes a suggestion, similar to English *How about . . . ?* or *What if . . . ?* It is especially common with either **nous** or **on** as the subject. With **tu** or **vous**, it can express impatience or irritation.

Si nous **sortions?**	*How about going out?*
Si on **partait** déjà?	*What if we leave now?*
—**Si** nous nous **dépêchions** un peu?	*How about if we hurry up?*
—Et **si** tu te **taisais?**	*And how about if you keep quiet?*

L'imprévu. *Dites combien de temps ces gens faisaient ce qu'ils faisaient quand quelque chose d'imprévu est arrivé. Traduisez les phrases en anglais. Suivez le modèle.*

MODÈLE   je / regarder la télé / une heure / Mon cousin a frappé à la porte.
→ Je regardais la télé depuis une heure quand mon cousin a frappé
à la porte.
OU Il y avait (Ça faisait) une heure que je regardais la télé quand mon
cousin a frappé à la porte.
I had been watching TV for an hour when my cousin knocked at the door.

1. vous / attendre le bus / vingt minutes / Jean-Claude est venu vous prendre avec sa voiture.

2. nous / étudier à la bibliothèque / six heures / Christine nous a invités à dîner chez elle.

3. Odile / dormir / dix minutes / Le téléphone a sonné.

4. Sylvain / entrer des données / deux heures / Il y a eu une panne d'électricité (*power failure*).

5. Brigitte / faire du jogging / une heure / Il a commencé à pleuvoir.

6. Alain / ranger ses affaires / dix minutes / Ses amis l'ont appelé pour jouer au football.

L **J'ai une idée!** *Marcelle s'ennuie. Son amie Claire lui propose des activités. Écrivez deux fois ses idées, une fois avec* **nous,** *la seconde avec* **on.** *Suivez le modèle.*

MODÈLE   aller au cinéma
→ Si nous allions au cinéma?
Si on allait au cinéma?

1. jouer aux cartes

2. acheter le journal

3. passer chez Françoise

4. regarder un film à la télé

5. manger au restaurant

6. commencer nos devoirs

Special Meanings of Certain Verbs

Some common verbs have different meanings in the imperfect and the passé composé.

savoir

Il **savait** l'adresse.   *He **knew** the address.*
Il **a su** l'adresse.   *He **found out** the address.*

connaître

Tu **connaissais** mon voisin?   ***Did** you **know** my neighbor?*
Tu **as connu** mon voisin?   ***Did** you **meet** my neighbor?*

pouvoir

Il **ne pouvait pas** sortir.	*He **couldn't** go out. (It was hard for him.)*
Il **n'a pas pu** sortir.	*He **couldn't** (and didn't) go out.*

vouloir

Je **voulais** partir.	*I **wanted** to leave.*
J'ai **voulu** partir.	*I **tried** to leave.*
Je **ne voulais pas** partir.	*I **didn't want** to leave.*
Je **n'ai pas voulu** partir.	*I **refused** to leave.*

avoir

Elle **avait** faim.	*She **was** hungry.*
Elle **a eu** faim.	*She **got** hungry.*

The imperfect forms of **pouvoir** and **vouloir** don't indicate whether the action of the infinitive took place or not.

M   *Comment dit-on cela en français?* Donnez l'équivalent français de ces phrases en anglais. Faites attention aux exemples ci-dessus.*

1. *Did you (vous) know the name of the street where she lives?*
   No, but I found it out this morning.

2. *Did they want to spend the day in town?*
   Yes, but they couldn't.

3. *I was able to work yesterday, but I refused to leave the house.*

4. *Did you (tu) get the letter yesterday?*
   No, I'd had the letter for a week.

5. *Did you (vous) meet the professor?*
   I knew him already.

N   *Une visite au musée.* Raconte*z cette histoire au passé en choisissant pour chaque verbe soit l'imparfait, soit le passé composé selon le cas.*

Je/J' _suis allé(e)_ (aller) au musée. Je/J'_____ (1. vouloir) voir les peintures de

la Renaissance. Je/J' _____ (2. entrer) d'abord dans les salles italiennes qui _____ (3. être)

à côté des salles françaises. Il y _____ (4. avoir) beaucoup de tableaux très intéressants.

Je/J'_____ (5. voir) des peintures fabuleuses. Après, je/j'_____ (6. passer) aux salles

françaises. Ensuite, je/j'_____ (7. monter) voir l'art du 20ème siècle. J'y _____ (8. trouver)

des œuvres fantastiques. Après une heure, je/j'_____ (9. descendre) à la librairie parce que

je/j'_____ (10. vouloir) acheter des cartes postales. J'y _____ (11. remarquer) deux livres

sur l'art qui me/m'_____ (12. intéresser) beaucoup, mais je ne/n'_____ (13. avoir) pas

assez d'argent pour les acheter. Je ne/n'_____ (14. acheter) que deux cartes postales.

Je/J'_____ (15. décider) de rentrer demain pour acheter les deux livres.

O *Fernand cherche du travail.* *Racontez cette histoire au passé en choisissant pour chaque verbe soit l'imparfait, soit le passé composé selon le cas.*

Fernand Bercot ___*voulait*___ (vouloir) travailler à Paris. Donc, il _____ (1. quitter) son

petit village dans la Gironde et il _____ (2. prendre) le train pour Paris. Il _____ (3. arriver)

dans la capitale il y a trois ans. Il n'_____ (4. avoir) même pas une chambre et il n'y

_____ (5. connaître) personne. Mais dans une semaine il _____ (6. trouver) un poste

de garçon de café. Il _____ (7. falloir) travailler beaucoup, mais il _____ (8. recevoir)

pas mal de pourboires. Il _____ (9. vivre) dans une chambre d'hôtel très modeste pour

faire des économies. Après un an et demi il _____ (10. renoncer) à son travail.

Il _____ (11. inviter) son frère Joseph à le rejoindre à Paris. Fernand _____ (12. mettre)

assez d'argent de côté pour monter un café. Son frère et lui _____ (13. ouvrir) un petit

bistrot dans le quinzième arrondissement. Ils _____ (14. être) ouvriers, mais maintenant

ils _____ (15. devenir) propriétaires d'un café!

NOTE CULTURELLE

- **La Gironde** est un département de l'ouest de la France dont le chef-lieu est le grand port atlantique de Bordeaux. Ce département est situé dans une grande région viticole qui produit des vins français très connus: Médoc, Saint-Émilion, Sauternes.
- **Paris** est divisé en vingt arrondissements, chacun possédant une mairie où se trouvent les bureaux administratifs. Il existe aussi un maire de la ville de Paris. Jacques Chirac, élu président de la France en 1995, avait été élu maire de Paris à trois reprises: en 1977, en 1983 et en 1989.

P *Activité orale. Hier, nous avons...* *Causez avec un(e) ami(e) au sujet de la journée que vous (et vos amis) avez passée hier. Pour chaque (ou pour presque chaque) action que vous mentionnez, décrivez aussi les circonstances: l'heure, le temps qu'il faisait, les actions des autres, etc. Comparez votre journée avec celle de votre ami(e).*

Pour parler un français authentique   **Speak Real French**

The Imperfect Tense

In the imperfect tense, four of the six forms are pronounced alike.

je	**parlais**	nous	parlions
tu	**parlais**	vous	parliez
il/elle	**parlait**	ils/elles	**parlaient**

je	**finissais**	nous	finissions
tu	**finissais**	vous	finissiez
il/elle	**finissait**	ils/elles	**finissaient**

je	**vendais**	nous	vendions
tu	**vendais**	vous	vendiez
il/elle	**vendait**	ils/elles	**vendaient**

In very formal French, these imperfect endings are pronounced with an open *e* sound, similar to the **ê** of **tête**. In contemporary spoken French, however, the verbs in boldface in the above tables end in closed **e**, the sound represented by **é**. This means that for **-er** verbs the following verb forms are pronounced alike: **parlais**, **parlait**, **parlaient**, **parler**, **parlez**, **parlé**. Thus, written French makes many distinctions that are not made in spoken French.

Compare these two forms.

> j'ai parlé
> je parlais

In written French, the two forms look nothing alike. In spoken French, however, the distinction is minimal.

> že par le
> žə par le

The contrast between the first vowel of the phrase carries the difference between imperfect and passé composé. The schwa of **je** drops in speech before a single consonant, so **je parlais** may be pronounced **j'parlais**. None of this is indicated in written French.

 Choose the form of the verb that completes each sentence correctly. All forms given are pronounced alike.

1. J'_____ au travail tous les jours.
   a. aller
   b. allez
   c. allais
   d. allé

2. Vous n'avez pas encore _____?
   a. commencé
   b. commencer
   c. commençais
   d. commencez

3. Elle _____ quand je suis entré.
   a. travaillait
   b. travaillé
   c. travaillez
   d. travailler

4. Où est-ce que vous _____ aujourd'hui?
   a. déjeuner
   b. déjeunaient
   c. déjeuné
   d. déjeunez

5. Hier j'ai _____ un bon film à la télé.
   a. regardé
   b. regardais
   c. regarder
   d. regardez

6. On dit qu'ils s'_____.
   a. aimé
   b. aimaient
   c. aimez
   d. aimer

Reflexive Verbs

Conjugation and Use of Reflexive Verbs

Reflexive verbs are called *pronominal verbs* in French, because they always appear with an object pronoun that refers to the same person or thing as the subject.

se réveiller *to wake up*

je	**me** réveille	nous	**nous** réveillons
tu	**te** réveilles	vous	**vous** réveillez
il/elle	**se** réveille	ils/elles	**se** réveillent
on	**se** réveille		

The reflexive pronoun usually precedes the conjugated verb.

—Je **me lève** toujours de bonne heure. *I always **get up** early.*
—Et est-ce que tu **te couches** aussi de bonne heure? *And do you also **go to bed** early?*
—Non, je ne **m'endors** pas avant minuit. *No, I don't **fall asleep** before midnight.*

Note that in a negative sentence, **ne** precedes the reflexive pronoun and **pas** follows the conjugated verb.

Reflexive verbs are used to express many routine actions.

se brosser les cheveux *to brush one's hair*
se brosser les dents *to brush one's teeth*
se coucher *to go to bed*
se couper les cheveux *to cut one's hair*
se couper/se limer les ongles *to cut/file one's nails*
se déshabiller *to get undressed*
s'endormir *to fall asleep*
s'habiller *to get dressed*
se laver *to wash up*

se laver la figure *to wash one's face*
se laver la tête *to wash one's hair*
se laver les mains *to wash one's hands*
se lever *to get up*
se maquiller *to put on makeup*
se peigner *to comb one's hair*
se raser *to shave*
se reposer *to rest*
se sécher les cheveux *to dry one's hair*

Note that when a body part receives the action of a reflexive verb, the definite article and not the possessive adjective is used to express possession.

A **Jumeaux (Twins).** *Jérôme et Paul sont des jumeaux. Paul décrit leur journée. Suivez le modèle.*

MODÈLE   se réveiller à 7 heures
→ Je me réveille à 7 heures. Jérôme se réveille à 7 heures aussi.

LE MATIN

1. se lever tout de suite
2. se brosser les dents
3. se peigner
4. se raser
5. s'habiller

LE SOIR

6. se laver les mains
7. se laver la figure
8. se reposer
9. se coucher à 11 heures
10. s'endormir tout de suite

B **C'est la mère des jumeaux qui parle.** *Maintenant c'est la mère de Jérôme et de Paul qui décrit leur journée typique. Suivez le modèle.*

MODÈLE   se réveiller à 7 heures
→ Ils se réveillent à 7 heures.

LE MATIN

1. se lever tout de suite
2. se brosser les dents
3. se peigner
4. se raser
5. s'habiller

LE SOIR

6. se laver les mains
7. se laver la figure
8. se reposer
9. se coucher à 11 heures
10. s'endormir tout de suite

C **Notre journée.** *Marthe et Vivienne décrivent une matinée typique. Employez dans chaque cas la première personne du pluriel pour savoir ce qu'elles font. Suivez le modèle.*

MODÈLE   se réveiller de bonne heure
→ Nous nous réveillons de bonne heure.

1. se lever immédiatement
2. se laver les mains et la figure
3. se brosser les dents
4. se laver la tête
5. se sécher les cheveux

6. se maquiller
7. se peigner
8. se brosser les cheveux
9. se limer les ongles
10. s'habiller avec soin

D   ***Au cinéma.*** *Jacques raconte sa sortie au cinéma avec ses amis. Formez des phrases au présent avec les éléments donnés pour voir ce qui se passe.*

Vocabulaire utile

s'approcher de *to approach*	**s'éloigner de** *to move away from*
s'arrêter *to stop*	**s'installer** *to move in, settle in*
s'asseoir *to sit down*	**se promener** *to take a walk*
se dépêcher *to hurry up*	**se réunir** *to get together*
se diriger vers *to head toward*	**se trouver** *to be located*

1. je / se réunir / avec mes amis

2. ils / se trouver / dans un café du centre

3. je / s'approcher / du café

4. mes amis / se lever

5. nous / s'éloigner du café

6. nous / se diriger / vers le cinéma

7. nous / se dépêcher

8. nous / s'arrêter au guichet pour prendre les billets

9. nous entrons dans le cinéma et nous / s'asseoir

The Infinitive of Reflexive Verbs

When the infinitive of a reflexive verb is used with another verb, such as **aller**, **pouvoir**, or **vouloir**, the reflexive pronoun precedes the infinitive and agrees with the subject.

—**Tu** vas **te** promener?	*Are **you** going to take a walk?*
—**Je** veux **me** promener, mais je ne peux pas.	*I want to take a walk, but I can't.*
—**Vous** devez **vous** dépêcher un peu.	***You** ought to hurry up.*
—**Nous** allons **nous** fâcher si vous ne vous taisez pas.	*We're going to get angry if you don't keep quiet.*

Such constructions are negated by putting **ne... pas** around the conjugated verb.

Je **ne** vais **pas** me promener.	*I'm **not** going to take a walk.*
Nous **ne** voulons **pas** nous dépêcher.	*We **don't** want to hurry.*

E **Sentiments.** *Exprimez les sentiments et les réactions des gens indiqués en utilisant un verbe à l'infinitif. Suivez le modèle.*

> MODÈLE   Jean / aller / s'amuser
> → Jean va s'amuser.

Les émotions

s'amuser *to have a good time*	**s'impatienter** *to get impatient*
s'animer *to feel more lively*	**s'inquiéter** *to worry*
se calmer *to calm down*	**se mettre en colère** *to get angry*
s'embêter *to be/get bored*	**s'offenser** *to get insulted/offended*
s'énerver *to get nervous/upset*	**se passionner (pour)** *to get excited (about)*
s'ennuyer *to be/get bored*	**se préoccuper** *to worry*
s'enthousiasmer *to get enthusiastic*	**se sentir** *to feel*
se fâcher *to get angry*	

1. je / ne pas vouloir / s'inquiéter

2. vous / devoir / se calmer

3. il / ne pas pouvoir / se sentir triste

4. elles / ne pas vouloir / s'ennuyer

5. tu / ne pas devoir / se mettre en colère

6. nous / ne pas aller / s'offenser

7. le professeur / aller / s'impatienter

8. tu / devoir / s'animer

F **Cette fois ça va être différent.** *Employez **aller** suivi d'un infinitif pour exprimer que cette fois les sentiments vont changer. Suivez le modèle.*

> MODÈLE   il / s'amuser
> → En général, il ne s'amuse pas, mais cette fois il va s'amuser.

1. je / se fâcher

2. elles / s'énerver

3. tu / s'impatienter

4. il / s'offenser

5. nous / s'inquiéter

6. vous / s'embêter

7. je / se sentir de trop (*in the way*)

8. tu / se passionner

G **Conseils psychologiques.** *Employez le verbe **devoir** suivi d'un infinitif pour donner des conseils pour maîtriser les émotions. Suivez le modèle.*

> MODÈLE   tu / ne pas devoir / s'énerver
> → Tu ne dois pas t'énerver.

1. vous / devoir / se calmer

2. elle / devoir / s'amuser un peu

3. je / devoir / se sentir heureux/heureuse

4. nous / ne pas devoir / se mettre en colère

5. ils / devoir / s'enthousiasmer

6. tu / ne pas devoir / s'impatienter

7. je / devoir / s'animer un peu

8. vous / ne pas devoir / s'offenser

The Passé Composé of Reflexive Verbs

All reflexive verbs are conjugated with **être** in the passé composé. The reflexive pronoun is placed immediately before the conjugated form of **être**, and the past participle agrees in gender and number with the reflexive pronoun if that pronoun is a direct object.

se laver *to wash up*			
je	**me suis lavé(e)**	nous	**nous sommes lavé(e)s**
tu	**t'es lavé(e)**	vous	**vous êtes lavé(e)(s)**
il	**s'est lavé**	ils	**se sont lavés**
elle	**s'est lavée**	elles	**se sont lavées**

When a direct object follows a reflexive verb (as in **se laver les mains**), the reflexive pronoun is an indirect object. In such cases, the past participle does not agree with the reflexive pronoun.

se laver les mains *to wash one's hands*			
je	**me suis lavé les mains**	nous	**nous sommes lavé les mains**
tu	**t'es lavé les mains**	vous	**vous êtes lavé les mains**
il	**s'est lavé les mains**	ils	**se sont lavé les mains**
elle	**s'est lavé les mains**	elles	**se sont lavé les mains**

In the negative, **ne** precedes the reflexive pronoun and **pas** follows the conjugated form of **être**.

Nicole **ne** s'est **pas** réveillée de bonne heure parce qu'elle **ne** s'est **pas** couchée de bonne heure.

Nicole didn't wake up early, because she didn't go to bed early.

H *Ne t'impatiente pas! Formez de petites conversations entre deux copines. La première veut savoir quand les choses vont se faire. La seconde lui répond qu'on les a déjà faites. Suivez le modèle.*

MODÈLE les enfants / se laver
→ Solange: Quand est-ce que les enfants vont se laver?
Annick: Ils se sont déjà lavés.

Vocabulaire utile
se charger de qqch *to take charge of something, be responsible for something*
se détendre *to relax*
se fatiguer *to get tired*
s'intéresser à qqn/à qqch *to be interested in someone/something*
se mettre à faire qqch *to begin to do something*
se mettre en route *to get going*
s'occuper de qqch *to take care of something*
se soigner *to take care of oneself*

1. tu / se mettre à préparer le dîner

2. les enfants / se coucher

3. Josette et toi / s'occuper du linge

4. tu / se reposer

5. Elvire / se laver la tête

6. tu / se limer les ongles

7. Carole et Paulette / se calmer

8. je / se brosser les cheveux

I **Pas encore.** *Madame Goulet est pressée parce que sa famille doit partir en vacances. Mais personne n'est prêt. Utilisez le passé composé avec* **pas encore** *pour exprimer les réponses à ses questions. Suivez le modèle.*

> MODÈLE   Marc, tu viens de te laver, n'est-ce pas?
> → Non, je ne me suis pas encore lavé.

1. Christine, tu viens de te lever, n'est-ce pas?

2. Chéri, tu viens de te raser, n'est-ce pas?

3. Marc et Christine, vous venez de vous brosser les dents, n'est-ce pas?

4. Christine, tu viens de te laver la tête, n'est-ce pas?

5. Chéri, tu viens de t'habiller, n'est-ce pas?

6. Marc et Christine, vous venez de vous peigner, n'est-ce pas?

J **Une excursion du lycée.** *Le lycée a organisé une excursion à Versailles pour les étudiants. Décrivez leur départ en formant des phrases au passé composé à partir des éléments donnés.*

1. Olivier et Jean / se réveiller de bonne heure

2. Christine / se laver la tête

3. Monique et Véronique / se préparer pour le départ

4. Mireille / se dépêcher comme une folle

5. Christian et Pierre / se charger de la nourriture

6. tous les étudiants / se réunir devant le lycée

7. ils / s'asseoir dans les autocars

8. les autocars / s'éloigner de l'établissement

K **Zéro de conduite.** *Grand-mère se plaint de la conduite de ses petits-enfants hier, quand toute la famille est venue lui rendre visite. Formez des phrases au passé composé pour voir ce qui est arrivé.*

La mauvaise conduite
se cacher *to hide*
s'échapper de *to run away from, escape from*
se mettre en panique *to fly into a panic*
se moquer de qqn/de qqch *to make fun of someone/something*
se mouiller *to get wet*
se plaindre de qqn/de qqch *to complain about someone/something*
se salir *to get dirty*

1. le petit Claude / se mouiller la chemise en buvant un Coca

2. Marlise / se salir dans le garage

3. les jumeaux / se moquer du voisin

4. les parents de Philippe / se mettre en panique

5. leur fils / s'échapper de la maison

6. Caroline / se plaindre de tout

7. le petit Baudoin / se cacher au sous-sol

8. Odile / se couper le doigt avec un couteau

9. moi / se fatiguer

10. je / se coucher de bonne heure

Reciprocal Reflexive Verbs

A plural reflexive pronoun may be used with a verb to express reciprocity (English: *each other*).

—Vous **vous parlez** souvent?	*Do you **speak to each other** often?*
—Oui, nous **nous téléphonons** tous les jours.	*Yes, we **phone each other** every day.*
—Marc et Constance **se voient** souvent?	*Do Marc and Constance **see each other** often?*
—Oui, ils **se donnent rendez-vous** après leur cours.	*Yes, they **make an appointment to see each other** after their class.*

The passé composé of a reciprocal verb is formed like the passé composé of any reflexive verb: with the auxiliary verb **être**. The past participle agrees with the reflexive pronoun if that pronoun is a direct object. In order to determine whether or not the reflexive pronoun is a direct object, consider whether the corresponding nonreflexive verb takes a direct or indirect object of the person. For instance, the following verbs take a direct object of the person.

aider quelqu'un *to help someone*
regarder quelqu'un *to look at someone*
voir quelqu'un *to see someone*

When the direct object is replaced by an object pronoun in the passé composé, the past participle agrees with it in gender and number.

Les enfants? Je **les** ai aidé**s**.	*The children? I helped **them**.*
Quand Marie est entrée, tout le monde **l**'a regardé**e**.	*When Marie came in, everyone looked at **her**.*
Les institutrices étaient là? Nous ne **les** avons pas vu**es**.	*The (female) elementary school teachers were there? We didn't see **them**.*

When these verbs are reflexive, the reflexive pronoun is a direct object and the past participle agrees with it.

Nous **nous** sommes aidés.	*We helped **each other**.*
Elles **se** sont regardées.	*They [fem.] looked at **each other**.*
Ils **se** sont vus.	*They saw **each other**.*

Here are examples of verbs that take an indirect object of the person.

donner (quelque chose) à quelqu'un *to give (something) to someone*
écrire à quelqu'un *to write to someone*
parler à quelqu'un *to talk to someone*

In verbs that take an indirect object of the person, there is no agreement in the passé composé when the indirect object noun is replaced by an indirect object pronoun.

Je **leur** ai donné mes coordonnées.	*I gave **them** my contact information.*
Christine est à Paris. Je **lui** ai écrit.	*Christine is in Paris. I have written **to her**.*
Nous avons vu Lise et Marthe, mais nous ne **leur** avons pas parlé.	*We saw Lise and Marthe, but we didn't speak **to them**.*

When these verbs are reflexive, the reflexive pronoun is an indirect object and the past participle does not agree with it.

Elles **se** sont **donné** des cadeaux.	*They [fem.] **gave each other** gifts.*
Nous **nous** sommes **écrit**.	*We **wrote to each other**.*
Ils **se** sont **parlé** au café.	*They **spoke to each other** at the café.*

Some Common Reciprocal Verbs

*s'acheter des cadeaux *to buy gifts for each other*
 s'aider *to help each other*
 s'aimer *to love each other*
 se comprendre *to understand each other*
 se connaître *to know each other*
 se détester *to hate each other*
*se donner rendez-vous *to make an appointment to see each other*
*s'écrire *to write to each other*
 s'entraider *to help each other*
*se mentir *to lie to each other*
*se parler *to speak to each other*
*se poser des questions *to ask each other questions*
 se regarder *to look at each other*
 se rencontrer *to meet, run into each other*
*se ressembler *to look alike*
*se téléphoner *to phone each other*
 se voir *to see each other*

---

*For these verbs, the reflexive pronoun is an indirect object.

L **Pas hier.** *Répondez à l'affirmatif aux questions qu'on vous pose, mais dites que hier c'était différent. Utilisez le passé composé et faites attention à l'accord du participe. Suivez le modèle.*

MODÈLE   Vous vous rencontrez souvent?
→ Oui, mais hier nous ne nous sommes pas rencontrés.

1. Vous vous voyez souvent?

2. Vous vous écrivez souvent?

3. Vous vous parlez souvent?

4. Vous vous téléphonez souvent?

5. Vous vous donnez souvent rendez-vous?

6. Vous vous aidez souvent?

7. Vous vous accompagnez souvent?

8. Vous vous invitez souvent?

M **Histoire d'amour.** *Racontez le triste amour de Félix et Geneviève. Utilisez le pronom* **ils** *et le passé composé dans chaque phrase. Remarquez qu'il y a des verbes qui ne sont pas pronominaux. Suivez le modèle.*

MODÈLE   se voir
→ Ils se sont vus.

Les rapports humains
se disputer *to argue*
s'entendre bien/mal avec qqn *to get along/not get along with someone*
se fiancer (avec qqn) *to get engaged (to someone)*
se marier (avec qqn) *to get married (to someone)*
rompre (avec qqn) *to break up (with someone)*
tomber amoureux/amoureuse de qqn *to fall in love with someone*

1. se connaître

2. se parler

3. se comprendre

4. tomber amoureux

5. s'acheter des petits cadeaux

6. se fiancer

7. après un temps / se disputer

8. se mentir

9. rompre

10. ne pas se marier

The Imperative of Reflexive Verbs

In negative commands, the reflexive pronoun precedes the verb.

Ne **t'**énerve pas!	*Don't get upset!*
Ne **vous** levez pas.	*Don't get up.*
Ne **nous** approchons pas.	*Let's not get closer.*

In affirmative commands, the reflexive pronoun is placed after the verb and connected to it by a hyphen. **Te** changes to **toi** when placed after the verb.

Asseyez-**vous**.	*Sit down.*
Dépêchons-**nous**.	*Let's hurry up.*
Habille-**toi** et mets-**toi** à travailler.	*Get dressed and start working.*

N *Quelle lenteur!* *Employez l'impératif des verbes pronominaux pour dire à un ami (et à deux amis) ce qu'ils doivent faire pour ne pas être en retard. Suivez le modèle.*

> MODÈLE   se réveiller
> → à un ami: Réveille-toi.
>   à deux amis: Réveillez-vous.

1. se lever
2. s'habiller
3. se dépêcher
4. se laver les mains
5. ne pas s'énerver

6. ne plus se reposer
7. ne pas se fâcher
8. ne pas se recoucher
9. se diriger vers la porte
10. se préparer pour partir

O *On s'encourage.* *Employez l'impératif de la première personne du pluriel pour dire à un ami ce qu'il faut faire pour ne pas être en retard. Suivez le modèle.*

> MODÈLE   se lever
> → Levons-nous.

1. se raser
2. s'habiller
3. se dépêcher
4. se laver les mains
5. ne pas s'énerver

6. ne plus se reposer
7. ne pas se fâcher
8. s'aider
9. se diriger vers la porte
10. se préparer pour partir

Other Reflexive Constructions and Reflexive Verbs

When inversion is used to form questions with reflexive verbs, the subject pronoun is placed after the verb; the reflexive pronoun remains before the verb. The use of inversion to form questions with reflexive verbs is limited to formal written style and very formal speech.

Vous intéressez-vous à l'art moderne?	*Are you interested in modern art?*
Les prisonniers **se sont-ils échappés?**	*Did the prisoners escape?*
Ne vous efforcez-vous pas de progresser?	*Aren't you striving to progress?*
Ne se sont-elles pas vues dans le Midi?	*Didn't they see each other in the south of France?*

In everyday speech and writing, the interrogative of reflexives is formed with **est-ce que** or by merely changing the intonation of the sentence.

Est que vous vous intéressez à l'art moderne? Vous vous intéressez à l'art moderne?	*Are you interested in modern art?*
Est-ce que les prisonniers se sont échappés? Les prisonniers se sont échappés?	*Did the prisoners escape?*
Est-ce que vous ne vous **efforcez** pas de progresser? Vous ne vous **efforcez** pas de progresser?	*Aren't you striving to progress?*
Est-ce qu'elles ne se sont pas vues dans le Midi? Elles ne se sont pas vues dans le Midi?	*Didn't they see each other in the south of France?*

A reflexive verb in the third person singular with an inanimate subject can sometimes be the equivalent of the English passive voice.

Ça ne **se fait** pas.	*That's not **done**.*
C'est un livre qui **se lit** beaucoup.	*It's a book that **is read** a lot.*
Cette ville **s'appelle** Valence.	*This city **is called** Valence.*

Some Additional Reflexive Verbs

s'adresser à qqn *to address, speak to, be aimed at*
s'en aller *to go away*
s'apercevoir de qqch *to notice something*
s'attendre à qqch *to expect something*
se débarrasser de qqn/de qqch *to get rid of someone/something*
se demander *to wonder*
se donner la peine de faire qqch *to take the trouble to do something*
se fier à qqn/qqch *to trust someone/something*
s'habituer à qqch *to get used to something, get accustomed to something*
se méfier de qqn/qqch *to distrust someone/something, be wary of someone/something*
se passer de qqch *to do without something*
se perdre *to get lost*
se priver de qqch *to deprive oneself of something*
se rappeler qqch *to recall/remember something*
se servir de qqch *to use something*
se soucier de qqn/qqch *to worry about someone/something, be concerned about someone/something*
se souvenir de qqn/qqch *to remember someone/something*
se tromper de qqch *to go to the wrong thing, select the wrong thing*

Posez vos questions! *Refaites ces questions dans la langue soignée* (formal) *en employant l'inversion.*

1. Est-ce que ce produit se vend bien?

2. Est-ce que les étudiants s'amusent au bal?

3. Est-ce que vous ne vous dirigez pas vers la sortie?

4. Est-ce qu'ils ne se sont pas approchés du guichet?

5. Est-ce que nous ne nous éloignons pas du centre de la ville?

6. Pourquoi est-ce que vos amis ne se sont plus réunis?

7. Pourquoi est-ce que tu ne t'intéresses plus au cinéma?

8. À quelle heure est-ce qu'elles se sont mises en route?

9. Est-ce qu'ils ne se sont pas offensés?

10. Est-ce qu'elle s'est souvenue de moi?

11. Pourquoi est-ce qu'elle ne s'est pas habituée à la vie française?

12. Est-ce que vous vous attendez à le voir?

Q **Comment est-ce que ça se dit?** *Employez des verbes pronominaux pour exprimer ces phrases en français.*

1. *They have gone away. I plan* (compter) *to go away too.*

2. *We took the wrong train.*

3. *This park is called* le jardin du Luxembourg.

4. *That is not said.*

5. *I am wary of dogs that I don't know.*

6. *He never used to worry about his work.*

7. *We trusted our friends.*

8. *Do you remember Professor Gauthier?*

9. *They didn't take the trouble to look for a good hotel.*

10. *I wonder if they got lost.*

R **Activité orale.** *Avec un(e) ami(e) décrivez votre journée—ce que vous faites le matin, comment vous arrivez au travail, les gens que vous y voyez et vos sentiments, ce que vous faites en rentrant chez vous, etc. Votre ami(e) décrira la sienne.*

9

Future and Conditional; Conditional Sentences (1)

The Future Tense

The future tense expresses an action that will take place in the future (English: *I will speak, we will finish*). The future tense of regular verbs is formed by adding the following endings to the infinitive: **-ai, -as, -a, -ons, -ez, -ont**.

parler

je	parler**ai**	nous	parler**ons**
tu	parler**as**	vous	parler**ez**
il/elle	parler**a**	ils/elles	parler**ont**

finir

je	finir**ai**	nous	finir**ons**
tu	finir**as**	vous	finir**ez**
il/elle	finir**a**	ils/elles	finir**ont**

Verbs whose infinitive ends in **-re** drop their final **-e** before the future-tense endings.

rendre

je	rendr**ai**	nous	rendr**ons**
tu	rendr**as**	vous	rendr**ez**
il/elle	rendr**a**	ils/elles	rendr**ont**

Some verbs have an irregular stem in the future tense. The endings are *regular* in all cases.

être	je **ser**ai	venir	je **viendr**ai	pouvoir	je **pourr**ai
faire	je **fer**ai	vouloir	je **voudr**ai	voir	je **verr**ai
aller	j'**ir**ai	acquérir	j'**acquérr**ai	devoir	je **devr**ai
avoir	j'**aur**ai	courir	je **courr**ai	recevoir	je **recevr**ai
savoir	je **saur**ai	envoyer	j'**enverr**ai	décevoir	je **décevr**ai
tenir	je **tiendr**ai	mourir	je **mourr**ai	pleuvoir	il **pleuvr**a

Related verbs have the same irregularities in their stems.

devenir	je **deviendr**ai
revenir	je **reviendr**ai

The future of **il faut** is **il faudra**. The future of **il y a** is **il y aura**.

Verbs that change a mute **e** to **è** before a mute **e** in the present tense (such as **acheter**) also change **e** to **è** in all forms of the future tense. Verbs that double their final consonant before a mute **e** in the present tense (such as **appeler**) have the same change in all persons of the future tense.

acheter	j'**achèter**ai
amener	j'**amèner**ai
appeler	j'**appeller**ai
jeter	je **jetter**ai

However, verbs such as **espérer** and **préférer** retain **é** in the future tense.

espérer	j'**espérer**ai
préférer	je **préférer**ai

The future of **s'asseoir** is either **je m'assiérai** or **je m'assoirai** (the latter without the **e** of the infinitive).

 C'est pour demain. *Tout ce qu'on allait faire aujourd'hui, on a remis* (postponed) *pour demain. Répondez à ces questions en suivant le modèle.*

MODÈLE   Jean ne fait pas les courses aujourd'hui?
→ Non, il fera les courses demain.

1. Mademoiselle, vous ne faites pas le ménage aujourd'hui?

2. Tes parents ne reviennent pas aujourd'hui?

3. Ton ami ne va pas au bureau aujourd'hui?

4. Je ne travaille pas aujourd'hui, monsieur?

5. Je ne réponds pas aujourd'hui?

6. Tu ne sais pas la réponse aujourd'hui?

7. Monsieur, je n'envoie pas le courriel aujourd'hui?

8. Nous n'emmenons pas les enfants au zoo aujourd'hui?

9. Les autres professeurs et vous, vous ne projetez pas le film aujourd'hui?

10. Les programmeurs ne complètent pas leur travail aujourd'hui?

 Je crois. *Serge, optimiste, parle avec un copain impatient. Serge croit que tout se réalisera. Écrivez ses réponses en suivant le modèle.*

MODÈLE   Un copain: Le prof vient ou ne vient pas?
Serge: Je crois qu'il viendra.

1. Je réussis ou je ne réussis pas?

2. Nos copains descendent ou ne descendent pas?

3. Théo va ou ne va pas?

4. Il neige ou il ne neige pas?

5. Tu sors ou tu ne sors pas?

6. Marie et moi, nous arrivons à l'heure ou nous n'arrivons pas à l'heure?

7. Tes parents nous prêtent la voiture ou ne nous prêtent pas la voiture?

8. Tu complètes tes devoirs ou tu ne complètes pas tes devoirs?

C *Je ne sais pas.* Dites dans chaque cas que vous ne savez pas si l'action arrivera. *Suivez le modèle.*

> MODÈLE Est-ce qu'il vient demain?
> → Je ne sais pas s'il viendra.

1. Est-ce qu'ils partent demain?

2. Est-ce que vous travaillez demain?

3. Est-ce que je passe l'examen demain?

4. Est-ce que le professeur revient demain?

5. Est-ce que les enfants vont à l'école demain?

6. Est-ce que tu conduis demain?

7. Est-ce que les étudiants lisent demain?

8. Est-ce qu'on projette un film demain?

9. Est-ce que tu veux venir demain?

10. Est-ce que ton copain peut rentrer demain?

D *Des projets pour l'été.* La famille Ramonet est très nombreuse. Le départ en Languedoc pour passer l'été n'est donc pas facile. Formez des phrases au futur à partir des éléments donnés pour dire ce que chaque membre de la famille fera pour faciliter ce départ.

1. maman / faire les valises

2. la fille aînée / s'occuper des petits

3. papa / se charger de la voiture

4. tout le monde / se réveiller à 7 heures du matin

5. tous les membres de la famille / se dépêcher

6. personne / se mettre en colère

7. les enfants / s'entraider

8. les grands-parents / préparer le petit déjeuner

9. la tante Marie / fermer les fenêtres

10. les Ramonet / se mettre en route vers 10 heures du matin

NOTE CULTURELLE

- **Le Languedoc-Roussillon** est une région du Midi située entre la Provence et la frontière espagnole. La ville la plus importante du Roussillon est Perpignan.
- Le Languedoc est connu pour son vignoble qui est responsable de 12% de la production mondiale du vin. Pour les touristes, le Languedoc offre la ville de Carcassonne, une forteresse médiévale très bien conservée et le fameux aqueduc romain, le pont du Gard.
- Le chef-lieu du Languedoc-Roussillon est Montpellier, ville universitaire et site d'une industrie électronique importante. D'autres villes importantes de la région sont Narbonne, Béziers et Sète.

Use of the Future After **quand** and Other Conjunctions

The future tense is used after **quand** (*when*), **lorsque** (*when*), **dès que** (*as soon as*), **aussitôt que** (*as soon as*), and **après que** (*after*) when a future event is implied. The main clause in these sentences is in either the future or the imperative, or uses **aller** + infinitive.

Téléphone-moi **quand tu seras** prêt.	*Phone me **when you're** ready.*
Je passerai te prendre **dès que tu m'appelleras**.	*I'll come by and pick you up **as soon as you call me**.*
Quand tu verras ma voiture, descends.	***When you see** my car, come downstairs to the street.*
Je te ramènerai **aussitôt que la réunion finira**.	*I'll bring you back **as soon as the meeting is over**.*

Note that English uses the present tense, not the future, in such clauses.

E *On se met en route. Odile Dulac explique quand sa famille fera les choses nécessaires pour partir à la montagne. Cette année les Dulac vont dans la région Midi-Pyrénées. Formez des phrases à partir des éléments donnés pour voir ce qu'elle dit. Mettez les propositions principales au futur.*

1. je / faire ma valise / dès que / le linge / être sec

2. les enfants / s'habiller / quand / ils / rentrer de l'école

3. nous / manger / quand / maman / revenir du marché

4. mon frère / mettre les valises dans la voiture / aussitôt que / papa / revenir de la station-service

5. nous / choisir la route / quand / je / trouver la carte

6. nous / partir / quand / faire beau

7. nous / chercher un hôtel / lorsque / nous / arriver à Aurillac

8. je / se coucher / aussitôt que / nous / être dans l'hôtel

NOTE CULTURELLE

- La région **Midi-Pyrénées** se situe entre les pays aquitains et le Languedoc, dans les Pyrénées centrales. Luchon est une station thermale très connue, très fréquentée par les touristes.
- La ville la plus importante et le chef-lieu de la région est Toulouse. Centre de la civilisation provençale au moyen âge et gouvernée par les comtes de Toulouse, la ville a souffert à l'époque de la croisade albigeoise.
- Aujourd'hui Toulouse est un grand centre industriel et scientifique, spécialisé dans l'aéronautique. On y construit les avions Airbus et les fusées spatiales Ariane.

F   *Conseils et ordres.* *Employez l'impératif et le futur pour donner des conseils et des ordres. Suivez le modèle.*

MODÈLE   CONSEIL/ORDRE   **Quand**
         (à ton ami Pierre) s'asseoir   quand / le professeur / entrer
         → Assieds-toi quand le professeur entrera.

CONSEIL/ORDRE	**Quand**
1. (à tes amis) sortir	dès que / la cloche / sonner
2. (à ton amie Lise) téléphoner	aussitôt que / Albert / arriver
3. (à tes amis) se mettre à prendre des notes	quand / le professeur / commencer sa conférence
4. (à ton petit frère) descendre à la cuisine	quand / je / t'appeler
5. (à Jean-Luc et Ghislaine) venir me voir	quand / vous / pouvoir
6. (à ta sœur) fermer la porte à clé	quand / tu / s'en aller
7. (à Mme Chiclet) dire bonjour de ma part à votre fils	quand / vous / le voir
8. (à tes parents) lire mon courriel	dès que / vous / la recevoir

The Conditional

The conditional expresses what might happen or what would happen if certain conditions existed. It is formed by adding the endings of the imperfect tense to the infinitive or to the irregular future tense stem.

parler

je	parler**ais**	nous	parler**ions**
tu	parler**ais**	vous	parler**iez**
il/elle	parler**ait**	ils/elles	parler**aient**

finir

je	finir**ais**	nous	finir**ions**
tu	finir**ais**	vous	finir**iez**
il/elle	finir**ait**	ils/elles	finir**aient**

rendre

je	rendr**ais**	nous	rendr**ions**
tu	rendr**ais**	vous	rendr**iez**
il/elle	rendr**ait**	ils/elles	rendr**aient**

être

je	ser**ais**	nous	ser**ions**
tu	ser**ais**	vous	ser**iez**
il/elle	ser**ait**	ils/elles	ser**aient**

The same spelling changes that appear in the future appear in the conditional.

acheter   j'**achèter**ais
appeler   j'**appeller**ais
préférer   je **préférer**ais

The conditional of **il faut** is **il faudrait**. The conditional of **il y a** is **il y aurait**.

The conditional tense is the equivalent of English *would* + verb. It should not be confused with the use of *would* to describe a repeated action in the past (imperfect tense).

| Si tu voulais te baigner, on **irait** à la plage. | If you wanted to go swimming, we **would go** to the beach. |
| On **allait** à la plage tous les jours quand on était petits. | We **would go** to the beach every day when we were children. |

G ***Si on pouvait.*** *On ferait les choses dont on a envie si on pouvait. Employez le conditionnel du verbe principal et l'imparfait de* **pouvoir** *pour exprimer cette idée en suivant le modèle.*

MODÈLE   Jean a envie de partir.
→ Oui, il partirait s'il pouvait.

1. J'ai envie de rentrer.

2. Monique et Danielle ont envie de faire du ski.

3. Tu as envie de devenir poète.

4. Odile et moi, nous avons envie de nous voir tous les jours.

5. J'ai envie de me mettre en route.

6. Richard a envie de se promener.

7. Sylvie et toi, vous avez envie d'acheter du pain.

8. Mon copain et moi, nous avons envie d'être de retour.

H *Moi non plus.* *Quand on vous dit ce que vos amis n'ont pas fait, dites dans chaque cas que vous ne feriez pas ces choses non plus. Employez le conditionnel dans vos réponses. Suivez le modèle.*

> MODÈLE   Je ne me suis pas baigné dans ce lac.
> → Moi non plus, je ne me baignerais pas dans ce lac.

1. Charles n'a pas pris la voiture.

2. Martine n'a pas fait la vaisselle.

3. Olivier et Chantal ne se sont pas assis dans le jardin.

4. Je n'ai pas regardé la télé aujourd'hui.

5. Les enfants n'ont pas enlevé leur pull.

6. Le collège n'a pas projeté ce film.

7. Les étudiants n'ont pas répété ces slogans.

8. Solange n'a pas couru.

I *Impossible!* *Employez le conditionnel pour dire dans chaque cas que la nouvelle qu'on vient de vous annoncer est sûrement fausse. Suivez le modèle.*

> MODÈLE   On dit que Pierre est parti.
> → Impossible! Il ne partirait pas.

1. On dit que vous avez renoncé à votre travail.

2. On dit que Catherine a rejeté notre offre.

3. On dit que Philippe s'est levé pendant la classe.

4. On dit que les professeurs ont fait grève.

5. On dit que tu exagères.

6. On dit que j'ai perdu les billets.

7. On dit que Laurent est tombé en skiant.

8. On dit que le petit Baudoin a jeté son dîner à la poubelle.

Conditional Sentences (1)

A conditional sentence consists of two clauses: an *if*-clause (**si**-clause) and a result clause.

If an event is likely to happen, the present is used in the **si**-clause and the present, future, or imperative is used in the result clause.

S'il **pleut**, nous **restons** chez nous.	*If it **rains**, we **stay** home.*
Viens me voir si tu **as** le temps.	***Come** see me if you **have** time.*
Si tu **t'en vas**, tes parents **se fâcheront**.	*If you **leave**, your parents **will get angry**.*

If an event is unlikely to happen or is contrary to fact, the imperfect is used in the **si**-clause and the conditional is used in the result clause.

Je t'**aiderais** si je **pouvais**.

*I'd **help** you if I **could**.* (FACT: I can't help you. But if I could, I would.)

S'il **parlait** espagnol, il **s'habituerait** à la vie mexicaine.

*If he **spoke** Spanish, he **would get used** to Mexican life.* (FACT: He doesn't speak Spanish. But if he did, he would get used to Mexican life.)

Conditional Sentences: Summary of Tenses

si-CLAUSE	RESULT CLAUSE
Present	Present, future, or imperative
Imperfect	Conditional

J   *Des progrès personnels pour Jean-Pierre. Jean-Pierre doit se transformer pour être un jeune homme à la page. Employez des phrases composées d'une supposition (si) à l'imparfait et d'une proposition principale au conditionnel pour exprimer ce que Jean-Pierre doit faire. Suivez le modèle.*

MODÈLE   Jean-Pierre ne lit jamais le journal. Il ne sait pas ce qui se passe dans le monde.
    →   Si Jean-Pierre lisait le journal, il saurait ce qui se passe dans le monde.

1. Jean-Pierre ne s'habille pas bien. Les autres étudiants se moquent de lui.

2. Jean-Pierre ne fait pas de sport. Il ne connaît pas beaucoup de monde.

3. Jean-Pierre ne s'intéresse pas à ses études. Il n'est pas préparé en classe.

4. Jean-Pierre s'absente souvent. Les professeurs se fâchent contre lui.

5. Jean-Pierre lit des bandes dessinées (*comics*) en classe. Les profs sont furieux.

6. Jean-Pierre mange toujours seul. Il ne parle pas avec les autres étudiants.

K   *Déménagement. Les Fantin essaient de décider où placer leurs meubles dans leur nouvelle maison. Exprimez leurs idées avec une phrase composée d'une supposition au présent et d'une proposition principale au futur. Suivez le modèle.*

MODÈLE   on / mettre la chaîne stéréo dans le séjour :
    on / pouvoir écouter des disques ensemble
    →   Si on met la chaîne stéréo dans le séjour, on pourra écouter des disques ensemble.

1. maman / installer la machine à laver au sous-sol : nous / avoir plus de place dans la cuisine

2. je / mettre la lampe à côté du fauteuil : je / pouvoir lire

3. nous / nettoyer le tapis : nous / le mettre dans le salon

4. tu / trouver la table en plastique : tu / pouvoir la mettre sur la terrasse

5. on / laisser l'ordinateur dans ma chambre : je / faire mes devoirs sans embêter les autres

6. les déménageurs / monter une étagère dans ma chambre : je / ranger tous mes livres

L *Il y a toujours des problèmes quand on déménage.* Refaites chaque phrase en supposition avec **si** à l'imparfait + proposition principale au conditionnel pour exprimer tout ce qui manque dans la nouvelle maison des Didier. Suivez le modèle.

MODÈLE   On n'a pas de lave-vaisselle. On fait la vaisselle à la main.
           → Si on avait un lave-vaisselle, on ne ferait pas la vaisselle à la main.

1. On n'a pas deux postes de télé. On ne peut pas regarder la télé dans le séjour.

2. Cette maison n'a pas de grenier (*attic*). Il n'y a pas de place pour les boîtes.

3. La cheminée ne fonctionne pas. Nous ne pouvons pas faire un feu.

4. On n'a pas de tableaux dans le salon. Le salon n'est pas accueillant (*cozy*).

5. Je n'ai pas de chaîne stéréo dans ma chambre. J'écoute mes disques dans le séjour.

6. Le frigo est tellement petit. Maman doit faire les courses plusieurs fois par semaine.

7. Tu ne décroches (*take down*) pas les rideaux. Je ne peux pas les laver.

8. Cette fenêtre ne se ferme pas bien. Il fait froid dans ma chambre.

M *Problèmes de santé.* Quelles seraient les réactions de ces amis à des problèmes de santé hypothétiques? Composez des phrases avec une supposition avec **si** à l'imparfait et une proposition principale au conditionnel à partir des éléments donnés. Suivez le modèle.

MODÈLE   **Si**   PROPOSITION PRINCIPALE
           Marie / se couper le doigt   elle / mettre un pansement
           → Si Marie se coupait le doigt, elle mettrait un pansement.

Comment est-ce qu'on se soignerait?

aller pieds nus *to go barefoot*
attraper un rhume *to catch a cold*
avoir mal à la tête *to have a headache*
le comprimé d'aspirine *aspirin tablet*
se couper au doigt *to cut one's finger*
être en forme *to be in shape*

se faire mal (au pied) *to hurt oneself (one's foot)*
maigrir *to lose weight*
mettre un pansement *to put on a bandage*
ordonner *to prescribe*
tomber malade *to get sick*

Si	PROPOSITION PRINCIPALE
1. je / se sentir mal	je / aller chez le médecin
2. il me faut / maigrir	je / ne manger que des légumes et des fruits
3. il / sortir sous la pluie	il / attraper un rhume
4. elle / tomber malade	elle / se reposer
5. nous / aller pieds nus	nous / se faire mal au pied
6. tu / avoir mal à la tête	tu / prendre des comprimés d'aspirine
7. le médecin / m'ordonner des antibiotiques	je / ne pas les prendre
8. je / être en forme	je / ne pas se fatiguer tellement

N *Activité orale.* *Discutez avec un(e) ami(e) de vos projets pour l'avenir. Employez le futur pour les choses que vous comptez faire et des phrases avec* **si** *pour exprimer les circonstances nécessaires pour réaliser vos projets. Employez le conditionnel pour les conditions qui sont hypothétiques ou peu probables. Suivez le modèle.*

MODÈLES Quand j'aurai dix-huit ans, j'irai à l'université.
Si j'ai de la chance, on me donnera une bourse d'études.
Si j'étais riche, je n'aurais pas besoin d'une bourse d'études.

Pour parler un français authentique	Speak Real French

Pronunciation of the Future and Conditional

All forms of the future and conditional have an /r/ sound before the ending. In **-er** and **-re** verbs whose stems end in a single pronounced consonant, it is this /r/ sound that distinguishes the conditional from the imperfect in the three persons of the singular and the third person plural. Compare the following forms.

IMPERFECT	CONDITIONAL
je passais	je passerais
tu t'arrêtais	tu t'arrêterais
il coupait	il couperait
elles invitaient	elles inviteraient
je vendais	je vendrais
tu attendais	tu attendrais
il interrompait	il interromprait
ils entendaient	ils entendraient

In modern spoken French, the sounds /é/ and /è/ do not contrast when they are the last sounds of a word. In word-final position, both are pronounced /é/. Thus, although in very formal pronunciation the future and conditional **je** forms are distinguished by the contrast between /é/ and /è/, the forms merge in speech in today's French and both end in the sound /é/.

FUTURE	CONDITIONAL
je parlerai	je parlerais
je finirai	je finirais
je défendrai	je défendrais
je ferai	je ferais
je serai	je serais
je viendrai	je viendrais
j'aurai	j'aurais
je verrai	je verrais

Pluperfect, Future Perfect, and Past Conditional; Conditional Sentences (2)

The Pluperfect (**Le plus-que-parfait**)

The pluperfect tense (English: *had done something*) consists of the imperfect of the auxiliary verb (either **avoir** or **être**, depending on the verb) plus the past participle.

chercher

j'	**avais cherché**	nous	**avions cherché**
tu	**avais cherché**	vous	**aviez cherché**
il/elle	**avait cherché**	ils/elles	**avaient cherché**

arriver

j'	**étais arrivé(e)**	nous	**étions arrivé(e)s**
tu	**étais arrivé(e)**	vous	**étiez arrivé(e)(s)**
il	**était arrivé**	ils	**étaient arrivés**
elle	**était arrivée**	elles	**étaient arrivées**

Reflexive verbs are conjugated with **être** in the pluperfect, just as they are in the passé composé.

se réveiller

je	**m'étais réveillé(e)**	nous	**nous étions réveillé(e)s**
tu	**t'étais réveillé(e)**	vous	**vous étiez réveillé(e)(s)**
il	**s'était réveillé**	ils	**s'étaient réveillés**
elle	**s'était réveillée**	elles	**s'étaient réveillées**

The rules for agreement of the past participle in all the compound tenses are the same as in the passé composé.

The pluperfect expresses a past action that occurred before another past action that is either mentioned in the same sentence or understood from context.

—Jean n'a pas mangé avec vous?	*Jean didn't eat with you?*
—Non. Quand Jean est arrivé, nous **avions** déjà **mangé**.	*No. When Jean arrived, we **had** already eaten.*

—Pourquoi est-ce que tu n'as pas répondu au téléphone? Tu ne t'**étais** pas encore **réveillé**?
—Si, je **m'étais** déjà **levé**.

*Why didn't you answer the telephone? **Hadn't** you **awakened** yet?*

*Yes, I **had** already **gotten up**.*

Je lui ai demandé s'il **avait lu** le livre. Il m'a répondu qu'il ne l'**avait** pas encore **acheté**.

*I asked him if he **had read** the book. He answered me that he **hadn't** yet **bought** it.*

A *Jacques était absent.* Lisez l'histoire de la classe du professeur Jourdain ce matin. Refaites chaque phrase au passé. Les verbes au présent passeront au passé composé; les verbes au passé composé passeront au plus-que-parfait.

1. Les étudiants ont pris leur place quand le professeur Jourdain entre.

2. Le professeur a déjà commencé à parler quand Marc sort son cahier.

3. Rachelle s'est endormie quand le professeur commence à poser des questions.

4. Le professeur a fini sa conférence quand la cloche sonne.

5. Nous nous sommes assis dans la cantine quand Jacques arrive.

6. Il nous demande si nous avons assisté à la classe du professeur Jourdain.

7. Hélène lui répond que nous avons tous été présents.

8. Je lui prête les notes que j'ai prises.

B *Explications.* On n'a pas fait ces choses hier parce qu'on les avait déjà faites avant-hier. Employez le plus-que-parfait dans vos explications. Suivez le modèle.

MODÈLE   Pourquoi est-ce que Claude n'a pas apporté les fleurs hier?
          → C'est qu'il avait déjà apporté les fleurs avant-hier.

1. Pourquoi est-ce que Joëlle ne t'a pas téléphoné hier?

2. Pourquoi est-ce que Renée n'est pas venue te voir hier?

3. Pourquoi est-ce que les garçons n'ont pas demandé le nom du médecin hier?

4. Pourquoi est-ce que tu n'as pas passé ton permis de conduire hier?

5. Pourquoi est-ce que Jeanne et Martine n'ont pas fait leur travail hier?

6. Pourquoi est-ce que tu n'as pas posté la lettre hier?

7. Pourquoi est-ce que Charles n'a pas fait le plein hier?

8. Pourquoi est-ce que ta mère n'a pas balayé la cuisine hier?

C *Déjà fait à 8 heures et demie du matin.* Employez le plus-que-parfait pour exprimer tout ce qu'on avait déjà fait à 8 heures et demie quand les amis ont sonné à la porte. Suivez le modèle.

MODÈLE   je / se réveiller
          → Quand mes amis ont sonné à 8 h 30, je m'étais réveillé(e).

1. ma sœur / prendre une douche

2. ma mère / préparer le petit déjeuner

3. je / se lever

4. mon amie Ghislaine / téléphoner deux fois

5. mon père / ne pas partir pour le bureau

6. je / relire mes notes de biologie

7. mes frères / mettre leurs dossiers dans leurs serviettes (*briefcases*)

8. je / ne pas s'habiller

D *C'est ce qu'elle a demandé.* *On peut supposer que Gilberte veut savoir toutes ces choses parce qu'elle a posé des questions au sujet de chacune. Exprimez cette idée en utilisant le plus-que-parfait, comme dans le modèle.*

MODÈLE   Tu crois que Gilberte veut savoir si nous avons réservé une table?
→ Elle m'a demandé si nous avions réservé une table.

1. Tu crois que Gilberte veut savoir si nous avons invité Suzanne?

2. Tu crois que Gilberte veut savoir si Marc a fini le projet?

3. Tu crois que Gilberte veut savoir si j'ai trouvé un emploi?

4. Tu crois que Gilberte veut savoir si Marie et Claire ont choisi une spécialisation?

5. Tu crois que Gilberte veut savoir si nos amis se sont réunis hier?

6. Tu crois que Gilberte veut savoir si M. Jourdain s'est fâché?

7. Tu crois que Gilberte veut savoir si Paul et Christine se sont fiancés?

8. Tu crois que Gilberte veut savoir si nous nous sommes trompés de train?

The Future Perfect (**Le futur antérieur**)

The future perfect tense (English: *will have done something*) consists of the future of the auxiliary verb (**avoir** or **être**) plus the past participle.

chercher

j'	**aurai cherché**	nous	**aurons cherché**
tu	**auras cherché**	vous	**aurez cherché**
il/elle	**aura cherché**	ils/elles	**auront cherché**

arriver

je	**serai arrivé(e)**	nous	**serons arrivé(e)s**
tu	**seras arrivé(e)**	vous	**serez arrivé(e)(s)**
il	**sera arrivé**	ils	**seront arrivés**
elle	**sera arrivée**	elles	**seront arrivées**

se réveiller

je	**me serai réveillé(e)**	nous	**nous serons réveillé(e)s**
tu	**te seras réveillé(e)**	vous	**vous serez réveillé(e)(s)**
il	**se sera réveillé**	ils	**se seront réveillés**
elle	**se sera réveillée**	elles	**se seront réveillées**

The future perfect expresses a future action that will have been completed before another future action takes place or before an implied or specified time in the future.

J'**aurai fini** vers 5 heures du soir.	*I **will have finished** around 5 P.M.*
Elle **sera arrivée** avant nous.	*She **will have arrived** before us.*
Ils **se seront installés** avant le mois de septembre.	*They **will have moved in** before the month of September.*

The future perfect is used after the conjunctions **quand**, **lorsque**, **dès que**, **aussitôt que**, and **après que** when the verb in the main clause is in the future tense.

Je te téléphonerai **quand la lettre sera arrivée**.	*I'll phone you **when the letter arrives**.*
Nous partirons **aussitôt que Chantal aura fini** son travail.	*We'll leave **as soon as Chantal has finished** her work.*

E   ***Qui aura fait quoi?*** *Votre ami et vous, vous vous dirigez vers la grande fête de fin d'année. Vous expliquez à votre ami que tout doit marcher comme sur des roulettes* (come off beautifully) *parce que tout a été très bien organisé. Employez le futur antérieur pour lui dire qui se sera chargé de chaque tache essentielle.*

1. Marie-France / préparer les hors-d'œuvre

2. Claude et Alain / aller chercher les boissons

3. Sylvie / mettre les couverts

4. Jean-Paul / choisir la musique

5. Sophie et Odile / inviter tout le monde

6. Hervé et Nathalie / décorer la salle

7. Marguerite / acheter les gobelets (*paper cups*)

8. Robert / organiser les attractions (*entertainment*)

F   ***Trop tard.*** *Utilisez le futur antérieur après* **quand** *pour dire que dans chaque cas il sera trop tard. Employez le futur dans la proposition principale. Suivez le modèle.*

MODÈLE   tu / arriver : je / sortir
          → Tu arriveras quand je serai sorti.

1. il / m'offrir un coup de main : je / finir

2. elle / sonner à la porte : nous / se coucher

3. tu / venir : tout le monde / partir

4. ils / trouver la carte : nous / se perdre

5. nous / arriver : ils / fermer le restaurant

6. il /nous renseigner : nous / trouver la solution

7. elle / apporter le pain : nous / finir de manger

8. tu / venir nous prendre en voiture : nous / partir en autocar

G *Récompensé ou puni?* *Expliquez pourquoi ces gens seront récompensés ou punis à partir des éléments proposés. Employez le futur dans la proposition principale et le futur antérieur dans la proposition introduite par* **parce que***. Suivez le modèle.*

> MODÈLE tu / être grondé *parce que* tu / ne rien faire
> → Tu seras grondé parce que tu n'auras rien fait.

Récompenses et punitions

agir *to act*	**gronder** *to scold*
comme il faut *properly*	**louer** *to praise*
se conduire *to behave*	**récompenser** *to reward*
donner un prix *to give a prize*	**sécher un cours** *to cut class*

1. tu / recevoir une bonne note *parce que* tu / étudier sérieusement

2. on / donner un prix à Marc *parce qu'*il / rédiger la meilleure composition

3. on / récompenser les étudiants *parce qu'*ils / se conduire comme il faut

4. les journaux / louer cet agent de police *parce qu'*il / agir héroïquement

5. le petit Pierrot / recevoir une bonne correction *parce qu'*il / ne pas ranger ses affaires

6. ses parents / gronder Michèle *parce qu'*elle / sécher ses cours

7. je / répondre à toutes les questions de l'examen *parce que* je / comprendre la matière

8. tout le monde / être déçu *parce que* nos cousins / ne pas arriver

H *En famille.* *Laurent Duval raconte une soirée que sa famille passera ensemble. Formez des phrases à partir des éléments proposés pour savoir ce qu'il dit. Employez le futur dans la proposition principale et le futur antérieur dans la proposition relative. Faites attention à l'accord du participe passé. Suivez le modèle.*

> MODÈLE nous / prendre des hors-d'œuvre *que* ma sœur et moi / préparer
> → Nous prendrons des hors-d'œuvre que ma sœur et moi,
>   nous aurons préparés.

1. nous / manger un dîner magnifique *que* nous / cuisiner

2. je / écouter le disque compact *que* je / acheter

3. maman / servir un dessert formidable avec la pâtisserie *qu'*elle / acheter

4. ma sœur / nous raconter l'histoire du roman *qu'*elle / lire

5. mon père / lire des articles dans la revue *qu'*il / acheter

6. nous / tous regarder le film *que* nous / louer

7. mon père et moi, nous / parler des articles *qu'*il / lire

8. ma sœur / chanter les nouvelles chansons *qu'*elle / apprendre à l'école

The Conditional Perfect (**Le conditionnel passé**)

The conditional perfect (English: *would have done something*) consists of the conditional of the auxiliary verb (**avoir** or **être**) plus the past participle.

chercher

j'	**aurais cherché**	nous	**aurions cherché**
tu	**aurais cherché**	vous	**auriez cherché**
il/elle	**aurait cherché**	ils/elles	**auraient cherché**

arriver

je	**serais arrivé(e)**	nous	**serions arrivé(e)s**
tu	**serais arrivé(e)**	vous	**seriez arrivé(e)(s)**
il	**serait arrivé**	ils	**seraient arrivés**
elle	**serait arrivée**	elles	**seraient arrivées**

se réveiller

je	**me serais réveillé(e)**	nous	**nous serions réveillé(e)s**
tu	**te serais réveillé(e)**	vous	**vous seriez réveillé(e)(s)**
il	**se serait réveillé**	ils	**se seraient réveillés**
elle	**se serait réveillée**	elles	**se seraient réveillées**

The conditional perfect usually labels an event that *did not take place* in the past.

—Tu m'**aurais aidé**?　　　　　　　　　　*Would you **have helped** me?*
—J'**aurais** tout **fait** pour t'aider.　　　*I **would have done** everything to help you.*

—Vous **vous seriez souvenu** de lui?　　*Would you **have remembered** him?*
—Non, je **ne l'aurais pas reconnu**.　　　*No, I **wouldn't have recognized** him.*

I　*Je n'aurais pas fait une chose pareille. Vous n'auriez pas fait tout ce que vos copains ont fait. Dites-le en employant le conditionnel passé. Suivez le modèle.*

　　　MODÈLE　　Je me suis baigné dans le fleuve.
　　　　　　　　→ Moi, je ne me serais pas baigné(e) dans le fleuve.

1. Philippe s'est couché à 5 heures du matin.

2. Claudette a pris rendez-vous avec le directeur.

3. Mireille et Louis se sont mis en route sous la pluie.

4. Alain a fait dix kilomètres à pied.

5. Christine a cueilli des fleurs dans le jardin public.

6. Serge et Frédéric ont cru à l'histoire que Marc a racontée.

7. Lise et Blanche ont dépensé tout leur argent.

8. Chantal a oublié la date de la réception.

J   *Eux, ils l'auraient fait.*   *Marcel avait peur de faire ce qu'il fallait faire. Les autres copains n'auraient pas eu peur. Exprimez cette idée en employant le conditionnel passé. Suivez le modèle.*

> MODÈLE   J'avais peur de parler avec le professeur. (Cécile)
>   → Vraiment? Cécile aurait parlé avec le professeur.

1. J'avais peur de conduire la voiture d'André. (Guillaume)

2. J'avais peur de descendre. (Jacqueline et Martin)

3. J'avais peur d'interrompre. (Vincent et moi)

4. J'avais peur de répondre. (moi)

5. J'avais peur d'employer ce mot. (Albert)

6. J'avais peur de plonger. (Simone et moi)

7. J'avais peur de déranger Georges. (Ségolène)

8. J'avais peur de me disputer avec lui. (Solange et Marie)

Conditional Sentences (2)

To express a hypothetical situation that is contrary to a past fact, French uses the pluperfect in the **si**-clause and the past conditional in the result clause.

—Jean-Claude n'est pas arrivé.	*Jean-Claude hasn't arrived.*
—S'il **était arrivé**, nous **aurions dîné** ensemble.	*If he **had arrived**, we **would have had dinner** together.*
—Je n'ai pas étudié.	*I didn't study.*
—Si tu **avais étudié**, tu **aurais réussi** les examens.	*If you **had studied**, you **would have passed** the exams.*
—Alice ne nous a pas vus.	*Alice didn't see us.*
—C'est vrai. Si elle nous **avait vus**, elle **se serait approchée** de notre table.	*That's true. If she **had seen** us, she **would have come over** to our table.*

K   *Moi, je l'aurais fait aussi.*   *Dites que vous auriez fait toutes ces choses si Berthe les avait faites. Suivez le modèle.*

> MODÈLE   Berthe n'est pas sortie hier.
>   → Mais si elle était sortie hier, moi aussi, je serais sorti(e).

1. Berthe n'est pas allée en ville hier.

2. Berthe n'a pas acheté de livres hier.

3. Berthe ne s'est pas promenée hier.

4. Berthe n'a pas envoyé ses paquets hier.

5. Berthe n'a pas pris son billet hier.

6. Berthe ne s'est pas préparée pour partir hier.

7. Berthe n'a pas écouté le cédé hier.

8. Berthe n'a pas travaillé hier.

L *Si on avait fini notre travail!* *Qu'est-ce que les copains auraient fait s'ils avaient fini leurs devoirs? Employez une phrase avec une proposition subordonnée au plus-que-parfait commençant par* **si** *et une proposition indépendante au conditionnel passé. Suivez le modèle.*

MODÈLE   Marc n'a pas appris le nouveau vocabulaire. (aller au cinéma)
→ Si Marc avait appris le nouveau vocabulaire, il serait allé au cinéma.

1. Rachelle n'a pas rédigé sa composition. (se réunir avec ses amis)

2. Philippe n'a pas relu ses leçons de chimie. (pouvoir jouer au football)

3. Louise et Danielle n'ont pas préparé le compte rendu. (aller aux grands magasins)

4. Olivier et Jean-Luc ne sont pas allés au laboratoire. (regarder la télé)

5. Françoise et Guy n'ont pas étudié l'histoire du dix-septième siècle. (aller danser)

6. Mireille n'a pas fait les problèmes de maths. (sortir avec Charles)

7. Monique et Édouard n'ont pas révisé leurs notes de littérature française. (dîner en ville)

8. Jean-François n'a pas appris le poème par cœur. (jouer aux jeux vidéo)

M *Résumés.* *Résumez chaque échange par une phrase composée d'une proposition subordonnée au plus-que-parfait commençant par* **si** *et une proposition indépendante au conditionnel passé. Suivez le modèle.*

MODÈLE   Thierry: Pourquoi est-ce que tu n'as pas répondu à mon courriel?
Georges: Je ne l'ai pas reçue.
→ Georges aurait répondu au courriel de Thierry s'il l'avait reçue.

1. Yves: Pourquoi est-ce que tu ne m'as pas salué à la cantine?
   Michèle: Je ne t'ai pas vu.

2. Roger: Pourquoi est-ce que tu ne m'as pas téléphoné?
   Sylvie: J'ai passé toute la journée à la bibliothèque.

3. Judith: Pourquoi est-ce que tu ne m'as pas dit qu'il y avait une réunion aujourd'hui?
   Damien: Je ne m'en suis pas souvenu.

4. Julie: Pourquoi est-ce que tu n'as pas suivi ton régime?
   Ariane: J'ai eu envie de manger du chocolat.

5. Sonia: Pourquoi est-ce que tu n'as pas fait le ménage?
   Nicolas: Je n'ai pas eu le temps.

6. Roland: Pourquoi est-ce que tu n'as pas pris ta bicyclette?
   Patrick: Je me suis foulé la cheville (*sprained my ankle*).

7. Grégoire: Pourquoi est-ce que Virginie et toi, vous n'êtes pas sortis?
   Paul: Nous avons dû étudier.

8. Hélène: Pourquoi est-ce que tu n'es pas venu au bureau?
   Louis: Je suis allé chez le médecin.

N *Création.* *Les personnes indiquées ont fait des choses surprenantes. Expliquez pourquoi en employant une phrase composée d'une proposition subordonnée au plus-que-parfait commençant par* **si** *et une proposition indépendante au conditionnel passé. Suivez le modèle.*

MODÈLE   Le professeur ne s'est pas fâché contre Pierrot.
          → Il se serait fâché contre Pierrot s'il avait entendu les paroles de Pierrot
          (s'il avait vu les dessins de Pierrot, etc.).

1. Christine ne s'est pas amusée à la soirée.

2. Les touristes ne se sont pas mis en route hier.

3. M. Marsaud ne s'est pas chargé de la collecte.

4. Tu n'as pas assisté au concert.

5. Le médecin ne m'a pas ordonné des antibiotiques.

6. Émile n'a pas ses devoirs.

7. Charlotte n'est pas venue nous voir.

8. Bernard et Stéphane n'ont pas joué au basket aujourd'hui.

O *Activité orale.* *Discutez avec un(e) ami(e) de comment votre vie aurait été différente si votre famille et vous, vous aviez fait les choses d'une façon différente. Employez des phrases avec* **si** *pour exprimer les possibilités.*

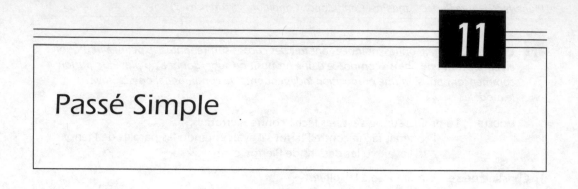

Passé Simple

Formation and Use of the Passé Simple

The passé simple is a literary tense used only in formal speeches and writing. Like the passé composé, it expresses an action that was completed in the past. The passé simple of regular -**er** verbs is formed by dropping the -**er** from the infinitive and adding the endings -**ai**, -**as**, -**a**, -**âmes**, -**âtes**, -**èrent**.

parler

je	parl**ai**	nous	parl**âmes**
tu	parl**as**	vous	parl**âtes**
il/elle	parl**a**	ils/elles	parl**èrent**

In the passé simple, **aller** is conjugated like a regular -er verb.

In all forms of the passé simple except the **ils** form, infinitives ending in -**cer** change **c** to **ç** and infinitives ending in -**ger** insert an **e**.

lancer

je	lan**çai**	nous	lan**çâmes**
tu	lan**ças**	vous	lan**çâtes**
il/elle	lan**ça**	ils/elles	lan**cèrent**

manger

je	mang**eai**	nous	mang**eâmes**
tu	mang**eas**	vous	mang**eâtes**
il/elle	mang**ea**	ils/elles	mang**èrent**

The passé simple of regular -**ir** and -**re** verbs is formed by dropping the infinitive ending and adding -**is**, -**is**, -**it**, -**îmes**, -**îtes**, -**irent**.

finir

je	fin**is**	nous	fin**îmes**
tu	fin**is**	vous	fin**îtes**
il/elle	fin**it**	ils/elles	fin**irent**

rendre

je	rend**is**	nous	rend**îmes**
tu	rend**is**	vous	rend**îtes**
il/elle	rend**it**	ils/elles	rend**irent**

Irregular **-ir** verbs like **dormir** and **partir** form the passé simple like **finir**: **je dormis**, **je partis**. Irregular **-re** verbs like **battre** and **suivre** form the passé simple like **rendre**: **je battis**, **je suivis**.

A *Au passé simple!* *Transformez ces formes verbales du passé composé au passé simple.*

1. j'ai gagné
2. tu as commencé
3. elle a choisi
4. elles t'ont attendu
5. vous avez espéré
6. tu as nagé
7. il m'a encouragé
8. nous avons déménagé
9. je suis descendu
10. tu as annoncé
11. ils ont rangé
12. elles ont défendu
13. vous avez obéi
14. nous avons entendu
15. j'ai remplacé
16. on a rédigé
17. nous avons réfléchi
18. vous avez essayé
19. tu es allé
20. nous avons partagé

The Passé Simple of Irregular Verbs

Some irregular verbs form the passé simple using the same endings as regular **-ir** and **-re** verbs.

INFINITIVE	STEM	PASSÉ SIMPLE
s'asseoir	**ass-**	je **m'assis**
conduire	**conduis-**	je **conduisis**
dire	**d-**	je **dis**
écrire	**écriv-**	j'**écrivis**
faire	**f-**	je **fis**
joindre	**joign-**	je **joignis**
mettre	**m-**	je **mis**
naître	**naqu-**	je **naquis**
peindre	**peign-**	je **peignis**
prendre	**pr-**	je **pris**
rire	**r-**	je **ris**
voir	**v-**	je **vis**

Most irregular verbs that have a past participle ending in **-u** have a stem that resembles their past participle. The endings for such verbs are **-s**, **-s**, **-t**, **-ˆmes**, **-ˆtes**, **-rent**. They follow the pattern of **avoir**.

avoir

j'	**eus**	nous	**eûmes**
tu	**eus**	vous	**eûtes**
il/elle	**eut**	ils/elles	**eurent**

INFINITIVE	STEM	PASSÉ SIMPLE
boire	**bu-**	je **bus**
connaître	**connu-**	je **connus**
courir	**couru-**	je **courus**
croire	**cru-**	je **crus**
devoir	**du-**	je **dus**
falloir	**fallu-**	il **fallut**
lire	**lu-**	je **lus**
pleuvoir	**plu-**	il **plut**
pouvoir	**pu-**	je **pus**
recevoir	**reçu-**	je **reçus**
savoir	**su-**	je **sus**
valoir	**valu-**	il **valut**
vivre	**vécu-**	je **vécus**
vouloir	**voulu-**	je **voulus**

Some verbs have special forms in the passé simple.

être

je	**fus**	nous	**fûmes**
tu	**fus**	vous	**fûtes**
il/elle	**fut**	ils/elles	**furent**

mourir

je	**mourus**	nous	**mourûmes**
tu	**mourus**	vous	**mourûtes**
il/elle	**mourut**	ils/elles	**moururent**

Verbs like **venir**

je	**vins**	nous	**vînmes**
tu	**vins**	vous	**vîntes**
il/elle	**vint**	ils/elles	**vinrent**

B *Transformation.* *Refaites cette petite histoire au passé simple.*

1. La nuit est tombée.

2. La ville est devenue silencieuse.

3. Les habitants sont rentrés chez eux.

4. On a fermé les magasins.

5. Je suis entré dans un bistrot.

6. Je me suis assis à une petite table.

7. J'ai attendu Michèle.

8. Elle a voulu me voir.

9. Elle m'a rejoint à 7 heures.

10. Nous avons pris un café ensemble.

11. Nous sommes sortis.

12. Nous nous sommes promenés dans la ville endormie.

13. Michèle m'a dit:

14. «J'ai décidé de te quitter.»

15. Elle a rompu avec moi.

16. Je n'ai rien pu faire.

17. Je suis rentré chez moi.

18. J'ai pleuré.

C *Transformation.* *Refaites cette petite histoire au passé simple.*

1. Marthe est sortie de sa maison.

2. Elle a marché à travers champ.

3. Elle s'est approchée du fleuve.

4. Elle y a vu trois amis.

5. Ils l'ont saluée.

6. Ils l'ont invitée à manger avec eux.

7. Elle a accepté.

8. Elle s'est assise avec eux.

9. Ils ont partagé leur déjeuner avec elle.

10. Soudain, le temps a changé.

11. Il a commencé à pleuvoir.

12. Les quatre amis sont revenus en ville.

13. Ils se sont mouillés un peu.

14. Ils ont cherché un café.

15. Ils ont commandé un chocolat.

16. Ils ont bu leur chocolat ensemble.

Present Participles; Uses of the Infinitive

The Present Participle

The French present participle corresponds to the English *-ing* form of a verb (*going, seeing, doing*).

The present participle of most verbs is formed by dropping -**ons** from the present tense **nous** form and adding -**ant**.

parler	nous parlon̸s̸ → **parlant**		lire	nous lison̸s̸ → **lisant**	
finir	nous finisson̸s̸ → **finissant**		prendre	nous prenon̸s̸ → **prenant**	
rendre	nous rendon̸s̸ → **rendant**		écrire	nous écrivon̸s̸ → **écrivant**	

This means that the final consonant of the stem is pronounced in all present participles.

Only three verbs have irregular present participles.

avoir	**ayant**
être	**étant**
savoir	**sachant**

A present participle may be used as an adjective or a verb. When used as an adjective, a present participle usually follows the noun or pronoun it modifies and agrees with it in gender and number.

de l'eau **courante** (< courir)	***running** water*
les numéros **gagnants** (< gagner)	*the **winning** numbers*
des histoires **touchantes** (< toucher)	***touching** stories*

When used as a verb, the present participle often follows the preposition **en**.

- **En** + present participle may express an action that is happening at the same time as the action of the main verb.

Ici on ne parle pas **en travaillant**.	*Here people don't talk **while working**.*
En entrant dans le café, nous avons vu notre amie Diane.	***Upon entering** the café, we saw our friend Diane.*

- It may also express how or why something is done.

On ne maigrit pas **en mangeant** des glaces.	*You don't get thinner **by eating** ice cream.*

J'ai fait des progrès en français **en lisant** beaucoup.	*I made progress in French **through reading** a lot.*

The present participle may also be used without **en**.

Ayant peur d'arriver en retard, nous sommes partis de très bonne heure.	***Being afraid** to arrive late, we left very early.*

The present participle may be used instead of a relative clause. In this case it is invariable. This construction is typical of formal speech and writing.

les trains **venant** de l'étranger (**venant** = qui viennent)	*trains **coming** from abroad*
des employés **parlant** français (**parlant** = qui parlent)	*employees **speaking** French*
un autobus **montant** le boulevard (**montant** = qui monte)	*a bus **going up** the boulevard*

A ***Des conseils.*** *Marie-Josette donne des conseils à son petit frère qui entre au collège. Refaites chacune de ses phrases en changeant la proposition commençant par **si** au gérondif. Suivez le modèle.*

MODÈLE   Tu apprendras beaucoup si tu fais attention.
→ Tu apprendras beaucoup en faisant attention.

1. Tu auras une bonne note si tu fais tes devoirs de maths tous les jours.

2. Tu arriveras à l'heure si tu quittes la maison à 7 heures et demie.

3. Si on apprend toutes les dates par cœur, on évite les problèmes dans le cours d'histoire.

4. Si tu écoutes des programmes en anglais à la radio, tu te prépareras pour l'examen oral.

5. On évite la fatigue si on organise son travail.

6. Si on regarde très peu la télé, on peut toujours finir son travail.

B ***La langue administrative.*** *Pour écrire des phrases typiques des avis officiels, remplacez la proposition subordonnée par le participe présent correspondant. Puisque ce participe est une forme verbale, il ne s'accorde pas avec le substantif. Suivez le modèle.*

MODÈLE   Les visiteurs qui désirent visiter le musée sont priés d'attendre à gauche.
→ Les visiteurs désirant visiter le musée sont priés d'attendre à gauche.

1. Les voyageurs qui partent pour le Nord sont priés de passer au quai numéro 3.

2. Nous annonçons un retard pour tous les avions qui proviennent d'Afrique.

3. Le docteur Gobert verra les malades qui souffrent d'un problème gastrique.

4. Les étudiants qui passent leurs examens demain doivent arriver au lycée à 8 heures.

5. C'est un manuel d'anglais qui contient tout le vocabulaire essentiel.

6. Voici une carte qui montre le site des centrales nucléaires.

Uses of the Infinitive

In French, the infinitive can serve as the subject of a sentence. English usually uses the *-ing* form of the verb in this case.

Voir, c'est **croire**.   *Seeing is believing.*

Apprendre le français en six mois   *Learning French in six months is not easy!*
n'est pas facile!

Vivre à Paris, c'est mon rêve.   *Living in Paris is my dream.*

The infinitive can also follow another verb. Depending on which verb it follows, it may or may not be preceded by a preposition. The following verbs are followed directly by an infinitive.

aimer *to like*	**espérer** *to hope*
aimer mieux *to prefer*	**oser** *to dare*
aller *to be going to*	**penser** *to intend*
avoir beau *to do (something) in vain*	**pouvoir** *to be able*
compter *to intend*	**préférer** *to prefer*
désirer *to want*	**savoir** *to know how*
détester *to hate*	**vouloir** *to want*
devoir *should, must, ought*	

—**Tu comptes partir** en vacances   *Do you intend to leave for vacation*
en février?   *in February?*

—Non, **je déteste voyager** en hiver.   *No, I hate traveling in the winter.*

—**Tu préfères y aller** en été?   *Do you prefer to go in the summer?*

—**J'aime mieux prendre** mes   *I prefer to take my vacation in the*
vacances au printemps.   *springtime.*

Verbs of motion are followed directly by an infinitive.

—**Je descends faire les courses.**   *I'm going down to do the shopping.*
Tu as besoin de quelque chose?   *Do you need anything?*

—**Tu peux aller** me **chercher** un   *Can you go get me a French newspaper?*
journal français?

The expressions **il faut** (*one must, you have to*) and **il vaut mieux** (*it's better to*) are also followed directly by the infinitive. These expressions are not conjugated for person: impersonal **il** is the only possible subject. They are conjugated for tense, however.

IMPERFECT	**il fallait**	**il valait mieux**
PASSÉ COMPOSÉ	**il a fallu**	**il a mieux valu**
FUTURE	**il faudra**	**il vaudra mieux**
CONDITIONAL	**il faudrait**	**il vaudrait mieux**

C ***Les fêtes et les célébrations.*** *Exercez-vous à employer la construction verbe + infinitif en ajoutant les verbes entre parenthèses aux phrases. Vous verrez comment les Maurois et leurs amis passent l'année. Suivez le modèle.*

MODÈLE   Les Maurois restent chez eux le jour de Noël. (préférer)
→ Les Maurois préfèrent rester chez eux le jour de Noël.

L'année des Français

le 1er janvier	Le jour de l'An. On s'offre de petits cadeaux appelés «étrennes».
le 6 janvier	La fête des Rois. Célébration de l'arrivée des Mages au berceau (*cradle*) de Jésus-Christ. On fête cette journée en mangeant un gâteau plat appelé «la galette des Rois» qui a une fève (*bean*) cachée. La personne qui trouve la fève dans son morceau est nommée le roi ou la reine de la fête.
le 8 mai	On commémore la victoire des Alliés et la fin de la Deuxième Guerre mondiale en Europe. On commémore la fin de la Première Guerre mondiale le 11 novembre, anniversaire de l'Armistice de 1918.
l'Ascension	Fête religieuse célébrée le sixième jeudi après Pâques.
la Pentecôte	Fête religieuse célébrée dix jours après l'Ascension, toujours un lundi. Pour beaucoup de Parisiens, c'est l'occasion de passer une fin de semaine de trois jours à la campagne.
le 14 juillet	La fête nationale française. Il y a un défilé militaire aux Champs-Elysées à Paris et on danse dans les rues. On commémore la prise de la Bastille, événement qui a marqué le début de la Révolution française.
le 15 août	L'Assomption. On célèbre la fête de la Sainte Vierge.
le 1er novembre	Le Toussaint, ou la Fête de tous les saints. Le 2 novembre est le jour des Morts. On va dans les cimetières fleurir les tombes (*put flowers on the graves*).
le 24 décembre	La veillée de Noël. Célébrée en famille avec un grand repas (le réveillon). On va aussi à l'église pour la messe de minuit.
le 25 décembre	Noël. Dans les familles, on se réunit autour du sapin (*fir tree*) où on a placé des cadeaux.
le 31 décembre	La Saint-Sylvestre. On célèbre avec un réveillon et on se souhaite une bonne année.

1. Les Maurois font un grand réveillon pour la Saint-Sylvestre. (aimer)
2. Ils s'offrent des étrennes le jour de l'An. (aller)
3. Le 6 janvier ils invitent des amis pour manger la galette des Rois. (espérer)
4. La grand-mère passe le dimanche de Pâques avec eux. (vouloir)
5. Le 8 mai ils vont en Normandie pour commémorer la victoire des Alliés en 1945. (compter)
6. Leurs amis les Dufau les invitent pour la Pentecôte. (devoir)
7. Eux, ils invitent les Dufau à Paris pour le 14 juillet. (penser)
8. Pour l'Assomption ils sont dans leur maison à la campagne. (désirer)
9. Ils vont fleurir les tombes de leurs parents décédés (*deceased*) le 2 novembre. (devoir)
10. Ils vont à la messe de minuit le 24 décembre. (aller)

D *Au bord de la mer. Ajoutez les verbes entre parenthèses à ces phrases pour voir comment un groupe d'amis a passé ses vacances au bord de la mer. Employez le même temps verbal que celui de la phrase donnée.*

1. Philippe nageait tous les jours. (vouloir)

2. Alice et Géraldine ont fait du tourisme. (pouvoir)

3. Georges ne nageait pas très bien. (savoir)

4. Il s'éloignait de la plage. (ne pas oser)

5. Claudette et Brigitte jouaient au tennis. (préférer)

6. Louis visitait les petits villages des alentours. (aimer)

7. Solange a acheté des souvenirs. (ne pas pouvoir)

8. Richard a écrit beaucoup de lettres. (devoir)

Verb + à + Infinitive

Some verbs require the preposition **à** before a following infinitive.

s'amuser à *to enjoy oneself (by doing)*
apprendre à *to learn how to*
arriver à *to manage to*
s'attendre à *to expect to*
avoir à *to have to*
chercher à *to try to*
commencer à *to begin to*
se consacrer à *to devote oneself to*
consentir à *to consent to*
continuer à *to continue*
se décider à *to make up one's mind to*
s'ennuyer à *to get/be bored (doing something)*
s'exercer à *to practice*
s'habituer à *to get used to*

hésiter à *to hesitate to*
s'intéresser à *to be interested in*
se mettre à *to begin to*
s'obstiner à *to persist stubbornly in*
parvenir à *to manage to, succeed in*
passer son temps à *to spend one's time (doing something)*
penser à *to be thinking of (doing something)*
se préparer à *to get ready to*
se résigner à *to resign oneself to*
réussir à *to succeed in*
songer à *to be thinking of (doing something)*
tendre à *to tend to*
tenir à *to insist on*

—Henri **s'obstine à causer** avec tous les touristes allemands.

—Il **s'exerce à parler** allemand.

—Il **parviendra à chasser** tous les touristes de Paris.

—Tu exagères. Les touristes **s'amusent à converser** avec lui.

*Henri **persists in chatting** with all the German tourists.*

*He's **practicing speaking** German.*

*He'll **succeed in chasing** all the tourists away from Paris.*

*You're exaggerating. The tourists **enjoy conversing** with him.*

Some verbs require a direct object before **à** + infinitive.

aider qqn à faire qqch *to help someone do something*
autoriser qqn à faire qqch *to authorize someone to do something*
encourager qqn à faire qqch *to encourage someone to do something*
engager qqn à faire qqch *to urge someone to do something*
forcer qqn à faire qqch *to force someone to do something*

inviter qqn à faire qqch *to invite someone to do something*
obliger qqn à faire qqch *to oblige someone to do something*

—J'ai invité les Deschênes à passer
  la Pentecôte avec nous.
—Ils vous aideront à préparer les
  repas. Ils adorent faire la cuisine.

I invited the Deschênes to spend
  Pentecost with us.
They'll help you prepare meals.
  They love to cook.

With **apprendre** when it means *to teach* and with **enseigner**, an indirect object is required before **à** + infinitive.

apprendre/enseigner à qqn à faire qqch *to teach someone to do something*

E *La soirée de Ghislaine.* *Ghislaine veut donner une soirée chez elle. Complétez le récit de ses préparatifs en ajoutant la préposition à aux phrases où elle manque. Si la préposition n'est pas nécessaire, mettez un X.*

1. Nous songeons _____ organiser une soirée.

2. Je tiens _____ donner une soirée formidable.

3. Michèle va _____ préparer des sandwichs.

4. Alfred et Robert doivent _____ s'occuper des boissons.

5. Ils tendent _____ oublier tout ce qu'ils ont à acheter.

6. Olivier invitera ses amis _____ venir.

7. Moi, je me consacrerai _____ mettre de l'ordre dans notre appartement.

8. Ma mère sait _____ faire une délicieuse tarte au citron.

9. Je l'aiderai _____ en faire deux ou trois.

F *On modifie un peu le message.* *Refaites chacune des phrases avec les éléments proposés entre parenthèses pour connaître les occupations et préoccupations d'un groupe d'étudiants. Suivez les modèles.*

MODÈLES Vous sortez. (pouvoir)
         → Vous pouvez sortir.

         Vous sortez. (on / obliger)
         → On vous oblige à sortir.

1. Nous lisons un livre par semaine. (le professeur / encourager)

2. Je rédige mes comptes rendus à l'ordinateur. (aimer mieux)

3. Jacques finira son compte rendu demain. (réussir)

4. Philomène fait de l'allemand. (son chef / engager)

5. Vous cherchez du travail. (l'administration de l'école / autoriser)

6. Henri et Jules reçoivent une mauvaise note en maths. (se résigner)

7. Chantal révise ses notes d'histoire. (continuer)

8. Odile recopie ses notes. (passer son temps)

Verb + **de** + Infinitive

Some verbs and expressions are joined to a following infinitive by the preposition **de**.

s'abstenir de *to refrain from*	**entreprendre de** *to undertake to*
accepter de *to agree to*	**essayer de** *to try to*
s'arrêter de *to stop*	**s'étonner de** *to marvel at*
avoir l'intention de *to intend to*	**éviter de** *to avoid*
avoir peur de *to be afraid of*	**s'excuser de** *to apologize for*
avoir raison de *to be right to*	**finir de** *to finish*
avoir tort de *to be wrong to*	**se flatter de** *to claim to (be able to)*
brûler de *to be burning/dying to*	**mériter de** *to deserve to*
se charger de *to make sure to; to see*	**oublier de** *to forget to*
to it (that something is done)	**parler de** *to talk about*
choisir de *to choose to*	**promettre de** *to promise to*
craindre de *to fear*	**se proposer de** *to set out to, mean to, intend to*
décider de *to decide to*	**refuser de** *to refuse to*
se dépêcher de *to hurry to*	**regretter de** *to regret*
s'empêcher de *to refrain from*	**résoudre de** *to resolve to*
s'empresser de *to hurry/rush to*	**risquer de** *to risk, run the risk of*

Venir de means *to have just (done something).*

> Je **viens de voir** Jacquot.   I **have just seen** Jacquot.

Note the following uses of prepositions other than **à** or **de** before an infinitive.

> **finir par faire qqch** *to end/wind up doing something*
> **commencer par faire qqch** *to begin by doing something*

Study the following pairs of contrasting examples.

> Il **commence à chercher** du travail.   He's **beginning to look for** work.
> Il **commence par chercher** du travail.   He's **beginning by looking for** work.
>
> Il **a fini de** nous **aider**.   He **finished helping** us.
> Il **a fini par** nous **aider**.   He **wound up helping** us.

G   *Élections au lycée. Nous essayons d'organiser les élections aux comités des délégués de classe* (student council), *mais ce n'est pas facile. Complétez les phrases suivantes avec les prépositions qui manquent pour savoir ce qui se passe. Si aucune préposition n'est nécessaire, mettez un X.*

1. Les étudiants se proposent _____ organiser les élections aux comités des délégués de classe.

2. Ils se mettent _____ chercher des candidats.

3. Ils comptent _____ procéder aux élections (*hold the election*) au mois de novembre.

4. Antoinette Dubois veut _____ se porter candidate.

5. Elle ne mérite pas _____ être élue.

6. Nous encourageons d'autres étudiants _____ se présenter.

7. Mais ils ne s'empressent pas _____ se porter candidats.

8. Je viens _____ parler avec Lise Léotard.

9. Elle s'intéresse un peu _____ participer aux comités.

10. Si elle se décide _____ se présenter,

11. il faudra _____ organiser sa campagne.

12. Mais en ce moment, nous craignons _____ ne pas avoir assez de candidats.

H   ***Dix jours à Paris.*** *Un groupe d'étudiants passe dix jours à Paris. Les étudiants sont pressés de tout voir et de tout faire, et chacun s'intéresse à quelque chose de différent. Formez des phrases avec les éléments donnés pour voir comment ils profitent de leur séjour.*

1. Loïc et Charles / tenir / voir un match de football

2. Marie-Noëlle / s'empresser / s'acheter des livres

3. Richard / descendre tous les jours / acheter des journaux

4. Albert / se flatter / connaître parfaitement toutes les lignes du métro

5. Berthe et Christine / entreprendre / organiser un pique-nique au Bois de Boulogne

6. Philippe / compter / visiter le marché aux timbres

7. Chantal / passer son temps / regarder les robes aux grands magasins

8. Tous les étudiants / brûler / visiter le Louvre

9. Martin / essayer / organiser une journée à la campagne

10. Paulette et Mireille / espérer / avoir le temps de voir Montmartre

I   ***Changement d'habitudes.*** *Jean-Pierre a eu des difficultés au lycée cette année. Son oncle raconte une conversation qu'il a eue avec son neveu. Exprimez la narration de l'oncle en français en faisant attention à l'enlacement du verbe et de l'infinitif.*

1. *I have just spoken with Jean-Pierre.*

2. *I explained to him that he risks wasting the school year* (l'année scolaire).

3. *I encouraged him to begin studying seriously.*

4. *He must refrain from going out every day.*

5. *He promised to pay attention in class.*

6. *He apologized for getting* (avoir eu) *bad grades.*

7. *He's not going to waste any more time watching TV.*

8. *He has made up his mind to be a good student.*

9. *I intend to speak with Jean-Pierre next week.*

10. *We will try to talk every week until the end of the school year.*

Verb + Object + *de* + Infinitive

A group of verbs that take **de** before the following infinitive take a direct object as well.

accuser qqn de faire qqch *to accuse someone of doing something*
convaincre qqn de faire qqch *to convince someone to do something*
décourager qqn de faire qqch *to discourage someone from doing something*
empêcher qqn de faire qqch *to prevent someone from doing something*
féliciter qqn d'avoir fait qqch *to congratulate someone for having done something*
persuader qqn de faire qqch *to persuade someone to do something*
prier qqn de faire qqch *to beg someone to do something*
remercier qqn de faire qqch *to thank someone for doing something*

Another group of verbs that take **de** before the following infinitive take an indirect object.

commander à qqn de faire qqch *to order someone to do something*
conseiller à qqn de faire qqch *to advise someone to do something*
déconseiller à qqn de faire qqch *to advise someone not to do something*
défendre à qqn de faire qqch *to forbid someone to do something*
demander à qqn de faire qqch *to ask someone to do something*
dire à qqn de faire qqch *to tell someone to do something*
interdire à qqn de faire qqch *to forbid someone to do something*
ordonner à qqn de faire qqch *to order someone to do something*
pardonner à qqn de faire qqch *to forgive someone for doing something*
permettre à qqn de faire qqch *to allow someone to do something*
promettre à qqn de faire qqch *to promise someone to do something*
proposer à qqn de faire qqch *to suggest to someone to do something*
reprocher à qqn de faire qqch *to reproach someone for doing something*
suggérer à qqn de faire qqch *to suggest to someone to do something*

J   *Comment aider nos amis?* Il y a beaucoup de copains qui ont des difficultés à la faculté. Sophie et Daniel s'ingénient à trouver des idées pour les aider. Écrivez leurs solutions en utilisant **il faut** et les mots proposés entre parenthèses. Suivez le modèle.

MODÈLE   Marc n'ouvre jamais le manuel d'histoire. (convaincre / le lire)
          → Il faut le convaincre de le lire.

1. Régine ne révise jamais son vocabulaire anglais. (encourager / apprendre les mots)

2. Christophe s'endort en classe. (commander / faire attention)

3. Brigitte n'est jamais chez elle et elle n'étudie pas. (déconseiller / sortir tous les jours)

4. Olivier ne participe pas aux discussions. (persuader / répondre)

5. Chantal et Robert parlent tout le temps pendant la classe. (dire / se taire)

6. Gérard et Louis ne pensent qu'au football. (conseiller / se concentrer sur leurs études)

7. Philippe dit qu'il ne comprend rien à la géométrie. (aider / résoudre les problèmes)

8. Baudoin et Micheline pensent s'absenter le jour de l'examen. (dissuader / le faire)

K **En famille.** *Les membres de la famille Chéron s'aiment bien et essaient de s'entraider et de se conseiller. Utilisez le vocabulaire et les éléments proposés pour décrire leurs rapports familiaux. Employez le passé composé. Suivez le modèle.*

MODÈLE la tante Rosette / conseiller / son neveu Pierrot / se coucher tôt
→ La tante Rosette a conseillé à son neveu Pierrot de se coucher tôt.

La famille
le père *father*
la mère *mother*
le fils *son*
la fille *daughter*
le frère (aîné/cadet) *(older/younger) brother*
la sœur (aînée/cadette) *(older/younger) sister*
le grand-père *grandfather*
la grand-mère *grandmother*
le petit-fils *grandson*
la petite-fille *granddaughter*
l'oncle *uncle*
la tante *aunt*
le neveu *nephew*
la nièce *niece*
le cousin *male cousin*
la cousine *female cousin*
le beau-père *father-in-law, stepfather*
la belle-mère *mother-in-law, stepmother*
les beaux-parents *in-laws*
le beau-fils, le gendre *son-in-law**
la belle-fille, la bru *daughter-in-law**
le beau-frère *brother-in-law*
la belle-sœur *sister-in-law*
le demi-frère *stepbrother, half-brother*
la demi-sœur *stepsister, half-sister*

1. le grand-père / convaincre / son gendre Guillaume / ne pas quitter son travail

2. les enfants de Guillaume et Sylvie / s'empresser / apporter des fleurs à la tante Émilie

3. le petit Bertrand / demander / sa mère / lui acheter une bicyclette

4. la grand-mère / pardonner / sa petite-fille Giselle / avoir oublié son anniversaire

5. Guillaume et Sylvie / féliciter / leur fille Christine / avoir eu 18 à l'examen de philo

6. l'oncle François / enseigner / sa nièce / se servir de l'ordinateur

7. Anne-Marie / interdire / sa fille Mireille / sortir avec Frédéric

8. Nadine / prier / ses parents / l'emmener au bord de la mer

9. Sylvie / inviter / ses beaux-parents / dîner

10. Guillaume / proposer / ses parents / passer leurs vacances avec sa famille

---

***Beau-fils** and **belle-fille** can also mean *stepson* and *stepdaughter*.

L **Et chez vous?** *Comment est-ce qu'on vit dans votre famille? Choisissez des mots des trois colonnes pour faire huit phrases qui décrivent les rapports familiaux chez vous. Faites attention aux objets directs et indirects et aux prépositions employées devant l'infinitif.*

mon père/ma mère	aider	aider à faire le ménage
mes parents	conseiller	conduire prudemment
mon grand-père	déconseiller	faire les courses pour lui/elle/eux/elles
ma grand-mère	défendre	jouer aux jeux vidéo
mes grands-parents	demander	manger en famille le dimanche
mon frère (aîné/cadet)	empêcher	nettoyer ma chambre
ma sœur (aînée/cadette)	encourager	prendre mes études au sérieux
mon oncle/ma tante	ordonner	ranger mes affaires
mon cousin/ma cousine	permettre	se coucher tôt en semaine
	proposer	trop parler au téléphone

Adjective or Noun + Preposition + Infinitive

Most adjectives and nouns take **de** before a following infinitive.

—Tu étais **surprise d'apprendre** que notre équipe a perdu le match?

*Were you **surprised to learn** that our team lost the game?*

—Oui. Mais ils sont **sûrs de gagner** le match de dimanche.

*Yes. But they're **sure to win** the game on Sunday.*

—Sans doute. Ils ont **un** grand **désir de gagner**.

*No doubt. They have **a** great **desire to win**.*

Some adjectives and nouns take **à**, however.

être déterminé(e) à *to be determined to*
être prêt(e) à *to be ready to*
être le premier/le troisième/le seul/le dernier (la première/la troisième/ la seule/la dernière) à *to be the first/third/only/last to*

Je suis **déterminée à être la première à avoir** 20 à l'examen de maths.

*I'm **determined to be the first to get** a 20 on the math test.*

Adjectives modified by **trop** or **assez** take **pour** before a following infinitive.

—Pierrot est **trop petit pour comprendre**.

*Pierrot is **too little to understand**.*

—Mais il est **assez intelligent pour se conduire** comme il faut.

*But he is **intelligent enough to behave** the way he ought to.*

M *À compléter.* *Complétez les phrases suivantes avec la préposition qui manque.*

1. Marie n'est pas prête _____ passer son examen de chimie.

2. Elle dit qu'elle est sûre _____ ne pas y réussir.

3. Mais elle est déterminée _____ passer l'été à réviser la chimie.

4. Je serais enchanté _____ vous aider à faire le ménage.

5. Je serais le premier _____ vous aider si je pouvais.

6. Mais je suis trop maladroit (*clumsy*) _____ vous être utile.

7. Je ne suis pas heureux _____ voir le petit Albert jouer aux jeux vidéo.

8. C'est une mauvaise idée _____ laisser un enfant perdre son temps de cette façon.

9. Il est le seul élève de sa classe _____ passer tant de temps devant l'écran.

10. Il est assez intelligent _____ comprendre l'importance de ce que je lui dis.

Faire + Infinitive

To express the idea that one person has, gets, or causes another person to do something, French uses the verb **faire** followed by an infinitive. This construction is called the *causative.*

—Tu **as fait redécorer** ton appartement?	*Have you **had** your apartment **redecorated**?*
—J'**ai fait repeindre** le salon, c'est tout.	*I **had** the living room **repainted**, that's all.*
—La voiture est en panne. Je ne peux pas la **faire démarrer**.	*The car isn't working. I can't **get** it **to start**.*
—Il faut la **faire réparer**, alors.	*Then we have to **have** it **repaired**.*

The person you have do the work or perform the action may appear at the end of the sentence if there is no other object.

Mme Ducros fait étudier **ses enfants**.	*Mrs. Ducros makes **her children** study.*
L'institutrice fait chanter **ses élèves**.	*The schoolteacher has **her pupils** sing.*

When the sentence contains two objects, the object of the infinitive is direct and the object of **faire** is indirect. The indirect object may be preceded by **par** or **à**.

J'ai fait repeindre mon appartement **par M. Jollivet.** J'ai fait repeindre mon appartement **à M. Jollivet.**	*I had **Mr. Jollivet** repaint my apartment.*

One or both of the objects in the above example can be replaced by an object pronoun. The object pronouns always precede **faire**.

Je **le lui** ai fait repeindre.	*I had **him** repaint **it**.*

In this construction, the past participle of **faire** does not agree with a preceding direct object.

N *Problèmes du logement.* *Les Giraud viennent d'acheter une maison à Grenoble.
La maison est charmante, mais les Giraud découvrent qu'il y a beaucoup de travail
à faire avant qu'ils puissent emménager. Lisez la liste des problèmes et employez* **il faut**
*et le causatif pour dire ce qu'il faut faire dans chaque cas pour rendre la maison habitable.
Suivez le modèle.*

MODÈLE   La peinture de la cuisine est vieille. (repeindre)
→ Il faut la faire repeindre.

Pour aménager une maison

crevassé *cracked* (of ground)   **marcher** *to work* (of an appliance)
débarrasser *to clear out*   **le papier (peint)** *wallpaper*
se décoller *to peel off*   **plâtrer** *to plaster*
installer *to install*   **remplacer** *to replace*
se lézarder *to crack* (of a wall)   **retapisser** *to repaper*
la lumière *light*

1. Le papier du salon se décolle. (retapisser)

2. La lumière dans la salle à manger ne marche pas. (réparer)

3. Le plancher des chambres à coucher est très sale. (nettoyer)

4. La fenêtre du balcon est cassée. (remplacer)

5. Le trottoir est crevassé. (paver)

6. Les murs se lézardent. (plâtrer)

7. Le garage est plein de vieux meubles. (débarrasser)

NOTE CULTURELLE

La ville de **Grenoble**, située dans les Alpes, est une belle ville cosmopolite.
Grenoble est une ville universitaire qui compte environ 40 000 étudiants. À
Grenoble on trouve aussi le Centre de Recherches Nucléaires où travaillent
ensemble des scientifiques français et étrangers. Pour les vacances d'hiver
Grenoble est une destination préférée parce que les stations de ski aux alentours de la ville sont nombreuses et excellentes. Capitale de la région appelée
le Dauphiné, Grenoble était le lieu des Jeux olympiques en 1968. La population de l'agglomération urbaine de Grenoble dépasse les 580 000 habitants.

O *Une institutrice de première* (**first-rate**). *Mlle Arnaud est une institutrice excellente
qui sait faire progresser ses élèves. Employez le causatif pour exprimer sa façon de résoudre
les problèmes de ses élèves et d'organiser sa classe. Suivez le modèle.*

MODÈLE   Jérôme jette des papiers par terre. (balayer la salle de classe)
→ Mlle Arnaud lui fait balayer la salle de classe.

1. Catherine n'aime pas parler en classe. (réciter des poèmes)

2. André a peur de parler devant tout le monde. (présenter son travail devant un petit
groupe)

3. Monique et Suzanne bavardent en classe. (écrire une composition)

4. Samuel ne comprend pas les problèmes de maths. (relire l'explication dans son livre)

5. Les élèves sont fatigués après un examen. (regarder un film)

6. Quelques élèves apprennent plus vite que les autres. (aider leurs camarades)

7. Le directeur arrive à la porte de sa salle de classe. (observer une leçon de français)

8. Nous nous intéressons à la musique. (écouter la chanson que les élèves ont apprise)

P   *Les causes.* *Votre ami fait des observations. Vous lui signalez la personne ou la chose qui est la cause des actions qu'il remarque. Suivez le modèle.*

MODÈLE   Les étudiants travaillaient. (leur professeur)
     → Leur professeur les a fait travailler.

Quelques actions

démarrer *to start* (of a car)	**rire** *to laugh*
grelotter *to shiver*	**soupirer** *to sigh*
pleurer *to cry*	**sourire** *to smile*
pousser *to grow*	**trembler** *to shake, tremble*
rager *to fume (with anger)*	

1. Élise pleurait. (son petit ami)

2. Les fenêtres tremblaient. (le vent)

3. J'ai vu les belles roses qui poussaient chez ton voisin. (mon voisin)

4. Les élèves lisaient. (leur institutrice)

5. Les enfants riaient. (le clown)

6. La voiture démarrait. (le mécanicien)

7. La mère souriait. (ses enfants)

8. La vieille dame soupirait. (la chaleur)

9. Le chien grelottait. (le froid)

10. Le client rageait. (la vendeuse)

Q   *Activité orale.* *Posez des questions à un(e) ami(e) sur ce qu'on l'encourage à faire, sur ce qu'on lui permet de faire, sur ce qu'on lui demande de faire, sur ce qu'on lui fait faire, etc. Employez des tournures avec l'infinitif. Votre ami(e) vous répondra en employant ces structures et vous posera des questions pareilles à son tour.*

II

Nouns and Their Modifiers; Pronouns

Nouns: Gender, Number, and Articles; Uses of Articles

Gender and Number of Nouns; Definite and Indefinite Articles

In traditional grammar, a noun is a word that names a person, place, thing, idea, or quality. We can also define a noun by the structures in which it occurs. In French, a noun is a word that can fill the blank slots in constructions such as the ones that follow.

le/la/l'/un/une _____ est
les/des _____ sont

French nouns are usually preceded by a determiner. The most common determiners are the definite and indefinite articles. The indefinite article (*a, an* in English) serves to introduce a noun into the discourse. The definite article (*the* in English) identifies something already introduced into the discourse that the speaker assumes is known to the person he or she is talking to.

—Tu sais? J'ai acheté **une** voiture.	*You know? I bought **a** car.*
—C'est vrai? Et où est **la** voiture?	*Really? And where is **the** car?*
Je voudrais la voir.	*I'd like to see it.*

French nouns are either masculine or feminine. Most nouns add -s to form the plural. There are four forms of the French definite article.

	MASCULINE	FEMININE
SINGULAR	**le** crayon	**la** table
	l'homme	**l'**école
PLURAL	**les** crayons	**les** tables
	les hommes	**les** écoles

Note that both masculine and feminine singular nouns beginning with a vowel or mute **h** take the definite article **l'**.

There are three forms of the French indefinite article.

	MASCULINE	FEMININE
SINGULAR	**un** crayon	**une** table
	un homme	**une** école
PLURAL	**des** crayons	**des** tables
	des hommes	**des** écoles

English has no plural indefinite article. French **des** is often equivalent to *some* or *any*.

A **À l'école.** *Ajoutez à chaque substantif l'article défini et écrivez le syntagme* (phrase) *au pluriel. Suivez le modèle.*

> MODÈLE   garçon
>   → le garçon / les garçons

1. cahier
2. calculette
3. étudiant
4. serviette
5. papier
6. stylo
7. leçon
8. calendrier
9. bibliothèque
10. dictionnaire
11. histoire
12. cloche
13. exposé
14. cantine
15. magnétoscope

B **Au magasin de vêtements.** *Ajoutez à chaque substantif l'article indéfini et écrivez le syntagme au pluriel. Suivez le modèle.*

> MODÈLE   chapeau
>   → un chapeau / des chapeaux

1. pull
2. chemise
3. pantalon
4. cravate
5. rayon
6. vendeur
7. vendeuse
8. robe
9. maillot de bain
10. veste
11. costume
12. chemisier
13. solde
14. blouson
15. anorak

Plural Nouns

Most French nouns form their plural by adding -**s**. There are some exceptions.

Singular nouns ending in -**s**, -**x**, or -**z** do not change form in the plural.

le cour**s**	→ les cour**s**
une foi**s**	→ des foi**s**
le moi**s**	→ les moi**s**
un pri**x**	→ des pri**x**
la voi**x**	→ les voi**x**
le ne**z**	→ les ne**z**

Most nouns ending in -**al** have a plural form ending in -**aux**.

l'anim**al**	→ les anim**aux**
le chev**al**	→ les chev**aux**
le génér**al**	→ les génér**aux**
l'hôpit**al**	→ les hôpit**aux**
l'idé**al**	→ les idé**aux**
le journ**al**	→ les journ**aux**

There are some exceptions: **le b**al → **les b**als, **le carnav**al → **les carnav**als, **le festiv**al → **les festiv**als, **le récit**al → **les récit**als.

Nouns ending in -**au**, -**eau**, or -**eu** add -**x** to form the plural.

le bat**eau**	→ les bat**eaux**
le bur**eau**	→ les bur**eaux**
le chev**eu**	→ les chev**eux**
le j**eu**	→ les j**eux**

An exception is **le pn**eu (*tire*) → **les pn**eus.

Most nouns ending in -**ou** add -**s** to form the plural.

le cl**ou**	*nail*	→ les cl**ous**
le tr**ou**	*hole*	→ les tr**ous**

A few exceptions add -**x**: **le bij**ou → **les bij**oux, **le ch**ou → **les ch**oux, **le gen**ou → **les gen**oux.

Some nouns have irregular plurals.

le ciel	→ les **cieux**
l'œil	→ les **yeux**
le travail	→ les **travaux**
monsieur	→ **messieurs**
madame	→ **mesdames**
mademoiselle	→ **mesdemoiselles**

Family names in French do not change form in the plural.

—Vous connaissez **les Durand**?	*Do you know **the Durands**?*
—Non, mais je sais qu'ils sont les voisins **des Chevalier**.	*No, but I know that they are neighbors of the Chevaliers.*

Some nouns are used mainly in the plural.

> **les ciseaux** *scissors*
> **les frais** *expenses, cost*
> **les mathématiques, les maths** *math*
> **les mœurs** *morals*
> **les vacances** *vacation*

Some nouns, especially abstract nouns, have no plural.

> **la foi** *faith*
> **la paix** *peace*
> **la patience** *patience*

Numbers and letters used as nouns also have no plural.

> «Femme» s'écrit avec deux **m**.   *"Femme" is written with two **m**'s.*
>
> Il y a deux **cinq** dans mon numéro.   *There are two **fives** in my phone number.*

Remember that most French nouns are pronounced the same in their singular and plural forms.

C   **Pas un mais deux.** *Répondez dans chaque cas que vous cherchez/voulez/avez deux, pas un des substantifs mentionnés. Suivez le modèle.*

> MODÈLE   Vous cherchez un stylo?
>   → Je cherche deux stylos.

1. Vous voulez un chapeau?
2. Vous assistez au festival?
3. Vous avez un neveu?
4. Votre nom s'écrit avec un *l*?
5. Vous cherchez un monsieur?
6. Vous étudiez un vitrail?
7. Vous prononcez un discours?
8. Vous cherchez un métal?
9. Vous prenez un morceau?
10. Vous visitez un pays?
11. Vous avez un choix?
12. Vous préparez un repas?
13. Vous lisez un journal?
14. Vous changez un pneu?
15. Vous avez un rival?

Determining the Gender of Nouns

Most nouns referring to males are masculine. Most nouns referring to females are feminine.

un homme	une femme
un garçon	une fille
un père	une mère
un oncle	une tante

Many feminine nouns are formed by adding **-e** to the masculine form.

un saint	→	une saint**e**
un rival	→	une rival**e**
un cousin	→	une cousin**e**
un marchand	→	une marchand**e**
un employé	→	une employé**e**
un ami	→	une ami**e**

In other cases, the masculine ending is changed to a feminine ending.

-ien	→	**-ienne**	un Ital**ien**	→	une Ital**ienne**
-on	→	**-onne**	un patr**on**	→	une patr**onne**
-eur	→	**-euse**	un vend**eur**	→	une vend**euse**
-teur	→	**-trice**	un ac**teur**	→	une ac**trice**
-er	→	**-ère**	un bouch**er**	→	une bouch**ère**
-ier	→	**-ière**	un épic**ier**	→	une épic**ière**

The suffix **-esse** forms the feminine of some masculine nouns.

un prince	→	une princ**esse**
un dieu	→	une dé**esse**

Many nouns have the same form for both masculine and feminine; only the article changes to indicate the gender of the person referred to.

un/une artiste
un/une camarade
un/une élève
un/une enfant

Some nouns are masculine even when they refer to women.

un poète	un médecin
un auteur	un ministre
un docteur	un peintre
un écrivain	un professeur
un ingénieur	un sculpteur
un juge	un témoin *witness*

Ma femme est **un auteur** très connu.	*My wife is **a** very famous **author**.*
Ta sœur est **un** très bon **peintre**.	*Your sister is **a** very good **painter**.*

Other nouns are grammatically feminine even when they refer to men.

une brute	une vedette *film star*
une personne	une victime

—Marc est **une personne** sympathique, n'est-ce pas?
*Mark is **a** nice **person**, isn't he?*

—Tu trouves? Tout le monde dit que c'est **une brute**.
*You think so? Everyone says that he's **a beast**.*

Nowadays, there is a tendency to create specific feminine forms for all nouns of profession. Forms such as **une auteuse/une autrice**, **une écrivaine**, **une ingénieure**, and **une témoin** can occasionally be found in writing but are not universally accepted. In school slang, however, **la professeur** and **la prof** are common.

D *À compléter.* *Choisissez le mot qui complète ces phrases.*

1. Dans mon quartier l'_____ (épicier / épicière) et son mari sont très aimables.

2. Élizabeth est devenue _____ (pharmacien / pharmacienne).

3. Cette étudiante est _____ (un / une) artiste formidable.

4. Notre ami Frédéric est _____ (un / une) des victimes de l'accident.

5. Tu connais _____ (le / la) violiniste? Il est italien, je crois.

6. On dit que Joseph Mercier est _____ (le / la) vedette de l'année.

7. Leur fille est _____ (un / une) enfant de sept ans.

8. Ma mère est _____ (le / la) seul ingénieur de l'équipe.

E *Elle aussi.* *Écrivez que les femmes mentionnées ont les mêmes caractéristiques que les hommes. Suivez le modèle.*

MODÈLE   Jacquot est clarinettiste. (sa sœur)
          → Sa sœur est clarinettiste aussi.

1. Albert est musicien. (Marguerite)

2. Louis? Il est épicier. (Émilie)

3. Mon cousin est un élève de cette école primaire. (ma nièce)

4. Charles? C'est un Breton. (Éloïse)

5. Jean-Paul Sartre est un écrivain célèbre. (Simone de Beauvoir)

6. Pierre a été victime de son imprudence. (Hélène)

7. Maurice est un instituteur formidable. (Lise)

8. M. Chauvin est le propriétaire de l'établissement. (Mme Chauvin)

9. Son mari est l'avocat de la défense. (sa femme)

10. Olivier est un médecin respecté. (Chantal)

11. Cet homme est aviateur. (cette femme)

12. Roger est un nageur formidable. (Mireille)

13. Paul est notre champion. (Caroline)

14. Je connais M. Duval, le commerçant. (Mme Mercier)

Determining the Gender of Nouns (Continued)

Although many French nouns give no clue to their gender (**le peuple**, **la foule**), some have endings that do indicate gender.

Masculine Endings

-age	un avantage, un orage, un voyage (BUT **la page**, **la plage**)
-eau	un bateau, un cadeau, un couteau (BUT **l'eau** [*fem.*], **la peau**)
-et	le jouet, le secret, le sujet
-ing	le camping, le dancing, le shopping
-isme	le socialisme, le communisme, le tourisme
-ment	un bâtiment, le commencement, un monument
-oir	un espoir, le mouchoir, le trottoir
-ou	le bijou, le clou, le genou

Feminine Endings

-ace	la glace, la menace, la surface
-ade	une ambassade, une promenade, une salade (BUT **le stade**)
-ance	la brillance, la chance, l'importance
-esse	la jeunesse, la politesse, la promesse
-ette	une bicyclette, la calculette, la cassette
-ière	la frontière, la lumière, la manière
-ine	une aspirine, la cuisine, la piscine (BUT **le magazine**)
-ise	une chemise, une surprise, une valise
-sion	la décision, l'inversion, la télévision
-té	la liberté, la société, la spécialité
-tion	la nation, la production, la programmation
-tude	une attitude, la gratitude, la solitude
-ure	une aventure, la lecture, la voiture

Some nouns can be either masculine or feminine, depending on their meaning.

le critique *critic*
la critique *criticism, review*

le livre *book*
la livre *pound*

le poste *job; radio or TV set*
la poste *mail, postal service*

le tour *tour, trip*
la tour *tower*

le voile *veil*
la voile *sail*

F   *Masculin ou féminin?*   *Choisissez l'article correct dans chaque cas.*

1. François s'est acheté _____ (un / une) mobylette.

2. Ce que tu as dit est vraiment _____ (un / une) compliment.

3. La natation est _____ (un / une) activité agréable.

4. _____ (Un / Une) côtelette d'agneau, s'il vous plaît.

5. _____ (Le / La) cyclisme est un sport important en France.

6. _____ (Quel / Quelle) émission comptez-vous regarder ce soir?

7. Je n'ai pas compris _____ (le / la) message.

8. Le pharmacien m'a donné _____ (un / une) ordonnance.

9. Elle aime _____ (le / la) peinture.

10. Est-ce que tu as vu _____ (le / la) stade?

11. Le petit Georges a mangé _____ (un / une) tartine.

12. J'ai perdu _____ (mon / ma) rasoir.

13. Il dit toujours _____ (le / la) vérité.

14. Vous avez lu _____ (le / la) critique du film?

15. Je veux voir les informations. Est-ce que je peux allumer _____ (le / la) poste?

16. Elle a acheté _____ (un / une) livre de pommes.

17. _____ (Un / Une) voile couvrait le visage de la mariée (*bride*).

18. Ce bateau a fait _____ (le / la) tour du monde.

C'est Versus il/elle est

French has two constructions to identify a noun referring to a person (*he's a . . .* , *she's a . . .*).

1 · **Il est/Elle est** or **ils sont/elles sont** is used before an unmodified noun of profession, religion, or nationality. Note that no indefinite article is used in this construction.

—**Il est** médecin?	*Is he a doctor?*
—Non, sa femme est médecin. Lui, **il est** scientifique.	*No, his wife is a doctor. He's a scientist.*
—**Ils sont** protestants, les Duvalier?	*Are the Duvaliers Protestants?*
—Lui, **il est** protestant. Elle, **elle est** catholique.	*He's a Protestant. She's a Catholic.*

2 · If the noun is modified (even by just an article), **c'est** or **ce sont** must be used. **C'est un/une** is the most common construction to identify things.

—**C'est** un avocat?	*Is he a lawyer?*
—Non, **ce n'est pas** un avocat. **C'est** un juge.	*No, **he's not** a lawyer. **He's** a judge.*
—**Ce sont** des soldats?	*Are they soldiers?*
—Non, **ce sont** des pilotes.	*No, **they're** pilots.*

G *Identifications.* *Complétez ces phrases en indiquant le choix correct.*

1. _____ (C'est / Il est) un journal français.

2. _____ (C'est / Elle est) vendeuse.

3. _____ (Ce sont / Ils sont) français.

4. _____ (Ce sont / Ils sont) des commerçants.

5. _____ (C'est / Il est) le propriétaire de la boutique.

6. _____ (C'est / Elle est) une salade délicieuse.

7. _____ (C'est / Elle est) notre patronne.

8. _____ (C'est / Elle est) vedette de cinéma.

9. _____ (C'est / Il est) architecte.

10. _____ (Ce sont / Ils sont) professeurs.

The Partitive

The partitive article is an indefinite article used to express an indefinite quantity or part of something (English: *some, any*). The partitive article consists of **de + le, la**, or **l'**. **De + le** contracts to **du**. The plural of the partitive article is **des**.

du lait	**de la** patience	**de l'**eau	**des** sandwichs
du pain	**de la** crème	**de l'**or	**des** pommes

After a negative, the partitive article is **de (d')** unless the verb is **être**. If the verb is **être**, the partitive article retains its full form. **De (d')** also replaces the indefinite article after a negative.

—Tu **n'**as **pas** encore acheté **de** pain!	*You haven't bought **any** bread yet!*
—Tu **n'**as vraiment **pas de** patience.	*You really don't have **any** patience.*
—C'est du lait, ça?	*Is that milk?*
—Non, **ce n'est pas du** lait. C'est de la crème.	*No, **it's not** milk. It's cream.*
—Tu as **une** voiture?	*Do you have **a** car?*
—Non, je **n'**ai **pas de** voiture.	*No, I don't have **a** car.*

When the preposition **de** is an integral part of an expression (for example, **avoir besoin de qqch** (*to need something*)), the partitive is not used.

Nous avons besoin **de** pain.   *We need bread.*

In expressions with **de, de** + article refers to a specific entity, something that the speaker assumes is known to the person he or she is talking to.

Nous avons besoin **du** pain.   *We need the bread.*

H   *Il ne reste rien à la charcuterie.*   *Jean-Claude est entré chez le charcutier du quartier pour acheter quelque chose à manger, mais il ne reste rien dans la boutique. Écrivez des échanges entre l'employé et Jean-Claude en suivant le modèle.*

> MODÈLE   œufs durs
> → —Vous avez des œufs durs?
> —Non, monsieur. Il n'y a plus d'œufs durs.

1. jambon
2. salade niçoise
3. fromage
4. carottes râpées

5. saucisson
6. saumon fumé
7. quiches
8. sandwichs

I   *On a fait les courses à moitié.*   *Tout le monde est sorti acheter à manger, mais personne n'a acheté tout ce qu'il fallait. Employez le partitif pour le dire, en suivant le modèle.*

> MODÈLE   Marc / acheter / lait / eau minérale
> → Marc a acheté du lait, mais il n'a pas acheté d'eau minérale.

1. Suzanne / chercher / farine / œufs
2. moi / rapporter / pain / beurre
3. Laurent / trouver / champignons / salade
4. Élisabeth / prendre / pommes / oranges
5. toi et moi / acheter / petits pois / haricots verts
6. vous / rapporter / fromage / yaourt
7. toi / chercher / viande / poulet
8. les garçons / prendre / lait / Coca

J   *C'est quoi, ça?*   *Antoinette ne reconnaît pas tous les plats qu'on a préparés. Elle demande à son amie de lui expliquer ce qu'ils sont. Suivez le modèle.*

> MODÈLE   crème / yaourt
> → —C'est de la crème, ça?
> —Non, ce n'est pas de la crème. C'est du yaourt.

1. bœuf / porc
2. poulet / dindon
3. haricots verts / endives
4. riz / couscous
5. vin / champagne
6. thon / saumon
7. bouillabaisse / soupe à l'oignon
8. crème caramel / glace

NOTE CULTURELLE

- Le **couscous** est un plat nord-africain, diffusé en France par le contact avec l'Afrique du Nord et par les immigrés maghrébins en France. C'est une spécialité à base de semoule à laquelle on ajoute de la viande et des légumes. Souvent on y ajoute aussi des merguez, de petites saucisses nord-africaines d'un goût très relevé.
- La **bouillabaisse** est un plat typique de Marseille (et de toute la Provence). On la prépare à partir de poissons variés et de fruits de mer que l'on fait cuire dans de l'eau ou du vin blanc. On y ajoute de l'ail et des condiments pour relever la saveur du poisson et des fruits de mer.
- La **crème caramel** est un dessert qui ressemble au flan espagnol. Il est préparé à base de crème et de sucre fondu et roussi par l'action du feu.

Expressions of Quantity

After expressions of quantity, **de** without the article is used instead of the partitive.

assez de	*enough*
autant de	*as much, as many*
beaucoup de	*much, many*
combien de?	*how much? how many?*
moins de	*less*
peu de	*few, little, not much*
plus de	*more*
tant de	*so much, so many*
trop de	*too much, too many*
un peu de	*a little (bit of)*

De is also used in expressions of weights and measures such as the following.

une boîte de	*a box of*
une bouteille de	*a bottle of*
un kilo de	*a kilo of*
une livre de	*a pound of*

—J'ai **deux bouteilles de** lait.	*I have **two bottles of** milk.*
—Alors, j'ai **autant de** lait que toi.	*Then I have **as much** milk as you do.*
—**Combien de** viande as-tu achetée?	***How much** meat did you buy?*
—J'ai pris **un kilo de** bœuf et **une livre de** jambon.	*I got **a kilo of** beef and **a pound of** ham.*

However, if the noun following the preposition **de** is specific in any of the above cases, the definite article is used, and will contract with the preposition.

Peu **des** étudiants ont compris.	*Few **of the** students understood.*
Les enfants ont mangé beaucoup **du** chocolat que je leur ai donné.	*The children ate much **of the** chocolate that I gave them.*

La plupart (*most*) and **bien** (*a lot*) are followed by **de** + article.

—Il étudie **la plupart du** temps?	*Does he study **most of the** time?*
—Oui, il a **bien des** livres à lire.	*Yes, he has **a lot of** books to read.*

The phrase **ne** + verb + **que** (*only*) is not really a negative and is followed by the partitive.

Tu **ne** dis **que des** sottises.	*You're saying **only** silly things.*

Note the use of the partitive with school subjects after the verb **faire**.

faire des maths	*to study (major in) math*
faire de la physique	*to study (major in) physics*

In formal style, **de** replaces the partitive before an adjective that *precedes* the noun.

Nous avons fait **de grands** efforts.	*We made **great** efforts.*

This rule is increasingly disregarded in all styles.

Elle a acheté **des belles** fleurs.	*She bought **some beautiful** flowers.*

However, **d'autres** is used in all styles.

—Avez-vous **d'autres** projets?	*Do you have **other** plans?*
—Oui, on en a **d'autres**.	*Yes, we have **others**.*

K   *À compléter.* Indiquez lequel des articles proposés est le choix correct.

1. Il prend _____ (du / de) thé.

2. Tu as besoin _____ (du / de) courage.

3. Ils m'ont servi _____ (des / de) côtelettes de veau.

4. Moi, je ne mange pas _____ (un / du / de) veau.

5. Elle ne fait que _____ (de / des) bêtises.

6. Nous cherchons _____ (des / de) crayons.

7. Ce soir on prépare _____ (du / de) poulet.

8. Combien _____ (des / de) cours suivez-vous?

9. Nous avons autant _____ (des / de) problèmes que vous.

10. Achète une livre _____ (des / de) poires.

11. La plupart _____ (des / de) étudiants sont sympathiques.

12. Les professeurs donnent trop _____ (du / de) travail.

13. Il ne lit plus les mêmes livres. Il en lit _____ (d' / des) autres.

14. Bien _____ (des / de) jounalistes ont écrit à ce sujet.

L *Comment est-ce que ça se dit?* *Traduisez les échanges suivants en français.*

1. *We need coffee.*
   I bought coffee.
   How much coffee did you buy?
   Enough coffee. And I bought three hundred grams of tea too.

2. *Most of the books that I read were interesting.*
   Too many of the books that I read were boring.

Uses of Articles

The definite article designates a specific noun.

—Je vais te montrer **le dessert**.	*I'm going to show you **the dessert**.*
—**Le dessert** que tu as préparé?	*The dessert you prepared?*

The French definite article labels nouns used in a general sense. English nouns are used without any article in this meaning.

La démocratie et **la liberté** sont des traits essentiels de la France.	*Democracy and freedom are basic characteristics of France.*

Contrast the general and specific uses of the definite article in the following example.

J'adore **la viande**, mais je n'aime pas **la viande** qu'on sert dans ce bistrot.	*I love **meat** (general), but I don't like **the meat** they serve in that bistro (specific).*

In a restaurant, the definite article is often used when ordering.

Pour moi, **le rosbif** et pour mon ami, **le canard à l'orange**.	*I'll have **roast beef**, and my friend will have **duck in orange sauce**.*

The French indefinite article is used much the way its English equivalent is. However, it is not used after **il/elle est** when followed by an unmodified noun of profession, nationality, or religion.

Les Bois sont professionnels. Lui, **il est avocat** et elle, **elle est professeur**.	*The Bois are professionals. **He's a lawyer** and **she's a teacher**.*

In a restaurant, the indefinite article is often used to designate a serving of something.

Un café et **un** petit rouge, s'il vous plaît.	*A cup of coffee and a glass of red wine, please.*

The partitive article before names of foods and beverages designates an indefinite quantity. English may or may not use the words *some* or *any* in these cases.

—Tu veux boire **du** chocolat?	*Would you like to drink hot chocolate?*
—Non, merci. Tu as **du** café?	*No, thanks. Do you have **any** coffee?*

Compare the uses of the articles with the word **thé** in the following sentences.

Le thé est une boisson d'origine orientale.	**Tea** *is a drink that comes from the Orient.* (general)
J'aime **le thé** que vous avez acheté.	*I like **the tea** that you bought.* (specific)
Un thé, s'il vous plaît.	*A **cup of tea**, please.* (a standard serving, said to a waiter)
Après mon dîner, je bois **du thé**.	*After my dinner, I drink **tea**.* (indefinite quantity)

After the prepositions **avec** and **sans**, no article is used unless the noun is modified.

—Il a écouté **avec** attention.	*He listened **with** attention (attentively).*
—Et il a rédigé une composition **sans** fautes.	*And he wrote a composition **without** mistakes.*
Il a agi **avec** courage.	*He acted courageously.*
Il a agi **avec un** courage admirable.	*He acted **with** admirable courage.*

M   *Qu'est-ce qui manque?*   *Complétez les phrases suivantes avec l'article qui manque. Si aucun article n'est nécessaire, mettez un X.*

1. Pour moi, _____ coq au vin et _____ pommes de terre à la lyonnaise.

2. Tu ne veux pas _____ bœuf?

3. Non, je mange très peu _____ viande. Je préfère _____ poulet.

4. Garçon! _____ limonade et _____ citron pressé, s'il vous plaît.

5. Je regrette, mais nous n'avons plus _____ citron pressé.

6. Alors, _____ jus d'orange.

7. Pour un étudiant en médecine, _____ diligence est très importante.

8. Il lui faut un peu de _____ repos aussi.

9. Mais, en général, _____ étudiants en médecine ont très peu de _____ temps pour se reposer.

10. Tu aimes _____ cinéma français?

11. Oui, il y a _____ films qui m'ont beaucoup plu. Mais je crois que je préfère _____ films italiens.

12. On passe _____ nouveaux films italiens au Pathé cette semaine. Tu veux aller les voir?

13. Oui, bien sûr. Mais j'ai tant _____ travail. On va voir. Si j'ai _____ temps libre, on ira au Pathé.

14. _____ ordinateur est essentiel dans _____ bureaux modernes.

15. C'est pour ça que beaucoup _____ étudiants font _____ informatique.

16. _____ informatique est une des matières les plus étudiées aujourd'hui.

17. La plupart _____ étudiants ont un ordinateur dans leur chambre.

18. _____ jeux électroniques sont aussi appréciés que _____ logiciels scientifiques.

N   **Comment?** *Traduisez les phrases suivantes en français. Choisissez parmi les substantifs suivants pour traduire les adverbes anglais par une phrase prépositive commençant par* **avec** *ou* **sans**.

attention	joie
courage	peur
haine	soin
intelligence	tendresse

1. *He spoke intelligently.*

2. *She acted courageously.*

3. *We set out* (se mettre en route) *fearlessly.*

4. *He answered hatefully.*

5. *He played joylessly.*

6. *He wrote* (rédiger) *his composition carelessly.*

7. *She spoke to him tenderly.*

8. *He listened attentively.*

O   **Activité orale.** *Jouez une scène au restaurant avec un(e) ami(e). Posez des questions au garçon et commandez les plats et les boissons. Faites attention à l'emploi des articles.*

Stressed Pronouns; Subject-Verb Agreement

Stressed Pronouns—Forms and Usage

Stressed pronouns are used to emphasize a noun or pronoun used as a subject or object, or to replace a noun used as a subject or object.

	SINGULAR	PLURAL
FIRST PERSON	**moi**	**nous**
SECOND PERSON	**toi**	**vous**
THIRD PERSON	**lui/elle**	**eux/elles**

Moi, **je** fais du latin, mais **lui**, **il** fait du grec.	*I'm taking Latin, but **he's** taking Greek.*
—**Nous**, **on** travaille aujourd'hui. Et **toi**?	*We're working today. What about **you**?*
—Je vais à la plage, **moi**.	*I'm going to the beach.*

A stressed pronoun may stand alone in answer to a question.

—Qui fait le ménage aujourd'hui? Toi?	*Who's doing the housework today? You?*
—Pas moi. **Eux**.	*Not me. **They are**.*

The stressed pronouns are used after **c'est** and **ce sont** to identify people.

C'est moi / C'est toi / C'est lui / C'est elle / C'est nous / C'est vous.

BUT

Ce sont eux / Ce sont elles.

Colloquially, one says **C'est eux / C'est elles**; in the negative, **Ce n'est pas eux. / Ce n'est pas elles**. Note also the questions **Qui est-ce?** (formal) and **C'est qui?** (informal).

The stressed pronouns are used after prepositions.

—Tu pars **sans elle**?	*Are you leaving **without her**?*
—Pas du tout. Elle vient **chez moi** et nous partons ensemble.	*Not at all. She's coming **to my house**, and we're leaving together.*

The stressed pronouns are also used after **ne... que**.

Je **ne** connais **que toi** à Paris.	***You're the only one** I know in Paris.*
Il n'aime **qu'eux**.	*He likes **only them**.*

The stressed pronoun **soi** (*himself/herself/themselves*) is used to avoid ambiguity.

Chacun pour **soi**.	*Every man for **himself**.*
Il ne faut pas parler toujours de **lui**.	*One shouldn't talk about **him** all the time.*
Il ne faut pas parler toujours de **soi**.	*One shouldn't talk about **oneself** all the time.*

 A *Vacances.* *Formez des phrases exprimant un contraste avec les éléments proposés. Employez des pronoms disjoints. Suivez le modèle.*

MODÈLE   je / aller au bord de la mer : ils / aller à la montagne
   → Moi, je vais au bord de la mer. Eux, ils vont à la montagne.

1. nous / partir en Italie : elles / partir en Grèce

2. je / prendre le train : ils / partir en voiture

3. tu / faire de l'alpinisme : il / faire de la natation

4. mes cousins / aller à la campagne : on (= nous) / aller leur rendre visite

5. je / avoir trois semaines de vacances : vous / avoir un mois

6. je / préférer voyager seul : tu / préférer voyager en groupe

7. on (= nous) / compter faire du cyclisme : il / vouloir faire du tourisme

8. elle / faire un stage linguistique en Allemagne : tu / te détendre

B *Tu as tort!* *Un copain vous dit des choses erronées sur vos habitudes, vos allées et venues, etc. Corrigez ses impressions en formant une phrase négative. Mettez le pronom **moi** à la fin. Suivez le modèle.*

MODÈLE   Je sais que tu aimes les films d'horreur.
   → Tu as tort! Je n'aime pas les films d'horreur, moi.

1. Je sais que tu sors avec Émilie.

2. Je sais que tu te lèves à 8 heures.

3. Je sais que tu dors en classe.

4. Je sais que tu joues de la clarinette.

5. Je sais que tu cherches du travail.

6. Je sais que tu vas chez Olivier après les cours.

C *Mon ami Philippe? Jamais!* *Un copain a des impressions fausses sur votre ami Philippe. Corrigez ses idées avec une phrase négative au passé composé contenant le mot **jamais**. Mettez le pronom **lui** à la fin. Suivez le modèle.*

MODÈLE   Ton ami Philippe sort avec Odile.
   → Qu'est-ce que tu dis? Il n'est jamais sorti avec Odile, lui.

1. Ton ami Philippe dort en classe.

2. Ton ami Philippe est toujours en retard.

3. Ton ami Philippe interrompt le professeur.

4. Ton ami Philippe se dispute avec Serge.

5. Ton ami Philippe se moque des cours.

6. Ton ami Philippe dérange les autres étudiants.

 D   *Réponses mystérieuses.*   *Un copain curieux vous pose beaucoup de questions. Répondez-lui au négatif, en remplaçant la personne en italique par le pronom disjoint convenable. Suivez le modèle.*

MODÈLE   Tu es arrivé avec *Richard*?
            →   Non, je ne suis pas arrivé avec lui.

1. Ce cadeau est pour *moi*?

2. Tu comptes dîner avec *Janine et François*?

3. Tu as l'intention de passer chez *Paulette*?

4. Je peux compter sur *toi*?

5. Est-ce que Suzanne a été invitée par *Jacques*?

6. Est-ce que le professeur est fâché contre *Alice et toi*?

7. Est-ce que tu t'assieds derrière *Adrienne*?

8. Est-ce que tu as une attitude hostile envers *mes copains*?

E   *Qui est-ce?*   *Écrivez des échanges pour vérifier l'identité des gens que vous voyez. Employez* **c'est/ce sont** *et un pronom disjoint selon le modèle.*

MODÈLE   les Durand là-bas / les Devaux
            → —Ce sont les Durand là-bas?
                —Non, ce n'est pas eux. Ce sont les Devaux.

1. toi dans la photo / ma sœur Barbara

2. moi le suivant (*next*) / lui

3. M. Charpentier assis sur le banc / notre voisin M. Beauchamp

4. Adèle Malmaison dans la boutique / Mlle Lachaux

5. nos amis là, à l'entrée du lycée / d'autres étudiants

6. Gisèle et Marie-Claire à l'arrêt d'autobus / Christine et Yvette

F   *Il n'y a pas d'autres.*   *Répondez aux questions suivantes à l'affirmatif. Utilisez l'expression* **ne... que** *suivi d'un pronom disjoint pour indiquer que la personne (les personnes) mentionnée(s) est (sont) le seul objet du sentiment exprimé. Suivez le modèle.*

MODÈLE   Elle invite M. Breuil?
            →   Oui. Elle n'invite que lui.

1. Tu m'aimes?

2. On respecte cet agent de police?

3. Les étudiants admirent le professeur Triquet?

4. Les juges estiment cette avocate?

5. Vous nous aidez?

6. Il apprécie les musiciens de cet orchestre?

7. Ils encouragent leurs filles?

8. Il amène sa sœur?

G *Joyeux anniversaire.* *Complétez ce paragraphe avec les pronoms qui manquent (disjoints et conjoints) pour savoir ce qu'on a fait pour fêter l'anniversaire de Florence.*

Demain, c'est l'anniversaire de Florence et moi, (1) _____ voulais organiser une surboum

pour (2) _____. J'ai téléphoné à mon amie Hélène. (3) _____, elle adore les fêtes,

et je savais qu'elle voudrait m'aider. «Qui est-ce que tu veux inviter?» m'a-t-elle demandé.

«Aide-(4) _____ à faire la liste, lui ai-je répondu. On invite Serge?»

—Oui, (5) _____, il est très sympathique et il aime danser.

—On invite Philippe et Charles?

—Oui, (6) _____, ce sont de grands blagueurs et ils font rire tout le monde.

—Et le cadeau de Florence? Qu'est-ce qu'on doit acheter pour (7) _____? Je n'ai vraiment

pas d'idées, (8) _____. Tu peux proposer quelque chose, (9) _____?

—On va demander à Janine et à Claire. Elles, (10) _____ ont toujours de bonnes idées

quand il s'agit de cadeaux.

Nous nous sommes réunies avec Janine et Claire et nous sommes allées avec (11) _____

aux grands magasins. Tout était très cher, et (12) _____, on n'avait pas beaucoup d'argent.

Tout d'un coup, Janine a dit: «Regarde! Des foulards de soie en solde. Allons les regarder.»

Nous en avons choisi un pour Florence et la vendeuse a fait un joli paquet.

La fête de Florence a été un grand succès. Nous avions invité une vingtaine d'amis et ils

sont tous venus. Florence a été vraiment très émue, et le foulard lui a beaucoup plu.

—Vous êtes vraiment de très bonnes amies, (13) _____. Vous m'avez rendue très

heureuse.

—Non, c'est (14) _____ la bonne amie, Florence. C'est un plaisir de faire tout ça pour

(15) _____.

Subject-Verb Agreement with Stressed Pronouns and Other Special Cases

After the phrase **c'est** + stressed pronoun + **qui**, the verb agrees with the stressed pronoun.

—**C'est toi qui t'en vas?**	*Are you the one who's leaving?*
—Non. **C'est moi qui suis** de garde.	*No. I'm the one who's on duty.*
Ce sont eux qui partent.	*They're the ones who are leaving.*
—**C'est vous qui faites** du japonais?	*Are you the ones who are studying Japanese?*
—Non. **C'est nous qui étudions** le russe.	*No. We're the ones who are studying Russian.*

Compound subjects linked by **et** or **ou** or **ni... ni...** are usually followed by a third person plural verb. When the subject is linked by **ni... ni...**, **ne** precedes the verb.

L'argent ou l'influence sont utiles.	*Money or influence is useful.*
Ni l'un ni l'autre ne viendront nous voir.	*Neither one will come to see us.*

However, the phrase **l'un ou l'autre** (*one or the other*) is followed by a singular verb.

L'un ou l'autre viendra nous voir.	*One or the other will come to see us.*

The third person plural is used after expressions of quantity, such as **beaucoup**, **la plupart**, **trop**, **combien**, **une foule**, **une multitude**. But the singular is used after **la foule de**.

Beaucoup (de touristes) **visitent** la ville.	*Many (tourists) visit the city.*
Une foule d'employés sont allés voir le directeur.	*A crowd of employees went to see the director.*
La foule d'employés a été reçue par lui.	*The crowd of employees was received by him.*

After approximate numbers ending in **-aine** and fractions, either the singular or the plural is used.

Une vingtaine d'ingénieurs travaille/ travaillent ici.	*About twenty engineers work here.*
La moitié arrive/arrivent à l'heure.	*Half arrive on time.*

H   *Quel verbe?* *Choisissez la forme du verbe qui complète les phrases.*

Qualités et émotions

l'amitié [fem.] *friendship*	**la générosité** *generosity*
l'amour [masc.] *love*	**la haine** *hatred*
les apparences [fem.] *appearances*	**le malheur** *unhappiness, misfortune*
le bonheur *happiness*	**la paresse** *laziness*
le courage *courage*	**la peur** *fear*
l'exactitude [fem.] *punctuality, exactness*	**la politesse** *politeness*
la force *strength*	**la prudence** *caution*

1. L'amitié et l'amour _____ (est / sont) des sentiments importants.

2. Ni son courage ni sa force ne _____ (l'a / l'ont) sauvé.

3. La haine ou la peur _____ (est / sont) responsables de son malheur.

4. C'est toi qui _____ (fais / fait) la vaisselle aujourd'hui.

5. Beaucoup d'assiettes sales _____ (t'attend / t'attendent) à la cuisine.

6. Combien _____ (vit / vivent) dans la peur dans ce pauvre pays?

7. L'exactitude et la prudence _____ (est / sont) les traits principaux de son caractère.

8. Il y a beaucoup d'étudiants ici. Le quart _____ (vient / viennent) de l'étranger.

9. C'est vous qui _____ (peut / pouvez) m'aider.

10. Voilà Olivier et Baudoin. L'un ou l'autre _____ (viendra / viendront) ce soir.

I **En français!** *Traduisez ces phrases en français.*

1. *He's buying bread. We're buying wine.*

2. *We saw Julien and Colette. We went over to* (s'approcher de) *them.*

3. *Gérard thinks only about himself.*

4. *Are you the one who teaches history?*

5. *We came in after him but before you* (tu).

6. *Many received our invitations, but only half accepted.*

7. *And I thought you were inviting only me!*

8. *There are Marc and Serge. One or the other knows the answer.*

J **Activité orale.** *Montrez des photos de famille à un(e) ami(e). Il (Elle) vous posera des questions au sujet des personnes photographiées: «C'est toi? C'est ta cousine Agnès?» Utilisez autant de pronoms disjoints que possible dans les questions et les réponses.*

Possessive and Demonstrative Adjectives and Pronouns

Possession and Possessive Adjectives

Possession in French is expressed by the preposition **de**. **De** is repeated before each owner.

la maison **de** mon oncle	*my uncle's house*
les cahiers **de** Janine et **d'**Alice	*Janine's and Alice's notebooks*

French possessive adjectives agree in gender and number with the noun they modify.

Before Masculine Singular Nouns

mon vélo	**notre** vélo
ton vélo	**votre** vélo
son vélo	**leur** vélo

Before Feminine Singular Nouns

ma calculatrice	**notre** calculatrice
ta calculatrice	**votre** calculatrice
sa calculatrice	**leur** calculatrice

Before All Plural Nouns

mes vélos, **mes** calculatrices	**nos** vélos, **nos** calculatrices
tes vélos, **tes** calculatrices	**vos** vélos, **vos** calculatrices
ses vélos, **ses** calculatrices	**leurs** vélos, **leurs** calculatrices

The possessive adjectives **son**, **sa**, **ses** may mean *his*, *her*, or *its*, depending on the owner. The form of the adjective agrees with the noun possessed.

Marie a **son** vélo et Pierre a **sa** moto.	*Marie has **her** bike and Pierre has **his** motorcycle.*

Before a feminine noun beginning with a vowel or mute **h**, the masculine forms **mon**, **ton**, **son** replace **ma**, **ta**, **sa**.

mon adresse
ton école
son histoire

To emphasize or clarify a possessor, French uses the preposition **à** plus a stressed pronoun.

—Monique et Philippe ont pris sa voiture.   *Monique and Philippe took his/her car.*

—Sa voiture **à lui** ou sa voiture **à elle**?   ***His*** *car or* ***her*** *car?*

Mon ordinateur **à moi** est plus rapide que leur ordinateur **à eux**.   ***My*** *computer is faster than* ***their*** *computer.*

The word **propre** (*own*) may also be used to add emphasis.

Je l'ai vu de mes **propres** yeux.   *I saw it with my* ***own*** *eyes.*

A   *Voilà.* *Utilisez* **voilà** *suivi d'un adjectif possessif pour signaler à votre amie que les objets dont elle parle sont tout près. Suivez le modèle.*

> MODÈLE   Tu as un livre?
> → Oui. Voilà mon livre.

1. Édouard a une voiture?

2. Nous avons une calculatrice?

3. Nos copains ont des disques?

4. Tu as des cartes?

5. J'ai des lettres?

6. Odile a un chien?

7. Marc et Chantal ont des billets?

8. Les étudiants ont une salle de réunion?

9. Jean-Marc a un sac à dos?

10. Nathalie a un ordinateur?

B   *C'est sûrement à quelqu'un d'autre.* *Dites dans chaque cas que le véhicule n'est pas à la personne proposée. Utilisez les adjectifs possessifs dans vos réponses. Suivez le modèle.*

> MODÈLE   La jeep est à vous?
> → Non. Ce n'est pas ma jeep.

Les véhicules

un autobus *bus*	**une caravane** *trailer camper*
un bateau *boat*	**une mobylette** *moped*
une bicyclette *bicycle*	**une moto** *motorcycle*
un camion *truck*	**une voiture de sport** *sports car*

1. La moto est à tes cousins?

2. Les voitures de sport sont à ton frère?

3. La caravane est à toi et à ta famille?

4. La mobylette est à Paul?

5. L'autobus est à la compagnie?

6. Le camion est à vous deux?

7. Le bateau est à toi?

8. La bicyclette est à Yves?

C *À qui?* *Vous entendez une phrase dans laquelle l'identité du possesseur est ambiguë. Demandez des précisions au moyen de la préposition* **à** *et d'un pronom disjoint. Suivez le modèle.*

MODÈLE   Christine et Maurice sont venus avec ses parents.
            → Ses parents à elle ou ses parents à lui?

1. Voilà Jacques et Madeleine avec sa mère.

2. Monsieur Lachaux et sa nouvelle épouse vivent avec ses enfants.

3. Les garçons et les filles sont arrivés dans leur voiture.

4. J'ai vu Olivier et Suzanne avec son cousin.

5. Quand je vous ai vus, Anne-Marie et toi, vous promeniez un chien.

6. Il veut revoir Paulette avant son départ.

D *Le bureau du club des étudiants en biologie.* *Les étudiants en biologie ont organisé un club et l'école leur a donné une petite salle pour installer leur bureau. Annette raconte ce que chaque étudiant a apporté au bureau. Employez des adjectifs possessifs pour savoir ce qu'elle dit. Suivez le modèle.*

MODÈLE   Georges / enveloppes
            → Georges a donné ses enveloppes.

Au bureau

une affiche *poster*	**un feutre** *felt-tipped pen*
un annuaire *telephone book*	**une imprimante** *printer*
un calendrier *calendar*	**du papier à lettres** *stationery*
un dictionnaire scientifique *science dictionary*	**un répondeur** *answering machine*

1. Roger / affiche

2. Louise et Simone / répondeur

3. Charles / feutres

4. Hélène / imprimante

5. le professeur de biologie / papier à lettres

6. Albert et vous / calendrier

7. moi / annuaire

8. toi / dictionnaire scientifique

Possessive Pronouns

The English possessive pronouns are *mine, yours, his, hers, ours,* and *theirs.* Those forms are used to replace a possessive adjective and noun. The French possessive pronouns consist of the definite article and a special possessive form. A possessive pronoun agrees in gender and number with the noun it replaces.

MASCULINE SINGULAR	FEMININE SINGULAR	MASCULINE PLURAL	FEMININE PLURAL
le mien	la mienne	les miens	les miennes
le tien	la tienne	les tiens	les tiennes
le sien	la sienne	les siens	les siennes
le nôtre	la nôtre	les nôtres	
le vôtre	la vôtre	les vôtres	
le leur	la leur	les leurs	

Le sien, la sienne, les siens, les siennes may mean *his, hers,* or *its,* depending on the owner. The form of the pronoun agrees with the noun it replaces.

Moi, j'ai **ma calculatrice**, mais Pierre n'a pas **la sienne**.	*I have **my calculator**, but Pierre doesn't have **his**.*
Nous aimons **notre quartier**, mais elle préfère **le sien**.	*We like **our neighborhood**, but she prefers **hers**.*

The articles **le** and **les** of the possessive pronouns contract with **à** and **de**.

—Tu penses à mon problème?	*Are you thinking about my problem?*
—Non. Je pense **au mien**.	*No. I'm thinking **about mine**.*
—Elle se souvient de nos idées?	*Does she remember our ideas?*
—Non. Elle se souvient **des siennes**.	*No. She remembers **hers**.*

E   *On a tout laissé au bureau.* *Employez un pronom possessif dans chaque cas pour dire que tout le monde a laissé ses affaires au bureau. Suivez le modèle.*

MODÈLE   toi / calculatrice / moi
→ Toi, tu as ta calculatrice, mais moi, j'ai laissé la mienne au bureau.

1. moi / portable / Françoise

2. nous / téléphones mobiles / nos collègues

3. toi / serviette / le directeur

4. David / dossiers / Christine

5. Odile / disquettes / moi

6. vous / carte mémoire (*memory stick*) / nous

7. mes amis / agendas / vous

8. la secrétaire / carnet d'adresses / toi

Ici et en bas. *La moitié des choses cherchées est ici, l'autre moitié est en bas. Employez des pronoms possessifs pour le dire, comme dans le modèle.*

> MODÈLE   Je cherche tes livres et les livres de Jean-Pierre.
> → Les miens sont ici, les siens sont en bas.

1. Je cherche mes copies et les copies des élèves.

2. Je cherche votre carte de crédit et la carte de crédit de Renée.

3. Je cherche notre carnet de chèques et le carnet de chèques de Rémi.

4. Je cherche tes photographies et les photographies de Paul.

5. Je cherche mes clés et les clés de nos amis.

6. Je cherche mon manteau et le manteau de Jacqueline.

 C'est le mien. *Répondez aux questions suivantes avec la préposition de la question et le pronom possessif correspondant. Suivez le modèle.*

> MODÈLE   Avec quel professeur parles-tu?
> → Avec le mien.

1. À quels amis téléphones-tu?

2. Dans quel laboratoire travaillent-ils?

3. De quelles clarinettes jouez-vous, vous deux?

4. À quelle tragédie pense-t-il?

5. De quelles affaires s'occupe-t-elle?

6. Contre quels étudiants le professeur est-il fâché?

7. De quel stylo vous servez-vous?

H **Contrastes.** *Un groupe de camarades de classe parle des différences qu'ils ont trouvées entre eux en faisant connaissance pendant la première semaine de l'année scolaire. Exprimez ce qu'ils disent en français.*

1. *Pierre and I use calculators. His is old, mine is new.*

2. *My English teacher is nice, yours is unpleasant.*

3. *Christine's backpack is red, mine is green.*

4. *My friends are better in math* (plus calés en maths) *than yours (are).*

5. *Your tests are hard. Ours are harder.*

6. *Solange's report* (compte rendu) *is long. Mine is longer.*

7. *My day* (journée) *is shorter than theirs.*

8. *The school's computers are more powerful* (puissants) *than his (are).*

I   *Activité orale.* *Avec un(e) camarade, jouez l'exercice précédent. Trouvez les différences et les ressemblances entre vous deux. Après, présentez les résultats de votre discussion à un(e) troisième camarade en employant autant de possessifs que possible.*

Demonstrative Adjectives

A demonstrative adjective points out a specific person or thing (*this* book, *that* story, *these* cassettes, *those* stores). The French demonstrative adjective by itself does not distinguish between *this* and *that*.

The French demonstrative adjective has four forms. The form agrees with the noun it modifies.

	MASCULINE		FEMININE	
SINGULAR	**ce** crayon	*this/that pencil*	**cette** table	*this/that table*
	cet homme	*this/that man*		
PLURAL	**ces** crayons	*these/those pencils*	**ces** tables	*these/those tables*

Note that before a masculine singular noun beginning with a vowel or mute **h**, the form **cet** is used.

To distinguish between *this* and *that*, **-ci** is added to a noun to mean *this* or *these* and **-là** is added to mean *that* or *those*.

—Votre classe lit **ce** livre-**ci** ou **ce** livre-**là**?   *Is your class reading **this** book or **that** book?*

—Nous lisons **ce** livre-**ci**. **Ces** romans-**là** sont pour l'année prochaine.   *We're reading **this** book. **Those** novels are for next year.*

J   *Dans le rayon d'informatique.* *Julie cherche un nouvel ordinateur et des accessoires. Elle demande au vendeur le prix de tout ce qu'elle voit. Écrivez ce qu'elle dit avec des adjectifs démonstratifs comme dans le modèle.*

MODÈLE   moniteur
     → Vous pouvez me dire le prix de ce moniteur, s'il vous plaît?

L'ordinateur
le clavier *keyboard*
le disque dur *hard drive*
la disquette *diskette*
le lecteur de CD-ROM *CD-ROM drive*

le logiciel *software package*
la souris *mouse*
l'unité de disque [fem.] *disk drive*

1. ordinateur

2. unité de disque

3. disquettes

4. logiciel

5. lecteur de CD-ROM

6. disque dur

7. clavier

8. souris

K *Préférences.* Utilisez l'adjectif démonstratif convenable avec le suffixe -**là** pour indiquer quel objet on préfère dans chaque cas. Suivez le modèle.

MODÈLE   Tu aimes la cravate de Jacques?
→ Oui, mais je préfère cette cravate-là.

1. Les étudiants aiment les livres d'histoire?

2. Tu aimes l'anorak de Fabien?

3. Germaine aime le chapeau de Colette?

4. Ta copine et toi, vous aimez les bijoux de Mme Deschamps?

5. Les voisins aiment leur appartement?

6. Tu aimes les quartiers du centre?

7. Tu aimes l'immeuble où habite Jean-Claude?

L *Choisissez!* Vous travaillez dans le rayon de vêtements d'un grand magasin. Utilisez les adjectifs démonstratifs suivis des suffixes -**ci** et -**là** pour demander des précisions aux clients quand ils veulent voir quelque chose. Suivez le modèle.

MODÈLE   Je voudrais voir ce foulard, s'il vous plaît.
→ Ce foulard-ci ou ce foulard-là?

1. Montrez-moi le pantalon, s'il vous plaît.

2. Je pourrais voir l'imperméable, s'il vous plaît.

3. Les chaussettes que vous avez derrière vous m'intéressent.

4. Voudriez-vous me montrer la robe bleue, s'il vous plaît.

5. Je voudrais essayer l'anorak, s'il vous plaît.

6. Ce tee-shirt ferait mon affaire.

7. Je voudrais voir les sandales, s'il vous plaît.

8. Vous me permettez d'essayer la veste jaune, s'il vous plaît.

Demonstrative Pronouns

French demonstrative pronouns (English: *this one, that one, the one; these, those, the ones*) agree with the noun they refer to.

	MASCULINE	FEMININE
SINGULAR	celui	celle
PLURAL	ceux	celles

As with demonstrative adjectives, -**ci** or -**là** can be added to the noun to distinguish between *this/that* and *these/those.*

—Quel logiciel recommandez-vous?   *Which software package do you recommend?*
—**Celui-ci** est plus utile que **celui-là**.   *This one is more useful than that one.*

—Quelle est la différence entre les imprimantes?	*What is the difference between these printers?*
—**Celles-ci** sont plus chères que **celles-là**.	*These are more expensive than **those**.*

Demonstrative pronoun + **-ci** and demonstrative pronoun + **-là** are also used to mean *the latter* and *the former*, respectively. The pronouns agree with the nouns they refer to. In French, *the latter* (**-ci**) precedes *the former* (**-là**).

L'industrie et l'agriculture sont importantes en France. **Celle-ci** emploie moins d'ouvriers que **celle-là**.	*Industry and agriculture are important in France. **The latter** employs fewer workers than **the former**.*

A demonstrative pronoun may be followed by the relative pronoun **qui** or **que** to mean *the one(s)*. The demonstrative pronoun may also be followed by **de** to signal possession.

—Quel livre a-t-il pris? **Celui qui** était sur la chaise?	*Which book did he take? **The one that** was on the chair?*
—Oui, c'était **celui qu**'il cherchait.	*Yes. That was **the one that** he was looking for.*
—Mais c'était **celui de mon frère**.	*But it was **my brother's**.*
—J'ai lu les revues françaises; **celles qui** étaient sur votre bureau.	*I read the French magazines; **the ones that** were on your desk.*
—**Celles de la** nouvelle **étudiante française**?	*The new **French student's**?*
—Oui. **Celles qu**'elle a apportées de France.	*Yes. **The ones that** she brought from France.*

The pronouns **ceci** (*this*) and **cela** (*that*) refer to situations rather than to specific nouns. In modern French, **cela** (or **ça** in spoken language) tends to be used instead of **ceci**.

—Et avec **ceci**?	*Anything else?*
—**Cela** suffit, merci.	*That's enough, thank you.*
—Il a perdu son travail. C'est dur, **ça**.	*He lost his job. That's a very difficult situation.*
—Oui, mais c'est **ça**, la vie!	*Yes, but **that's** life!*

M *Un client difficile.* À la charcuterie, Jean-Marc n'aime rien de ce qu'on lui montre. Écrivez ce qu'il dit en utilisant les pronoms démonstratifs. Suivez le modèle.

MODÈLE   Vous voulez un peu de ce fromage, monsieur?
→ Non, pas celui-là.

1. Vous voulez un peu de cette salade niçoise, monsieur?

2. Vous voulez un peu de ce jambon, monsieur?

3. Vous voulez un peu de ce saucisson, monsieur?

4. Vous aimez ces biscuits, monsieur?

5. Vous voulez quelques tranches (*slices*) de cette quiche, monsieur?

6. Vous voulez un peu de cette choucroute, monsieur?

7. Vous aimez les crudités, monsieur?

8. Vous voulez un peu de ce rosbif, monsieur?

 Les affaires qui traînent. *Formez des échanges qui identifient les possesseurs des objets que les étudiants ont laissé traîner dans la salle de permanence* (study hall). *Suivez le modèle.*

> MODÈLE   bonnet gris / Philippe / Stéphane
> → —Qui a oublié ce bonnet gris? Philippe?
>   —Non, je crois que c'est celui de Stéphane.

1. Walkman / Gisèle / Josette

2. stylo / Colin / Luc

3. chaussures / Fabien / Martin

4. gants / Julie / Hélène

5. cahiers / Eugénie et Colette / Élisabeth et Monique

6. calculatrice / Gérard / Paul

7. lunettes / Loïc / Thomas

 Quel bon goût. *Gabrielle aime tout ce que son amie Thérèse achète, possède, emploie, etc. Utilisez les pronoms démonstratifs et les verbes entre parenthèses pour voir ce qu'elle dit. Suivez le modèle.*

> MODÈLE   Tu aimes les pulls en coton? (porter)
> → Pas tellement. Mais j'aime celui que tu portes.

1. Tu aimes les petits pois? (préparer)

2. Tu aimes la musique des années quarante? (jouer)

3. Tu aimes les voitures allemandes? (conduire)

4. Tu aimes la soupe à l'oignon? (servir)

5. Tu aimes les lunettes de soleil? (porter)

6. Tu aimes les spaghettis? (faire)

7. Tu aimes les sandales? (acheter)

P **En français!** *Écrivez l'équivalent français des phrases suivantes.*

1. *This exercise is not well done. This is unacceptable.*

2. *This book is more difficult than that one.*

3. *They always arrive late. I don't like that.*

4. *The port of Marseilles* and the port of Cherbourg are important. The former is bigger than the latter.* [Switch in French to *The latter is less big than the former.*]

5. *Whose suitcases are these?*
   That one belongs to me.

6. *I didn't say that. I don't think like that.*

Q ***Activité orale.*** *Jouez une scène de départ avec un(e) ami(e). L'ami(e) vous aide à faire les valises et vous demande s'il faut emporter les choses qu'il (elle) voit dans votre chambre. Vous précisez dans chaque cas que vous emportez quelque chose d'autre. Employez autant d'adjectifs et de pronoms démonstratifs et possessifs que possible. Par exemple:* **Cette brosse-là n'est pas la mienne. Je vais emporter celle-ci.**

---

*FRENCH	ENGLISH
Marseille	*Marseilles*
Lyon	*Lyons*

The names of these two cities have no final -s in French.

Interrogative Adjectives and Pronouns, and Other Question Words

Interrogative Adjectives

The interrogative adjective **quel** (*which, what*) agrees in gender and number with the noun it modifies.

	MASCULINE		FEMININE	
SINGULAR	**Quel** train?	*Which train?*	**Quelle** classe?	*Which class?*
PLURAL	**Quels** trains?	*Which trains?*	**Quelles** classes?	*Which classes?*

Quel(le)(s) may be preceded by a preposition.

> **De quel** livre est-ce que vous parlez?　　*What book are you talking about?*
>
> **Pour quelle** compagnie travaille-t-il?　　*What company does he work for?*

In French, prepositions must always stand before their noun object; they cannot appear at the end of the sentence, the way prepositions in English often do. Similarly, the prepositional phrase in French cannot be broken up the way prepositional phrases in English frequently are.

Quel(le)(s) is used before forms of **être** in sentences where English uses *what*.

> **Quelle** est la différence?　　*What's the difference?*
>
> **Quelles** sont vos idées?　　*What are your ideas?*

When a phrase consisting of **quel(le)(s)** + noun precedes a form of the passé composé or other compound tense and the verb is conjugated with **avoir**, the past participle agrees with the noun if the noun is the direct object of the verb.

> **Quels films** est-ce que tu as loués?　　*Which films did you rent?*
>
> **Quelle chanson** est-ce qu'il a jouée?　　*Which song did he play?*

BUT

> **Quelle chanson** a joué tout à l'heure?　　*What song just played?*

In the last sentence, no agreement is made between **quelle chanson** and the past participle, because **chanson** is the subject of the verb, not the direct object.

Quel(le)(s) may also be used in exclamations. The implication may be either positive or negative.

Quelle catastrophe!	***What a*** *catastrophe!*
Quels restaurants!	***What*** *restaurants!*

 A ***Pour préciser.*** *Utilisez l'adjectif interrogatif* **quel** *pour demander des précisions sur les objets qu'on mentionne. Suivez le modèle.*

> MODÈLE   Jacqueline s'est renseignée sur les possibilités.
> → Sur quelles possibilités?

1. Philippe m'a prêté le vélo.

2. Jocelyne et Vivienne ont écouté les CD.

3. Lucette a joué avec la raquette.

4. J'ai conduit la voiture.

5. Tu me donnes la carte, s'il te plaît.

6. Marc est sur la moto.

7. Montrez-moi la chambre.

8. J'ai perdu les jumelles (*binoculars*).

9. Serge se sert de la caméra.

10. Moi, je me sers de l'appareil-photo.

B ***Des précisions.*** *Dans chaque cas, demandez qu'on précise de quel article il s'agit. Utilisez l'adjectif interrogatif* **quel** *et faites attention aux prépositions et à l'accord du participe passé. Suivez le modèle.*

> MODÈLE   Simone a acheté des livres.
> → Quels livres a-t-elle achetés?

1. Monique a pris des billets.

2. Alain et Crispin sont entrés dans un magasin d'informatique.

3. Gabrielle a besoin d'une disquette.

4. Les étudiants ont parlé avec un de leurs professeurs.

5. Marc a réussi à un examen difficile.

6. Yves a reçu une mauvaise note dans une de ses classes.

7. Mes parents ont acheté des médicaments.

8. Les enfants ont regardé des émissions à la télé.

C *Exclamations!* *Choisissez l'exclamation convenable dans chaque cas en écrivant la forme correcte de* **quel** *devant un seul des deux substantifs proposés.*

1. Le cousin de Marie-Christine est blessé dans un accident de la route.

    a. _____ tragédie!

    b. _____ courage!

2. Eugène a gagné 40 000 euros à la loterie!

    a. _____ horreur!

    b. _____ chance!

3. Le toit de leur maison s'est effondré (*caved in*).

    a. _____ malheur!

    b. _____ merveille!

4. Germaine a séché (*cut*) tous ses cours cette semaine.

    a. _____ bêtise!

    b. _____ diligence!

5. Il y a eu un tremblement de terre en Italie.

    a. _____ plaisir!

    b. _____ catastrophe!

6. Les grands-parents de François lui ont donné de l'argent pour acheter ses livres.

    a. _____ générosité!

    b. _____ politesse!

7. Julien refuse de travailler.

    a. _____ paresse!

    b. _____ talent!

Interrogative Pronoun **lequel**

A French interrogative pronoun agrees in gender and number with the noun it refers to.

	MASCULINE		FEMININE	
SINGULAR	**lequel**	*which (one)*	**laquelle**	*which (one)*
PLURAL	**lesquels**	*which (ones)*	**lesquelles**	*which (ones)*

—Un de nos élèves est tombé malade.   *One of our students got sick.*
—**Lequel?**   ***Which one?***

—Mon frère travaille dans une banque.   *My brother works in a bank.*
—**Dans laquelle?**   ***In which one?***

—Il y a deux robes qui sont pour toi.   *There are two dresses that are for you.*
—**Lesquelles?**   ***Which ones?***

When the interrogative pronoun **lequel/laquelle/lesquel(le)s** precedes a form of the passé composé or other compound tense and the verb is conjugated with **avoir**, the past participle agrees with the interrogative pronoun if that pronoun is the direct object of the verb.

—Elle a beaucoup de robes.	*She has many dresses.*
—Laquelle a-t-elle mis**e**?	*Which one did she put on?*
—Ils m'ont offert beaucoup de livres intéressants.	*They offered me a lot of interesting books.*
—Lesquel**s** est-ce que tu as choisi**s**?	*Which ones did you choose?*

The prepositions **à** and **de** contract with the interrogative pronoun.

—Nous allons à un pays étranger.	*We are going to a foreign country.*
—**Auquel?**	***To which one?***
—J'ai besoin de ces journaux.	*I need those newspapers.*
—**Desquels?** Il y en a tant.	***Which ones?*** *There are so many.*

  Ça m'intéresse. *Demandez à votre ami(e) quel objet l'intéresse. Employez le pronom interrogatif et le pronom démonstratif dans vos réponses, comme dans le modèle.*

> MODÈLE　Ce livre m'intéresse.
> → Lequel? Celul-là?

1. Ce film m'intéresse.

2. Ces revues m'intéressent.

3. Ce club d'informatique m'intéresse.

4. Ces émissions m'intéressent.

5. Cette photo m'intéresse.

6. Ces disques m'intéressent.

7. Cet itinéraire m'intéresse.

E　**Exactement.** *Posez des questions avec le pronom interrogatif* **lequel** *pour savoir exactement de quel objet il s'agit. Suivez le modèle et faites attention aux contractions obligatoires.*

> MODÈLE　Il cherche les chaussures de sport.
> → Lesquelles cherche-t-il exactement?

1. Je veux l'anorak.

2. Elle met les bottes.

3. Nous lavons les pulls.

4. J'ai besoin des chaussettes de laine.

5. Elle cherche les collants.

6. Ils pensent aux vêtements.

7. Je prends le blue-jean.

F *En colonie de vacances. Les affaires des jeunes gens qui font un séjour dans cette colonie de vacances sont en pagaille. Les animateurs essaient de les restituer, ce qui n'est pas facile. Utilisez les pronoms interrogatifs, démonstratifs et possessifs pour écrire les réponses des jeunes gens aux questions des animateurs. Suivez le modèle.*

MODÈLE   Ce sont tes valises, Claudette?
→ Lesquelles? Ah, non. Celles-là ne sont pas les miennes.

On part en colonie

la colonie de vacances *summer camp*
le couteau de poche *pocketknife*
la couverture *blanket*
les jumelles *binoculars*
la lampe de poche *flashlight*

la raquette de tennis *tennis racket*
le sac à dos *backpack*
le sac de couchage *sleeping bag*
la tente *tent*

1. C'est ta raquette de tennis, Baudouin?

2. Ce sont tes pulls, Richard?

3. C'est le sac à dos d'Yvette?

4. Ce sont vos sacs de couchage, Marc et Paul?

5. Ce sont les lettres de Christine et Mireille?

6. C'est ta lampe de poche, Colin?

7. Ce sont vos couvertures, Ombeline et Josette?

8. Ce sont tes jumelles, Alice?

9. C'est ton couteau de poche, Serge?

10. C'est la tente de Michèle?

Interrogative Pronouns **who, whom, what,** and Other Question Words

When *who* is the subject of the verb, it is usually rendered by **qui** in questions. No inversion of subject and verb takes place in this case.

Qui habite dans cet immeuble?   *Who lives in that apartment house?*

Qui veut de l'eau minérale?   *Who wants some mineral water?*

Qui as the subject of the sentence may be replaced by **qui est-ce qui.**

Qui est-ce qui me demande au   *Who wants to speak to me on the phone?*
téléphone?

When *whom* is the direct object of the verb, **qui** may be used as the interrogative pronoun, followed by inversion. This construction, like all constructions using inversion, is characteristic of formal style.

Qui voulez-vous voir?   *Whom do you wish to see?*

Qui cherche-t-il?   *Whom is he looking for?*

In all styles, when *whom* is the direct object of the verb, it may be expressed using **qui est-ce que**. The subject and verb are not inverted after **qui est-ce que**.

Qui est-ce que vous connaissez ici?	*Whom do you know here?*
Qui est-ce qu'ils ont appelé?	*Whom did they call?*

What as the subject of the sentence is expressed by **qu'est-ce qui**.

Qu'est-ce qui t'a fait mal?	*What hurt you?*
Qu'est-ce qui t'embête?	*What is annoying you?*

What as the direct object of the verb is expressed by **qu'est-ce que**. The subject and verb are not inverted after **qu'est-ce que**.

Qu'est-ce que vous avez acheté?	*What did you buy?*
Qu'est-ce que j'ai fait?	*What did I do?*
Qu'est-ce que tu as pris comme dessert?	*What did you have for dessert?*

In formal style, **qu'est-ce que** may be replaced by **que** if the subject of the sentence is a pronoun. The subject and verb must be inverted after **que**.

Que désirez-vous?	***What would you like?***
Qu'ont-ils décidé?	***What have they decided?***

If the subject of the sentence is a noun, **qu'est-ce que** is more common than **que**.*

Qu'est-ce que les touristes ont vu?	*What did the tourists see?*
Qu'est-ce que le professeur a dit?	*What did the teacher say?*

The interrogative pronoun **qui** is used after prepositions. However, the interrogative pronoun **que** is replaced by **quoi** when it follows a preposition.

À qui avez-vous demandé le chemin? **À qui est-ce que** vous avez demandé le chemin?	*Who(m) did you ask directions **of**?*
Sur qui peut-elle compter? **Sur qui est-ce qu'**elle peut compter?	*Who(m) can she rely **on**?*
À quoi pensez-vous? **À quoi est-ce que** vous pensez?	*What are you thinking **about**?*
De quoi ont-ils besoin? **De quoi est-ce qu'**ils ont besoin?	*What do they need?*

Here is a summary of the French equivalents of *who(m)* and *what*.

	SUBJECT	OBJECT	AFTER PREPOSITION
who(m)	Qui?/Qui est-ce qui?	Qui?/Qui est-ce que?	qui
what	Qu'est-ce qui?	Que?/Qu'est-ce que?	quoi

---

*Inversion of the verb and noun subject is possible after **que** if the noun subject is short: **Que veulent ce gens-là?** *What do those people want?*

Other Question Words

combien?	*how many? how much?*
comment?	*how?*
depuis combien de temps?	*how long?*
depuis quand?	*since when?*
lequel? laquelle? lesquel(le)s?	*which one(s)?*
où?	*where?*
d'où?	*from where?*
pourquoi?	*why?*
quand?	*when?*
quel + noun?	*which _____?*

Other interrogatives (*question words*) can be used with inversion or **est-ce que**. The forms with inversion are characteristic of formal style.

Quand est-ce que vous viendrez? **Quand** viendrez-vous?	**When** *will you come?*
Comment est-ce qu'il le fera? **Comment** le fera-t-il?	**How** *will he do it?*
Combien est-ce que vous me devez? **Combien** me devez-vous?	**How much** *do you owe me?*
Pourquoi est-ce que tu ne l'as pas vendu? **Pourquoi** ne l'as-tu pas vendu?	**Why** *didn't you sell it?*

In very formal style, a noun subject followed by an inverted pronoun and verb may follow an interrogative.

Qui le juge a-t-il accusé?	**Whom has the judge** *accused?*
Pourquoi ce candidat n'a-t-il pas été élu?	**Why wasn't this candidate** *elected?*
Dans quelle revue cet article sera-t-il publié?	**In which magazine will this article** *be published?*

After all interrogatives except for **qui**[*] and **pourquoi**, French allows inversion of the subject and verb without adding a pronoun, as long as the verb is in a simple tense (the simple future, present, or passé simple) and there is no direct or indirect object after the verb and subject.

Quand **viendra Lise**?	When **will Lise arrive?**
Depuis quand **étudie votre frère**?	How long **has your brother been studying?**
Combien de parfums **produit la France**?	How many perfumes **does France produce?**
Quelle langue **parlent vos amis**?	What language **do your friends speak?**

---

[*]After the interrogative **qui**, inversion of a noun subject and verb places the noun subject in the position of the direct object: Qui **aime Paul?** = *Who loves Paul?* (NOT *Who(m) does Paul love?*).

BUT

Pourquoi **est-ce que Jean est sorti?**	*Why **did Jean go out?***
Quelle langue **est-ce que vos amis parlent** à leurs parents?	*What language **do your friends speak** with their parents?*

OR

Pourquoi **Jean est-il sorti?**	*Why **did Jean go out?***
Quelle langue **vos amis parlent-ils** à leurs parents?	*What language **do your friends speak** with their parents?*

In informal French, there are different rules for question formation. These patterns are less acceptable in formal situations or in writing, but they are extremely common in speech.

- **Est-ce que** is dropped, but no inversion takes place.

Quand tu viens?	*When are you coming?*
Pourquoi tu dis ça?	*Why do you say that?*
Comment ils vont faire ça?	*How are they going to do that?*
Où tu les as retrouvés?	*Where did you meet up with them?*

Que cannot be used in the preceding construction.

- The question word is not placed at the front of the sentence, but left where the element it asks about normally appears. **Que** is replaced by **quoi** in this structure.

Il vient **à trois heures.**	*He's coming **at three o'clock.***
Il vient **à quelle heure?**	***What time** is he coming?*
Il part **demain.**	*He's leaving **tomorrow.***
Il part **quand?**	***When** is he leaving?*
Ça coûte **cent euros.**	*It costs **one hundred euros.***
Ça coûte **combien?**	***How much** does it cost?*
Ils font **leurs devoirs.**	*They're doing **their homework.***
Ils font **quoi?**	***What** are they doing?*
Il veut **une tarte.**	*He wants **a pastry.***
Il veut **quoi?**	***What** does he want?*

G *Des questions.* *Complétez les questions suivantes avec le pronom qui manque.*

1. _____ (*Who*) travaille ici?

2. _____ (*What*) tu as fait hier?

3. _____ (*What*) vous avez acheté pour le déjeuner?

4. _____ (*What*) vous intéresse?

5. Avec _____ (*whom*) tu es sorti?

6. Sur _____ (*what*) avez-vous écrit?

H *Posez vos questions.* *Indiquez le mot qui manque pour formuler une question correcte.*

1. _____ voyez-vous?
   a. Qui est-ce que
   b. Qui est-ce qui
   c. Qui
   d. Qu'est-ce que

2. _____ tu cherches dans ce tiroir?
   a. Qu'est-ce que
   b. Que
   c. Quoi
   d. Qu'est-ce qui

3. Sur _____ insiste-t-elle?
   a. que
   b. qu'est-ce que
   c. qu'est-ce qui
   d. quoi

4. À quelle heure _____ le train?
   a. part-il
   b. part
   c. il part
   d. est-ce que part

5. Tu as acheté _____?
   a. que
   b. qu'est-ce que
   c. est-ce que
   d. quoi

6. _____ allé _____?
   a. Est-il / où
   b. Où / est-il
   c. Il est / où
   d. Où est / il

7. De _____ parlez-vous?
   a. quoi
   b. quoi est-ce que
   c. que
   d. qu'est-ce que

8. _____ commandent ces clients?
   a. Qu'est-ce que
   b. Que
   c. Quoi
   d. Qui

I   *Le style soutenu.* *Refaites chaque question dans un style plus formel en enlevant* **est-ce que***. Faites toutes les modifications nécessaires. Suivez le modèle.*

> MODÈLE   Où est-ce qu'elle habite?
> → Où habite-t-elle?

1. Qu'est-ce qu'ils ont préparé?

2. Qui est-ce que Marie a vu?

3. Quand est-ce que vos amis ont loué cet appartement?

4. Quel logiciel est-ce que tu recommandes?

5. Dans quel hôtel est-ce que Céline va rester?

6. Pourquoi est-ce que cet enfant pleure?

7. Combien est-ce qu'elles ont payé?

J   *Oh, Jacqueline!* *Jean-Claude s'intéresse à Jacqueline, la cousine de son ami Gérard. Il veut se renseigner sur elle, sur ses goûts, et ainsi de suite. Lisez les informations que Gérard lui a données. Écrivez les questions que Jean-Claude a posées pour obtenir les réponses ci-dessous. Utilisez un style familier, selon le modèle.*

> MODÈLE   Ma cousine s'appelle Jacqueline.
> → Ta cousine s'appelle comment?

1. Elle habite Paris.

2. Elle arrive dans une semaine.

3. Jacqueline voyage avec son frère.

4. Elle va rester un mois avec nous.

5. Jacqueline s'intéresse à la chimie.

6. Elle aime la cuisine japonaise.

7. Elle aime faire de la voile.

8. Jacqueline a besoin d'une voiture.

K   *Activité orale.* *Jouez l'activité F avec un(e) camarade en employant les objets qu'on trouve dans la salle de classe et vos affaires personnelles. Vous pouvez varier la structure des questions et des réponses, pourvu que vous utilisiez tous les pronoms que vous avez appris.*

Adjectives, Comparatives, and Superlatives

Gender of Adjectives

Adjectives give information about nouns and pronouns (a *small* box, a *different* book). French adjectives agree in gender and number with the noun or pronoun they modify. Most masculine adjectives add **-e** to form the feminine.

bleu *blue*	→	bleu**e**
compliqué *complicated*	→	compliqué**e**
espagnol *Spanish*	→	espagnol**e**
grand *big*	→	grand**e**
gris *gray*	→	gris**e**
noir *black*	→	noir**e**
petit *little, small*	→	petit**e**
poli *polite*	→	poli**e**
prochain *next*	→	prochain**e**

Several groups of adjectives do not follow this rule.

Adjectives with a masculine form ending in **-e** do not change form in the feminine.

bizarr**e** *strange, peculiar*	→	bizarr**e**
difficil**e** *difficult*	→	difficil**e**
drôl**e** *funny*	→	drôl**e**
jaun**e** *yellow*	→	jaun**e**
logiqu**e** *logical*	→	logiqu**e**
roug**e** *red*	→	roug**e**

Most masculine adjectives ending in **-x** have feminine forms ending in **-se**.

dangereu**x** *dangerous*	→	dangereu**se**
génereu**x** *generous*	→	génereu**se**
heureu**x** *happy*	→	heureu**se**
merveilleu**x** *marvelous*	→	merveilleu**se**
nerveu**x** *nervous*	→	nerveu**se**
sérieu**x** *serious*	→	sérieu**se**

Masculine adjectives ending in **-f** have feminine forms ending in **-ve**.

acti**f** *active*	→	acti**ve**
naï**f** *naïve*	→	naï**ve**
neu**f** *new*	→	neu**ve**
sporti**f** *athletic*	→	sporti**ve**

Adjectives ending in **-el**, **-en**, or **-on** double the final consonant before adding **-e**.

actu**el** *present, present-day*	→	actu**elle**
cru**el** *cruel*	→	cru**elle**
canadi**en** *Canadian*	→	canadi**enne**
europé**en** *European*	→	europé**enne**
b**on** *good*	→	b**onne**
mign**on** *cute*	→	mign**onne**

Gentil (*nice, friendly*), **pareil** (*similar*), and **nul** (*none, not any*) also double the final **-l** before adding **-e**: **gentille**, **pareille**, **nulle**. The double **l** is pronounced /y/ in **gentille** and **pareille**, but /l/ in **nulle**.

Some masculine adjectives ending in **-s** have feminine forms ending in **-sse**.

ba**s** *low*	→	ba**sse**
épai**s** *thick*	→	épai**sse**
gra**s** *fat, fatty*	→	gra**sse**
gro**s** *big, fat*	→	gro**sse**

Some masculine adjectives ending in **-et** have feminine forms ending in **-ète**.

compl**et** *complete*	→	compl**ète**
discr**et** *discreet*	→	discr**ète**
inqui**et** *restless, upset*	→	inqui**ète**
secr**et** *secretive*	→	secr**ète**

Some masculine adjectives ending in **-et** or **-ot** double the final **-t** before adding **-e**.

coqu**et** *flirtatious*	→	coqu**ette**
mu**et** *mute*	→	mu**ette**
s**ot** *foolish*	→	s**otte**

Masculine adjectives ending in **-er** have feminine forms ending in **-ère**.

am**er** *bitter*	→	am**ère**
derni**er** *last*	→	derni**ère**
étrang**er** *foreign*	→	étrang**ère**
lég**er** *light*	→	lég**ère**

Masculine adjectives derived from verbs and ending in **-eur** have feminine forms ending in **-euse**.

flatt**eur** *flattering*	→	flatt**euse**
tromp**eur** *deceptive*	→	tromp**euse**

Some adjectives have irregular feminine forms.

beau *beautiful, handsome*	→	**belle**
blanc *white*	→	**blanche**
bref *brief*	→	**brève**
doux *sweet, gentle, soft*	→	**douce**
faux *false*	→	**fausse**
favori *favorite*	→	**favorite**
fou *mad, crazy*	→	**folle**
frais *fresh*	→	**fraîche**
franc *frank*	→	**franche**
grec *Greek*	→	**grecque**
long *long*	→	**longue**
nouveau *new*	→	**nouvelle**
public *public*	→	**publique**
roux *redheaded*	→	**rousse**
sec *dry*	→	**sèche**
vieux *old*	→	**vieille**

Some adjectives are invariable. They do not change form to reflect gender or number.

un pantalon **chic**	*stylish pants*
une robe **chic**	*a stylish dress*
des chaussures **marron**	*brown shoes*
des chaussettes **marron**	*brown socks*

Adjectives of color derived from nouns, such as **marron**, **orange**, and **rose**, are invariable.

In a phrase referring to color that contains the word **clair** (*light*) or **foncé** (*dark*), both the adjective of color and the word **clair** or **foncé** are invariable.

une robe **vert clair**	*a light green dress*
des jupes **bleu foncé**	*dark blue skirts*

A   ***Tous les deux.*** *Répondez aux questions en disant que la deuxième chose ou personne mentionnée a la même caractéristique que la première. Suivez le modèle.*

> MODÈLE   Ce lycée est grand. Et cette école?
> → Elle est grande aussi.

1. Ce pain est très frais. Et cette tarte?

2. Ce café est amer. Et votre bière?

3. Mon voisin est très sot. Et votre voisine?

4. Ce compte rendu est complet. Et cette page?

5. Ce tableau est ancien. Et cette sculpture?

6. Le frère de Rosette est brun. Et sa sœur?

7. Le concert est merveilleux. Et la pièce de théâtre?

8. Le président est très discret. Et sa secrétaire?

9. Son père est roux. Et sa tante?

10. Le film est sensationnel. Et la musique?

11. Leur cousin est sportif. Et leur cousine?

12. Leur fils est mignon. Et leur fille?

B **Substitution.** *Refaites les locutions suivantes en faisant les substitutions indiquées. Suivez le modèle.*

MODÈLE   un garçon intelligent (fille)
           → une fille intelligente

1. le gouvernement actuel (administration)

2. une histoire drôle (récit)

3. un chapeau chic (écharpe)

4. une conclusion logique (résultat)

5. le théâtre grec (langue)

6. l'ordre public (opinion)

7. un enfant nerveux (mère)

8. une valise légère (paquet)

9. une chanson favorite (film)

10. un fromage exquis (viande)

11. un calme trompeur (tranquillité)

12. un goût délicat (nourriture)

Plural of Adjectives

Most French adjectives are made plural by adding -s to the masculine or feminine singular form.

bon	→	bons
noir	→	noirs
drôle	→	drôles
poli	→	polis
blanche	→	blanches
heureuse	→	heureuses

Masculine singular adjectives ending in -s or -x do not change form in the plural.

des gâteaux délicieux	*delicious cakes*
des bâtiments bas	*low buildings*

Adjectives ending in -eau, such as **beau** and **nouveau**, add -x to form the masculine plural.

de beaux jardins*	*beautiful gardens*
des mots nouveaux	*new words*

Most masculine singular adjectives ending in -al have plural forms ending in -aux.

des plans géniaux	*brilliant plans*
des problèmes sociaux	*social problems*

---

* In formal style, **de** can replace the partitive before an adjective that precedes the noun. See page 140.

But the adjectives **banal**, **fatal**, **final**, **natal**, and **naval** form the masculine plural by adding -s.

les examens finals   *final exams*
leurs pays natals   *their native countries*

C **Pas un mais deux.** *Répondez dans chaque cas qu'il s'agit de deux choses, pas d'une seule. Suivez le modèle.*

MODÈLE   Tu as vu un beau monument?
→ J'ai vu deux beaux monuments.

1. Tu vas passer un examen oral?

2. Tu as vu un film affreux?

3. Il y a un gros immeuble dans cette rue?

4. Tu as l'examen final aujourd'hui?

5. Il a un cousin roux?

6. Il a écrit un livre banal?

7. Il étudie un cas spécial?

8. Ils ont fait un voyage dangereux?

9. Tu as appris un mot nouveau?

10. Il y a un œuf frais dans le frigo?

11. Nous allons visiter un monument national?

12. Tu as acheté un produit local?

D **On court les magasins.** *Vous demandez des choses dans différents magasins. Qu'est-ce le vendeur ou la vendeuse vous répond? Suivez le modèle.*

MODÈLE   Je cherche une robe longue.
→ Voici les robes longues.

1. Je cherche un parfum français.

2. Je voudrais un légume frais.

3. J'ai besoin d'un journal espagnol.

4. Je veux acheter un fromage crémeux.

5. Montrez-moi, s'il vous plaît, un fromage gras.

6. J'ai besoin d'un pantalon gris.

7. Vous avez un foulard bleu?

8. Je voudrais lire un roman québécois.

E *La vie intellectuelle.* *Formez des phrases qui seraient utiles dans des discussions intellectuelles en ajoutant la forme correcte des adjectifs aux substantifs donnés.*

1. actuel

   a. les élections _____

   b. l'économie _____

   c. les conflits _____

2. international

   a. des efforts _____

   b. des organisations _____

   c. une entreprise _____

3. grec

   a. la poésie _____

   b. les régions _____

   c. les dialectes [*masc.*] _____

4. classique

   a. la musique _____

   b. les philosophes _____

   c. les chansons _____

5. religieux

   a. une croyance _____

   b. des sentiments _____

   c. des conceptions _____

6. européen

   a. l'union _____

   b. les pays _____

   c. les langues _____

7. concret

   a. des exemples _____

   b. une application _____

   c. des actions _____

8. étranger

   a. des influences _____

   b. la littérature _____

   c. les ambassadeurs _____

9. fictif (*fictional*)

   a. des personnages _____

   b. une situation _____

   c. des histoires _____

10. naval

   a. l'école _____

   b. des combats _____

   c. les bases _____

Position of Adjectives

Most French adjectives follow the noun they modify.

C'est un garçon **intelligent**.	*He's an **intelligent** boy.*
C'est une femme **cultivée**.	*She's a **cultured** woman.*

Some common adjectives referring to beauty, age, goodness, and size usually precede the noun.

beau *beautiful, handsome*	**joli** *pretty*
bon *good*	**long** *long*
gentil *nice, friendly*	**mauvais** *bad*
grand *big*	**nouveau** *new*
gros *big, fat*	**petit** *small*
jeune *young*	**vieux** *old*

Nous sommes arrivés à ce **petit** hôtel après un **long** voyage.	*We arrived at this **small** hotel after a **long** trip.*

Special forms of **beau**, **nouveau**, and **vieux** are used before masculine singular nouns beginning with a vowel.

un **beau** bâtiment	*a beautiful building*
un **bel** immeuble	*a beautiful apartment house*
un **nouveau** bâtiment	*a new building*
un **nouvel** immeuble	*a new apartment house*
un **vieux** bâtiment	*an old building*
un **vieil** immeuble	*an old apartment house*

Ordinal numbers and some other common adjectives usually precede the noun they modify.

autre *other*	**premier** *first*	
chaque *each*	**quelques** [pl.] *a few*	
plusieurs *several*	**tel** *such*	

Prenez la **troisième** rue à gauche.	*Turn left at the **third** street.*
Chaque étudiant a **plusieurs** livres.	***Each** student has **several** books.*

When more than one adjective is used to describe a noun, each adjective is placed in its usual position. If two adjectives occupy the same position before or after the noun, they are joined by **et**.

un **bon** compte rendu **intéressant**	*a **good**, **interesting** report*
un compte rendu **intéressant et compréhensif**	*an **interesting**, **comprehensive** report*
un **long et mauvais** compte rendu	*a **long**, **bad** report*

Some adjectives can either follow or precede a noun, but their meaning changes depending on their position. Usually, they have a literal meaning when they follow the noun and a figurative meaning when they precede it.

un **ancien** combattant	*a **former** soldier (veteran)*
une ville **ancienne**	*an **old** (**ancient**) city*
un **brave** homme	*a **decent** man*
un soldat **brave**	*a **brave** soldier*
certains pays	***certain** (**some**) countries*
un échec **certain**	*a **sure** failure*
mon **cher** ami	*my **dear** friend*
une voiture **chère**	*an **expensive** car*
la **dernière** fois	*the **last** (**final**) time*
l'année **dernière**	*last (**the preceding**) year*
la **même** idée	*the **same** idea*
le jour **même**	*the **very** day*
un **pauvre** homme	*a **poor** (**unfortunate**) man*
un homme **pauvre**	*a **poor** (**penniless**) man*

la **prochaine** fois	*the **next** (**following**) time*
la semaine **prochaine**	***next** week*
ma **propre** chambre	*my **own** room*
une chambre **propre**	*a **clean** room*
un **sale** quartier	*a **nasty** (**awful**) neighborhood*
un quartier **sale**	*a **dirty** neighborhood*
la **seule** femme	*the **only** woman*
une femme **seule**	*a woman **alone***
un **simple** citoyen	*an **ordinary** citizen*
un texte **simple**	*a **simple** text*
un **vrai** ami	*a **real** friend*
une histoire **vraie**	*a **true** story*

F **Identifiez.** *Complétez les réponses de Micheline aux questions de son amie Solange en écrivant un des adjectifs de la liste ci-dessus. Faites attention au placement de l'adjectif pour exprimer l'idée communiquée par chaque échange entre les deux amies. Suivez le modèle.*

MODÈLE   Solange: Ta nouvelle jupe a coûté beaucoup d'argent?
            Micheline: Oui, c'est une _____ jupe _chère_.

1. Solange: Tu as déjà étudié avec M. Deschênes?

   Micheline: Oui, c'est mon _____ professeur _____.

2. Solange: Tu es allée en Bretagne il y a un mois?

   Micheline: Oui, j'y suis allée le _____ mois _____.

3. Solange: Tes voisins les Durand n'ont pas beaucoup d'argent, n'est-ce pas?

   Micheline: C'est vrai. C'est une _____ famille _____.

4. Solange: Tu n'as pas fait de fautes à l'examen de maths?

   Micheline: J'étais la _____ étudiante/l'étudiante _____ à résoudre tous les problèmes.

5. Solange: Hélène est toujours disposée à nous aider.

   Micheline: Oui, c'est une _____ amie _____.

6. Solange: Olivier ne nettoie jamais son appartement.

   Micheline: Tu as raison. C'est un _____ appartement _____.

7. Solange: Tous les détails de l'histoire sont exacts.

   Micheline: Oui, c'est une _____ histoire _____.

8. Solange: Tes parents t'ont offert une bicyclette pour ton anniversaire, n'est-ce pas?

   Micheline: Oui, j'a ma _____ bicyclette _____ maintenant.

G *Décrivons!* *Formez des descriptions en partant des éléments donnés. Faites attention au genre, au nombre et aux formes spéciales des adjectifs. Utilisez* **de** *dans chaque cas (voir page 140). Suivez le modèle.*

MODÈLE   jeune / professeurs
            → de jeunes professeurs

1. beau / terrasse

2. vieux / églises

3. vieux / objet

4. nouveau / ordinateur

5. nouveau / industrie

6. vieux / instruments

7. beau / îles

8. beau / accent

9. nouveau / usines

10. beau / animaux

11. vieux / assiette

12. nouveau / avions

H *À l'école avec Odile.* *Odile décrit ses compagnons, ses professeurs, ses classes et le lycée où elle étudie. Pour voir ce qu'elle dit, ajoutez les adjectifs entre parenthèses aux phrases pour modifier les substantifs en italique. Faites attention à l'accord et au placement des adjectifs. Suivez le modèle.*

MODÈLE   Mon professeur de français est une *femme*. (intelligent, cultivé)
            → Mon professeur de français est une femme intelligente et cultivée.

1. Nous assistons aux conférences dans une *salle*. (grand, ancien)

2. Pour la classe d'anglais nous préparons des *exposés*. (petit, intéressant)

3. Dans la classe de maths nous subissons des *épreuves*. (long, difficile)

4. Derrière le lycée il y a un *jardin*. (petit, joli)

5. J'y vais souvent avec mon ami Philippe. C'est un *garçon*. (beau, gentil)

6. Nous parlons des *poèmes* qu'il faut préparer. (nouveau, français)

7. Il y a des *professeurs* au lycée. (plusieurs, excellent)

8. Ils font des *cours*. (passionnant, utile)

I *Et maintenant il s'agit de vous.* *Décrivez ces aspects de votre vie en ajoutant deux adjectifs à chaque phrase pour modifier les substantifs en italique.*

1. Mon ami X est un *garçon*.

2. Mon amie X est une *fille*.

3. Mon professeur d'anglais est un *homme*/une *femme*.

4. J'habite dans une *maison*/un *appartement*.

5. J'habite dans un *quartier*.

6. J'aime les *chansons*.

7. Mes amis et moi, nous aimons les *films*.

8. Je préfère les *conversations*.

Comparison of Adjectives, Adverbs, Nouns, and Verbs

One object or person may be seen as having more, less, or the same amount of a characteristic as another object or person. To express this, French and English use comparative constructions.

To make comparisons of superiority, French uses the construction **plus** + adjective + **que**.

Le boulevard est **plus large que** notre rue.	*The boulevard is **wider than** our street.*

To make comparisons of inferiority, French uses the construction **moins** + adjective + **que**.

Mais le boulevard est **moins large que** l'autoroute.	*But the boulevard is **less wide than** (**not as wide as**) the superhighway.*

To make comparisons of equality, French uses the construction **aussi** + adjective + **que**.

Le boulevard est **aussi large que** l'avenue de la République.	*The boulevard is **as wide as** the Avenue of the Republic.*

The adjectives **bon** and **mauvais** have irregular comparative forms.

bon(ne)(s)　→　**meilleur(e)(s)**
mauvais(e)(s)　→　**pire(s)**

Ce restaurant est **meilleur que** l'autre.	*This restaurant is **better than** the other one.*
Le bruit est **pire** ici **que** dans mon quartier.	*The noise is **worse** here **than** in my neighborhood.*

Adverbs are compared in the same way as adjectives.

Elle répond **plus poliment que** lui.	*She answers **more politely than** he does.*
Elle répond **moins poliment que** lui.	*She answers **less politely than** he does.*
Elle répond **aussi poliment que** lui.	*She answers **as politely as** he does.*

The adverbs **bien** and **mal** have irregular comparative forms: **mieux** (*better*) and **pire** (*worse*). **Pire** may be replaced by **plus mal**. The comparative of **beaucoup** is **plus**, and the comparative of **peu** is **moins**.

—On dit que M. Morot enseigne **mieux que** Mme Richard.	*They say that Mr. Morot teaches **better than** Mrs. Richard.*
—J'en doute. Ses étudiants écrivent **pire** (**plus mal**) **que** les étudiants de Mme Richard.	*I doubt it. His students write **worse than** Mrs. Richard's students do.*

When verbs are compared, **autant** replaces **aussi** in comparisons of equality.

Je travaille **plus/moins que** toi.	*I work **more/less than** you do.*
Je travaille **autant que** toi.	*I work **as much as** you do.*

The comparison of nouns resembles the comparison of verbs. **De** is used before the noun.

Il a **plus/moins de soucis que** nous.	He has **more/fewer worries than** we do.
Il a **autant de soucis que** nous.	He has **as many worries as** we do.

In comparisons, **que** may be followed by a noun, a stressed pronoun, a demonstrative or possessive pronoun, a prepositional phrase, or an adjective. In the last case, the adjective functions as a noun.

Le chemisier jaune est plus chic que **le vert**.	The yellow blouse is more stylish than **the green one**.
Les petits enfants étudient autant que **les grands**.	The little children study as much as **the big ones**.
Ce roman est moins intéressant que **ceux de l'autre auteur**.	This novel is not as interesting as **the ones by the other author**.

J   *Notre ville.*   *Faites les comparaisons indiquées par le signe arithmétique. Suivez le modèle.*

> MODÈLE   le lycée / − vieux / l'école primaire
> → Le lycée est moins vieux que l'école primaire.

1. le stade / + grand / la salle de concert

2. les cinémas / + nombreux / les théâtres

3. la faculté de médecine / = importante / la faculté de droit

4. le jardin zoologique reçoit / = visiteurs / la bibliothèque municipale

5. le musée scientifique / − grand / le musée d'art

6. les restaurants ici / = chers / les restaurants parisiens

7. les rues de la vieille ville / + étroites / les rues des quartiers modernes

8. le quartier des affaires / − animé / le quartier des étudiants

9. la piscine municipale / + bonne / la plage au bord du fleuve

10. la maison de la culture offre / = activités / le centre communautaire (*community center*)

K   *Un moment difficile à l'université.*   *Ces étudiants sont très occupés. Exprimez ce qu'ils font en employant la comparaison des substantifs (**plus de**, **moins de**, **autant de**). Suivez les modèles.*

> MODÈLES   Richard lit trois romans. Odile en lit deux.
> → Richard lit plus de romans qu'Odile.
>
> Richard lit trois romans. Odile en lit quatre.
> → Richard lit moins de romans qu'Odile.
>
> Richard lit trois romans. Odile en lit trois aussi.
> → Richard lit autant de romans qu'Odile.

1. Frédéric suit cinq cours. Marc en suit quatre.

2. Sylvie écrit deux thèmes. Robert en écrit un.

3. Monique subit trois examens. Marcelle en subit quatre.

4. Maurice résout (*solves*) trois problèmes de maths. Philippe en résout trois aussi.

5. Marie-Laure étudie deux langues étrangères. Alfred en étudie deux aussi.

6. Claudine apprend trois poèmes. Chantal en apprend quatre.

7. Hervé analyse cinq œuvres. Charles en analyse quatre.

8. Julie fait six expériences de chimie. Serge en fait six aussi.

L **Les impressions.** *Un(e) ami(e) vous dit ses impressions. Vous les contradisez moyennant des comparaisons, selon les indications données. Faites attention aux signes arithmétiques et suivez les modèles.*

MODÈLES J'ai l'impression que Corinne ne travaille pas beaucoup. (+ / les autres)
→ Ce n'est pas vrai. Elle travaille plus que les autres.

J'ai l'impression que Corinne ne travaille pas beaucoup. (= / les autres)
→ Ce n'est pas vrai. Elle travaille autant que les autres.

1. J'ai l'impression que ton frère dort trop. (− / moi)

2. J'ai l'impression que Danielle n'étudie pas beaucoup. (+ / Éliane)

3. J'ai l'impression que notre professeur parle trop. (− / le professeur de Justine)

4. J'ai l'impression que ton chien ne mange pas beaucoup. (= / les autres chiens)

5. J'ai l'impression que tu ne lis pas beaucoup. (+ / toi)

6. J'ai l'impression que Paul ne comprend pas beaucoup. (= / les autres étudiants)

M **Les professeurs parlent de leurs étudiants.** *Exprimez ces idées avec le comparatif des adverbes en refaisant les phrases selon les modèles.*

MODÈLES Jacques travaille sérieusement. Laurent, pas tellement.
→ Jacques travaille plus sérieusement que Laurent.

Jacques travaille sérieusement. Laurent, même plus.
→ Jacques travaille moins sérieusement que Laurent.

Jacques travaille sérieusement. Laurent aussi.
→ Jacques travaille aussi sérieusement que Laurent.

1. Monique répond intelligemment. Christine, même plus.

2. Édouard rédige soigneusement. Louis, pas tellement.

3. Nicole travaille rapidement. Lucien aussi.

4. Anne-Marie écoute attentivement. Guillaume, aussi.

5. Gérard oublie souvent. Paulette, même plus.

6. François se comporte bien. Georges, pas tellement.

N *Et vous?* *Faites des comparaisons entre cette année à l'école et l'année dernière quant aux choses indiquées. Utilisez des pronoms démonstratifs après* **que** *et faites attention à la forme des adjectifs. Suivez le modèle.*

MODÈLE   mes classes / difficile
                → Mes classes sont plus/moins/aussi difficiles que celles de l'année dernière.

1. nos manuels / intéressant

2. mes camarades de classe / sympathique

3. les professeurs / exigeant

4. les devoirs / facile

5. la nourriture qu'on sert à la cantine (*lunchroom*) / bon

6. mon horaire / commode

7. la classe de français / passionnant

8. les bals qu'on organise / amusant

O *Comparez.* *Choisissez des éléments des trois colonnes pour exprimer des comparaisons basées sur votre expérience personnelle.*

ma chambre	grand	la chambre de X
ma maison	petit	la maison de X
mon appartement	joli	l'appartement de X
mes disques compacts	beau	les disques compacts de X
mon école	laid	l'école de X
ma rue	moderne	la rue de X
mon quartier	intéressant	le quartier de X
mes amis	bon	les amis de X
mes professeurs	mauvais	les professeurs de l'année dernière
mes classes	tranquille	mes cousins
mes devoirs	bruyant	les classes de X
	sale	les devoirs de X
	propre	les devoirs donnés par X
	sympathique	
	gentil	
	intelligent	
	difficile	
	facile	
	passionnant	
	ennuyeux	

P *Ces vacances—meilleures ou pires?* *Les membres de la famille Grandet reviennent de leurs vacances en Auvergne. Ils les comparent avec les vacances en Bretagne l'année dernière. En partant des éléments donnés, écrivez les phrases qu'ils disent. L'élément après* **que**, *c'est-à-dire, le deuxième terme de la comparaison, doit être un pronom. Suivez le modèle.*

> MODÈLE   la piscine qu'on avait en Bretagne était / + grand /
>   la piscine qu'on avait en Auvergne
>   → La piscine qu'on avait en Bretagne était plus grande que celle qu'on avait
>   en Auvergne.

1. le voyage en train était / + long / le voyage de l'année dernière

2. l'hôtel en Auvergne était / + luxueux / l'hôtel où on est descendu en Bretagne

3. le paysage auvergnat était / + montagneux / le paysage de Bretagne

4. le poisson en Bretagne était / + bon / le poisson qu'on a servi en Auvergne

5. les grandes randonnées qu'on a faites en Auvergne étaient / + intéressant /
   les grandes randonnées qu'on a faites en Bretagne

6. les restaurants en Auvergne étaient / − cher / les restaurants de Bretagne

7. les nuits en Auvergne étaient / + frais / les nuits de Bretagne

Superlative of Adjectives, Adverbs, and Nouns

The superlative of an adjective is formed by placing the definite article before **plus** or **moins** and the adjective. When the adjective follows the noun, the definite article appears both before the noun and before **plus** or **moins**.

—Où se trouve **le restaurant le plus connu** ici?

*Where is **the most well-known restaurant** here?*

—**Les restaurants les plus célèbres** et **les plus chers** se trouvent dans ce quartier.

*The most famous and **the most expensive restaurants** are found in this neighborhood.*

The English preposition *in* after a superlative is translated by **de**.

—Quel est le magasin le plus élégant **de** cette ville?

*What is the most elegant store **in** this city?*

—On dit que «Chez Cartier» est un des magasins les plus élégants **du** pays.

*They say that Chez Cartier is one of the most elegant stores **in** the whole country.*

If an adjective usually precedes the noun, its superlative form also precedes the noun. Only one definite article is required.

Chantal est **la meilleure élève** de la classe.

*Chantal is **the best student** in the class.*

Paris est **la plus grande ville** de France.

*Paris is **the biggest city** in France.*

The superlative of an adverb is formed with **le plus** or **le moins**.

—Lise s'exprime **le plus clairement** de tous les élèves. | *Lise expresses herself **the most clearly** of all the pupils.*
—Et elle parle **le moins lentement** aussi. | *And she speaks **the least slowly** too.*

The superlatives of **bien** and **mal** are irregular: **le mieux** (*the best*), **le pis** (*the worst*). In modern usage, **le plus mal** is used instead of **le pis**.

—On dit que ce professeur enseigne **le mieux**. | *They say that this teacher teaches **best**.*
—J'en doute. Ses étudiants écrivent **le plus mal de** tous. | *I doubt it. His students write **the worst** of all.*

The phrases **le plus** (*the most*) and **le moins** (*the least*) can be used after verbs. These are the superlatives of **beaucoup** and **peu**, respectively.

—C'est Alain qui travaille **le plus**. | *Alain is the one who works **the most**.*
—Et qui gagne **le moins**. | *And who earns **the least**.*

The phrases **le plus de** (*the most*) and **le moins de** (*the least, the fewest*) are used before nouns.

—Toi, tu manges **le plus de** viande. | *You eat **the most** meat.*
—Et **le moins de** légumes. | *And **the fewest** vegetables.*

Q *Notre classe. Formez des superlatifs pour décrire les étudiants de la classe. Faites attention aux signes arithmétiques. Suivez le modèle.*

MODÈLE   Charles / − attentif
        → Charles est le moins attentif.

1. Marylène / + diligent

2. Jacques et Pierre / − obéissant

3. Solange / + sympathique

4. Irène et Marie / − travailleur

5. Olivier / + intelligent

6. Anne-Marie / + bavard

7. Jean-Paul / + charmant

8. Colette et Brigitte / − préparé

R *Visite de la ville. Rachelle fait visiter sa ville à ses amis. Elle leur explique tout en employant des superlatifs. Écrivez ce qu'elle leur dit. Suivez le modèle.*

MODÈLE   c'est / bibliothèque / important / ville
        → C'est la bibliothèque la plus importante de la ville.

1. voilà / place / imposant / ville

2. ici vous voyez / cathédrale / ancien / région

3. en face il y a / université / connu / pays

4. c'est / rue / long / ville

5. dans cette rue il y a / magasins / beau / région

6. voilà / charcuterie / apprécié / quartier

7. devant nous il y a / hôtel / international / pays

8. dans cette rue se trouvent / cafés / fréquenté / ville

9. ici vous voyez / maison / vieux / ville

10. voilà / stade / grand / région

S   *La classe de littérature.* *Le professeur et les étudiants expliquent les aspects superlatifs des œuvres qu'ils lisent. Suivez le modèle.*

MODÈLE   roman / émouvant / siècle
→ C'est le roman le plus émouvant du siècle.

1. poème / connu / littérature européenne

2. pièce de théâtre / représenté / année

3. comédie / applaudi / théâtre national

4. roman / vendu / la littérature moderne

5. tragédie / estimé / notre théâtre

6. poète / merveilleux / son siècle

7. romancier / lu / monde

8. dramaturge / apprécié / notre époque

T   *Les meilleurs et les pires.* *Dans ce groupe d'étudiants il y a des jeunes extraordinaires. Exprimez leurs distinctions (pas toutes sont positives) avec le superlatif des adverbes. Faites attention aux signes arithmétiques et suivez le modèle.*

MODÈLE   Jean / courir / vite (+)
→ C'est Jean qui court le plus vite.

1. Lucie / parler / poliment (+)

2. Olivier / travaille / efficacement (−)

3. Albert / étudier / sérieusement (−)

4. Suzanne / chanter / bien (+)

5. Hélène / arriver en retard / souvent (+)

6. Roger / répondre / calmement (+)

U **Vos opinions.** *Écrivez des phrases en français pour identifier les choses ou les personnes spécifiées. Suivez le modèle.*

> MODÈLE   *the most interesting class this year*
> → La classe la plus intéressante cette année est la classe de littérature américaine.

1. *the hardest book you are reading*

2. *the worst song of the year*

3. *the student who studies most seriously*

4. *the member of your family who eats most quickly*

5. *the friendliest teacher in the school*

6. *the most expensive store in town*

7. *the best compact disc or tape you have*

8. *the restaurant you like the most*

V **Activité orale.** *Décrivez votre maison ou appartement, votre voiture, votre famille à un(e) ami(e). Ne vous limitez pas à décrire—faites aussi des comparaisons entre les pièces de votre logement, entre votre voiture et celle de vos amis, etc.*

| Pour parler un français authentique | Speak Real French |

Adjectives

From the point of view of spoken French, there are several categories of adjectives.

- Adjectives ending in **-é**, **-i**, or a consonant + **u**, as well as some adjectives of nationality, have four written forms but only one spoken form.

un quartier animé	des quartiers animés
une rue animée	des rues animées
un garçon poli	des garçons polis
une fille polie	des filles polies
un homme têtu (*stubborn*)	des hommes têtus
une femme têtue	des femmes têtues
un port espagnol	des ports espagnols
une région espagnole	des régions espagnoles

- Adjectives with two spoken forms have a pronounced final consonant in the feminine that is absent in the masculine. Most of these adjectives have four written forms. The masculine singular and plural are pronounced alike, and the feminine singular and plural are pronounced alike. The feminine is given first in these pairs.

Final Consonant /t/ in the Feminine

une voiture verte	des voitures vertes
un camion vert	des camions verts
une fille intelligente	des filles intelligentes
un garçon intelligent	des garçons intelligents

Sometimes, the spelling makes it difficult to see that the adjective belongs to this category.

Final Consonant /s/ in the Feminine

une matière grasse	des matières grasses
le foie gras	des foies gras

Final Consonant /z/ in the Feminine

une jupe grise	des jupes grises
un pantalon gris	des pantalons gris
une famille heureuse	des familles heureuses
un couple heureux	des couples heureux

Final Consonant /sh/ in the Feminine

une fleur fraîche	des fleurs fraîches
un fruit frais	des fruits frais

If the final consonant of the feminine form is not pronounced, /è/ changes to /é/ in the corresponding masculine form.

une équipe inquiète	des équipes inquiètes
un joueur inquiet	des joueurs inquiets
une valise légère	des valises légères
un paquet léger	des paquets légers

If the final consonant of the feminine form is /n/, the corresponding masculine form often ends in a nasal vowel.

une bière italienne	des bières italiennes
un vin italien	des vins italiens
une bonne journée	des bonnes journées
un bon séjour	des bons séjours

French spelling can be misleading about the pronunciation of masculine and feminine forms of adjectives. For instance, the following masculine singular adjectives consist of an initial consonant and the nasal vowel /õ/. In other words, they rhyme with **bon** /bõ/.

long	/lõ/
rond	/rõ/

In the feminine form, the underlying final consonant is pronounced.

bonne	/bən/
longue	/lõg/
ronde	/rõd/

The adjectives **blanc**, **franc**, and **grand** function similarly. To form the masculine, the final consonant of the feminine form drops and the masculine form therefore ends in a nasal vowel.

FEMININE		MASCULINE	
blanche	/blãsh/	blanc	/blã/
franche	/frãsh/	franc	/frã/
grande	/grãd/	grand	/grã/

 Activité orale. *Faites les substitutions indiquées. Utilisez la forme masculine correspondante de l'adjectif en transformant les phrases. Faites attention à la prononciation. Suivez le modèle.*

> MODÈLE   La pluie est forte.
>   le vent
>   → Le vent est fort.

1. une œuvre importante
   un programme

2. une table ronde
   un lit

3. Cette histoire est longue.
   ce film

4. une écharpe blanche
   un foulard

5. une analyse complète
   un système

6. La ville est grande.
   le quartier

7. une entreprise américaine
   un directeur

8. Cette viande est bonne.
   ce poisson

9. de l'eau fraîche
   du vin

10. une grosse surprise
    un _____ problème

Object Pronouns

Direct Object Pronouns

The direct object is the person or thing that serves as the complement of the verb. It is connected to it without a preposition.

Je vois **Jean**.	*I see **John**.*
Nous ne voyons pas **le magasin**.	*We don't see **the store**.*
J'ouvre **mon livre**.	*I open **my book**.*
Elle porte **ses lunettes**.	*She's wearing **her glasses**.*

Once a direct object noun has been introduced into the discourse (conversation or written document), it may be replaced by a direct object pronoun.

Direct Object Pronouns

	SINGULAR		PLURAL	
FIRST PERSON	**me**	*me*	**nous**	*us*
SECOND PERSON	**te**	*you*	**vous**	*you*
THIRD PERSON	**le**	*him/it*	**les**	*them*
	la	*her/it*		

Direct object pronouns precede the conjugated verb. Note that before a verb beginning with a vowel or mute **h**, the pronouns **me, te, le, la** become **m', t', l'**.

—Est-ce que tu achètes **ce livre**?	*Are you buying **that book**?*
—Non. Je **le** regarde tout simplement.	*No. I'm just looking at **it**.*
—**Me** retrouvez-vous en ville?	*Will you meet **me** in town?*
—Oui. Nous **t'**attendons au café de la Gare.	*Yes. We'll wait for **you** at the Café de la Gare.*
—Tu aimes **ces nouvelles chansons**?	*Do you like **these new songs**?*
—Pas du tout. Je **les** déteste.	*Not at all. I hate **them**.*
—**Ta chambre** est vraiment propre.	***Your room** is really clean.*
—Je **l'**ai nettoyée ce matin.	*I cleaned **it** this morning.*

When a verb is followed by an infinitive, the direct object pronoun comes before the verb of which it is the direct object—usually the infinitive.

—Vous pouvez **nous** déposer en ville?	*Can you drop **us** off downtown?*
—Je regrette, mais je ne peux pas **vous** prendre.	*I'm sorry, but I can't take **you** (give **you** a lift).*
—Je peux **t'**aider?	*Can I help **you**?*
—Oui, merci. Tu vois cette chaise? Tu peux **la** monter au deuxième étage.	*Yes, thank you. Do you see this chair? You can take **it** up to the third floor.*

Direct object pronouns precede the auxiliary verb in compound tenses. Remember that a past participle agrees in gender and number with a direct object noun or pronoun that precedes it.

—As-tu vu **Daniel**?	*Have you seen **Daniel**?*
—Je **l'**ai cherché, mais je ne **l'**ai pas trouvé.	*I looked for **him**, but I didn't find **him**.*
—Je **t'**ai appelé, mais tu ne **m'**as pas entendu.	*I called **you**, but you didn't hear **me**.*
—Si. Je **t'**ai salué, mais tu ne **m'**as pas vu.	*Yes I did. I waved hello to **you**, but you didn't see **me**.*
—Et **les lettres**? Où est-ce que vous **les** avez mises?	*What about **the letters**? Where did you put **them**?*
—Je **les** ai jet**ées** à la poubelle. Je croyais que vous **les** aviez déjà lues.	*I threw **them** in the garbage. I thought that you had already read **them**.*

Several verbs that take indirect objects in English take direct objects in French.

attendre qqn/qqch *to wait for someone/something*
chercher qqn/qqch *to look for someone/something*
demander qqch *to ask for something*
écouter qqn/qqch *to listen to someone/something*
payer qqch *to pay for something*
regarder qqn/qqch *to look at someone/something*

 Au magasin de vêtements. *Ombeline est dans une boutique. Continuez le récit de ce qu'elle fait pour acheter les vêtements qu'il lui faut en utilisant les verbes entre parenthèses et les pronoms de complément direct. Suivez le modèle.*

MODÈLE   Voilà la porte du magasin. (ouvrir)
          → Elle l'ouvre.

1. Voilà les robes. (regarder)

2. Voilà une robe dans sa taille. (essayer)

3. La robe ne lui plaît pas. (ne pas prendre)

4. Elle aime ce chemisier. (acheter)

5. Elle veut voir les foulards en soie. (chercher)

6. Elle trouve un foulard qui va bien avec son nouveau chemisier. (prendre)

7. Elle passe au rayon des chapeaux. (regarder)

8. Il y a deux chapeaux qui l'intéressent. (essayer)

9. Ils sont très chers. (ne pas acheter)

10. Mais elle va acheter le foulard. (payer)

 Emménagement. *La famille Jonquières est en train d'emménager dans leur nouvelle maison. Mme Jonquières répond aux questions des déménageurs sur l'emplacement des meubles. Employez les mots entre parenthèses pour écrire ses réponses et remplacez les compléments directs par des pronoms. Suivez le modèle.*

MODÈLE   Et le lave-vaisselle, madame? (installer / cuisine)
→ Vous pouvez l'installer dans la cuisine.

1. Et ce sofa, madame? (mettre / salon)

2. Et ce lit, madame? (monter / à la chambre de mon fils)

3. Et la machine à laver? (descendre / au sous-sol)

4. Et cette chaîne stéréo? (laisser / salon)

5. Et cette table? (placer / salle à manger)

6. Et ces vêtements? (mettre / penderie)

7. Et cet ordinateur? (monter / à la chambre de ma fille)

8. Et ces fauteuils? (laisser / salon)

C **Pas possible!** *Michel répond au négatif aux questions de son ami. Écrivez ce qu'il dit avec le pronom convenable. Suivez le modèle.*

MODÈLE   Tu m'aides?
→ Non, je ne peux pas t'aider.

1. Tu me déposes en ville?

2. Tu m'emmènes à la poste?

3. Tu me raccompagnes?

4. Tu m'attends?

5. Tu nous rejoins, Sara et moi?

6. Tu nous appelles?

7. Tu nous invites?

8. Tu nous présentes?

D **On s'organise.** *Les étudiants s'organisent pour nettoyer le foyer d'étudiants avant de partir pour l'été. Employez le(s) nom(s) entre parenthèses pour répondre aux questions. Remplacez les compléments directs des questions par des pronoms et employez la construction **aller** + infinitif. Suivez le modèle.*

> MODÈLE   Qui fait le linge? (Jean-Claude)
> → Jean-Claude va le faire.

Le nettoyage

balayer *to sweep*	**nettoyer** *to clean*
la casserole *pot*	**les ordures** [fem.] *garbage*
épousseter (j'époussette) *to dust*	**le parquet** *wooden floor*
faire le linge *to do the laundry*	**passer l'aspirateur** *to run the vacuum cleaner*
faire le lit *to make the bed*	**la poêle** *frying pan*
faire les carreaux *to wash the windows*	**récurer** *to scour*
laver *to wash*	**sortir** *to take out*
les meubles [masc.] *furniture*	**les toilettes** [fem.] *bathroom*

1. Qui balaie la cuisine? (Sabine)

2. Qui lave les verres? (Marc et David)

3. Qui nettoie les toilettes? (Élisabeth et Stéphanie)

4. Qui fait les lits? (moi)

5. Qui sort les ordures? (Édouard)

6. Qui passe l'aspirateur? (Barbara)

7. Qui époussette les meubles? (Charles et Michèle)

8. Qui fait les carreaux? (Odile et François)

9. Qui récure les casseroles et les poêles? (Louis et Denise)

10. Et qui lave tous les parquets? (toi!)

E **Tout est déjà fait.** *Répondez au passé composé aux questions de votre ami sur le travail au bureau. Remplacez les compléments directs des questions par des pronoms. Faites attention à l'accord du participe passé. Suivez le modèle.*

> MODÈLE   Tu ne lis pas le document?
> → Je l'ai déjà lu.

1. Tu n'écris pas la réponse?

2. Marc et Paul ne rédigent pas le contrat?

3. Catherine et toi, vous ne faites pas les problèmes de maths?

4. Lise n'écrit pas les programmes?

5. Tu n'étudies pas l'application?

6. Christine ne fait pas l'expérience au laboratoire?

7. Olivier ne révise pas les données?

8. Baudoin et Philippe ne téléchargent pas les feuilles de calcul (*spreadsheets*)?

9. Tu n'écoutes pas les informations par Internet?

10. Tu ne relis pas les manuels?

Indirect Object Pronouns

An indirect object is the person to whom or for whom an action is done. It is connected to its verb by the preposition **à**.

J'écris **à Jean**.	*I write (**to**) **John**.*
Les élèves parlent **au professeur**.	*The students talk **to the teacher**.*
Nous donnons des cadeaux **à nos amis**.	*We give gifts **to our friends**.*

The French indirect object pronouns refer only to people. **Lui** may mean either *to/for him* or *to/for her*, depending on its context.

Indirect Object Pronouns

	SINGULAR	PLURAL
FIRST PERSON	**me**	**nous**
SECOND PERSON	**te**	**vous**
THIRD PERSON	**lui**	**leur**

The indirect object pronouns follow the same rules for position as the direct object pronouns.

—Les parents de cet enfant ont de la chance. Il **leur** obéit toujours.	*That child's parents are lucky. He always obeys **them**.*
—C'est vrai. Il ne **leur** désobéit jamais.	*That's true. He never disobeys **them**.*
—Ce chapeau **vous** va très bien.	*That hat looks very good **on you**.*
—Il **vous** plaît?	*Do **you** like it?*
—Et Louis? Il a faim?	*What about Louis? Is he hungry?*
—Oui. Je **lui** prépare un sandwich.	*Yes. I'm making a sandwich **for him**.*
—Je vais **leur** téléphoner ce soir.	*I'm going to phone **them** this evening.*
—S'ils ne sont pas là, tu peux **leur** laisser un message au répondeur.	*If they're not there, you can leave **them** a message on the answering machine.*

Several verbs that take direct objects or have other constructions in English take indirect objects in French.

aller bien à qqn *to look nice on someone*
convenir à qqn *to suit someone, be convenient for someone*
désobéir à qqn *to disobey someone*
obéir à qqn *to obey someone*
plaire à qqn *to please someone*
répondre à qqn *to answer someone*
téléphoner à qqn *to call/phone someone*

Many verbs take two objects: a direct object (a thing) and an indirect object (a person).

apporter qqch à qqn *to bring something to someone*
demander qqch à qqn *to ask someone for something*
dire qqch à qqn *to tell/say something to someone*
donner qqch à qqn *to give something to someone*
envoyer qqch à qqn *to send something to someone*

expliquer qqch à qqn *to explain something to someone*
laisser qqch à qqn *to leave something for someone*
montrer qqch à qqn *to show something to someone*
offrir qqch à qqn *to give something to someone (as a gift)*
passer qqch à qqn *to pass something to someone*
permettre qqch à qqn *to allow someone to do something*
prêter qqch à qqn *to lend something to someone*
promettre qqch à qqn *to promise something to someone*
rendre qqch à qqn *to give something back to someone*
vendre qqch à qqn *to sell something to someone*

Note that in **présenter qqn à qqn** (*to introduce someone to someone*), both the direct and the indirect objects refer to people.

With several French verbs, **à** is the equivalent of English *from*.

acheter qqch à qqn *to buy something from someone*
arracher qqch à qqn *to snatch something from someone*
cacher qqch à qqn *to hide something from someone*
emprunter qqch à qqn *to borrow something from someone*
enlever qqch à qqn *to take something away from someone*
louer qqch à qqn *to rent something from someone*
prendre qqch à qqn *to take something from someone*
voler qqch à qqn *to steal something from someone*

Sentences such as **Je lui ai acheté la voiture** may mean either *I bought the car **from** him/ her* or *I bought the car **for** him/her,* depending on the context.

F   *Oui et non. Employez les mots entre parenthèses et un pronom complément d'objet indirect pour dire dans chaque cas ce qu'on ne fait pas. Suivez le modèle.*

MODÈLE   Je prête mon crayon à Luc. (mon stylo)
→ Je ne lui prête pas mon stylo.

1. Nous donnons des conseils à nos voisins. (argent)

2. Annette me montre ses photos. (logiciels)

3. J'ai écrit une carte postale à mes cousins. (courriel)

4. Les Dufau vendent leur maison aux Masson. (voiture)

5. Je vais offrir une montre à ma petite amie. (collier)

6. Vous envoyez des dessins à votre frère. (affiches)

7. Mon chien m'apporte le journal. (mes pantoufles)

8. Il a dit son adresse au médecin. (son numéro de téléphone)

9. Le professeur a expliqué les problèmes à ses étudiants. (la méthode)

10. Je vais demander la voiture à mon père. (argent pour l'essence)

G *Ce qu'il faut faire.* *Les employés d'un grand bureau demandent à leur chef ce qu'ils doivent faire aujourd'hui. Il leur répond avec l'expression* **il faut** *et un pronom complément d'objet indirect. Suivez le modèle pour savoir exactement ce qu'il dit.*

MODÈLE   Et pour nos clients en Tunisie? (envoyer le rapport)
→ Il faut leur envoyer le rapport.

Les affaires

l'agence [fem.] *agency*	**la note** *bill*
l'annonce [fem.] *ad*	**le produit** *product*
le banquier/la banquière *banker*	**le rapport** *report*
la cargaison *shipment*	**régler la note** *to pay the bill, settle the account*
le fournisseur/la fournisseuse *supplier*	**le représentant/la représentante** *representative*
la gamme *range, line*	**le vendeur/la vendeuse** *salesperson*

1. Et pour M. Delavigne? (écrire une lettre)

2. Et pour nos fournisseurs en Allemagne? (payer la dernière cargaison de marchandises)

3. Les Régnier n'ont pas encore réglé la note. (envoyer la note encore une fois)

4. M. Sarda a déjà appelé deux fois ce matin. (prêter trois cent mille francs)

5. Les gens de l'agence Autos-Jour ont téléphoné. (louer trois voitures et un camion)

6. Votre banquier a téléphoné. (emprunter un million de francs)

7. La représentante du journal est arrivée. (montrer les nouvelles annonces)

8. Nos vendeurs vont arriver à 11 heures. (présenter la nouvelle gamme de produits)

H *Conseils et recommandations.* *Un groupe de copains parlent des camarades qui avaient besoin d'aide. Écrivez les solutions qu'ils ont trouvées en formant des phrases au passé composé avec des pronoms compléments d'objet indirect. Suivez le modèle.*

MODÈLE   Émile aimait bien mon ordinateur.
tu donner / une heure au clavier (*keyboard*)
→ Tu lui as donné une heure au clavier.

1. Marguerite ne pouvait pas aller à pied au lycée.
son père / prêter la voiture

2. Albert a perdu sa montre.
nous / offrir une montre pour son anniversaire

3. Monique ne comprenait pas ce texte.
moi, je / expliquer les idées du livre

4. Richard et Serge voulaient jouer au football.
nous / demander de jouer avec nous

5. Nathalie est malade et ne peut pas sortir.
vous / apporter des revues et des journaux

6. Sylvie et Maude voulaient étudier pour l'examen d'histoire.
nous / rendre les livres que nous leur avions empruntés

7. Mathieu a été absent hier. Il a manqué tous ses cours.
nous / montrer nos notes

8. Hélène et Robert sont maintenant en Corse.
   moi, je / envoyer une lettre

9. Solange nous a écrit il y a deux semaines.
   nous / répondre

10. Alfred et Gilles ne savaient pas qu'il y a une fête vendredi.
    nous / téléphoner

Pronoun y

A preposition of location (**à**, **en**, **dans**, **sur**, **sous**, **devant**, **derrière**, etc.) plus a noun referring to a place or thing can be replaced by **y**.

—Vous allez tous **à Paris**?	*Are you all going **to Paris**?*
—Oui, nous **y** passons nos vacances.	*Yes, we're spending our vacation **there**.*
—As-tu répondu **à son message**?	*Have you answered **his message**?*
—Oui. J'**y** ai déjà répondu.	*Yes. I have already answered **it**.*
—Tu travailles **dans ce bureau**?	*Do you work **in this office**?*
—Non, je n'**y** travaille plus.	*No, I don't work **there** anymore.*
—Où est la monnaie? **Sur la table**?	*Where's the change? **On the table**?*
—Oui. J'**y** ai laissé l'argent.	*Yes. I left the money **there**.*

Y may refer to an entire phrase, clause, or idea. Sometimes **y** has no direct English equivalent. The reflexive pronouns **me**, **te**, **se** elide to **m'**, **t'**, **s'** before **y**.

—Tu **t'**es déjà mise **à travailler**, Christine?	*Have you already started working, Christine?*
—Non, je ne **m'y** suis pas encore mise.	*No, I haven't started yet.*
—Il est difficile de traverser la rue parce qu'il y a tant de voitures.	*It's hard to cross the street because there are so many cars.*
—Tu as raison. Il faut **y** prendre garde. (**y** = **aux voitures**)	*You're right. We have to be careful (**of them**). (**prendre garde à qqch**)*
—Alice n'aime pas son travail.	*Alice doesn't like her work.*
—Elle doit **y** renoncer. (**y** = **à son travail**)	*She ought to quit. (**renoncer à qqch**)*
—Les idées de cet auteur sont difficiles.	*This author's ideas are difficult.*
—J'**y** réfléchis beaucoup. (**y** = **aux idées**)	*I think **about them** a lot. (**réfléchir à qqch**)*

 Jamais de la vie! *Les gens ne font jamais ces activités. Dites-le en employant le pronom* **y**. *Suivez le modèle.*

MODÈLE   Tu vas souvent à Lille?
          → Non, je n'y vais jamais.

1. Lucie travaille au sous-sol?

2. Maurice et François étudient à la terrasse du café du coin?

3. Ton petit ami attend devant le cinéma?

4. Vos parents passent leurs vacances au bord de la mer?

5. Vous achetez à manger dans cette charcuterie?

6. Les enfants jouent derrière l'immeuble?

7. Les voisins se réunissent sur le toit?

8. Tu laisses tes livres sur l'escalier?

9. Tu manges parfois dans la voiture?

10. Les étudiants viennent souvent à ce restaurant?

J *Conseillez et rassurez.* *Votre amie exprime ses doutes. Employez l'expression* **il faut**, *le pronom* **y** *et le verbe ou l'expression entre parenthèses pour lui donner un conseil ou pour la rassurer. Suivez le modèle.*

MODÈLE   J'ai du mal à me concentrer sur le livre de philosophie. (faire attention)
→ Il faut y faire attention.

1. Je n'ai pas encore fait de projets de vacances. (penser)

2. Je suis inquiète au sujet de mon avenir. (réfléchir)

3. On dit que les rues de cette ville sont dangereuses la nuit. (prendre garde)

4. Notre plan ne pourra pas réussir. (renoncer)

5. Cette matière m'ennuie. C'est pour ça que mes notes sont mauvaises. (s'intéresser)

6. Je ne sais pas si je pourrai devenir médecin. (rêver)

7. J'ai des doutes sur ses explications. (croire)

8. On m'attend au bureau du professeur. (aller)

Pronoun **en**

An indefinite or a partitive article plus a noun can be replaced by the pronoun **en**. **En** often means *some* or *any* in this context.

—Tu veux **du jus**?	*Do you want **any juice**?*
—Non, je n'**en** veux pas.	*No, I don't want **any**.*
—Connaissez-vous **des professeurs** ici?	*Do you know **any teachers** here?*
—Oui, j'**en** connais.	*Yes, I know **some**.*

En may replace nouns used with expressions of quantity or numbers. In such cases, **en** may have no direct English equivalent.

—As-tu beaucoup **de travail**?	*Do you have a lot **of work**?*
—J'**en** ai trop. (**en** = **de travail**)	*I have too much.*
—Robert a des frères?	*Does Robert have any brothers?*
—Oui, il **en** a trois.	*Yes, he has three (**brothers**).*
—Tu n'as que trois cents francs?	*You have only three hundred francs?*
—J'**en** ai perdu deux cents.	*I lost two hundred (**francs**).*

En may replace the construction **de** + noun or infinitive.

—Pauline est-elle revenue **de France**?
*Has Pauline come back **from France**?*

—Elle **en** revient jeudi.
*She's coming back (**from there**) Thursday.*

—Les étés passés en Bretagne étaient merveilleux, n'est-ce pas?
The summers spent in Brittany were wonderful, weren't they?

—Oui. Je m'**en** souviens.
(**en** = **des étés**)
*Oh, yes. I remember **them**.*

—Ton fils a-t-il peur **de nager dans l'océan**?
*Is your son afraid **to swim in the ocean**?*

—Oui. Il **en** a peur.
*Yes. He's afraid (**to do it**).*

The pronoun **en** follows the same rules for position as direct and indirect object pronouns. In compound tenses, the past participle does not agree with **en**.

K *Votre ville. Répondez aux questions suivantes. Employez le pronom **en** dans vos réponses. Vos réponses peuvent être négatives ou affirmatives, selon le cas.*

Vocabulaire urbain

bordé de *lined with*
de luxe *luxury* [adj.]
encombré de *blocked by, congested with*
un espace vert *a green space, park*
manquer de *to lack, be short of*
se méfier de *to be wary/distrustful of*

le promeneur *stroller, walker*
regorger de *to be bursting with*
la sécurité personnelle *personal safety*
se soucier de *to worry about*
se vanter de *to boast of*

1. Est-ce que la ville se vante de ses musées?

2. Est-ce que les magasins regorgent de vêtements de luxe?

3. Est-ce que les rues sont pleines de promeneurs?

4. Est-ce qu'il faut se soucier de sa sécurité personnelle?

5. Est-ce que vous vous méfiez de la ville la nuit?

6. Est-ce que les trottoirs sont bordés d'arbres?

7. Est-ce que les rues sont encombrées de véhicules?

8. Est-ce que votre ville manque d'espaces verts?

 *Rectification. Votre ami(e) se trompe sur les quantités. Corrigez ce qu'il (elle) vous dit avec les chiffres donnés et le pronom **en**. Suivez le modèle.*

MODÈLE   Paulette a deux frères, n'est-ce pas? (4)
           → Non, elle en a quatre.

1. Il y a vingt élèves dans cette classe, n'est-ce pas? (32)

2. Stéphane gagne mille cinq francs par semaine, n'est-ce pas? (2100)

3. Vous avez cent vingt pages à lire, n'est-ce pas? (250)

4. Nous avons parcouru (*covered, traveled*) quatre cents kilomètres, n'est-ce pas? (300)

5. Tu as eu soixante-dix dollars d'amende (*fine*), n'est-ce pas? (90)

6. Leur nouvelle maison a trois salles de bains, n'est-ce pas? (5)

7. Nous allons acheter dix biftecks, n'est-ce pas? (15)

8. Tu veux une douzaine d'œufs, n'est-ce pas? (deux douzaines)

M *C'est déjà fait.* *Répondez aux questions de votre ami(e) sur ce qui se passe à l'université en disant que tout s'est déjà accompli. Utilisez le pronom **en** dans chaque cas. Suivez le modèle.*

MODÈLE Pierre va-t-il acheter des livres?
→ Il en a déjà acheté.

1. Chantal et Odile comptent-elles suivre des cours de chimie?

2. L'étudiant va-t-il se plaindre de ses classes?

3. Est-ce que Bernard va être accablé de travail?

4. M. Dumarier va-t-il se charger des inscriptions?

5. Est-ce que Mme Martel va jouer du piano?

6. François va-t-il se mêler des affaires des autres étudiants?

7. Est-ce que Michel compte faire du japonais?

8. Anne-Marie peut-elle demander des conseils sur son programme d'études?

9. Est-ce que Gilbert va revenir de la faculté?

10. Le professeur Froissard va-t-il donner des devoirs?

Double Object Pronouns

When a sentence contains two object pronouns, the pronouns take the following order.

me					
te	le, l'				
se	*before* la, l'	*before*	lui	*before* y *before* en	
nous	les		leur		
vous					

Double object pronouns follow the same rules of position as single object pronouns.

—Est-ce que ton père te prête la voiture? | *Does your father lend you the car?*
—Non, il ne **me la** prête jamais. | *No, he never lends **it to me**.*
—Tu vas donner les cadeaux aux enfants? | *Are you going to give the gifts to the children?*
—Oui, je vais **les leur** donner. | *Yes, I'm going to give **them to them**.*
—Marcelle a sa calculatrice? | *Does Marcelle have her calculator?*
—Oui, je **la lui** ai rendue hier. | *Yes, I returned **it to her** yesterday.*

—Nos cousins ont besoin d'argent.   *Our cousins need money.*
—Nous pouvons **leur en** envoyer.   *We can send **them some**.*

—C'est une très belle avenue.   *This is a very beautiful avenue.*
—Oui, nous **nous y** promenons   *Yes, we often take a walk **here**.*
souvent.

N *Ce qu'il faut faire.* *Employez les verbes entre parenthèses et deux pronoms compléments d'objet pour dire ce qu'il faut faire (ou ce qu'on va faire) dans chaque cas. Suivez le modèle.*

MODÈLE   Odile ne sait pas l'adresse de Philippe. (je / aller / dire)
→ Je vais la lui dire.

1. Marie-France ne reçoit pas de courriels. (nous / devoir / écrire)

2. Serge veut voir ces documents. (je / aller / prêter)

3. Ousmane a besoin de son manuel de chimie. (nous / devoir / rendre)

4. Rachelle prend le déjeuner au bistrot d'en face. (tu / pouvoir / retrouver)

5. Suzanne et Ghislaine veulent voir tes photos. (je / avoir l'intention de / montrer)

6. Yves et Marc cherchent des affiches. (il faut / donner)

7. Je ne comprends pas ces mots. (je / aller / expliquer)

8. Nous voudrions du parfum de France. (Marguerite / pouvoir / rapporter)

9. Les enfants adorent le jardin. (vous / pouvoir / amener)

10. La vie ici n'est pas facile. (nous / devoir / s'habituer)

O *Mais si!* *Votre ami se trompe. Les choses qui, selon lui, n'arrivent pas sont déjà arrivées. Dites-le-lui en employant le passé composé et deux pronoms compléments d'objet. Suivez le modèle.*

MODÈLE   Sabine n'offre jamais de cadeaux à ses frères.
→ Mais si! Elle leur en a déjà offert.

1. Albert ne sert jamais de boissons à ses invités.

2. Tu ne donnes jamais de conseils à Philippe.

3. Serge et Robert ne s'opposent pas au programme politique de notre parti.

4. Marc et Justine ne se servent jamais de cet ordinateur.

5. Louise et toi, vous ne vous rendez pas compte du problème.

6. Olivier ne nous rend jamais les choses qu'il nous emprunte.

7. Cette femme ne lit jamais de livres à ses enfants.

8. Ces parents n'enseignent pas le français à leurs enfants.

9. Ce professeur ne propose jamais de thèmes intéressants à ses étudiants.

10. Toi, tu ne m'envoies jamais de cartes postales.

P ***Proposons des solutions.*** *Employez* **si** *suivi de l'imparfait, les mots entre parenthèses et deux pronoms compléments d'objet pour proposer des solutions aux problèmes posés par votre amie. Suivez le modèle.*

> MODÈLE   Nathalie n'a pas de romans en français. (envoyer deux ou trois)
> → Si on lui en envoyait deux ou trois?

1. Maurice et Frédéric admirent nos disques compacts. (prêter)

2. Monique est à la bibliothèque de Beaubourg. (retrouver)

3. Madeleine et Lise n'ont pas la voiture pour aller au travail aujourd'hui. (amener)

4. Jean-Paul aime les croissants que nous faisons. (apporter une demi-douzaine)

5. Agnès sort du bureau à 5 heures. (aller attendre)

6. Cette rue a l'air dangereux. (s'éloigner)

7. Nous avons une lettre à écrire et cet ordinateur est libre. (se servir pour la rédiger)

8. Philippe et son frère nous ont demandé le journal d'hier. (donner)

9. Eugénie a tous nos livres d'histoire. (demander)

10. Charles et sa femme s'intéressent à notre lecteur de disques compacts. (vendre)

Restrictions on the Use of Object Pronouns

The object pronouns **me, te, nous, vous, lui, leur** cannot follow a reflexive pronoun. The preposition **à** or **de** plus a stressed pronoun is used instead. **En** does not replace **de** plus animate noun when the **de** is part of a verbal expression, as in **s'approcher de** and **avoir peur de**. Compare the following pairs of sentences.

> Je me fie **à ce dictionnaire**. → Je m'y fie.
> Je me fie **à ce médecin**. → Je me fie **à lui**.

> J'ai peur **des avions**. → J'en ai peur.
> J'ai peur **de nos professeurs**. → J'ai peur **d'eux**.

> Nous nous approchons **de la ville**. → Nous nous **en** approchons.
> Nous nous approchons **de notre père**. → Nous nous approchons **de lui**.

 Oui, bien sûr. *Répondez aux questions de votre ami(e) à l'affirmatif. Remplacez les mots en italique par le pronom convenable. Suivez le modèle.*

> MODÈLE   Est-ce que vous vous fiez *à votre mémoire*?
> → Oui, nous nous y fions.

1. Est-ce que tu te fies *à tes amis*?

2. Est-ce que Paulette s'intéresse *à la géologie*?

3. Est-ce que Jean-Luc s'intéresse *à Paulette*?

4. Est-ce que le petit Victor a honte *de ce qu'il a fait*?

5. Est-ce que son père a honte *du petit Victor*?

6. Est-ce que tu te souviens *de ton séjour en Espagne*?

7. Est-ce que tu te souviens *des gens que tu y as connus*?

8. Est-ce que le détective doute *de l'explication de M. Arnaud*?

9. Est-ce que le détective se doute *de M. Arnaud*?

10. Est-ce que vous avez peur *des voyages en bateau*?

Object Pronouns in Affirmative Commands

In affirmative commands, object pronouns follow the verb and are joined to it with a hyphen. **Me** and **te** become **moi** and **toi** after a command form.

Dites-**nous** ce qui est arrivé.   *Tell **us** what happened.*

Les journaux? Mettez-**les** sur la table.   *The newspapers? Put **them** on the table.*

Aide-**moi**!   *Help **me**!*

Although the final **-s** of the **tu** form is usually dropped in the imperative of **-er** verbs, it is restored (and pronounced) before **y** and **en** in affirmative commands.

—J'ai envie de manger des pommes.   *I feel like eating apples.*
—Achète**s-en**.   *Buy **some**.*

—J'aime mes vacances en Bretagne.   *I love my vacation in Brittany.*
—Reste**s-y** plus longtemps.   *Stay **there** longer.*

When an affirmative command contains two object pronouns, the pronouns take the order shown below. **Moi + en** becomes **m'en** and **toi + en** becomes **t'en** in affirmative commands.

		moi				
le, l'		toi				
la, l'	before	lui	before	y	before	en
les		nous				
		vous				
		leur				

—Je viens de recevoir mes photos.   *I've just received my photos.*
—Montre-**les-moi**.   *Show **them to me**.*

—Regarde, j'ai du jus de fruits.   *Look, I have some fruit juice.*
—Donne-**m'en**. J'ai très soif.   *Give **me some**. I'm very thirsty.*

—Je peux me servir de ton stylo?   *May I use your pen?*
—Volontiers. Sers-**t'en**.   *Gladly. Use **it**.*

In affirmative commands, **y** is replaced by **là** or **là-bas** after **me/moi**, **te/toi**, **le**, **la** if **y** refers to a place.

—Tu vas être à la bibliothèque?   *Are you going to be at the library?*
—Oui, attends-**moi là-bas**.   *Yes, wait for **me there**.*

In negative commands, object pronouns have their usual position before the conjugated verb.

Ne **les** mettez pas sur la table.   *Don't put **them** on the table.*

R **On donne des ordres.** *Répondez aux questions par l'impératif des verbes entre parenthèses, si possible. Remplacez les substantifs des questions par des pronoms compléments d'objet. Suivez le modèle.*

MODÈLE   Ces bonbons ont l'air délicieux.
              (tu / prendre / plusieurs)
              → Prends-en plusieurs.

1. Je ne veux plus rester ici. (tu / s'en aller)

2. Veux-tu que je te dépose devant la faculté? (tu / déposer)

3. J'ai de la salade. En veux-tu? (tu / donner)

4. Nous n'aimons pas le programme du nouveau directeur. (vous / s'opposer)

5. Ces gens me rendent nerveux. (tu / s'éloigner)

6. Je vais m'habiller dans la salle de bains. Ça va? (tu / s'habiller)

7. Devons-nous nous arrêter à côté du parc? (vous / s'arrêter)

8. Qui va s'occuper du dîner? (tu / se charger)

9. Je crois que j'ai votre disquette. (vous / rendre)

S **En français.** *Exprimez les idées suivantes en français.*

1. *I asked him for his literature book, but he didn't give it to me.*

2. *He doesn't have his car anymore because someone stole it from him.*

3. *These people are interested in your house. Sell* (vous) *it to them.*

4. *We asked the teacher questions about the lesson, but he didn't answer them.*

5. *I looked for French newspapers and found two. I'll show them to you* (tu).

6. *She's on the third floor. Go* (tu) *up (to there) and you'll see her.*

7. *The children were playing on the roof, but they have come down (from there).*

8. *You've made soup. Bring me some and I'll taste* (essayer) *it.*

T **Activité orale.** *Parlez avec un(e) ami(e) au sujet des choses et objets que vous avez et des plats que vous aimez manger. Formez les questions pour évoquer des réponses qui contiennent un ou deux pronoms compléments d'objet.*

III

Other Elements of the Sentence

Numbers; Time; Dates

Cardinal Numbers to 99

The cardinal numbers from 0 to 20 are as follows.

0	zéro		
1	un, une	11	onze
2	deux	12	douze
3	trois	13	treize
4	quatre	14	quatorze
5	cinq	15	quinze
6	six	16	seize
7	sept	17	dix-sept
8	huit	18	dix-huit
9	neuf	19	dix-neuf
10	dix	20	vingt

Un and **une** are the only numbers that agree in gender with a following noun. The forms for *one* are the same as the indefinite article.

From 20 to 59, French counts by tens, as does English. Note that **un(e)** is joined to the multiples of ten by **et**. The other units (2 through 9) are joined by a hyphen.

21	vingt et un(e)	32	trente-deux
22	vingt-deux	33	trente-trois
23	vingt-trois	40	quarante
24	vingt-quatre	41	quarante et un(e)
25	vingt-cinq	42	quarante-deux
26	vingt-six	43	quarante-trois
27	vingt-sept	50	cinquante
28	vingt-huit	51	cinquante et un(e)
29	vingt-neuf	52	cinquante-deux
30	trente	53	cinquante-trois
31	trente et un(e)		

Une is used instead of **un** before a feminine noun: **vingt et une pages**, **cinquante et une femmes**.

The **-t** of **vingt** is clearly pronounced in the numbers 21–29.

From 60 to 99, French counts by twenties. The units 1 through 19 are added to the multiple of twenty. **Un(e)** is joined by a hyphen, not by **et**, to **quatre-vingts**. Note also that **quatre-vingts** loses its final **-s** before another number.

60	soixante	74	soixante-quatorze	87	quatre-vingt-sept
61	soixante et un(e)	75	soixante-quinze	88	quatre-vingt-huit
62	soixante-deux	76	soixante-seize	89	quatre-vingt-neuf
63	soixante-trois	77	soixante-dix-sept	90	quatre-vingt-dix
64	soixante-quatre	78	soixante-dix-huit	91	quatre-vingt-onze
65	soixante-cinq	79	soixante-dix-neuf	92	quatre-vingt-douze
66	soixante-six	80	quatre-vingts	93	quatre-vingt-treize
67	soixante-sept	81	quatre-vingt-un(e)	94	quatre-vingt-quatorze
68	soixante-huit	82	quatre-vingt-deux	95	quatre-vingt-quinze
69	soixante-neuf	83	quatre-vingt-trois	96	quatre-vingt-seize
70	soixante-dix	84	quatre-vingt-quatre	97	quatre-vingt-dix-sept
71	soixante et onze	85	quatre-vingt-cinq	98	quatre-vingt-dix-huit
72	soixante-douze	86	quatre-vingt-six	99	quatre-vingt-dix-neuf
73	soixante-treize				

The **-t** of **vingt** is *not* pronounced in the numbers 80–99.

A *Dix de plus. Votre ami(e) se trompe. Chaque chiffre qu'il (elle) mentionne doit être majorée de dix. Corrigez ses calculs. Suivez le modèle.*

> MODÈLE   Je crois qu'il y a vingt-deux étudiants dans cette classe.
> → Non. Il y a trente-deux étudiants.

1. Je crois que nous avons besoin de soixante et un livres.

2. Je crois que ça coûte soixante-neuf dollars.

3. Je crois que cette ville est à quarante-huit kilomètres d'ici.

4. Je crois que son oncle a cinquante-six ans.

5. Je crois qu'ils ont passé soixante-treize jours en Suisse.

6. Je crois que tu as reçu un chèque pour quatre-vingts francs.

7. Je crois que je dois téléphoner à quatre-vingt-une personnes.

8. Je crois que nos amis arrivent le seize avril.

B *Corrections. Corrigez les numéros selon les indications données entre parenthèses. Écrivez les numéros en lettres. Suivez le modèle.*

> MODÈLE   Il habite 23, rue de la Paix. (33)
> → Non. Il habite trente-trois, rue de la Paix.

1. Son numéro de téléphone est le 03.87.34.44.56. (le 03.87.34.44.57)

2. Il a payé 77 francs. (99)

3. La grand-mère d'Yvette a 65 ans. (76)

4. Ils ont invité 60 personnes à la réception. (82)

5. Dans cette cité (*housing development*) il y a 82 appartements. (95)

6. Nous avons fait 68 kilomètres à vélo. (74)

7. La charcuterie a coûté 70 francs. (80)

8. Des représentants de 85 pays sont venus au congrès (*convention*) international. (98)

Cardinal Numbers 100 and Above

Round multiples of 100 are written with a final **-s**. However, the final **-s** of **cents** drops before another number.

100	cent	201	deux cent un
200	deux cents	326	trois cent vingt-six
300	trois cents	572	cinq cent soixante-douze

The word for *thousand*, **mille**, is invariable. Note that neither **cent** (*hundred*) nor **mille** (*thousand*) is preceded by **un**. (Compare English *one* hundred, *one* thousand.)

1.000	mille	100 000	cent mille
1.001	mille un	200 000	deux cent mille
1.200	mille deux cents, douze cents	582 478	cinq cent quatre-vingt-deux mille
2.000	deux mille		quatre cent soixante-dix-huit
3.500	trois mille cinq cents		
10.000	dix mille		

French uses a period or a space to separate thousands where English uses a comma. The comma is used in French numbers as a decimal point: **2,5** = **deux virgule cinq**.

The French word **million** is a noun and is followed by **de** before another noun. However, if other numbers come between **million** and the noun, **de** is not used. Note that **cent** is pluralized directly before the word **million**.

un million de livres	*1,000,000 books*
deux millions d'habitants	*2,000,000 inhabitants*
trois millions trois cent mille étudiants	*3,300,000 students*
deux cents millions de Russes	*200,000,000 Russians*
deux cent soixante-cinq millions d'Américains	*265,000,000 Americans*

The French word for *billion* is **un milliard**. **Milliard** is a noun like **million**: **cinq milliards d'êtres humains**. The French term **un billion** means *a trillion*.

C   *Autour du monde. Voici les chiffres de la population de plusieurs pays. Écrivez ces chiffres en lettres. Suivez le modèle.*

> MODÈLE   La France: 65 500 000
> → La France a soixante-cinq millions cinq cent mille habitants.

1. l'Espagne: 46 030 000

2. le Danemark: 5 500 000

3. le Japon: 127 300 000

4. la Chine: 1 350 000 000

5. l'Argentine: 40 100 000

6. la Suisse: 7 800 000

7. le Nigeria: 154 800 000

8. le Viêt-nam: 85 800 000

D *La population urbaine française.* *Employez les chiffres des dernières années pour comparer la population des villes avec celle de l'agglomération urbaine* (metropolitan area). *Écrivez les nombres en lettres. Suivez le modèle.*

MODÈLE	VILLE	AGGL. URB. (2007)	VILLE (2006)
	Grenoble	427 659	158 746

→ L'agglomération urbaine de Grenoble a quatre cent vingt-sept mille six cent cinquante-neuf habitants dont cent cinquante-huit mille sept cent quarante-six habitent dans la ville même.

	VILLE	AGGL. URB. (2007)	VILLE (2006)
1.	Paris	10 142 983	2 201 578
2.	Marseille	1 418 481	847 084
3.	Lyon	1 417 463	480 778
4.	Lille	1 016 205	232 432
5.	Nice	940 018	350 735
6.	Toulouse	850 876	444 392
7.	Bordeaux	800 117	235 878
8.	Nantes	568 743	290 871
9.	Strasbourg	440 264	276 867
10.	Montpellier	318 223	254 974

E *Maintenant c'est à vous de faire des recherches démographiques.*
Trouvez la population de six villes américaines ou canadiennes, dont trois au-dessus d'un million d'habitants et trois au-dessous. Écrivez le nom de chaque ville et sa population en chiffres et en lettres.

Ordinal Numbers

To form most ordinal numbers (*first, second, third,* etc.), the suffix **-ième** is added to the cardinal number. One exception is **un/une**, for which the ordinal number is **premier/ première**. Numbers ending in **-e** drop the **-e** before adding **-ième**. The ordinal **second(e)** is synonymous with **deuxième**. Note the spellings of the words for *fifth* and *ninth*.

deuxième *second*	**dix-septième** *seventeenth*
quatrième *fourth*	**vingtième** *twentieth*
cinquième *fifth*	**centième** *hundredth*
huitième *eighth*	**millième** *thousandth*
neuvième *ninth*	**quatorze centième** *fourteen hundredth*
dixième *tenth*	**trois mille cinq centième** *thirty-five hundredth*
quatorzième *fourteenth*	

The word **premier/première** is only used to mean *first*. Ordinals such as *twenty-first* and *one hundred first* are formed regularly.

vingt et unième *twenty-first*	**quatre-vingt-unième** *eighty-first*
soixante et onzième *seventy-first*	**cent unième** *one hundred first*

Ordinal numbers are abbreviated as follows: **1er**, **1ère**, **2e**, **3e**, etc.

Ordinal numbers are used to express fractions, except for **la moitié** (*half*), **le tiers** (*third*), and **le quart** (*fourth*).

le quart des élèves	*a quarter* of the students
les cinq sixièmes des enseignants	*five sixths* of the teaching staff

French uses cardinal numbers, not ordinal numbers, for dates and after the names of kings and queens (except for *first*, when **premier/première** is used).

le premier juin	*June 1*
le vingt-cinq août	*August 25*
Henri **IV** (= **Quatre**)	*Henry the Fourth*
Charles **II** (= **Deux**)	*Charles the Second*

French uses the suffix **-aine** to create nouns designating approximate numbers.

une dixaine de lettres	*about ten* letters
une vingtaine d'étudiants	*about twenty* students
des centaines de gagnants	*hundreds* of winners

F   *Mon Dieu, que c'est haut!*   *Un groupe de jeunes Français fait un stage à Chicago. Ils travaillent tous dans un énorme gratte-ciel. L'un d'eux, Gilbert, écrit à sa famille à Paris et donne des précisions «d'altitude» sur lui-même et sur ses amis. Attention: Dans les bâtiments français, **le premier étage** est l'équivalent du deuxième étage aux États-Unis. L'étage qui est au niveau du trottoir s'appelle **le rez-de-chaussée**. Gilbert emploie le système français. Suivez le modèle.*

MODÈLE   Alberte / 13
       → Alberte travaille au douzième étage.

1. moi / 74
2. Gilles / 22
3. Dorothée / 96
4. Richard et Maurice / 40
5. Paulette / 19
6. Suzanne et Émilie / 85
7. Marc / 46
8. Josette / 80

G   *En français!*   *Traduisez les phrases suivantes en français.*

1. *the forty-fifth day*
2. *a third of the children*
3. *the fifty-ninth lesson*
4. *the hundredth letter*
5. *three eighths of the students*
6. *about thirty books*
7. *the three thousandth issue* (le numéro)
8. *Louis the Ninth*

NOTE CULTURELLE

On emploie les nombres ordinaux en France pour les années d'éducation secondaire, mais à l'inverse de l'anglais. Au point de vue d'un Américain, on compte à rebours. Les étudiants commencent le collège en sixième et terminent en troisième. Le lycée va de la seconde à la première et la dernière année s'appelle «terminale».

Telling Time

To ask the time in French, the question **Quelle heure est-il?** (or more colloquially, **Il est quelle heure?**) is used. The response is the phrase **il est** followed by the hour.

Il est **une heure**.	*It's one o'clock.*
Il est **onze heures**.	*It's eleven o'clock.*

Minutes past the hour until the half hour are added directly to the hour. The words **quart** and **demie** are joined by **et**.

Il est **quatre heures cinq**.	*It's five past four.*
Il est **quatre heures et quart**.	*It's a quarter past four.*
Il est **quatre heures vingt**.	*It's twenty past four.*
Il est **quatre heures et demie**.	*It's four thirty.*

Minutes before the hour are expressed by the word **moins**. **Moins le quart** means *a quarter to the hour.*

Il est cinq heures **moins vingt**.	*It's twenty to five.*
Il est cinq heures **moins le quart**.	*It's a quarter to five.*

For *twelve noon*, French uses **il est midi**, and for *twelve midnight*, **il est minuit**. Minutes past these hours are expressed as above.

Il est **midi moins le quart**.	*It's a quarter to twelve (A.M.).*
Il est **midi et demi**.	*It's twelve thirty (P.M.).*
Il est **minuit dix**.	*It's ten past twelve (A.M.).*
Il est **minuit et quart**.	*It's a quarter past twelve (A.M.).*

The preposition **à** is used to indicate the time at which something happens.

—**À** quelle heure est-elle arrivée?	*What time did she arrive?*
—**À** huit heures moins le quart.	*At a quarter to eight.*

Some Useful Expressions Relating to Clock Time

Il est six heures **pile**.	*It's six o'clock **sharp**.*
Il est **tard/tôt**.	*It's **late/early**.*
Il se lève **tard**.	*He gets up **late**.*
Il se couche **tôt/de bonne heure**.	*He goes to bed **early**.*
Je suis **en retard/en avance**.	*I'm **late/early**.*
Je suis **à l'heure**.	*I'm **on time**.*
Ma montre **avance** (de cinq minutes).	*My watch **is** (five minutes) **fast**.*
Ma montre **retarde** (de cinq minutes).	*My watch **is** (five minutes) **slow**.*

être matinal(e)	to be an early riser
se coucher tôt	to go to bed early
faire la grasse matinée	to sleep late, sleep in

French uses a 24-hour clock for official purposes, such as transportation and entertainment schedules. In this system of telling time, **douze heures** and **vingt-quatre heures** replace **midi** and **minuit**, respectively. Minutes after the hour are counted from one to fifty-nine. **Et**, **moins**, **quart**, and **demie** are not used. Phrases such as **du matin**, **de l'après-midi**, **du soir**, and **de la nuit**, which are French equivalents of A.M. and P.M., are also not used in the 24-hour system.

La première séance du film est à **18 h 14**.	*The first showing of the film is at* **6:14** *P.M.*
Le train pour Berlin part à **13 h 48**.	*The train for Berlin leaves at* **1:48** *P.M.*
Le départ est prévu pour **0 h 35**.	*Departure is scheduled for* **12:35** *A.M.*
Boutique fermée entre **12 h** et **14 h**.	*Shop closed between* **noon** *and* **2** *P.M.*

H **La famille Raynaud revient des vacances.** *Le jour du retour des Raynaud a été très mouvementé. Écrivez ce qui s'est passé et à quelle heure. Suivez le modèle.*

MODÈLE   6 h / les enfants / se lever
→ Il est six heures. Les enfants se lèvent.

1. 7 h / Mme Raynaud / mettre les dernières choses dans les valises

2. 7 h 30 / les Raynaud / prendre le petit déjeuner à l'hôtel

3. 8 h 20 / le chasseur (*bellhop*) / descendre leurs bagages

4. 8 h 35 / M. Raynaud / appeler un taxi

5. 9 h 05 / les Raynaud / arriver à la gare

6. 9 h 15 / le petit Charles / tomber et se faire mal au genou

7. 9 h 30 / le pharmacien de la gare / mettre un pansement sur le genou de Charles

8. 9 h 45 / les Raynaud / prendre leurs places dans le train pour Paris

9. 9 h 55 / le train / partir

10. 3 h 20 / ils / arriver à Paris

I **La journée de M. Cavalli, épicier.** *M. Léon Cavalli est propriétaire d'une épicerie à Lille. Il décrit sa journée. Reconstruisez ces phrases à partir des éléments donnés pour savoir ce qui est arrivé et à quelle heure. Suivez le modèle.*

MODÈLE   moi / se lever / 5 h 30
→ Je me suis levé à cinq heures et demie.

1. moi / arriver à la boutique / 6 h 15

2. la livraison (*delivery*) du lait et des œufs / venir / 6 h 35

3. mes commis (*clerks*) / arriver / 6 h 50

4. nous / ouvrir l'épicerie / 7 h pile

5. la première cliente / franchir le seuil (*cross the threshold*) / 7 h 10

6. ma sœur / passer me voir / 10 h 45

7. nous / fermer pour le déjeuner / 1 h 40

8. moi / rouvrir ma boutique / 3 h 30

NOTE CULTURELLE

Lille est une importante ville française située dans le nord du pays tout près de la frontière belge. Avec les villes de Tourcoing et de Roubaix, Lille forme une grande agglomération de plus d'un million de personnes.

 À la gare de Genève. *Voici une liste de départs des trains en gare de Genève. Lisez la liste et répondez aux questions en employant l'heure officielle.*

HEURE	POUR	VOIE
5 58	Zurich	4
9 05	Genève-Aéroport	3
10 22	Lyon-Perrache	7
13 08	Dortmund (Allemagne)	6
14 06	La Plaine	5
15 35	Milan (Italie)	8
16 50	Paris	8
17 22	Lausanne	4
19 10	Paris	8
19 25	Zurich	4
20 25	Naples (Italie)	4
21 58	Bern	4
22 50	Barcelone (Espagne)	7
23 02	Zagreb (Croatie)	4
23 12	Nice	7
23 15	Genève-Aéroport	3

1. Quels trains y a-t-il pour Paris?

2. À quelle heure y a-t-il un train pour La Plaine?

3. À quelle heure part le train pour Zurich?

4. Quels trains y a-t-il pour l'Italie?

5. À quelle heure peut-on prendre le train pour Bern?

6. Quels trains y a-t-il pour des villes françaises à part Paris?

7. À quelle heure doit-on prendre le train s'il faut prendre l'avion à onze heures du matin?

8. Quel train y a-t-il pour l'Allemagne? pour l'Espagne?

9. Vous voulez arriver à Zurich le soir. Quel train prendrez-vous?

10. Quand y a-t-il un train pour Lausanne?

Days, Dates, and Years

Here are the words for the days of the week and the months and seasons of the year.

Les jours de la semaine

lundi *Monday*	**vendredi** *Friday*
mardi *Tuesday*	**samedi** *Saturday*
mercredi *Wednesday*	**dimanche** *Sunday*
jeudi *Thursday*	

Les mois de l'année

janvier *January*	**mai** *May*	**septembre** *September*
février *February*	**juin** *June*	**octobre** *October*
mars *March*	**juillet** *July*	**novembre** *November*
avril *April*	**août** *August*	**décembre** *December*

Les saisons

le printemps *spring*
l'été *summer*
l'automne *fall, autumn*
l'hiver *winter*

To specify *when* something happens, French uses several patterns.

- No preposition is used before days of the week.

Il arrivera **lundi**.	*He'll arrive **on Monday**.*
Je l'ai vue **dimanche**.	*I saw her **on Sunday**.*

- **Le** is used before the days of the week to indicate repeated or regular action.

—Je n'ai pas de cours **le mardi**.	*I don't have classes **on Tuesdays**.*
—Et moi, je travaille **le vendredi**.	*And I work **on Fridays**.*

- The preposition **en** is used before months of the year and the names of the seasons, except for **au printemps**.

—Tu prends tes vacances **en juillet**?	*Are you taking your vacation **in July**?*
—Non. Je n'aime pas partir **en été**. Je prends mes vacances **en mai**.	*No. I don't like to go on vacation **in the summer**. I take my vacation **in May**.*
—Tu as raison. C'est agréable, les vacances **au printemps**.	*You're right. Vacationing **in the spring** is very pleasant.*

To express dates, French uses cardinal numbers, except for **le premier**. The definite article **le** precedes the date. Note that as with days of the week, no preposition is used for *on*.

—Je croyais que tes cousins arrivaient **le trente novembre**.	*I thought your cousins were arriving **on November thirtieth**.*
—Non, c'était prévu pour **le premier décembre**.	*No, it was scheduled for **the first of December**.*

When dates are written in figures, the day precedes the month.

    4.3.98   *March 4, 1998*

Years are usually expressed in hundreds, although **mil** may also be used. **En** is used to express the year in which something happened.

    en dix-sept cent quatre-vingt-neuf $\Big\}$
    en mil sept cent quatre-vingt-neuf   *in 1789*

    Je suis né **en dix-neuf cent quatre-**   *I was born **in 1989**.*
      vingt-neuf.

As in English, the last two numbers are often used in speech to express the years of the present century.

    Elle est partie en **quatre-vingt-onze**.   *She left in '91.*

Some Useful Expressions Relating to the Days and Dates

Quelle est la date (aujourd'hui)?	*What's today's date?*
Le combien sommes-nous?	*What's today's date?*
C'est le premier juin.	*It's June first.*
Nous sommes le premier juin.	*It's June first.*
Quel jour sommes-nous?	*What day is it?*
C'est mercredi.	*It's Wednesday.*
Nous sommes mercredi aujourd'hui.	*It's Wednesday today.*
au début de juin	*at the beginning of June*
à la mi-juin	*in the middle of June*
vers la fin de juin	*toward the end of June*
des gens endimanchés	*people dressed in their Sunday best*
un peintre du dimanche	*an amateur painter*
Poisson d'avril!	*April fool!*
Il te rendra ton argent la semaine des quatre jeudis.	*You'll never get your money back from him.* (English: *in a month of Sundays*)

K   *L'année de Francine. Francine est une étudiante américaine qui écrit à Anne-Marie, son amie française. Dans sa lettre elle lui raconte tout ce qui s'est passé dans l'année. Avant d'écrire, elle fait une liste des dates importantes. Aidez-la en écrivant les dates en français.*

1. January 2: retour des vacances

2. January 24: examens finals

3. February 14: la Saint-Valentin—dîner avec Jean-Claude

4. March 10: bal au centre communautaire

5. April 1: poisson d'avril (*April Fool's Day*)

6. May 28: parade pour le jour des Morts au Champ d'Honneur (*Memorial Day*)

7. June 24: dernier jour de classes

8. July 4: jour de l'Indépendance (fête nationale)

9. July 16: boulot (*job*) commence (au restaurant)

10. August 30: j'ai rompu avec Jean-Claude

11. September 6: premier jour de cours—j'ai connu Philippe

12. November 25: Thanksgiving

L   *Histoire de France du dixième au dix-neuvième siècle.* *Écrivez ces dates importantes de l'histoire française. Suivez le modèle.*

    MODÈLE   Charlemagne couronné «empereur des Romains» par le pape Léon III:
             25.12.800
        → le vingt-cinq décembre huit cents

1. Hughes Capet élu roi à Noyon: 1.7.987

2. commencement de la première croisade: départ des croisés armés: 15.8.1096

3. bataille de Bouvines: Philippe Auguste bat Jean sans Terre et ses alliés: 27.7.1214

4. Jeanne d'Arc brûlée à Rouen: 30.5.1431

5. édit de Nantes: 15.4.1598

6. Louis XIV devient roi de France: 7.6.1654

7. prise de la Bastille: 14.7.1789

8. déclaration de l'Empire (Napoléon Empereur) par le Sénat: 18.5.1804

9. création de la Troisième République: 4.9.1870

M   *Examen d'histoire.* *Françoise étudie pour l'examen d'histoire contemporaine. Aidez-la en choisissant l'année correcte pour chaque événement donné. Écrivez votre réponse en lettres.*

1. début de la Première Guerre mondiale (1914 ou 1915)

2. fin de la Première Guerre mondiale (1918 ou 1919)

3. début de la crise économique mondiale (1927 ou 1929)

4. commencement de la Deuxième Guerre mondiale (1938 ou 1939)

5. chute (*fall*) de Paris (1940 ou 1941)

6. fin de la Seconde Guerre mondiale (1944 ou 1945)

7. De Gaulle devient Président de la Cinquième République (1957 ou 1958)

8. l'Algérie indépendante (1962 ou 1964)

NOTE CULTURELLE

Le général Charles de Gaulle a dirigé les Forces de la France Libre (c'est-à-dire, l'armée française en exil) pendant la Deuxième Guerre mondiale. En 1958, en pleine crise économique et coloniale (soulèvement de l'Algérie), de Gaulle est élu Président de la Cinquième République. Il a participé à la rédaction de la constitution de la Cinquième République qui a donné à la France un régime présidentiel.

 Et maintenant il s'agit de vous. *Faites une liste des dates de naissance (jour, mois, année) de vos frères et sœurs, de vos parents, de vos meilleurs amis. Écrivez les dates en lettres.*

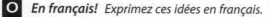 **En français!** *Exprimez ces idées en français.*

1. *What's today's date?*
   It's March twenty-first.

2. *He'll never come to see us. (= He'll come to see us in a month of Sundays.)*

3. *I'm only an amateur painter.*

4. *What day is it?*
   It's Saturday.

5. *You [pl.] are all dressed up (in your Sunday best).*

6. *I'm going to Italy in the spring.*

7. *What time is it?*
   It's eight o'clock sharp.
   Good. I'm early.

8. *Has John gotten up already?*
   No. He's not an early riser, you know.
   I know he likes to sleep in.

Activité orale. *Posez des questions à un(e) ami(e) sur les grands moments de sa vie: Quand a-t-il/elle emménagé ici, quand est-il/elle né(e), quand a-t-il/elle commencé à travailler, etc. Votre ami(e) vous posera le même genre de questions.*

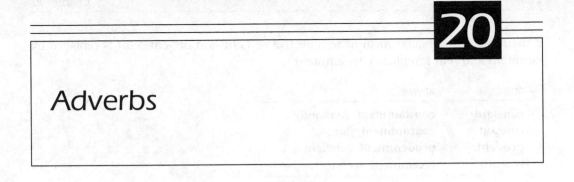

Adverbs

Adverbs of Manner

Adverbs give information about verbs, adjectives, other adverbs, or an entire sentence. Adverbs of manner tell how something is done.

Most adverbs of manner are formed by adding **-ment** to the feminine form of the adjective.

MASCULINE	FEMININE	ADVERB
actif	**active**	**activement** *actively*
amer	**amère**	**amèrement** *bitterly*
certain	**certaine**	**certainement** *certainly*
cruel	**cruelle**	**cruellement** *cruelly*
doux	**douce**	**doucement** *gently, softly*
franc	**franche**	**franchement** *frankly*
lent	**lente**	**lentement** *slowly*
public	**publique**	**publiquement** *publicly*
sérieux	**sérieuse**	**sérieusement** *seriously*

If the masculine singular form of an adjective ends in a vowel, **-ment** is added directly to that form.

MASCULINE	ADVERB
absolu	**absolument** *absolutely*
facile	**facilement** *easily*
poli	**poliment** *politely*
sincère	**sincèrement** *sincerely*
vrai	**vraiment** *really, truly*

If the masculine singular form of an adjective ends in **-ant** or **-ent**, **-ant** is replaced by **-amment** and **-ent** is replaced by **-emment**.

ADJECTIVE	ADVERB
constant	**constamment** *constantly*
courant	**couramment** *fluently*
prudent	**prudemment** *carefully*
récent	**récemment** *recently*

Some adjectives form adverbs by adding **-ément**.

ADJECTIVE	ADVERB
aveugle	**aveuglément** *blindly*
commun	**communément** *commonly*
confus	**confusément** *confusedly*
énorme	**énormément** *enormously*
intense	**intensément** *intensely*
obscur	**obscurément** *obscurely*
précis	**précisément** *precisely*
profond	**profondément** *profoundly, deeply*
uniforme	**uniformément** *uniformly*

A number of adjectives can be used as adverbs, mostly in set phrases. The masculine singular form of the adjective is used.

parler (tout) bas	*to speak (very) softly*
acheter/vendre cher	*to buy/sell at a high price*
coûter cher	*to cost a lot*
payer cher	*to pay a high price for*
s'arrêter court	*to stop short*
aller tout droit	*to go straight ahead*
travailler dur	*to work hard*
parler fort	*to yell*
crier fort	*to cry out loudly*
lire tout haut	*to read aloud*
mettre la radio plus haut	*to turn the radio up louder*

Some adverbs are irregular.

ADJECTIVE	ADVERB
bon	**bien** *well*
mauvais	**mal** *badly*
meilleur	**mieux** *better*
pire	**pis** *worse*
bref	**brièvement** *briefly*
gai	**gaiement** *gaily*
gentil	**gentiment** *gently*

Some other common adverbs of manner do not end in **-ment**.

ainsi *thus*
debout *up, awake, standing up*
exprès *on purpose*
vite *quickly*
volontiers *gladly*

 A *Pour décrire des actions.* *Formez les adverbes qui correspondent aux adjectifs suivants. Après cet exercice, vous serez prêt(e) à décrire une vaste gamme d'actions. Suivez le modèle.*

MODÈLE   personnel
          → personnellement

1. affreux
2. intelligent
3. correct
4. possible
5. gentil
6. triste
7. massif
8. gai
9. confus
10. fréquent

11. moral
12. pratique
13. généreux
14. actuel
15. évident
16. léger
17. long
18. précis
19. exact
20. complet

B *Comment est-ce qu'ils ont parlé?* *Formez des adverbes pour décrire comment ces personnes s'adressent au professeur. Suivez le modèle.*

MODÈLE   Sarah est sincère quand elle parle avec le professeur?
          → Oui, elle lui parle sincèrement.

1. Frédéric est nerveux quand il parle avec le professeur?
2. Lise est confuse quand elle parle avec le professeur?
3. Paul est honnête quand il parle avec le professeur?
4. Anne et Barbara sont tristes quand elles parlent avec le professeur?
5. Luc et Jean-Claude sont furieux quand ils parlent avec le professeur?
6. Thérèse est patiente quand elle parle avec le professeur?
7. Odile et Marc sont polis quand ils parlent avec le professeur?
8. Fanny est discrète quand elle parle avec le professeur?
9. Éric et Jacques sont intenses quand ils parlent avec le professeur?
10. Serge est gentil quand il parle avec le professeur?

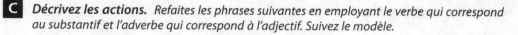

C **_Décrivez les actions._** *Refaites les phrases suivantes en employant le verbe qui correspond au substantif et l'adverbe qui correspond à l'adjectif. Suivez le modèle.*

MODÈLE   Est-ce que les réponses de Victor sont intelligentes?
→ Oui, il répond intelligemment.

1. Est-ce que le travail de Paulette est diligent?

2. Est-ce que les réactions de son frère sont violentes?

3. Est-ce que les dessins de cette artiste sont bons?

4. Est-ce que les sorties de votre sœur sont fréquentes?

5. Est-ce que la prononciation des ces élèves est mauvaise?

6. Est-ce que son amour pour elle est aveugle?

7. Est-ce que les punitions de l'institutrice sont uniformes?

8. Est-ce que les réflexions de ce philosophe sont profondes?

The Use and Position of Adverbs of Manner

Adverbs of manner ending in -**ment** and the adverbs **bien**, **mal**, **mieux**, **pis**, and **vite** usually directly follow the verb they modify. In compound tenses, short adverbs usually follow the auxiliary verb, and longer adverbs usually follow the past participle.

—Julie et Bruno se disputent **constammant**.	*Julie and Bruno argue **constantly**.*
—Après le dîner, ils se sont disputés **amèrement** et Julie a **vite** quitté le salon.	*After dinner they argued **bitterly**, and Julie **quickly** left the living room.*

When an adverb modifies an adjective or another adverb, it precedes the word it modifies.

Cette lettre est **très importante**.	*This letter is **very important**.*
Les spectateurs étaient **profondément émus**.	*The audience was **deeply moved**.*

Adverbs of manner ending in -**ment** can be replaced by **avec** plus the corresponding noun.

amèrement	→ **avec amertume**
discrètement	→ **avec discrétion**
joyeusement	→ **avec joie**
violemment	→ **avec violence**

Sans + noun is often the equivalent of English adverbs ending in *-lessly* or English adverbs formed from negative adjectives.

sans espoir	*hopelessly*
sans hésitation	*unhesitatingly*
sans honte	*shamelessly*
sans succès	*unsuccessfully*

D'une façon, **d'une manière**, **d'un ton**, or **d'un air** plus an adjective may be used in place of an adverb or when no adverb exists.

d'une façon compétente	*competently*
d'une manière compatible	*compatibly*
d'un air indécis	*indecisively*
d'un ton moqueur	*mockingly*

D *Formez vos phrases!* *Mettez les éléments donnés en ordre pour former des phrases correctes. Faites attention à la position des adverbes. Suivez le modèle.*

MODÈLE   expliqué / bien / problème / le / a / le professeur
→ Le professeur a bien expliqué le problème.

1. mal / le vocabulaire / prononces / tu

2. nettoie / la cuisine / elle / soigneusement

3. ridicule / trouvons / ce projet / complètement / nous

4. étroitement / sont / les membres de cette famille / unis

5. sans / marche / il / empressement

6. d'une façon / les enfants / se sont conduits / déplaisante

7. dur / Marcelle / à / travaille / la bibliothèque

8. une / acceptée / c'est / largement / idée

9. le / ont / ils / texte / compris / vite

10. m' / elle / répondu / a / brusquement

E *Pour reconnaître les adverbes.* *Les locutions suivantes peuvent être traduites par des adverbes en anglais. Écrivez pour chacune d'elles une traduction convenable.*

1. d'un ton insultant

2. sans doute

3. avec gentillesse

4. avec indignation

5. d'un ton sec

6. d'une façon extravagante

7. avec décision

8. avec intelligence

F *L'expression adverbiale.* *Consultez la liste des substantifs ci-dessous et employez-les avec les prépositions* **avec** *et* **sans** *pour traduire les adverbes anglais.*

la cérémonie *ceremony*   **l'imagination** *imagination*
la colère *anger*   **l'indifférence** *indifference*
l'effort *effort*   **le tact** *tact*
le goût *taste*   **la tolérance** *tolerance*

1. *effortlessly*

2. *tastefully*

3. *unimaginatively*

4. *unconcernedly*

5. *angrily*

6. *tolerantly*

7. *unceremoniously*

8. *tactlessly*

Adverbs of Time

Adverbs of time tell when or in what order something happens.

actuellement *at present*   **enfin** *at last, finally*
alors *then*   **ensuite** *next, following that*
après *after, afterwards*   **hier** *yesterday*
après-demain *the day after tomorrow* **jamais** *never*
aujourd'hui *today*   **longtemps** *for a long time*
auparavant *previously, beforehand* **maintenant** *now*
aussitôt *immediately*   **n'importe quand** *anytime*
autrefois *formerly, in the past* **parfois** *sometimes*
avant *before*   **précédemment** *previously*
avant-hier *the day before yesterday* **quelquefois** *sometimes*
bientôt *soon*   **rarement** *rarely, seldom*
d'abord *at first*   **récemment** *recently*
de bonne heure *early*   **souvent** *often*
déjà *already, ever*   **tard** *late*
demain *tomorrow*   **tôt** *early*
dernièrement *lately*   **toujours** *always*
désormais *from now on*   **tout à l'heure** *a short while ago;*
encore *still, yet, again*   *very soon*
encore une fois *again*   **tout de suite** *immediately*

Adverbs of time usually follow the verb, but they often occur at the beginning of sentences.

Je vais **quelquefois** au théâtre. }
Quelquefois je vais au théâtre.   ***Sometimes*** *I go to the theater.*

Il travaillait **auparavant** à Lille. }
Auparavant il travaillait à Lille. *He worked in Lille **previously**.*

Many phrases expressing points in time function as adverbial phrases.

le week-end	**le matin/l'après-midi**
en semaine *during the week*	**le soir/la nuit**
la semaine dernière/prochaine	**tous les jours**
toute la journée	**une fois, deux fois**, etc.
tous les ans	**une/deux fois par semaine/mois**
tous les mois	**mardi**
toutes les semaines	**le mardi**
le lendemain *the day after*	**mardi prochain**
la veille *the evening before*	**mardi dernier**

G   *Antonymes.* *Trouvez dans la deuxième colonne des antonymes pour les adverbes de temps de la première colonne.*

1. tard	a. autrefois
2. actuellement	b. avant
3. hier	c. jamais
4. souvent	d. demain
5. toujours	e. rarement
6. après	f. tôt

H   *Qu'est-ce vous faites et quand?* *En choisissant des éléments des trois groupes (ou en ajoutant d'autres éléments), écrivez dix phrases qui parlent de vos activités et de celles des gens que vous connaissez.*

moi, je	arriver	auparavant
nous	partir	tout de suite
mes parents	se lever	_____ fois par semaine
mon frère/ma sœur	se coucher	tous les jours
mon meilleur ami _____	faire ses devoirs	le matin/soir
ma meilleure amie _____	rentrer	l'après-midi
mon petit ami _____	faire du jogging	tous les matins/soirs
ma petite amie _____	faire du sport	le samedi/dimanche
les autres étudiants	aller au cinéma	quelquefois
il y a des étudiants qui	nous faire passer un examen	dernièrement
le professeur	passer un examen	souvent
le directeur	sortir	hier/avant-hier
	travailler	demain/après-demain
		désormais

Adverbs of Place

Adverbs of place tell where something happens.

ailleurs	*elsewhere, somewhere else*	**ici**	*here*
d'ailleurs	*besides*	**là**	*there*
autour	*around*	**là-bas**	*over there*
dedans	*inside*	**loin**	*far away*
dehors	*outside*	**n'importe où**	*anywhere*
derrière	*behind*	**nulle part**	*nowhere*
dessous	*below*	**nulle part ailleurs**	*nowhere else*
dessus	*above*	**partout**	*everywhere*
devant	*in front*	**partout ailleurs**	*everywhere else*
en bas	*down, downstairs*	**près**	*near*
en haut	*up, upstairs*	**quelque part**	*somewhere*

In everyday language, both spoken and written, **ici** is often replaced by **là**.

> Je regrette, mais Mme Poirier n'est
> pas **là**.

> *I'm sorry, but Mrs. Poirier is not **here**.*

Là- can be added to some of the above adverbs of place.

là-dedans	*in there*
là-dessous	*underneath there*
là-dessus	*on top of it, on it*
là-haut	*up there*

I   **Antonymes.** *Trouvez dans la deuxième colonne des antonymes pour les adverbes de lieu de la première colonne.*

1. ici   a. dessus

2. dedans   b. nulle part

3. loin   c. derrière

4. dessous   d. dehors

5. partout   e. là

6. devant   f. en haut

7. en bas   g. près

J   **Une belle maison.** *Rendez plus précise cette description d'une belle maison en ajoutant les adverbes de lieu donnés entre parenthèses aux phrases. On peut placer ces adverbes à la fin de la phrase, et parfois au début aussi. Suivez le modèle.*

MODÈLE   Je remarque une maison. (là-bas)
         → Je remarque une maison là-bas.

1. C'est une jolie maison. Il y a des arbres. (autour)

2. Il y a un jardin. (derrière)

3. Je regarde le salon. (en bas)

4. Je voudrais voir les chambres (en haut)

5. Je cherche les propriétaires. (partout)

6. Je ne les vois pas. (nulle part)

7. Travaillent-ils? (dehors)

8. Je les entends. (quelque part)

9. Il y a deux voix. (tout près)

10. Les voilà. (devant)

 Du temps et du lieu. *Traduisez les conversations suivantes en français en faisant attention aux adverbes de temps et de lieu.*

1. *Yesterday I looked for my watch everywhere.*
   I saw it somewhere. Did you look (for it) upstairs?

2. *It rains here every week.*
   I know. I wish I lived elsewhere.

3. *I didn't go anywhere on Wednesday.*
   Neither did I. I seldom go out during the week.

4. *Formerly I used to do the marketing* (faire le marché) *every day.*
   At present you do the marketing once a week, right?

5. *I would go to see her anytime, anywhere.*
   You won't have to go far. There she is, over there.

Adverbial Phrases

Prepositional phrases often function as adverbs of time, place, and manner. The preposition **dès** and the compound preposition **à partir de** combine with time words to tell when something happened.

dès le matin	*from the morning on*
dès le début	*from the beginning*
dès mon retour	*as soon as I get back*
à partir d'aujourd'hui	*from today on*
à partir de demain	*from tomorrow on*
à partir d'hier	*starting yesterday*

Adverbial Phrases of Time with the Prepositions **dans** and **en**

dans l'avenir	*in the future*
dans le passé	*in the past*
dans un mois	*in a month*
dans un moment	*in a moment*
en ce moment	*at this time*
dans cinq minutes	*in five minutes* (*five minutes from now*)
en cinq minutes	*in five minutes* (time it takes to do something)

d'aujourd'hui en huit	*a week from today*
en avance	*early* (relative to a point in time)
en retard	*late* (relative to a point in time)

Adverbial Phrases with the Preposition à

Phrases of Time

à l'heure	*on time*
à temps	*in time*
à l'époque	*at the time, at that time*
à l'époque où nous sommes	*in this day and age*
à leur arrivée	*when they arrived*
à leur retour	*when they returned*

Phrases of Place

à droite	*to/on the right*
à gauche	*to/on the left*
à trois kilomètres de la ville	*three kilometers from the city*
à trois heures de Paris	*three hours from Paris*

Phrases of Manner

à merveille	*wonderfully*
à pied	*on foot*
à cheval	*on horseback*
à la hâte	*hastily, in a rush*
à peine	*hardly*

Adverbial Phrases with the Preposition de

d'habitude	*usually*
d'ordinaire	*usually*
de temps en temps	*from time to time*
du matin au soir	*from morning to night*
de bonne heure	*early*
de mois en mois	*from month to month*
de jour en jour	*from day to day*
marcher d'un bon pas	*to walk at a good pace*

Adverbial Phrases with the Preposition en

en avant	*in front, ahead*
en arrière	*in back*
en désordre	*in a mess*
en pagaille	*in a mess*
en face	*across the way*
en groupe	*in a group*
en plus	*moreover*
en tout cas	*in any case*
en train/autobus/avion/voiture	*by train/bus/plane/car*

Adverbial Phrases with the Preposition **par**

par hasard	*by chance*
par la force	*by force*
par écrit	*in writing*
par terre	*on the ground*
par ici	*this way*
par là	*that way*
par conséquent	*consequently*
par intervalles	*intermittently*
payer par chèque	*to pay by check*
par la poste	*through the mails, by mail*
par un temps pareil	*in such weather*

Adverbial Phrases with the Preposition **sans**

sans but	*aimlessly*
sans chaussures	*barefoot*
sans doute	*doubtlessly*
sans faute	*without fail*
sans mal	*without any trouble, without difficulty*

Adverbial Phrases with the Preposition **sur**

sur les 3 heures	*at about 3 o'clock*
sur le moment	*at first*
sur une année	*over (the period of) a year*
un jour sur deux	*every other day*

L *Mon rendez-vous.* *M. Perrin explique les difficultés qu'il a eues pour ne pas manquer son rendez-vous. Ajoutez les prépositions qui manquent pour savoir ce qui lui est arrivé.*

J'avais rendez-vous à 3 heures. Je ne voulais pas arriver (1) _____ retard. Je suis donc parti

(2) _____ les 2 heures pour arriver un peu (3) _____ avance. Il pleuvait. Je ne pouvais pas

aller (4) _____ pied (5) _____ un temps pareil. J'ai décidé d'aller (6) _____ autobus.

Mais l'autobus n'est pas venu. (7) _____ conséquent, j'ai pris un taxi. Je m'étais (8) _____

peine assis quand le taxi a eu un pneu crevé. Je suis descendu du taxi et j'ai commencé

à marcher (9) _____ un bon pas. Je me trouvais (10) _____ vingt minutes du bureau

où on m'attendait. Tout à fait (11) _____ hasard mon ami Michel est passé dans sa voiture.

Il a klaxonné pour attirer mon attention. Il m'a emmené (12) _____ voiture et on est arrivés

(13) _____ cinq minutes. Je suis arrivé (14) _____ temps!

M ***Les soucis d'un jeune professeur.*** *Alfred Saint-Martin est un jeune professeur d'histoire dans un lycée de Tours. Il a une classe difficile. Pour savoir ce qu'il en pense et ce qu'il compte faire, refaites les phrases suivantes en y ajoutant la traduction française des phrases adverbiales données entre parenthèses.*

1. J'ai fait un effort pour organiser la classe. (*right from the start*)

2. J'ai dit aux étudiants qu'il est défendu de venir en classe. (*barefoot*)

3. Je leur ai dit que je ne veux pas qu'ils laissent la salle de classe. (*in a mess*)

4. Ils ne doivent laisser ni leurs livres ni leurs papiers. (*on the ground*)

5. Jean-Claude Mercier vient au cours. (*every other day*)

6. Noëlle Chenu se promène dans les couloirs. (*aimlessly*)

7. Elle travaille un peu. (*intermittently*)

8. Elle prépare ses devoirs. (*hurriedly*)

9. Lise Monnet est la meilleure étudiante de la classe. (*doubtlessly*)

10. Elle travaille. (*wonderfully*)

11. Les autres étudiants l'admirent. (*usually*)

12. Nous avons une semaine de congé. (*starting tomorrow*)

13. Je vais faire un effort pour améliorer cette classe. (*as soon as we get back*)

14. Nous allons faire des excursions. (*from time to time*)

15. Nous irons à Versailles. (*in a group*)

16. Les vieilles méthodes ne sont pas toujours bonnes. (*in this day and age*)

17. Je jugerai cette expérience. (*over four months*)

Negatives and Indefinites

Negative Words

In Chapter 3, we reviewed the following positive and corresponding negative words.

encore, toujours	*still*	plus	*no more*
encore, davantage	*more*	plus	*no more, not anymore*
quelquefois	*sometimes*	jamais	*never*
toujours	*always*	jamais	*never*
souvent	*often*	jamais	*never*
quelqu'un	*someone, somebody*	personne	*no one, nobody*
quelque chose	*something*	rien	*nothing*
quelque part	*somewhere*	nulle part	*nowhere*

Here are some additional pairs of corresponding positive and negative expressions.

déjà	*ever*	jamais	*never*
déjà	*already*	pas encore	*not yet*
soit... soit, soit... ou	*either . . . or*	ni... ni	*neither . . . nor*
ou	*or*	ni	*neither, nor*

In both simple and compound tenses, **ne** precedes the conjugated verb and the negative word usually follows the conjugated verb.

—Est-ce que tu as **déjà** été en Belgique?	*Have you **ever** been to Belgium?*
—Non, je **n'**y suis **jamais** allé.	*No, I've **never** gone there.*
—Nous passerons l'été **soit** à Nice, **soit** en Espagne. Et vous?	*We'll spend the summer either in Nice or in Spain. How about you?*
—Nous **ne** partons **ni** dans le Midi, **ni** à l'étranger. Nous travaillons cet été.	*We won't be going **either** to the south of France **or** abroad. We're working this summer.*

More than one negative word can be used in a sentence: **ne... plus jamais** or **ne... jamais plus** (*never again*), **ne... plus rien** (*nothing else, nothing more*), **ne... plus personne** (*nobody else, no one anymore*), etc.

—Il **n'**y a **jamais personne** ici.	*There's **never anyone** here.*
—C'est qu'il **n'**y a **plus rien** à faire.	*That's because there's **nothing more** to do.*

231

Negative words can stand by themselves.

—Connais-tu beaucoup de monde ici?	*Do you know a lot of people here?*
—**Personne.**	***No one.***
—Qu'est-ce que vous cherchez?	*What are you looking for?*
—**Rien.**	***Nothing.***

Both **ne** and the negative words **pas**, **rien**, **jamais**, and **plus** precede an infinitive. **Personne**, however, follows an infinitive.

Je vous conseille de **ne pas** y **aller**.	*I advise you **not to go** there.*
Il m'a dit de **ne jamais revenir**.	*He told me **never to come back**.*
On passe la journée à **ne rien faire**.	*We spend the day **doing nothing**.*
Je préfère **ne voir personne**.	*I prefer **not to see anyone**.*

After the word **que** in comparisons, French uses negative words.

—J'ai l'impression que Vincent est **plus paresseux que jamais**.	*I have the impression that Vincent is **lazier than ever**.*
—Vous vous trompez. Il travaille **mieux que personne**.	*You're mistaken. He works **better than anyone**.*

Before adjectives, nouns, pronouns, or adverbs, **non** or **pas** is usually used. **Non** is more formal, **pas** is more colloquial.

—Tu es éreinté?	*Are you exhausted?*
—**Pas éreinté (Non éreinté).** Un peu fatigué.	***Not exhausted.*** *A little tired.*
Il travaille mardi, **pas jeudi (non jeudi)**.	*He's working Tuesday, **not Thursday**.*

A   *Hubert le rêveur.* *Hubert passe son temps à rêver. Essayez de le ramener à la réalité en employant les mots négatifs nécessaires. Suivez le modèle.*

> MODÈLE   Je gagne toujours à la loterie.
> → Ne dis pas d'idioties! Tu ne gagnes jamais à la loterie.

1. Quelqu'un me donnera un million de francs.

2. Quelques filles me croient le plus beau garçon du lycée.

3. J'ai souvent vingt à l'examen de philo.

4. La femme du Président de la République m'a envoyé quelque chose.

5. Mon père va m'offrir soit une Ferrari ou une Jaguar.

6. Il me reste toujours quelque chose de l'argent que j'ai reçu pour mon anniversaire.

7. Je connais quelqu'un à Istamboul.

8. Je connais quelqu'un à Singapour aussi.

9. J'irai quelque part avec Solange.

10. Si je n'aime pas mes cadeaux, on m'offrira quelque chose d'autre.

B *Marceline la trouble-fête* (**party-pooper**). *Marcelline est tellement pessimiste au sujet de la soirée qu'on a organisée qu'elle donne le cafard (depresses) à tout le monde. Écrivez les réactions de Marcelline aux idées de ses copains en employant les mots négatifs convenables. Suivez le modèle.*

MODÈLE   Tout le monde viendra à notre fête.
→ Personne ne viendra à notre fête.

1. Chacun apportera quelque chose à manger.

2. Nous boirons quelque chose.

3. Nous écouterons soit des cassettes soit des disques compacts.

4. Jeanine a déjà acheté du jus de fruits.

5. Olivier a une nouvelle cassette.

6. Odile amène toujours quelqu'un d'intéressant.

7. Ces soirées sont toujours amusantes.

8. Après la soirée, nous irons nous promener quelque part.

C *Comment est-ce que cela se dit?* *Traduisez les échanges suivants en français en faisant attention à l'emploi des mots négatifs.*

1. *Don't you have any more packages?*
   No. I don't have anything more.

2. *That pastry cook makes cakes better than anyone.*
   Yes. That's why he has more clients than ever.

3. *He never brings anything when we invite him to dinner.*
   Don't invite him ever again.

4. *Have you ever spoken with Alfred?*
   No. He doesn't understand either English or French. I prefer not to speak to him.

D *Tout change.* *Quels changements y a-t-il eu à l'école depuis que vous y allez? Faites une liste de cinq choses* **qu'on n'y fait plus**. *Par exemple,* **On ne sert plus de bonbons à la cantine.**

E *Jamais de la vie!* *Quelles choses sont interdites à l'école? Chez vous en famille? Au travail, si vous travaillez? Faites une liste de cinq choses* **qu'on n'y fait jamais.** *Par exemple,* **On ne fume jamais en classe.**

F *Les coutumes.* *Il y a des choses qu'on ne fait pas, non pas parce qu'elles sont interdites, mais parce que nos coutumes nous empêchent de les faire. Faites une liste de cinq choses* **que personne ne ferait.** *Par exemple,* **Personne ne viendrait à l'école en pyjama.** *Le ridicule n'est pas exclu, bien sûr.*

Indefinite Words and Expressions

Many English indefinite expressions begin with the word *some*. They are often the positive counterparts of negative words.

quelquefois	*sometimes*
quelqu'un	*someone, somebody*
quelque chose	*something*
quelque part	*somewhere*

The word *some* before a noun is expressed in French either by the partitive article or by **quelques**, which is more emphatic.

Je n'ai que **quelques** mots à vous dire.	*I have only **a few** words to say to you.*
Vous trouverez **quelques** idées intéressantes dans cet article.	*You'll find **some** interesting ideas in this article.*

When used emphatically, the pronoun *some* is rendered by **quelques-uns**, **quelques-unes**. The pronoun **en** usually appears in the sentence.

—As-tu acheté des journaux français?	*Did you buy any French newspapers?*
—J'**en** ai acheté **quelques-uns**.	*I bought **some** (= **a few**).*
—As-tu acheté des revues françaises?	*Did you buy any French magazines?*
—J'**en** ai acheté **quelques-unes**.	*I bought **some** (= **a few**).*

When *some* is the subject of the sentence and means *some people*, its French equivalent is **certains**. It often occurs in conjunction with **d'autres** (*others*).

Certains appuient cette nouvelle loi, **d'autres** sont contre.	***Some** support this new law, **others** are against (it).*

In everyday French, **certains** and **d'autres** as subjects are often replaced by **il y en a qui** and **il y en a d'autres qui**, respectively.

Il y en a qui appuient cette nouvelle loi, **il y en a d'autres qui** sont contre.	***Some** support this new law, **others** are against it.*

To express *someone or other, something or other, somewhere or other*, etc., French uses **je ne sais** plus the appropriate interrogative word.

je ne sais qui	*someone or other*
je ne sais quoi	*something or other*
je ne sais où	*somewhere or other*
je ne sais comment	*somehow*
je ne sais quel + *noun*	*some + noun + or other*
je ne sais quand	*sometime or other*
je ne sais pourquoi	*for some reason or other*
je ne sais combien	*I'm not sure how much/many*

—Jacqueline est allée **je ne sais où** aujourd'hui.	*Jacqueline went **somewhere or other** today.*
—Oui. Le dimanche elle va rendre visite à **je ne sais qui** à Fontainebleau.	*Yes. On Sundays she goes to visit **someone** in Fontainebleau.*

—Il s'est sauvé de l'accident **je ne sais comment**.	*Somehow or other he saved himself from the crash.*
—Quelle chance! Cette tragédie a fait **je ne sais combien** de victimes.	*What luck! That tragedy caused **I don't know how many** deaths.*

Any in the sense of *it doesn't matter which one* is expressed in French by **n'importe** followed by the appropriate interrogative word.

n'importe qui	*anyone*
n'importe quoi, quoi que ce soit	*anything*
n'importe où	*anywhere*
n'importe comment	*anyhow*
n'importe quel + *noun*	*any* + noun
n'importe lequel/laquelle/lesquels/lesquelles	*whichever one(s), any one(s)*
n'importe quand	*at any time*
n'importe combien	*any amount, no matter how much/many*

—Qu'est-ce que tu veux manger?	*What do you want to eat?*
—**N'importe quoi.**	***Anything.***
—Et où est-ce que tu veux aller après?	*And where do you want to go afterwards?*
—**N'importe où.**	***Anywhere.***

Remember that the English word *any* and the words it appears in (*anyone, anything, anywhere*) are translated by negative words in French if the sentence is negative, and by indefinite words and expressions if the sentence is positive. Contrast the following pairs of sentences.

—Est-ce qu'il en sait **quelque chose**?	*Does he know **anything** about it?*
—Non. Il **n'**en sait **rien**.	*No. He **doesn't** know **anything** about it.*
—Allez-vous **quelque part** cette semaine?	*Are you going **anywhere** this week?*
—Non, nous **n'**allons **nulle part**.	*No, we're **not** going **anywhere**.*

Sometimes when English *any* is used in a negative sentence, its French equivalent is one of the expressions with **n'importe**. The word *just* often appears before *any* in the English sentence in this case.

Je ne vais pas offrir **n'importe quoi**.	*I'm not going to give **just anything** as a gift.*
Nous ne voulons pas passer le temps avec **n'importe qui**.	*We don't want to spend time with **just anyone**.*

G *Exprimez votre indifférence. Répondez aux questions suivantes en employant une des expressions avec* **n'importe***. Par vos réponses vous montrez que le choix entre les possibilités vous est égal. Suivez le modèle.*

MODÈLE   Avec qui est-ce que je dois parler?
   → Avec n'importe qui.

1. Qu'est-ce que tu veux boire?

2. Où est-ce que tu veux manger?

3. Quel journal est-ce que je dois acheter?

4. Quand est-ce que tu veux partir?

5. À quel cinéma veux-tu aller?

6. Combien d'argent vas-tu payer?

7. Comment est-ce que tu comptes le convaincre?

8. À qui est-ce que nous pouvons demander le chemin?

 On n'est pas au courant. *Refaites les phrases suivantes en employant une des expressions avec* **je ne sais.** *Les deux phrases doivent signifier plus ou moins la même chose. Suivez le modèle.*

> MODÈLE   Elle va nous offrir quelque chose. Je n'ai pas la moindre idée de ce que c'est.
> → Elle va nous offrir je ne sais quoi.

1. Marc ne se souvient pas de la personne à qui il a donné le message.

2. On ignore avec quel professeur elle va parler.

3. Personne ne comprend pourquoi elles se sont mises en colère.

4. Personne ne savait combien de pilules le malade avait prises.

5. Je ne vois pas comment il a réussi aux examens.

6. On ne nous a pas dit quand nos cousins arriveraient.

I **En français, s'il vous plaît.** *Exprimez les idées suivantes en français. Faites attention aux particularités des mots indéfinis et négatifs.*

1. a. *You can find that bread in any bakery.*

   b. *There isn't any bakery around here.*

   c. *He works in some bakery.*

   d. *There are* **some** *bakeries in this neighborhood. Some are very good.*

2. a. *They're buying something.*

   b. *Are they buying anything?*

   c. *They're not buying anything.*

   d. *They're buying something (or other).*

   e. *They're not buying just anything.*

3. a. *We love these songs and are learning some of them.*

   b. *We're learning* **some** *songs.*

   c. *We can learn any songs.*

   d. *We can learn any one.*

   e. *We didn't learn any song (at all).*

4. a. *We can leave anytime.*

   b. *They're going to leave at some time or other.*

5. a. *Anyone can do that.*

   b. *No one can do that.*

   c. *Some can do that, others can't.*

Indefinite Words and Expressions (Continued)

When an indefinite or negative word or expression is followed by an adjective, the preposition **de** is placed between them. The adjective is always masculine singular.

quelqu'un/personne d'intelligent	*someone/no one intelligent*
quelque chose/rien de délicieux	*something/nothing delicious*
un je ne sais quoi de fascinant	*something fascinating*
Quoi de neuf?	*What's new?*

The phrase **d'autre** translates *else* with **quelqu'un**, **quelque chose**, **personne**, **rien**, and **quoi**: **quelqu'un/quelque chose/rien d'autre** (*someone/something/nothing else*), **Quoi d'autre?** (*What else?*). Note also **ailleurs** (*elsewhere*) and **nulle part ailleurs** (*nowhere else*).

De followed by a masculine singular adjective is also used after **qu'est-ce qu'il y a** and **ce qu'il y a**.

Qu'est-ce qu'il y a de plus amusant pour les enfants que le guignol?	**What is more fun** for children than a puppet show?

The word **chaque** means *each*. The corresponding pronoun (*each one*) is **chacun**, **chacune**.

—Avez-vous apporté quelque chose pour **chaque** enfant?	*Have you brought something for **each** child?*
—Oui, j'ai un cadeau pour **chacun**.	*Yes, I have a gift for **each** (one).*

The word **tout** has several uses in French. As an adjective it has four forms: **tout**, **toute**, **tous**, **toutes**.

- When **tout** directly precedes a singular noun, it means *every*.

Tout enfant doit aller à l'école.	**Every child** must go to school.

This is similar in meaning to **tous/toutes** + definite article + plural noun.

Tous les enfants doivent aller à l'école.	**All children** must go to school.

- **Tout/toute** + definite article + singular noun means *all the, the whole*. Compare **toute la ville** (*the whole city*) with **toute ville** (*every city*).

- Study the meanings of **tous/toutes les** + number.

Il vient **tous les trois mois**.	He comes **every three months** (**every third month**).
Prenez. C'est pour **tous les deux**.	Take it. It's for **both of you**.
Nous sommes sortis **tous les quatre**.	**All four of us** went out.

- **Tout** as a pronoun means *everything*.

J'espère que **tout** va bien.	I hope **everything** is all right.
Tout est en règle.	**Everything** is in order.

- **Tous** as a pronoun (final **-s** pronounced) means *everyone*. It is followed by a plural verb when it is the subject of the sentence.

Ils sont **tous** revenus.	They **all** came back.
Tous ont demandé de vous voir.	**Everyone** has asked to see you.

Tout le monde + singular verb is the most common way to express *everyone*. To express *the whole world*, French uses **le monde entier**.

Tout le monde a demandé de te voir.	**Everyone** has asked to see you.

- **Tout** as an adverb before an adjective means *quite, completely, fully*. It is invariable (**tout**, pronounced /tu/ (/tut/ before a vowel)) before a singular or plural masculine adjective, but shows gender and number agreement with a following feminine adjective. These agreements indicate that before a feminine adjective **tout** is pronounced /tut/.

Il est **tout** content.	He's **quite** happy.
Elle est **toute** contente.	She's **quite** happy.
Ces logiciels sont **tout** neufs.	These software packages are **brand** new.
Ces maisons sont **toutes** neuves.	These houses are **brand** new.

Before a feminine adjective beginning with a vowel or mute **h**, the agreement of **tout** in writing is optional, since the final **-t** is pronounced before the following vowel (*liaison*).

Elle a été **tout(e)** étonnée.	She was **thoroughly** amazed.
Elles sont **tout(es)** heureuses.	They are **completely** happy.

J **À compléter.** *Choisissez parmi les possibilités proposées celle qui complète correctement la phrase.*

1. Le médecin m'a dit de ne rien manger _____ sucré. (quelque chose / de / no word required)

2. Si Jean-Marc ne peut pas le faire, on va demander à quelqu'un _____. (d'autre / autre / ailleurs)

3. _____ étudiante doit rédiger une composition. (Chacune / Toutes les / Chaque / Chacun)

4. Je ne veux aller nulle part _____. (d'autre / autrement / ailleurs / autre)

5. Il y a trois belles églises dans la ville et nous les avons visitées _____. (tous / toutes / tout / chacune / chaque)

K   *En français, s'il vous plaît!* *Exprimez les phrases suivantes en français.*

1. *Everyone is happy now.*

2. *He takes a business trip every three weeks.*

3. *Give us something good to eat, Mom!*

4. *You should contact someone else.*

5. *I have three little (female) cousins and I want to buy a doll for each.*

6. *Every café serves croissants.*

7. *There's (= Il a…) something frightening (effrayant) about him.*

Idioms and Expressions with Negative and Indefinite Words

Expressions with jamais

à jamais	*forever*
à tout jamais	*forever and ever*
Jamais deux sans trois.	*Misfortunes always come in three's.*
Jamais de la vie!	*Not on your life!*
Il n'en manque jamais une!	*He's always blundering. He always puts his foot in it.*

Expressions with quelque(s)

Il est trois heures et quelques.	*It's a little past three.*
Je suis quelque peu déçu.	*I'm a little disappointed.*

Expressions with ni… ni

Cette histoire n'a ni queue ni tête.	*This story doesn't make any sense at all.*
Cela ne me fait ni chaud ni froid.	*It's all the same to me. I don't feel strongly about it.*

Expressions with rien

De rien.	*You're welcome.*
Ça ne fait rien.	*It doesn't matter. That's OK.* (answer to **Pardon.**)
Comme si de rien n'était.	*As if nothing had happened.*
Si cela ne vous fait rien.	*If you don't mind.*
Rien qu'à le voir, on sait qu'il est gentil.	*Just by looking at him, you know he's nice.*
Je veux te parler, rien que cinq minutes.	*I want to talk to you; it'll take just five minutes.*
Tu dis ça rien que pour m'embêter.	*You're saying that just to annoy me.*
Ce n'est pas pour rien qu'il t'a dit ça.	*It's not without good reason that he told you that.*
Rien ne sert de pleurer.	*It's no use crying.*
Cet article n'a rien à voir avec nos recherches.	*This article has nothing to do with our research.*

Il a peur d'un rien.   *He's afraid of every little thing.*
Un rien la fait rire.   *She laughs at every little thing.*
Moi, j'y mettrais un rien de poivre.   *I'd add a dash of pepper.*
C'est un/une rien du tout.   *He/She is a nobody. He/She is a worthless*
                                         person.

Expressions with **chacun**

Chacun son goût. / Chacun ses goûts.   *Everyone to his own taste.*
Chacun pour soi!   *Every man for himself!*
Chacun à son tour.   *Each one in his turn.*
Tout un chacun.   *Anyone at all. Everyone.*

Expressions with **certain**

d'un certain âge   *middle-aged*
Elle a un certain charme.   *She has a certain charm.*

Expressions with **ailleurs**

d'ailleurs   *moreover, besides*
partout ailleurs   *everywhere else*
Il est ailleurs. / Il a l'esprit ailleurs.   *He's miles away (not paying attention).*

Expressions with **nul**, etc.

un travail nul   *a worthless piece of work*
une composition nulle   *a worthless composition*
faire match nul   *to tie (sports)*
Il est nul/Elle est nulle en philosophie.   *He's/She's a very poor philosophy student.*
C'est une vraie nullité.   *He's (She's) a real wash-out.*

L   *Comment l'exprimer?* Choisissez la possibilité qui exprime l'idée indiquée.

1. *You want to tell a friend that he's not paying attention.*
   a. Tu es une vraie nullité.
   b. Tu as l'esprit ailleurs.

2. *You want to say that a certain place is not very selective in its admission policies.*
   a. On admet tout un chacun.
   b. C'est un rien du tout.

3. *You want to say that a friend is always making serious errors in judgment.*
   a. Rien qu'à le voir, on s'en rend compte.
   b. Il n'en manque jamais une.

4. *You react to a story that makes no sense to you.*
   a. Cette histoire n'a ni queue ni tête.
   b. Cette histoire ne me fait ni chaud ni froid.

5. *You reassure someone who said "excuse me" because he thought he stepped on your toe.*
   a. Si cela ne vous fait rien.
   b. Cela ne fait rien.

6. *You tell someone that you won't take much of her time.*
   a. Rien que cinq minutes.
   b. Une heure et quelques.

7. *You tell someone it's no use crying.*
   a. Rien ne sert de pleurer.
   b. Tu pleures pour un rien.

8. *You want to say that Mr. X is a nobody.*
   a. C'est un rien du tout.
   b. C'est un travail nul.

9. *You want to express a categorical refusal.*
   a. Comme si de rien n'était.
   b. Jamais de la vie!

10. *You want to deny any connection between something and yourself.*
    a. Cela ne me fait rien du tout.
    b. Ça n'a rien à voir avec moi.

M *Qu'est-ce que cela veut dire?* *Choisissez la possibilité qui exprime la même idée que la première phrase.*

1. Un rien l'effraie.
   a. Rien ne l'effraie.
   b. Tout l'effraie.

2. Mets un rien de sel dans la soupe.
   a. La soupe a besoin d'un peu de sel.
   b. Ne mets plus de sel dans la soupe.

3. C'est un homme d'un certain âge.
   a. Il a environ cinquante ans.
   b. Je sais exactement quel âge il a.

4. Il fait ça rien que pour nous faire peur.
   a. Il évite de faire des choses qui nous feraient peur.
   b. La seule raison pour laquelle il fait ça est pour nous faire peur.

5. Ils ont fait match nul.
   a. Les deux équipes n'ont pas joué.
   b. Les deux équipes ont eu le même nombre de points.

6. Rien qu'à l'entendre, on sait qu'elle a du talent.
   a. Si tu l'entendais seulement, tu te rendrais compte de son talent.
   b. En l'entendant, tu te rends compte qu'elle n'a pas de talent.

7. Il est trois heures et quelques.
   a. Il est presque quatre heures.
   b. Il est entre trois heures et trois heures dix.

8. Ce n'est pas pour rien que je t'ai dit ça.
   a. Je n'ai dit ça pour aucune raison.
   b. J'avais une très bonne raison pour te le dire.

Prepositions; Prepositions with Geographical Names

The Preposition à

A preposition is a word that links two elements of a sentence: **le livre** *de* **Janine**, **entrer** *dans* **la cuisine**, **parler** *à* **lui**, **finir** *de* **travailler**.

The preposition **à** has many uses in French. Remember its contractions: **à** + **le** → **au**, **à** + **les** → **aux**. **À** is also used before infinitives in many constructions (see Chapter 12). In addition, the preposition **à**

- Expresses direction and location in space

aller **à la banque**	*to go **to the bank***
être **à la banque**	*to be **at the bank***

- Labels distance in time and space

habiter **à quinze kilomètres de** Paris	*to live **fifteen kilometers from** Paris*
être **à trois heures de** Marseille	*to be **three hours from** Marseilles*

- Expresses the point in time at which something happens (clock time, age)

arriver **à 7 heures du soir**	*to arrive **at seven in the evening***
à dix-huit ans	*at **(the age of) eighteen years***
À quelle heure le train part-il?	***What time** does the train leave?*

- Expresses the manner or style in which something is done

manger **à la française**	*to eat **French style***
coucher **à quatre dans une chambre**	*to sleep **four to a room***

- Labels the principal ingredient in a dish or a characteristic feature of someone or something

un sandwich **au fromage**	*a **cheese** sandwich*
une glace **aux fraises**	***strawberry** ice cream*
la femme **au chapeau**	*the woman **in (wearing) the hat***
une chemise **à manches longues**	*a **long-sleeved** shirt*

- Expresses possession or belonging to someone

Ce stylo est **au prof.**	*This pen is **the teacher's**.*
C'est bien gentil **à toi.**	*That's really nice **of you**.*

■ Expresses the means by which something is done

fait **à la main**	*made **by hand***
aller **à bicyclette**	*to go **by bike***
aller **à pied**	*to go **on foot***
écrire **au crayon**	*to write **in pencil***

■ Is used in expressions of measurement

faire du 70 **à l'heure**	*to do 70 kilometers **an hour***
vendre **au kilo**	*to sell **by the kilogram***
vendre **au mètre**	*to sell **by the meter***
être payé **au mois**	*to be paid **by the month***
un à un	*one by one*
peu à peu	*little by little*

■ Indicates the purpose for which an object is intended

une tasse **à** thé	*a teacup*
sandwichs **à** emporter	*sandwiches to take out*

The preposition **à** also

■ Is used with nouns derived from verbs or with infinitives as a replacement for a subordinate clause

à mon arrivée	*when I got there* (*upon my arrival*)
à notre retour	*when we got back* (*upon our return*)
à l'entendre chanter	*when I heard him/her sing* (*upon hearing him/her sing*)
à la réflexion	*if you think about it* (*on second thought*)

■ Translates as *at* and *to* with certain nouns

à la demande de tous	***at** everyone's request*
à ma grande surprise/joie	***to** my great surprise/joy*
à sa consternation	***to** his dismay*

■ Expresses a standard for judging or knowing (and means *by, according to, from*)

reconnaître quelqu'un **à sa voix**	*to recognize someone **by his/her voice***
juger quelque chose **aux résultats**	*to judge something **by the results***
À ce que j'ai compris, il ne viendra pas.	***From what I understood**, he won't come.*

Some Idioms and Useful Expressions with the Preposition à

Location (Spatial and Figurative)

à côté	*next door, nearby*
à côté de	*next to*
à deux pas de chez moi	*right near my house*
être à la page	*to be up to date*
à la une	*on the front page*
Je ne me sens pas à la hauteur.	*I am not qualified for (equal to) the task.*
Qui est à l'appareil?	*Who's calling?*

Time

à la fois	*at the same time, at once*
à l'instant	*a moment ago*
à ses heures (libres)	*in one's free time*
à plusieurs reprises	*several times*
à tout moment	*all the time*

Manner

à souhait	*according to your wishes, as you would like it*
aimer quelqu'un à la folie	*to be mad/wild about someone*
à juste titre	*rightfully*
à l'endroit	*right side out* (of clothing)
à l'envers	*inside out* (of clothing)
être à l'étroit	*to be cramped for space*
étudier quelque chose à fond	*to study something thoroughly*
lire à haute voix	*to read aloud*
un vol à main armée	*armed robbery*
à la perfection	*perfectly, just right*
à titre confidentiel	*off the record*
à titre de père	*as a father, in my role as a father*
à tort	*wrongfully*
à tour de rôle	*in turn*

Price, Purpose, and Degree

avoir quelque chose à bon compte	*to get something cheap*
faire les choses à moitié	*to do things halfway*
à peine	*hardly*
acheter quelque chose à prix d'or	*to pay through the nose for something*
à tout prix	*at all costs*
à la longue	*in the long run*
tout au plus	*at the very most* (final **-s** of **plus** pronounced)

Sentences, Interjections, and Exclamations

au fait	*by the way*
à propos	*by the way*
À votre santé!	*To your health!*
À la poubelle!	*Get rid of it! Throw it out!*
Au feu!	*Fire!*
Au voleur!	*Stop! Thief!*
À la ligne.	*New paragraph.* (in dictation)
À quoi bon?	*What's the use?*
À suivre.	*To be continued.*
Au suivant!	*Next! Who's next?*

A ***Expliquez les différences.*** *Comprenez-vous la différence de sens qui existe entre les deux expressions de chaque paire? Expliquez-la en anglais.*

1. à la une / à la page

2. à plusieurs reprises / à la fois

3. à l'étroit / à la hauteur

4. une bouteille à lait / une bouteille de lait

5. au suivant / à suivre

B ***Synonymes ou antonymes?*** *Indiquez si les expressions suivantes sont synonymes ou antonymes.*

1. à juste titre / à tort

2. à tort / à la perfection

3. à l'appareil / au téléphone

4. à l'endroit / à l'envers

5. à propos / au fait

6. à bon compte / à prix d'or

7. à tour de rôle / tour à tour

C ***Comment est-ce que cela se dit?*** *Exprimez ces expressions en français.*

1. *chocolate ice cream*

2. *the man in the blue suit*

3. *to our great sadness*

4. *to sell by the pound*

5. *to recognize someone by his voice*

6. *off the record*

7. *in one's free time*

8. *to read aloud*

9. *two hundred meters from the movie theater*

10. *the girl with blond hair*

11. *in turn*

12. *at the very most*

D *On cause.* *Complétez ces échanges avec les expressions qui manquent.*

1. a. —Tu as le journal. Qu'est-ce qu'il y a _____? (*on the front page*)

   b. —Un vol _____ dans le métro. (*armed*)

2. a. —Tu sais, papa, j'aime Philippe _____. (*madly*)

   b. —Babette, ma fille, _____, je te dirai que tu es trop jeune. (*as a father*)

3. a. —Tu as eu cette robe _____? (*at a good price*)

   b. —Au contraire! Je l'ai achetée _____! (*through the nose*)

4. a. —Marie-Claude a appris son rôle _____. (*perfectly*)

   b. —Oui, elle ne fait pas les choses _____. (*halfway*)

The Preposition **de**

Like **à**, the preposition **de** has many uses in French. Remember its two contractions: **de** + **le** → **du**, **de** + **les** → **des**. **De** is also used as the partitive article (see Chapter 13) and before infinitives in many constructions (see Chapter 12). It also

- Expresses possession

le livre **de l'étudiant**	the **student's** book
les rues **de Paris**	the streets **of Paris**
le contenu **du livre**	the contents **of the book**

- Expresses starting point or origin

partir **de Paris**	to leave **from Paris**
sortir **de la boutique**	to go out **of the shop**
le train **de Lyon**	the train **from/to Lyons**
Il est **du Sénégal**.	He's **from Senegal**.

- Expresses the contents of something

une tasse **de thé**	a cup **of tea**
une collection **de poupées**	a **doll** collection

- Labels the characteristic feature of something (The English equivalent is often a compound noun (noun + noun).)

la société **de consommation**	the **consumer** society
une classe **d'anglais**	an **English** class

- Labels the cause of something

mourir **de faim**	to die **of hunger**
fatigué **du voyage**	tired **from the trip**

- Is used in the construction **changer de** + singular noun to express *to change* + singular or plural noun

changer **de train**	to change **trains**
changer **d'avion**	to change **planes**

changer **de direction**	*to change* **direction**
changer **d'avis/d'idée**	*to change* **one's mind**
changer **de vêtements**	*to change* **clothes**

- Labels the means

écrire **de la main gauche**	*to write* **with one's left hand**
faire quelque chose **de ses propres mains**	*to do something* **with one's own hands**

- Is used in many expressions of measurement

un bifteck **de 500 grammes**	*a* **five-hundred-gram** *steak*
une route longue **de 30 kilomètres**	*a* **thirty-kilometer**-*long road*
augmenter son salaire **de 1000 francs**	*to raise his/her salary* **by 1000 francs**
plus grand(e) **d'une tête**	*a* **head** *taller*
Ce fleuve a **850 mètres de large** et **100 mètres de profondeur**.	*This river is* **850 meters wide** *and* **100 meters deep**.

- Introduces phrases that express the manner in which something is done

connaître quelqu'un **de vue**	*to know someone* **by sight**
répéter **de mémoire**	*to repeat* **from memory**

- Introduces nouns in apposition

la région **de Bourgogne**	*the* **Burgundy** *region*
le nom **de Maubrey**	*the name* **Maubrey**
Quel temps **de chien!**	*What* **lousy** *weather!*

- Is used in some expressions of place and time

de ce côté	*on this side*
de l'autre côté	*on the other side*
du côté de la bibliothèque	*in the direction of the library*
de côté et d'autre	*here and there; on both sides*
du temps de Napoléon	*in Napoleon's time*
de nos jours	*in our day*
travailler **de** jour/nuit	*to work days/nights*
Ils n'ont rien fait **de** toute l'année.	*They've done nothing all year.*
Je n'ai rien fait de pareil **de** toute ma vie.	*I've done nothing like that in my entire life.*

Some Idioms and Useful Expressions with the Preposition de

Time

d'abord	*first*
trois jours de suite	*three days in a row*
de bonne heure	*early*
de bon matin	*early in the morning*

Appositions

C'est un drôle de numéro.	*He/She is a strange character.*
C'est une drôle d'idée.	*It's a strange idea.*
Espèce d'imbécile!	*You idiot!*

Origin, Manner, and Other Categories

du coup	*as a result*
ne pas être d'attaque	*not to feel up to it*
d'autre part	*on the other hand*
poser une question de but en blanc	*to ask a question just like that/point-blank/ suddenly*
se heurter de face/front	*to collide head-on*
un billet de faveur	*complimentary ticket*
du reste	*moreover*
C'est de la part de qui, s'il vous plaît?	*Who's calling, please?*
Cette pièce sert d'étude.	*This room is used as a study.*

E *Est-ce à ou de?* *Complétez ces phrases avec* **à** *ou* **de**. *Si aucune préposition n'est nécessaire, mettez un* X. *N'oubliez pas que dans certains cas il faudra employer les contractions* **au**, **aux**, **du**, **des**.

1. Elle est contente _____ notre travail.

2. J'ai soif. Je vais acheter une bouteille _____ jus de pomme.

3. Tu prends ton thé dans un verre _____ vin? Comme c'est bizarre.

4. Si tu veux écrire à tes parents, je te donnerai du papier _____ lettres.

5. Je lui ai demandé s'il voulait m'accompagner. Il a fait «non» _____ la tête.

6. _____ l'aide! Je suis tombé et je ne peux pas me lever!

7. Nous n'avons rien fait _____ toute la semaine.

8. Nous allons _____ côté de la place. Tu viens avec nous?

9. Ma chambre est longue _____ quatre mètres et a trois mètres _____ large.

F *Expliquez les différences.* *Comprenez-vous la différence de sens qui existe entre les deux expressions de chaque paire? Expliquez-la en anglais.*

1. de suite / à suivre

2. de hauteur / à la hauteur

3. à côté / de côté

4. Il est au Japon. / Il est du Japon.

5. une corbeille à papier / une corbeille de papier

6. travailler de jour / travailler à la journée

G *La vie en famille.* *Mme Gilbert écrit à son amie Vivienne Mauriac pour lui donner des nouvelles de sa famille. Pour savoir ce qu'elle dit, complétez sa lettre avec des prépositions ou des phrases commençant par* **à** *ou* **de**.

Ma chère Vivienne:

Tu me pardonneras de ne pas avoir écrit avant. Tout va très bien ici. Les enfants

grandissent. Mon fils Paul est déjà plus grand que moi _____ (1. *by a head*). Il dit qu'il

veut être pilote. C'est une _____ (2. *strange idea*), n'est-ce pas? J'espère qu'il va

_____ (3. *change his mind*).

Brigitte étudie à la _____ (4. *medical school*). Elle se lève tous les jours

_____ (5. *early in the morning*) pour lire. Ses cours sont difficiles et il faut qu'elle étudie

tout _____ (6. *thoroughly*). Paul va au lycée qui est _____ (7. *right near*) de chez nous.

Mon mari voyage beaucoup pour affaires. Demain il revient _____ (8. *from*) New York

et la semaine prochaine il prend le train _____ (9. *for*) Genève où il va passer une semaine.

Il n'a jamais autant voyagé _____ (10. *in his whole life*).

Et toi, qu'est-ce que tu deviens? J'attends de tes nouvelles avec impatience. Écris-moi.

Toutes mes amitiés,

Sylvie

H *Comprenez-vous?* *Laquelle des deux possibilités signifie plus ou moins la même chose que l'expression donnée?*

1. C'est un drôle de numéro.
   a. C'est une personne bizarre.
   b. Elle n'a pas de numéro de téléphone.

2. Je la connais de vue.
   a. Je la vois.
   b. Je sais qui c'est quand je la vois.

3. Jacquot est plus petit de trois centimètres.
   a. Jacquot mesure trois centimètres de moins que quelqu'un.
   b. Jacquot mesure moins de trois centimètres.

4. l'idiot de son mari
   a. Son mari est un idiot.
   b. Son mari a un idiot.

5. du côté de la gare
   a. tout près de la gare
   b. vers la gare

6. On a donné un billet de faveur à Marc.
   a. Marc n'a pas payé le billet.
   b. Marc n'a pas voulu le billet.

7. Il m'a posé la question de but en blanc.
   a. Il a hésité à me poser la question.
   b. Il m'a posé la question brusquement.

8. Mon oncle m'a servi de professeur de maths.
   a. Mon oncle a trouvé quelqu'un pour m'enseigner les maths.
   b. Mon oncle m'a enseigné les maths lui-même.

9. C'est une classe d'arabe.
   a. Les étudiants sont arabes.
   b. On y enseigne l'arabe.

10. C'est de la part de qui?
    a. Qui est à l'appareil?
    b. Qui est celui qui part?

The Prepositions **avec** and **sans**

The preposition **avec** expresses accompaniment, much like English *with*.

Attends, j'irai **avec toi**.	*Wait, I'll go **with you**.*
Je suis d'accord **avec vous**.	*I agree **with you**.*

Avec also

- Labels the cause of something

Avec l'inflation, tout le monde parle des prix.	***With inflation**, everyone is talking about prices.*
J'ai peur de conduire **avec toute cette neige**.	*I'm afraid to drive **with all this snow**.*

- Expresses *in addition to*

Et **avec cela (ça)**, madame?	***Anything else**, ma'am? (in a store)*
Il n'a pas étudié et **avec ça** il a séché le cours.	*He didn't study, and **on top of that** he cut class.*

Avec + noun is often the equivalent of an English adverb, as reviewed in Chapter 20.

avec joie	*joyfully*
avec colère	*angrily*

The preposition **sans** is the equivalent of English *without*.

Notre équipe a dû jouer **sans** notre meilleur joueur.	*Our team had to play **without** our best player.*
Sans argent on ne peut rien faire.	***Without** money, you can't do anything.*
Je me suis couché **sans** avoir fini mon travail.	*I went to bed **without** having finished my work.*

Sans can mean *if it weren't for . . .* or *but for . . .*

Sans ce plan, on se serait perdus.	***If it weren't for this street map**, we would have gotten lost.*

The preposition **sans** + noun is often the equivalent of an English adjective ending in -*less* or an adjective with a negative prefix such as *un-* or *in-*.

sans abri	*homeless*
sans domicile fixe (S.D.F.)	*homeless*
une situation **sans remède**	*a **hopeless** situation*
un film **sans intérêt**	*an **uninteresting** film*
une femme **sans préjugés**	*an **unprejudiced/unbiased** woman*
sans doute	*doubtless, doubtlessly*
sans effort	*effortless, effortlessly*

The use of **sans** with negative words eliminates the need for **ne**. The partitive article often becomes **de** after **sans** because of the implied negative meaning of the preposition.

sans parler à **personne**	***without** speaking to **anyone***
sans rien faire	***without** doing **anything***
sans jamais l'avoir vu	***without ever** having seen him*
sortir **sans** faire **de** bruit	*to go out **without** making **any** noise*

Some Idioms and Useful Expressions with the Prepositions **avec** and **sans**

se lever avec le jour	*to get up at the crack of dawn*
se fâcher avec quelqu'un	*to get angry with someone*
prendre des gants avec quelqu'un	*to handle someone with kid gloves*
se mettre en rapport/relation avec	*to get in touch with*
être sans le sou	*to be broke*
être sans travail/emploi	*to be out of work, be unemployed*
les sans-emploi	*the unemployed*
sans faute	*without fail*
sans plus	*that's all, nothing more*
sans aucun doute	*without a doubt*
sans ça	*otherwise*
être un sans-gêne	*to be inconsiderate*
sans oublier	*last but not least*
sans broncher	*without flinching*
Sans façons!	*Sincerely! Let's not stand on ceremony! I really mean it!*

I **Sans ou avec?** *Complétez les phrases françaises avec la préposition **sans** ou **avec** pour qu'elles aient à peu près le même sens que leur traduction anglaise.*

1. *He's an unimaginative man.* C'est un homme _____ imagination.

2. *She answered bitterly.* Elle a répondu _____ amertume.

3. *They write effortlessly.* Ils écrivent _____ effort.

4. *Come eat with us! I really mean it!* Viens manger avec nous! _____ façons!

5. *If it weren't for her, we wouldn't have finished the job.* _____ elle, nous n'aurions pas fini le travail.

6. *With the ice on the road, driving is difficult.* _____ le verglas, il est difficile de conduire.

7. *You have to handle him carefully.* Il faut le prendre _____ des gants.

8. *Don't go out barefoot.* Ne sors pas _____ chaussures.

9. *You have to speak sweetly to her.* Il faut lui parler _____ douceur.

10. *He threw himself into the fray unflinchingly.* Il s'est lancé au combat _____ broncher.

J **En français, s'il vous plaît!** *Donnez l'équivalent français de ces expressions. Utilisez* **avec** *ou* **sans** *dans chaque cas.*

1. *doubtless*	6. *lovingly*
2. *otherwise*	7. *kindly*
3. *to get up at the crack of dawn*	8. *broke, down and out*
4. *heartless*	9. *Anything else?*
5. *the unemployed*	10. *unhesitatingly*

The Prepositions **en** and **dans**

The prepositions **en** and **dans** both mean *in*. **En** is used directly before a noun; **dans** must be followed by an article (definite, indefinite, or partitive) or by some other determiner, such as a possessive or demonstrative adjective.

aller **en ville**	*to go **downtown***
dans la ville	*in the city*
être **en prison**	*to be **in jail***
dans cette prison	*in this jail*
habiter **en banlieue**	*to live **in the suburbs***
dans une banlieue éloignée	*in a distant suburb*

En is used to mean *as* or *like*.

Je te parle **en ami**.	*I'm speaking to you **as a friend**.*
Il agit **en prince**.	*He's acting **like a prince**.*

En also

- Expresses location within a period of time

en juillet	*in July*
en automne	*in the fall*
en 1996	*in 1996*
faire quelque chose **en** deux semaines	*to do something **in** two weeks*
de jour **en** jour	*from day to day, daily*

- Labels the means of transportation

voyager **en** train/avion	*to travel **by** train/plane*
rentrer **en** taxi/car	*to go back **by** cab/intercity bus*

- Marks condition or appearance

être **en** nage	*to be all sweated up*
être **en** bonne santé	*to be **in** good health*

être **en** pyjama	*to be **in** one's pajamas*
être **en** guerre	*to be **at** war*
en hâte	***in** a hurry*
en désordre	***in** disorder*
en pagaille	***in** a mess*
en jeu	***at** stake*

- Marks transformation into something else

transformer la ferme **en** atelier	*to transform the farm **into** a workshop*
se déguiser **en** prêtre	*to disguise oneself **as** a priest*
casser quelque chose **en** morceaux	*to break something **into** pieces*
traduire **en** italien	*to translate **into** Italian*

- Marks the material of which something is made (as does **de**)

un collier **en or**	*a **gold** necklace*
un couteau **en acier inoxydable**	*a **stainless steel** knife*
une jupe **en laine**	*a **wool** skirt*
C'est **en quoi?**	***What's** it **made of?***

- Is used before **plein** to mean *in the middle of*

en pleine ville	***right in the middle of** the city*
en plein hiver	***in the middle of** winter*
être **en plein** travail	*to be **in the middle of** one's work*

- Forms some common adverbial expressions

en haut/bas	*upstairs/downstairs*
en avant/arrière	*forward/backward*
en face	*opposite*
en tout cas	*in any case*
en plus	*besides, in addition*

Some Idioms and Useful Expressions with **en**

être en garde	*to be on guard*
être en tournée	*to be on tour (of a performer)*
être en vacances	*to be on vacation*
être en voyage	*to be on a trip*
en moyenne	*on the average*
croire en Dieu	*to believe in God*
avoir confiance en quelqu'un	*to have confidence in someone*
en direct	*live (TV/radio broadcast)*
en différé	*recorded (TV/radio broadcast)*
en danger	*in danger*
en semaine	*during the week*
être en pleine forme	*to be in good physical shape*
C'est sa mère en plus jeune.	*She's a younger version of her mother.*
Avez-vous cette serviette en cuir noir?	*Do you have this briefcase in black leather?*

Some Expressions in Which **en** Is Followed by an Article or Determiner

en l'honneur de	*in honor of*
en l'absence de	*in the absence of*
en mon nom	*in my name*
en sa faveur	*in his favor*

Dans is used to express location (English: *in*).

dans la boîte	***in** the box*
dans la rue	***in** the street*
dans la voiture	***in** the car*

Dans also

- Expresses location in time (English: *in, in the course of, during*)

dans la semaine	***during** the week* (cf. **en semaine**)
dans la journée	***during** the course of the day*
dans la soirée	***during** the course of the evening*
dans la matinée	***during** the morning*
dans l'après-midi	***during** the afternoon*
Tout sera prêt **dans** cinq jours.	*Everything will be ready **in** five days.*

- Expresses figurative location

dans la situation actuelle	***in** the present situation*
dans ces conditions	***given** these conditions*
être **dans** les affaires	*to be **in** business*

- Is used in contexts where English uses *from, on,* or *into*

boire **dans** une tasse	*to drink **from** a cup*
prendre quelque chose **dans** une boîte	*to take something **from** a box*
copier quelque chose **dans** un livre	*to copy something **from** a book*
dans l'avion	***on** the plane*
monter **dans** le train	*to get **on** the train*
mettre quelque chose **dans** le tiroir	*to put something **into** the drawer*
On s'est croisés **dans** l'escalier.	*We ran into each other **on** the stairs.*

Some Idioms and Useful Expressions with **dans**

partir/aller passer ses vacances dans les Alpes	*to leave for/spend one's vacation in the Alps*
errer dans les rues	*to wander through the streets*
errer dans la ville	*to wander through the city*
être dans le pétrin	*to be in a jam/fix*
coûter dans les mille euros	*to cost in the neighborhood of a thousand euros*
dans les coulisses	*behind the scenes*
dans le doute	*when in doubt*
dans le sens de la longueur	*lengthwise*

Ce n'est pas dans mes projets.

Qu'est-ce qui se passe dans sa tête?

I'm not planning to do that.

What's gotten into him? What can he be thinking of?

K **Est-ce en ou dans?** *Complétez les paragraphes suivants avec* **en** *ou* **dans**.

Le nouvel appartement des Truffaut

Les Truffaut ont acheté un nouvel appartement. Je crois qu'il leur a coûté (1) _____ les 500.000 mille euros. L'appartement n'est pas (2) _____ la ville de Paris parce qu'ils préfèrent habiter (3) _____ banlieue. Mais leur bureau est (4) _____ ville. Ils y vont (5) _____ train.

Christine Urbain parle de ses vacances

J'ai envie de partir (6) _____ vacances. J'aime passer mes vacances (7) _____ les Alpes. J'adore partir (8) _____ été. Il fait beau et je mets un short (9) _____ coton tous les jours. Je commence à faire mes préparatifs. Tout sera prêt (10) _____ cinq jours et je pourrai partir!

Un collègue en difficulté

Je ne sais pas ce qui se passe avec Édouard. Son bureau est (11) _____ pagaille. Lui qui était toujours (12) _____ pleine forme ne fait plus d'exercice. Je me demande ce qui se passe (13) _____ sa tête. Le chef n'a plus confiance (14) _____ lui. J'ai l'impression que son poste est (15) _____ jeu et Édouard ne semble pas s'en rendre compte.

Une réception diplomatique

Dimanche il y aura une réception (16) _____ l'honneur de l'ambassadeur du Maroc. La réception aura lieu (17) _____ l'après-midi. On invite (18) _____ moyenne une quarantaine de personnes. (19) _____ la situation actuelle, ces réceptions sont importantes. L'ambassade se trouve (20) _____ une rue tranquille.

L **Comment est-ce que cela se dit?** *Exprimez les expressions suivantes en français.*

1. *on the stairs*
2. *to be bathed in sweat*
3. *a taller version of his father*
4. *behind the scenes*
5. *upstairs*
6. *in the middle of the night*
7. *lengthwise*
8. *to be in a fix*
9. *to be in business*
10. *to be in pajamas*
11. *at war*
12. *What's it made of?*

Sur, sous, and Related Prepositions

Sur usually corresponds to English *on*, and **sous** corresponds to English *under*. However, there are cases where the two French prepositions have unexpected English equivalents.

Sur also

- Corresponds to English *at* or *in* in an expression of position

sur le stade	*at the stadium*
sur la place (du marché)	*at the marketplace*
sur la chaussée	*in the roadway*
sur le journal (*colloquial*)	*in the newspaper*
acheter quelque chose **sur** le marché	*to buy something at the market*
Il pleut **sur** toute la France.	*It's raining all over France.*

- Expresses approximate time

arriver **sur** les 3 heures	*to arrive at around 3 o'clock*
Elle va **sur** ses dix-huit ans.	*She's going on eighteen.*

- Expresses English *out of* in statements of proportion and measure

deux fois **sur** trois	*two times out of three*
une femme **sur** dix	*one woman in ten*
un jour **sur** trois	*every third day*
un lundi **sur** deux	*every other Monday*

- Labels the subject of a piece of writing or conversation (English: *about*)

un article **sur** la santé	*an article about health*
interroger le soldat **sur** son régiment	*to question the soldier about his regiment*

- Has many figurative and idiomatic uses

revenir **sur** ses pas	*to retrace one's steps*
être **sur** la bonne/mauvaise piste	*to be on the right/wrong track*
vivre les uns **sur** les autres	*to live one on top of the other*
La clé est restée **sur** la porte.	*The key was left in the door.*
Je n'ai pas les documents **sur** moi.	*I don't have the documents on me.*
Cet enfant a eu grippe **sur** grippe.	*This child has had one flu after the other.*
Il revient toujours **sur** la même question.	*He keeps going back to the same matter.*
Elle est revenue **sur** son idée.	*She thought better of it.*

Sous also

- Corresponds to English *at* or *in*

sous l'équateur	*at the equator*
sous la tente	*in the tent*
sous la pluie	*in the rain*
sous le soleil	*in the sunshine*

| avoir quelque chose **sous** les yeux | *to have something **before** one's eyes* |
| avoir quelque chose **sous** la main | *to have something **at** hand* |

- Expresses location in time, usually within a period or historical event

sous la Révolution	***at the time of** the Revolution*
sous le règne de Napoléon	***in** Napoleon's reign*
sous peu	*shortly*

- Has idiomatic uses

présenter **sous** un jour favorable	*to present **in** a favorable light*
sous peine d'amende	***on** penalty of a fine*
sous l'influence de	***under** the influence of*
sous une identité d'emprunt	***under** an assumed identity*
étudier la question **sous** tous les angles	*to study the question **from** every angle*

Sur and **sous** have corresponding adverbs: **dessus** (*over it, on top of it*) and **dessous** (*beneath it, underneath*).

| La chaise boîte. Ne mets pas ta valise **dessus**. | *The chair is uneven. Don't put your suitcase **on top of it**.* |
| Tu vois tous ces papiers? La lettre est **dessous**. | *Do you see all those papers? The letter is **underneath them**.* |

The adverbs have the compound forms **au-dessus** and **au-dessous**.

| habiter **au-dessus/au-dessous** | *to live **upstairs/downstairs*** |

Au-dessus de and **au-dessous de** are compound prepositions.

les enfants **au-dessus de** dix ans	*children **over** ten years of age*
rien **au-dessus de** 100 francs	*nothing **over** 100 francs*
les jeunes **au-dessous de** dix-huit ans	*young people **under** eighteen years old*
être **au-dessous de** sa tâche	*to be **not up to** one's task*
Il fait dix degrés **au-dessus de** zéro.	*It's ten degrees **above** zero.*
C'est **au-dessus de** mes forces.	*It's **too much** for me.*
Il croit que c'est **au-dessous de** lui de faire le ménage.	*He thinks that it's **beneath** him to do the housework.*

Par-dessus de and **en dessous de** also appear in some expressions.

par-dessus le marché	*on top of everything, in addition to everything*
faire quelque chose **en dessous**	*to do something underhanded*
être **en dessous** de la moyenne	*to be below average*
J'en ai **par-dessus** la tête.	*I'm fed up with it.*

Some Common Expressions with **dessus** and **dessous**

| aller bras dessus, bras dessous | *to walk arm in arm* |
| sens dessus-dessous | *topsy-turvy, in complete disorder* |

M *Exprimez en français!* *Écrivez les phrases suivantes en français.*

1. *I'm fed up with it.*

2. *Jacques and Marie walk arm in arm.*

3. *These students are below average.*

4. *The detective is on the right track.*

5. *We bought apples at the marketplace.*

6. *I like to take walks in the rain.*

7. *I'm free every other Saturday.*

8. *He works under an assumed identity.*

9. *She thinks work is beneath her.*

10. *Children below ten years of age don't pay.*

11. *It's too much for me.*

12. *He wrote an article about Tunisia.*

Entre, pour, and par

The preposition **entre** means *between*.

Il y a un jardin **entre** les deux maisons.	*There is a garden **between** the two houses.*

Entre also

- Has many figurative uses

entre parenthèses	*in parentheses*
entre guillemets	*in quotation marks*
entouré **entre** quatre murs	*shut in*
entre nous	*just between us*
Il n'y a rien de commun **entre** eux.	*They have nothing in common.*
J'ai cette revue **entre** les mains.	*I have that magazine in my hands.*

- Appears in some important idioms

entre chien et loup	*at twilight*
entre la poire et le fromage	*at the end of a meal*
parler **entre** ses dents	*to mumble*

Note the use of **d'entre** to translate *of* before a disjunctive pronoun after expressions of quantity, numbers, negative words, and interrogatives.

beaucoup **d'entre** nous	*many of us*
deux **d'entre** eux	*two of them*
personne **d'entre** nous	*none of us*
Qui **d'entre** vous?	*Who among you?*

The preposition **pour** usually translates into English as *for*.

J'ai apporté quelque chose **pour** toi.	*I've brought something for you.*

Pour means *for* with expressions of time. It usually indicates future time.

Je pars **pour** trois jours.	*I'm leaving for three days.*
J'en ai **pour** cinq minutes.	*I'll be done in five minutes.*

Pour also

- Means *to* or *in order to* before an infinitive

Tu ne dis ça que **pour** me fâcher.	*You're only saying that to make me angry.*

- Occurs in idiomatic expressions

garder le meilleur **pour** la fin	*to save the best for last*
un sirop **pour** la toux	*a cough syrup*
être **pour** la peine de mort	*to be for (in favor of) the death penalty*
Tant d'histoires **pour** si peu de chose!	*So much fuss over such a small thing!*
Et **pour** cause!	*And for good reason!*
Pour être fâché, je le suis!	*Talk about being angry, I am angry!*

Par usually translates into English as *through* or *by,* especially with the passive voice.

jeter quelque chose **par** la fenêtre	*to throw something out of the window*
un tableau peint **par** Louis David	*a picture painted by Louis David*
obtenir quelque chose **par** la force	*to get something by force*
Il est sortie **par** la porte de devant.	*He went out through the front door.*

Par also

- Denotes position in certain expressions of place and time

être/tomber **par** terre	*to be/fall on the ground*
deux fois **par** mois	*twice a month*
par les temps qui courent	*these days*
Tu ne vas pas sortir **par** un temps pareil!	*You're not going to go out in weather like this!*

- Occurs in idiomatic expressions

par ici	*this way*
par là	*that way*
par conséquent	*consequently*
par mégarde	*by accident*
par intervalles	*intermittently*
par cœur	*by heart*
faire quelque chose par amitié	*to do something out of friendship*
faire quelque chose par amour	*to do something out of love*
Il a fini par ennuyer tout le monde.	*He wound up annoying everyone.*

N   *La vie est parfois compliquée.* *Complétez les narrations suivantes avec les prépositions* **entre, pour** *ou* **par.**

La mère de Maurice est furieuse!

Ma mère est furieuse. (1) _____ être furieuse, elle l'est! Elle dit que c'est (2) _____ cause. Je vais vous dire ce qui s'est passé. J'étais avec mes amis. Il faisait très mauvais. Plusieurs (3) _____ nous sommes sortis (4) _____ la tempête. Moi, je me suis enrhumé. Maintenant je prends du sirop (5) _____ la toux et des pastilles (6) _____ la grippe. Et je garde le meilleur (7) _____ la fin. Ma mère a attrapé mon rhume. (8) _____ conséquent, elle prend le sirop et les pastilles avec moi.

Les problèmes de Philippe

(9) _____ nous, je crois que Philippe est déprimé. Il dit des bêtises (10) _____ mégarde et parle souvent (11) _____ ses dents. Il laisse ses papiers (12) _____ terre et il se fâche (13) _____ un rien. Il va finir (14) _____ ennuyer tout le monde.

Other Prepositions

Devant (*in front of*) and **derrière** (*behind*) are used to express position and location.

devant le lycée	***in front of*** *the high school*
derrière l'arbre	***behind*** *the tree*

Avant (*before*), like **après** (*after*), is used to talk about time.

avant huit heures	***before*** *eight o'clock*
après l'examen	***after*** *the test*

Avant becomes **avant de** before an infinitive.

avant de partir	***before*** *leaving*

Après is usually used with the perfect infinitive (**avoir** or **être** + past participle).

après avoir fini le travail	***after finishing*** *the work*
après être sorti(e)(s)	***after going out***

À travers means *through, across.*

partir **à travers** bois	*to set off* ***through*** *the woods*
voir le paysage **à travers** la vitre	*to see the scenery* ***through*** *the window*
partir **à travers** champs	*to set off* ***across*** *country*

Chez means *at the house of, at the store of,* or, figuratively, *with, among.*

passer le dimanche **chez mon oncle**	*to spend Sunday* ***at my uncle's house***
acheter du poulet **chez le boucher**	*to buy chicken* ***at the butcher's***
aller **chez le dentiste**	*to go* ***to the dentist***
C'est une coutume **chez les Allemands.**	*It's a custom* ***among the Germans.***

Contre means *against*.

s'appuyer **contre** le mur	*to lean **against** the wall*

Contre has other English equivalents in certain contexts.

se fâcher/être en colère **contre** quelqu'un	*to get/be angry **with** someone*
dix voix **contre** cinq	*ten votes **to** five*
échanger/troquer un livre **contre** un logiciel	*to exchange/swap a book **for** a software program*
Nous sommes tout à fait **contre**.	*We're totally **against** (it).*

Vers means *toward* in space and time; **envers** means *toward* figuratively, in the sense of an attitude or gesture toward someone.

aller **vers** Lille	*to go **toward** Lille*
vers cinq heures	***around** five o'clock*
votre gentillesse **envers** moi	*your kindness **toward** me*

Hors de and **en dehors de** mean *outside of* when referring to spatial position.

hors de l'appartement	***out of** the apartment*
en dehors de l'appartement	***outside (of)** the apartment*

Hors de and **hors** (in certain fixed expressions only) can be used figuratively.

hors d'haleine	***out of** breath*
hors de danger	***out of** danger*
hors jeu	***offside** (sports)*

Other Prepositions

à cause de *because of*	**parmi** *among*
au sujet de *about (on the subject of)*	**pendant** *during*
d'après *according to*	**près de** *near*
durant *during*	**quant à** *as for*
environ *about (approximately)*	**selon** *according to*
loin de *far from*	**suivant** *according to*
malgré *in spite of*	

O *Comprenez-vous? Écrivez l'équivalent anglais de ces phrases.*

1. On se verra vers 6 heures.

2. D'après le médecin, il n'est pas hors de danger.

3. On vit mieux en dehors de la ville.

4. Il a été très généreux envers ses enfants.

5. Elle regarde à travers la fenêtre.

6. Le professeur a parlé au sujet de l'examen.

7. Il me faut passer chez mon avocat.

8. Je te donne ces timbres contre cette pièce.

P   *Et en français?*   *Écrivez ces phrases en français.*

1. *according to the newspapers*
2. *during the class*
3. *in spite of the difficulty*
4. *near the station*
5. *as for me*
6. *three votes to two*

7. *about ten students*
8. *offside (out of play)*
9. *across country*
10. *with (among) French people*
11. *before going downstairs*
12. *after going downstairs*

Prepositions with Geographical Names

French uses the definite article before names of countries, provinces, regions, and continents.

    la France *France*   **le Midi** *the south of France*
    la Bretagne *Brittany*   **l'Europe** *Europe*

French uses the preposition **en** to express motion toward or location in a country (or province or region) if the place name is feminine singular. The definite article is not used.

    aller **en** Italie   *to go **to** Italy*
    partir **en** Pologne   *to leave **for** Poland*
    faire un voyage **en** Chine   *to take a trip **to** China*

En is also used before masculine singular countries beginning with a vowel. The definite article is not used.

    émigrer **en** Israël   *to emigrate **to** Israel*

NOTE **Israël** is not usually accompanied by the definite article: **Israël est un pays du Moyen-Orient.**

To express *from* with the above categories of place names, **de** or **d'** is substituted for **en**.

    revenir **d'**Italie   *to return **from** Italy*
    être **de** Pologne   *to be **from** Poland*
    partir **d'**Israël   *to leave **from** Israel*
    arriver **d'**Haïti   *to arrive **from** Haiti*

For masculine singular place names that do not begin with a vowel, and masculine and feminine plural place names, *to* or *in* is expressed by **à** plus the definite article (**au** or **aux**).

    aller/être **au** Portugal   *to go **to**/be **in** Portugal*
    aller/être **au** Japon   *to go **to**/be **in** Japan*
    aller/être **aux** États-Unis   *to go **to**/be **in** the United States*
    aller/être **aux** Antilles   *to go **to**/be **in** the West Indies*

To express *from* with the above place names, **de** plus the definite article (**du** or **des**) is used.

revenir **du** Danemark	*to come back **from** Denmark*
revenir **du** Canada	*to come back **from** Canada*
revenir **du** Viêt-nam	*to come back **from** Vietnam*
revenir **des** Pays-Bas	*to come back **from** the Netherlands*

With the names of most islands, French uses **à** (sometimes **à la** for feminine names) to express *to* and **de** (sometimes **de la**) to express *from*.

à (l'île) Maurice, **de** (l'île) Maurice	*to Mauritius, **from** Mauritius*
à la Réunion, **de la** Réunion	*to Reunion Island, **from** Reunion Island*
à Porto Rico, **de** Porto Rico	*to Puerto Rico, **from** Puerto Rico*
à la Guadeloupe, **de la** Guadeloupe	*to Guadeloupe, **from** Guadeloupe*
à la Martinique, **de la** Martinique	*to Martinique, **from** Martinique*

NOTE Some islands, however, take **en**: **en Sicile**, **en Corse**, **en Sardaigne**.

Before names of cities, French uses **à** to express *to* or *in* and **de** to express *from*.

à Montréal, **de** Montréal	*to/in Montreal, **from** Montreal*
à Genève, **de** Genève	*to/in Geneva, **from** Geneva*
à New York, **de** New York	*to/in New York, **from** New York*
à Saïgon, **de** Saïgon	*to/in Saigon, **from** Saigon*

Some cities have a definite article as part of their name: **Le Havre**, **La Rochelle**, **Le Caire** (*Cairo*), **La Havane** (*Havana*), **La Nouvelle-Orléans** (*New Orleans*). The article is kept when **à** or **de** is used with these names and the appropriate contractions are made.

Le Havre: **au** Havre, **du** Havre	*Le Havre: **to/in** Le Havre, **from** Le Havre*
La Rochelle: **à La** Rochelle, **de La** Rochelle	*La Rochelle: **to/in** La Rochelle, **from** La Rochelle*

All place names take the definite article when modified. **En** becomes **dans** when the article is used. The preposition **à** also changes to **dans** when the place name is modified.

> **dans** l'Europe du vingtième siècle   *in twentieth-century Europe*

French uses **en** to express *in* or *to* and **de** to express *from* before the following states that are grammatically feminine: **Californie**, **Caroline du Nord/Sud**, **Géorgie**, **Floride**, **Louisiane**, **Pennsylvanie**, **Virginie**, and **Virginie Occidentale**. The rest of the states are grammatically masculine, and either **dans le** or **au** may be used. Before states beginning with a vowel, **dans l'** or **en** may be used.

> **dans le** Texas, **au** Texas, **du** Texas
> **dans** l'Alabama, **en** Alabama, **de** l'Alabama, **d'**Alabama

Notice the differences in the prepositions used with provinces or states and cities with the same name.

le Québec, Québec	*Quebec Province, Quebec City*
au Québec, **à** Québec	*to/in Quebec Province, to/in Quebec City*
du Québec, **de** Québec	*from Quebec Province, from Quebec City*

Note also **le New York** (*New York State*) and **New York** (*New York City*), and **le Mexique** (*Mexico*) and **Mexico** (*Mexico City*).

Feminine Countries

l'Europe

l'Allemagne *Germany*	l'Espagne *Spain*	la République Tchèque
l'Angleterre *England*	la France *France*	*Czech Republic*
l'Autriche *Austria*	la Grèce *Greece*	la Russie *Russia*
la Belgique *Belgium*	l'Irlande *Ireland*	la Serbie *Serbia*
la Bosnie *Bosnia*	l'Italie *Italy*	la Slovaquie *Slovakia*
la Croatie *Croatia*	la Norvège *Norway*	la Suède *Sweden*
l'Écosse *Scotland*	la Pologne *Poland*	la Suisse *Switzerland*

l'Afrique

l'Afrique du Sud	l'Égypte *Egypt*	la Mozambique
South Africa	la Libye *Libya*	*Mozambique*
l'Algérie *Algeria*	la Mauritanie *Mauritania*	la Tunisie *Tunisia*
la Côte-d'Ivoire *Ivory Coast*		

l'Asie et l'Océanie

l'Arabie Saoudite	l'Inde *India*	les Philippines
Saudi Arabia	la Jordanie *Jordan*	*the Philippines*
l'Australie *Australia*	la Nouvelle-Zélande	la Syrie *Syria*
la Chine *China*	*New Zealand*	la Thaïlande *Thailand*
la Corée *Korea*		la Turquie *Turkey*

l'Amérique

les Antilles *West Indies*	la Colombie *Colombia*	la République Dominicaine
l'Argentine *Argentina*	Haïti *Haiti*	*Dominican Republic*

Masculine Countries

l'Europe

le Danemark *Denmark*	les Pays-Bas *Netherlands*
le Luxembourg *Luxemburg*	le Portugal *Portugal*

l'Afrique

le Congo *the Congo*	le Maroc *Morocco*	le Soudan *Sudan*
le Mali *Mali*	le Sénégal *Senegal*	le Zaïre *Zaire*

l'Asie et l'Océanie

le Cambodge *Cambodia*	Israël *Israel*	le Liban *Lebanon*
l'Irak *Iraq*	le Japon *Japan*	le Pakistan *Pakistan*
l'Iran *Iran*	le Koweït *Kuwait*	le Viêt-nam *Vietnam*

l'Amérique

le Brésil *Brazil*	le Chili *Chile*	le Mexique *Mexico*
le Canada *Canada*	les États-Unis	le Pérou *Peru*
	United States	

Q ***Des étudiants à l'étranger.*** *Un groupe de jeunes Belges fait un stage d'un an dans différents pays. Dites en chaque cas le pays et la ville où ils se trouvent. Suivez le modèle.*

> MODÈLE   Willie / France / Paris
> → Willie travaille en France, à Paris.

1. Monique / Canada / Québec

2. Olivier / États-Unis / La Nouvelle-Orléans

3. Mariek / Japon / Tokyo

4. Fernand / Brésil / Sao Paolo

5. Gérard / Mexique / Mexico

6. Stella / Haïti / Port-au-Prince

7. Luc / Sénégal / Dakar

8. Brigitte / Pays-Bas / Amsterdam

9. Sylvie / Égypte / Le Caire

10. Béatrice / Portugal / Lisbonne

11. Jan / Viêt-nam / Saïgon

12. Raymond / Israël / Jérusalem

R ***D'où sont-ils?*** *Faites des phrases pour exprimer l'origine de ces étudiants internationaux. Suivez le modèle.*

> MODÈLE   Jacques / France
> → Jacques est de France.

1. Fatima / Irak

2. Lise / Bruxelles

3. Martin et Santos / Chili

4. Sven / Danemark

5. Rosa et Laura / Naples

6. Mei-Li / Chine

7. Amalia / Mexico

8. Fred et Jane / Californie

9. Kimberly / Vermont

10. Odile / Luxembourg

11. Corazon / Philippines

12. Mies / Pays-Bas

13. Hanako et Hiro / Japon

14. Bill / États-Unis

15. Olivier / Le Havre

IV

Verbs in Two-Clause Sentences

Relative Clauses

The Relative Pronouns **qui** and **que**

A relative clause describes someone or something mentioned in the main clause. A relative clause begins with a relative pronoun, such as *who, whom, which,* or *that.* The noun that the relative pronoun refers to is called the antecedent. Relative clauses are in boldface italics in the examples below.

*the woman **who studies a lot***	*Who* is the relative pronoun; *woman* is the antecedent.
*the students **whom we helped***	*Whom* is the relative pronoun; *students* is the antecedent.
*the computer **that I use***	*That* is the relative pronoun; *computer* is the antecedent.

The French relative pronouns **qui** and **que** are used for both people and things. **Qui** is used when the relative pronoun is the subject of its clause. **Que** is used when the relative pronoun is the direct object of the verb in its clause.

la femme **qui étudie beaucoup**	**Qui** is the relative pronoun, subject of the verb **étudier**.
un ordinateur **qui est facile à utiliser**	**Qui** is the relative pronoun, subject of the verb **être**.
les étudiants **que nous avons aidés**	**Que** is the relative pronoun, direct object of the verb **aider**.
l'ordinateur **que j'ai utilisé**	**Que** is the relative pronoun, direct object of the verb **utiliser**.

NOTE In relative clauses introduced by **qui**, the verb agrees with **qui**, which has the same person and number as the antecedent.

Relative pronouns can never be omitted in French the way they often are in English.

l'homme **que** je connais	*the man (**whom**) I know*
les articles **que** je lis	*the articles (**that**) I read*

When the verb of the relative clause is in a compound tense conjugated with **avoir**, the past participle agrees with the relative pronoun **que**, which is a preceding direct object. The gender and number of **que** is determined by its antecedent.

les jeunes filles qu'il a invité**es**	*the girls whom he invited*
la robe que tu as mis**e**	*the dress you put on*

NOTE The relative pronoun **que** becomes **qu'** before a vowel or mute **h**.

When the verb of the relative clause is in a compound tense conjugated with **être**, the past participle agrees with the relative pronoun **qui**, because **qui** is the subject of the verb in the relative clause. The antecedent determines the gender and number of **qui**.

les étudiantes qui sont arrivé**es**	*the students who arrived*
l'assiette qui est tombé**e**	*the plate that fell*

A **Est-ce qui ou que?** *Complétez les phrases suivantes avec* **qui** *ou* **que**. *Toutes les phrases ont quelque chose à voir avec le monde du lycée.*

Le cours de philo

1. Voilà le professeur _____ enseigne le cours de philosophie.

2. C'est un cours _____ tout le monde aime bien.

3. Nous avons des lectures _____ sont très difficiles, mais passionnantes.

4. Les questions _____ le prof nous pose font penser.

5. Voilà Jean-Claude. C'est lui _____ reçoit les meilleures notes en philo.

6. Il dit que c'est une matière _____ le passionne.

7. Notre professeur est un homme _____ Jean-Claude admire beaucoup.

Le cours de chimie

8. Ma meilleure amie est une fille _____ s'appelle Géraldine.

9. C'est quelqu'un _____ je connais depuis longtemps.

10. C'est le cours de chimie _____ nous intéresse le plus.

11. Géraldine et moi, nous faisons tous les problèmes _____ le prof nous donne à résoudre.

12. Notre professeur est une femme _____ a écrit plusieurs livres de chimie.

13. Géraldine et moi, nous avons acheté un des bouquins _____ elle a écrit.

14. C'est un livre _____ est très utile pour l'étudiant.

15. C'est un livre _____ nous avons recommandé à tous nos amis.

16. Le prof de chimie est une femme _____ on respecte beaucoup.

B *Des précisions.* *Les propositions relatives, comme les adjectifs, servent à préciser, à identifier. Formez des propositions relatives pour mieux expliquer à votre ami(e) de qui ou de quoi il s'agit. Suivez les modèles.*

MODÈLES   Quel livre veux-tu? (Il y a un livre sur la table.)
→ Le livre qui est sur la table.

Quels gants est-ce Paulette va mettre? (Son petit ami lui a acheté des gants.)
→ Les gants que son petit ami lui a achetés.

La santé

agir *to work* (of medicine)	**ordonner** *to prescribe*
le cabinet *doctor's office*	**la pilule** *pill*
le centre diététique *health food store*	**la piqûre** *injection*
le comprimé *tablet*	**le régime** *diet*
conseiller *to advise, recommend*	**le sirop pour la toux** *cough syrup*
la crème *cream*	**suivre un régime** *to follow a diet*
donner le vertige à *to make dizzy*	**le vertige** *dizziness*
l'infirmière [fem.] *nurse*	**la vitamine** *vitamin*

1. Quel médecin est-ce que je dois aller voir? (Il a son cabinet dans ce bâtiment.)

2. Quels comprimés prends-tu? (Mon médecin m'a ordonné ces comprimés.)

3. Quel régime est-ce qu'il faut suivre? (J'ai trouvé un régime au centre diététique.)

4. Quel sirop pour la toux agit vite? (J'ai laissé un sirop sur la table.)

5. Quelle piqûre t'a fait mal? (L'infirmière m'a fait une piqûre hier.)

6. Quelles pilules t'ont donné le vertige? (J'ai pris les pilules hier.)

7. Quelle crème utilises-tu pour la peau? (Le pharmacien m'a conseillé une crème.)

8. Quelles vitamines prends-tu? (Les vitamines sont bonnes pour le cœur.)

C *Encore des précisions.* *La personne qui parle emploie des propositions relatives pour identifier la personne ou la chose à laquelle elle fait allusion. Suivez les modèles.*

MODÈLES   Quel ordinateur?
Olivier l'utilise.
→ L'ordinateur qu'Olivier utilise.
Il a beaucoup de mémoire.
→ L'ordinateur qui a beaucoup de mémoire.

1. Quel professeur?

a. Tous les étudiants l'adorent.

b. Il enseigne le français et l'espagnol.

c. Il vient de se marier.

d. Mes parents le connaissent.

2. Quelle maison?

   a. Jeanne et Richard l'ont achetée.

   b. Elle a un jardin et une piscine.

   c. On l'a construite en 1975.

   d. Elle est en briques.

3. Quels cadeaux?

   a. Mon frère et moi, nous les avons reçus il y a une semaine.

   b. Mon oncle et ma tante nous les ont envoyés.

   c. Je te les ai montrés hier.

   d. Ils t'ont beaucoup plu.

4. Quel restaurant?

   a. Nos amis l'ont ouvert l'année dernière.

   b. Il a une ambiance alsacienne.

   c. Il a des nappes rouges.

   d. Beaucoup d'artistes le fréquentent.

5. Quel sénateur?

   a. Le peuple l'a élu l'année dernière.

   b. Il a promis de combattre l'inflation.

   c. Il est marié avec une journaliste.

   d. Les ouvriers l'appuient.

Preposition + qui and lequel

The relative pronoun **qui** may serve as the object of a preposition. In such cases, it refers only to people. There is no agreement of the past participle in compound tenses when **qui** is preceded by a preposition.

l'homme **à qui** je donne le livre	*the man I'm giving the book **to***
la femme **à qui** nous pensons	*the woman **that** we're thinking **of***
les étudiants **à qui** j'ai parlé	*the students **whom** I spoke **to***

Lequel is the relative pronoun that refers primarily to things after a preposition. It agrees in gender and number with its antecedent.

	MASCULINE	FEMININE
SINGULAR	**lequel**	**laquelle**
PLURAL	**lesquels**	**lesquelles**

The prepositions **à** and **de** combine with the forms of **lequel** as follows.

	MASCULINE	FEMININE
SINGULAR	**auquel**, **duquel**	**à laquelle**, **de laquelle**
PLURAL	**auxquels**, **desquels**	**auxquelles**, **desquelles**

l'examen **auquel** j'ai réussi   *the test I passed* (**réussir à**)

la matière **à laquelle** je m'intéresse   *the subject I'm interested **in*** (**s'intéresser à**)

les bureaux **auxquels** vous téléphonez   *the offices you telephone* (**téléphoner à**)

les études **auxquelles** il s'applique   *the studies he applies himself **to*** (**s'appliquer à**)

D   ***Continuons à préciser.*** *Formez des phrases qui ont des propositions relatives commençant par* **à**. *N'oubliez pas la différence de construction qu'il faut respecter entre les antécédents animés et inanimés. Suivez le modèle.*

MODÈLE   Quel cours est bon? (J'ai assisté à un cours.)
      → Le cours auquel j'ai assisté.

1. Avec quelle fille Roland va-t-il sortir? (Il pense à une fille tout le temps.)

2. Quelle lettre vas-tu me montrer? (J'ai répondu à cette lettre.)

3. Quel débat as-tu écouté? (Nos copains ont pris part à ce débat.)

4. De quelles habitudes le médecin parle-t-il? (Il faut renoncer à ces habitudes.)

5. Avec quel homme est-ce qu'elle s'est mariée? (Elle se fiait à cet homme.)

6. Quels clients sont venus? (Nous avons téléphoné à ces clients.)

7. Quels détails aimez-vous? (Vous avez veillé à ces détails.)

8. Quelles méthodes as-tu recommandées? (Je crois à ces méthodes.)

E   ***Quel drame!*** *Complétez les phrases suivantes avec le pronom relatif convenable. Toutes les phrases font allusion aux éléments d'une histoire d'amour entre Élisabeth et Antoine.*

1. la lettre _____ Élisabeth a répondu

2. les parents _____ les deux jeunes gens n'ont pas obéi

3. le concert de rock _____ ils ont assisté

4. Georges, l'ami _____ Antoine se confiait

5. Odile, la fille _____ Antoine a connue dans la classe d'éducation civique

6. les rapports entre les deux _____ la jalousie d'Élisabeth a nui

7. les conversations avec Odile _____ Antoine a dû renoncer

8. la querelle d'amour _____ Georges s'est mêlé

9. la mauvaise situation _____ l'intervention de Georges a remédié

10. le rapprochement _____ a eu lieu entre Élisabeth et Antoine

Dont

The relative pronoun **dont** replaces the preposition **de** plus a relative pronoun. **Dont** immediately follows its antecedent and can refer to either people or things.

Dont is used when the verb or expression in the relative clause requires the preposition **de** before an object.

un professeur **dont** je me souviens	*a teacher (**whom**) I remember* (**se souvenir de**)
les affaires **dont** il s'occupe	*the matters **that** he's taking care **of*** (**s'occuper de**)
les employés **dont** j'ai besoin	*the employees **that** I need* (**avoir besoin de**)

Dont is used when **de** introduces a phrase that modifies another noun. (The English equivalent is usually *whose* or *of which*.)

un étudiant **dont** je connais les parents	*a student **whose** parents I know* (**les parents de l'étudiant**)
une idée **dont** on comprend l'importance	*an idea **whose** importance (the importance **of which**) we understand* (**l'importance de l'idée**)
un auteur **dont** j'ai lu tous les livres	*an author, all of **whose** books I have read* (**tous les livres de l'auteur**)

Notice the word order in the clause introduced by **dont**. Also notice that when **dont** is used to express possession, the definite article is used in place of a possessive adjective.

Dont is used with numbers and expressions of quantity.

des articles **dont** j'ai lu **quelques-uns**	*articles, **some of which** I've read* (**quelques-uns des articles**)
des étudiants **dont une dizaine** sont français	*some students, **about ten of whom** are French* (**une dizaine des étudiants**)
trois hommes **dont deux** médecins	*three men, **of whom two** are doctors* (**deux des trois hommes**)

De qui or **de** + a form of **lequel** may also be used to refer to people and things, but **dont** is usually the preferred form.

F   ***De qui s'agit-il exactement?*** *Précisez de qui il s'agit en employant une proposition relative qui commence par **dont**. Dans chaque cas, l'équivalent anglais commence par le mot whose. Suivez le modèle.*

MODÈLE   Quel journaliste? (Tout le monde lit ses articles.)
→ Le journaliste dont tout le monde lit les articles.

1. Quelle fille? (Sa mère est médecin.)

2. Quel ami? (Son oncle travaille au ministère.)

3. Quel sénateur? (Le pays entier a écouté son discours.)

4. Quels ouvriers? (Leur syndicat compte entreprendre une grève.)

5. Quels étudiants? (On a publié leur rapport.)

6. Quel professeur? (Son cours est toujours plein.)

7. Quelle infirmière? (Tout le monde admire son travail.)

8. Quelle programmeuse? (Ses logiciels se vendent très bien.)

9. Quels voisins? (Leurs enfants assistent à cette école.)

10. Quel groupe de rock? (Tous les jeunes écoutent ses chansons.)

 En une seule phrase, s'il vous plaît! *Faites de chaque paire de phrases une seule phrase en vous servant du pronom relatif convenable. Choisissez entre* **qui**, **que**, **à qui**, **auquel** *et* **dont**. *Suivez le modèle.*

> MODÈLE   La cordonnerie est le métier. Ils vivent de ce métier.
> → La cordonnerie est le métier dont ils vivent.

Un séjour dans une ville de province

1. Notre guide nous a montré un paysage. Nous nous sommes émerveillés de ce paysage.

2. Nous avons visité les murailles. La vieille ville est entourée de ces murailles.

3. Une amie nous a invités au festival de danse. Elle prenait part à ce festival.

4. Nous sommes allés voir une rue. On transformait cette rue en rue piétonne.

5. On est allés voir une comédie. On a beaucoup ri de cette comédie.

6. Nous avons essayé la cuisine régionale. La ville se vante de sa cuisine.

7. On nous a signalé l'absence d'une université. Nous nous sommes aperçus de cette absence.

8. C'est la vie universitaire. La ville manquait de vie universitaire.

9. Nous avions des amis dans la région. Nous avons téléphoné à ces amis.

10. Nous avons passé une belle journée avec eux. Nous nous souvenons encore de cette journée.

Une crise dans l'administration nationale

11. La crise est arrivée. Tout le monde avait peur de cette crise.

12. Un ministre faisait mal les fonctions. Il était responsable de ces fonctions.

13. C'était un homme respecté. Personne ne se doutait de lui.

14. Ce ministre est un homme bien en vue (*prominent*). La nation entière se fiait à lui.

15. On dit qu'il a donné des emplois à des gens non qualifiés. Plusieurs de ces gens étaient ses parents et amis.

16. Ils faisaient un travail. On commençait à se plaindre de ce travail.

17. Il y avait cent employés au ministère. On a congédié une trentaine de ces employés.

18. C'est la confiance de la nation. Le ministre a abusé de la confiance de la nation.

Other Relatives

Relative pronouns may follow other prepositions besides **à** and **de**. The relative pronoun **qui** is used to refer to people after all prepositions except **entre** and **parmi**. **Lequel** can be used to refer to both people and things, although **qui** is usually preferred for people. After **entre** and **parmi**, a form of **lequel** must be used.

Animate Antecedents

les amis sur qui je compte (ALSO **sur lesquels**)	*the friends I rely **on***
l'employée dont je vous ai parlé (ALSO **de qui, de laquelle**)	*the employee whom I spoke to you **about***
le cousin chez qui j'habite	*the cousin at whose house I live*
les deux jeunes filles entre lesquelles il s'est assis	*the two girls he sat **between***
les quatre garçons parmi lesquels Janine a choisi	*the four boys **among whom** Janine chose*

Inanimate Antecedents

la table sur laquelle j'ai posé mes affaires	*the table I put my things **on***
l'immeuble dans lequel elle habite	*the apartment house that she lives **in***
la tente sous laquelle j'ai dormi	*the tent that I slept **in***

Prepositions of location and direction plus a relative pronoun can be replaced by **où**.

la table où j'ai posé mes affaires	*the table **where** I put my things*
l'immeuble où elle habite	*the apartment house **where** she lives*

Où can also be used as a relative pronoun after time words. **Que** is also possible.

le jour où elle est partie } **le jour qu'**elle est partie }	*the day she left*

After a compound preposition ending with **de** (such as **à cause de**) or a noun phrase ending with **de** (such as **dans la classe de**), **dont** must be replaced by **qui** (for people) or a form of **de** + **lequel** (for both things and people).

la gare près de laquelle je travaille	*the station I work **near***
l'étudiante au sujet de qui je vous ai parlé	*the student **about whom** I spoke to you*
les voisins à cause de qui nous avons dû déménager	*the neighbors **because of whom** we had to move*
le voyage au cours duquel je l'ai connu	*the trip **during which** I met him*
une vallée au fond de laquelle se trouve un village	*a valley **at the bottom of which** there is a village*
des méthodes au moyen desquelles on peut mesurer la qualité de votre travail	*methods **by means of which** one can measure the quality of your work*

Le soleil est **une étoile autour de laquelle** tourne la terre.

*The sun is **a star around which** the earth turns.*

H *Le style soutenu. Traduisez les phrases suivantes en anglais. Elles ont toutes des propositions subordonnées compliquées et sont typiques du style journalistique ou littéraire.*

La conférence de presse

à la suite de *following*
au bout de *at the end of* (space)
au cours de *during, during the course of*
le chômage *unemployment*
défavorisé *underprivileged*

la démarche *step, measure*
se démettre de *to resign from*
fonder *to found*
prédire *to predict*
routier *pertaining to roads*

1. Le gouvernement a fait une démarche dont les conséquences sont à regretter.

2. Les agents de police ont fait un effort dont notre équipe reconnaît l'importance.

3. C'est une crise économique en conséquence de laquelle le chômage a augmenté.

4. On attend une déclaration du général sous les ordres de qui l'armée combattait.

5. Notre pays participe à un effort international dont on prédit le succès.

6. Elle a eu une maladie à la suite de laquelle elle a dû se démettre de son poste.

7. Ils ont fait une étude des conditions dans lesquelles vivent les défavorisés de notre ville.

8. Nous assistions à la conférence de presse au cours de laquelle on a annoncé les nouveaux projets de construction routière.

I *Gestion critiquée. Ajoutez le pronom relatif convenable à ces phrases pour savoir pourquoi Philippe Duhamel et Micheline Arnaud ne sont pas d'accord avec les plans de leur entreprise. Dans plusieurs cas il faut ajouter aussi la préposition qui manque.*

Vocabulaire utile
être d'accord avec *to be in agreement with*
se familiariser avec *to familiarize oneself with*
insister sur *to insist on*
se renseigner sur *to get information about*

1. Nous n'avons pas assisté à la réunion pendant _____ on a pris la décision.

2. Ils commencent un programme d'action _____ nous ne sommes pas d'accord.

3. Nous croyons qu'il produira des résultats _____ on ne s'attend pas.

4. Ils ne peuvent pas assurer la qualité _____ nous insistons.

5. Ils ne connaissent pas le marché _____ nous nous sommes familiarisés.

6. Il y a trop de choses _____ ils ne se sont pas renseignés.

7. C'est un projet contre _____ nous allons protester.

8. On va exposer toutes les mauvaises conséquences _____ nous nous méfions.

J *Au pays de mes ancêtres.* Christine montre à son amie Julie le village où elle est née et où sa famille a toujours vécu. Ajoutez le pronom relatif convenable à la conversation entre les deux filles. Dans plusieurs cas il faut ajouter aussi la préposition qui manque.

À la campagne
le chêne *oak tree*
la clôture *fence*
l'étang [masc.] *pond*
grimper aux arbres *to climb trees*
le jardin potager *vegetable garden*
le peuplier *poplar tree*

Christine: Viens, je vais te montrer la maison dans (1) _____ on habitait. La voilà.

Julie: La maison à côté de (2) _____ il y a deux chênes?

Christine: Justement. Ce sont les arbres (3) _____ on grimpait, mes frères et moi, quand on était petits et entre (4) _____ il y avait avant un petit banc en bois.

Julie: Est-ce que je peux voir ta chambre?

Christine: Oui, montons. La voilà, la chambre dans (5) _____ je couchais. Et voilà la fenêtre par (6) _____ je regardais la neige en hiver.

Julie: Et cette clôture?

Christine: C'est la clôture derrière (7) _____ il y a un champ.

Julie: Je vois un chemin à gauche.

Christine: Oui, c'est un chemin le long (8) _____ il y a des peupliers.

Julie: Tu ne m'as pas dit qu'il y avait aussi un étang?

Christine: Ah, oui, l'étang sur (9) _____ on patinait en hiver. On peut y aller, ce n'est pas loin. Et chemin faisant, je te présenterai aux voisins chez (10) _____ je passais beaucoup de temps. Ils avaient un fils (11) _____ j'étais amoureuse.

Julie: Et qu'est-ce qu'il est devenu, ce fils?

Christine: Il était beaucoup plus âgé que moi. Il a passé plusieurs années à Lyon au cours (12) _____ il s'est marié.

Relatives Without Antecedents

When there is no antecedent in the main clause, French uses **ce qui** if the relative is the subject of its clause and **ce que** if it is the direct object.

—Je ne vois pas **ce qui** t'inquiète.	*I don't see **what's** upsetting you.*
—**Ce qui** reste à faire me tracasse.	***What** there is left to do is worrying me.*
—Dis-moi **ce que** tu veux.	*Tell me **what** you want.*
—**Ce que** je préfère, c'est de partir.	***What** I prefer is to leave.*

When the verb of the relative clause requires the preposition **de** before an object, **ce dont** is used.

—Je n'ai pas trouvé **ce dont** j'avais besoin.	*I haven't found **what** I needed.* (**avoir besoin de**)
—Tu veux que je te prête **ce dont** je me sers?	*Do you want me to lend you **what** I use?* (**se servir de**)
Ce dont vous avez besoin est ce logiciel.	***What you need** is this software program.*
Voilà **ce dont ils sont convaincus**.	*There's **what they're convinced of**.*
J'ai compris **ce dont il était capable**.	*I understood **what he was capable of**.*

When the verb of the relative clause requires the preposition **à** before an object, **ce à quoi** is used.

On ne sait pas **ce à quoi il faut s'attendre**.	*We don't know **what to expect**.* (**s'attendre à**)
Comment deviner **ce à quoi ils pensent**?	*How can one guess **what they are thinking of**?* (**penser à**)
Il faut découvrir **ce à quoi tu es allergique**.	*They have to discover **what you are allergic to**.* (**être allergique à**)

Ce qui, **ce que**, and **ce dont** can also refer to a preceding clause.

Il arrive toujours à l'heure, **ce qui** me plaît.	*He always arrives on time, **which** I like.*
Il parle trois langues, **ce que** j'admire.	*He speaks three languages, **which** I admire.*
Il est très travailleur, **ce dont** on s'est aperçu.	*He's very hard-working, **which** people have noticed.*

Ce qui and **ce que** are used after **tout** to express *all that, everything that*.

Il m'a montré **tout ce qu'**il a écrit.	*He showed me **everything that** he wrote.*
Tout ce qui est sur la table est pour toi.	***All that** is on the table is for you.*

The demonstrative pronouns **celui**, **celle**, **ceux**, **celles** are common before the relative pronouns **qui** and **que**, and mean *he/she who, they who, the one(s) who, those who*.

Ceux qui le connaissent l'estiment.	***Those who** know him admire him.*
Celui qui désobéit sera puni.	***He who** disobeys will be punished.*
Il y a plusieurs étudiantes françaises, mais il faut parler avec **celles qui** connaissent Marseille.	*There are several (female) French students here, but you have to speak with **the ones who** are familiar with Marseilles.*

Note that in proverbs **qui** is often used by itself to mean *he who*.

Rira bien **qui** rira le dernier.	***He who** laughs last, laughs best.*
Qui aime bien châtie bien.	*Spare the rod, spoil the child. (**He who** loves, punishes.)*

K *À compléter.* *Complétez les phrases suivantes avec les pronoms relatifs qui manquent. Parfois l'équivalent anglais sera donné pour vous aider.*

1. —Avec qui comptes-tu parler? Avec Daniel ou Baudoin?

    —Peu importe. Avec _____ (*the one who*) je trouverai à la fac.

2. Tu veux un peu de _____ je mange?

3. _____ s'est passé est merveilleux.

4. Je trouve bête _____ (*everything that*) il dit.

5. Il s'est marié avec _____ (*the one who*) il a connue l'été dernier.

6. Il faut cacher _____ les enfants ont peur.

7. Nous n'avons pas accepté _____ ils nous ont offert.

8. Il dit qu'il aura de bonnes notes, _____ je doute.

9. Elle est très cultivée, _____ nous plaît.

10. Je ne comprends pas _____ vous allez étudier en Belgique.

11. On se demande _____ a pu l'offenser.

12. Je te remercie de tout _____ tu as fait pour moi.

L *Jacqueline est amoureuse.* *Jacqueline a un petit ami Luc, dont elle est amoureuse. Voici la lettre qu'elle écrit à son sujet à son amie Éliane. Complétez-la avec **ce qui**, **ce que** ou **ce dont**.*

Ma chère Éliane:

   Je te remercie de ta lettre. Luc et moi, on continue à sortir ensemble. Tu m'as demandé

(1) _____ il fait. Il est étudiant en sciences. (2) _____ l'intéresse, c'est la chimie.

Je comprends (3) _____ Luc étudie parce que je m'intéresse à la chimie aussi.

   Je vais t'expliquer (4) _____ nous faisons quand nous sortons. Nous allons beaucoup

au cinéma et au théâtre. (5) _____ nous attire, ce sont les films étrangers. Nous en voyons

beaucoup. (6) _____ nous avons besoin est un bon lecteur de DVD pour pouvoir en regarder

à la maison aussi. Tu comprends que Luc et moi, nous avons les mêmes goûts, (7) _____

est une bonne chose.

   Je ne sais pas (8) _____ nous allons faire pendant l'été. Luc veut faire un stage dans

une entreprise à Singapour, mais moi, je dois travailler ici. C'est-à-dire que nous ne nous

verrons pas pendant deux mois, (9) _____ j'ai peur. Luc me rassure en disant que deux mois,

ce n'est pas l'éternité, (10) _____ est vrai.

   Bon, Éliane, écris-moi et dis-moi tout (11) _____ tu fais maintenant. Tu m'as écrit que

tu penses à changer de faculté, (12) _____ je me doutais. Je sais que tu trouves la médecine moins intéressante maintenant. Qu'est-ce que tu comptes faire, alors? Écris-moi dès que tu auras une petite minute de libre.

Je t'embrasse,

Jacqueline

 M *Exercice d'ensemble.* *Joignez les deux phrases françaises en une seule au moyen d'un pronom relatif. Suivez le modèle.*

MODÈLE J'ai écouté un cédé. Je vais te le prêter.
→ J'ai écouté un cédé que je vais te prêter.

À *la recherche d'un nouvel emploi*

1. Élisabeth a un poste. Elle veut en démissionner.

2. Il y a d'autres emplois. Elle essaie de se renseigner là-dessus.

3. Elle manque de qualifications. Nous ne pouvons pas nous en passer dans mon bureau.

4. Elle a téléphoné à d'autres entreprises. Je lui en ai donné le nom.

5. Il y a des cours d'orientation (*guidance*). Elle y assiste.

6. Il y a de nouveaux logiciels (*software*) pour le bureau. Élisabeth se familiarise avec eux.

7. Elle a déjà trouvé une entreprise. Elle voudrait travailler pour cette entreprise.

Mon petit déjeuner

8. Je vais te montrer les choses. J'ai besoin de ces choses pour préparer mon petit déjeuner.

9. Voilà le réchaud (*hot plate*). Je fais mon café sur ce réchaud.

10. Voici le bol. Je bois mon café du matin dans un bol.

11. Voilà la boulangerie. J'achète mes croissants et mon pain dans cette boulangerie.

12. Voilà la porte de la boutique. Il y a une enseigne (*sign*) au-dessus de la porte.

N *En français. Exercice d'ensemble.* *Exprimez les idées suivantes en français.*

1. *I understood everything that they said.*

2. *Those who came early found seats.*

3. *There's the station near which she works.*

4. *Here is the café in front of which I saw her.*

5. *This is a book without which I can't finish my work.*

6. *I don't see the park that we are going toward.*

7. *We went to the city where she works.*

8. *We met the teacher our friend had talked about.*

9. *What he remembers is a secret.*

10. *What he participates in is interesting.*

The Present Subjunctive

Moods of Verbs

The mood of a verb indicates how the speaker views a statement. The indicative mood is used to express facts and describe reality. The imperative mood is used to express commands. And the subjunctive mood is used to express wishes, desires, necessities, emotions, opinions, doubts, suppositions, and other more subjective conditions.

Indicative Mood

Nous faisons nos devoirs.   *We do our homework.*

Imperative Mood

Faisons nos devoirs tout de suite!   *Let's do our homework right away!*

Subjunctive Mood

Le professeur exige **que nous fassions**   *The teacher demands **that we do** our*
     nos devoirs tous les soirs.   *homework every night.*

The subjunctive mood is used much more frequently in French than it is in English. It typically appears in dependent and relative clauses.

Forms of the Present Subjunctive

To form the present subjunctive of most verbs, drop the **-ons** ending from the present tense **nous** form and add the endings **-e, -es, -e, -ions, -iez, -ent**.

rentrer	finir	vendre
que je rentr**e**	que je finiss**e**	que je vend**e**
que tu rentr**es**	que tu finiss**es**	que tu vend**es**
qu'il/qu'elle rentr**e**	qu'il/qu'elle finiss**e**	qu'il/qu'elle vend**e**
que nous rentr**ions**	que nous finiss**ions**	que nous vend**ions**
que vous rentr**iez**	que vous finiss**iez**	que vous vend**iez**
qu'ils/qu'elles rentr**ent**	qu'ils/qu'elles finiss**ent**	qu'ils/qu'elles vend**ent**

Regular **-er** verbs that have changes in the vowel in the present tense stem, such as **acheter** and **compléter**, have those changes in the subjunctive as well.

que j'ach**è**te	que nous ach**e**tions
que je compl**è**te	que nous compl**é**tions

Most irregular verbs follow the same pattern as the regular verbs: the endings of the present subjunctive are added to the stem. Study the subjunctive of **lire**, **écrire**, and **joindre**.

lire	écrire	joindre
que je lise	que je écriv**e**	que je joign**e**
que tu lis**es**	que tu écriv**es**	que tu joign**es**
qu'il/qu'elle lise	qu'il/qu'elle écrive	qu'il/qu'elle joigne
que nous lis**ions**	que nous écriv**ions**	que nous joign**ions**
que vous lis**iez**	que vous écriv**iez**	que vous joign**iez**
qu'ils/qu'elles lis**ent**	qu'ils/qu'elles écriv**ent**	qu'ils/qu'elles joign**ent**

Irregular verbs such as **boire**, **venir**, and **prendre**, which have variations in the stem in the present indicative, show the same changes in the present subjunctive.

boire	venir	prendre
que je boiv**e**	que je vienn**e**	que je prenn**e**
que tu boiv**es**	que tu vienn**es**	que tu prenn**es**
qu'il/qu'elle boive	qu'il/qu'elle vienne	qu'il/qu'elle prenne
que nous buv**ions**	que nous ven**ions**	que nous pren**ions**
que vous buv**iez**	que vous ven**iez**	que vous pren**iez**
qu'ils/qu'elles boiv**ent**	qu'ils/qu'elles vienn**ent**	qu'ils/qu'elles prenn**ent**

The verbs **aller**, **avoir**, **être**, **vouloir**, **faire**, **pouvoir**, and **savoir** are irregular in the subjunctive.

Two Stems

aller	avoir
que j'**aille**	que j'**aie**
que tu **ailles**	que tu **aies**
qu'il/qu'elle **aille**	qu'il/qu'elle **ait**
que nous **allions**	que nous **ayons**
que vous **alliez**	que vous **ayez**
qu'ils/qu'elles **aillent**	qu'ils/qu'elles **aient**

être	vouloir
que je **sois**	que je **veuille**
que tu **sois**	que tu **veuilles**
qu'il/qu'elle **soit**	qu'il/qu'elle **veuille**
que nous **soyons**	que nous **voulions**
que vous **soyez**	que vous **vouliez**
qu'ils/qu'elles **soient**	qu'ils/qu'elles **veuillent**

One Stem

faire	pouvoir	savoir
que je **fasse**	que je **puisse**	que je **sache**
que tu **fasses**	que tu **puisses**	que tu **saches**
qu'il/qu'elle **fasse**	qu'il/qu'elle **puisse**	qu'il/qu'elle **sache**
que nous **fassions**	que nous **puissions**	que nous **sachions**
que vous **fassiez**	que vous **puissiez**	que vous **sachiez**
qu'ils/qu'elles **fassent**	qu'ils/qu'elles **puissent**	qu'ils/qu'elles **sachent**

The verb **valoir** is conjugated like **aller** in the present subjunctive.

que je **vaille**   que **nous valions**

Uses of the Subjunctive: Imposition of Will, Necessity, Getting Someone to Do Something

The subjunctive is used after verbs that express wanting, preferring, needing, making, or forcing someone to do something.

—Je ne **veux** pas **qu'il parte**.	*I don't **want him to leave**.*
—Alors **je vais empêcher qu'il s'en aille**.	*Then **I'll keep him from going away**.*
—**J'exige que** Baudoin **soit** là.	*I **demand that** Baudoin **be** here.*
—**Il faut que nous l'invitions**, alors.	*We **must invite him** then.*
—**Je suggère que** vous **traduisiez** l'article.	*I **suggest that** you **translate** the article.*
—**Il est nécessaire que** vous m'**aidiez**.	*It's **necessary for you to help** me.*

The following verbs are followed by the subjunctive.

aimer mieux que *to prefer*	**ordonner que** *to order*
attendre que *to wait until, wait for*	**permettre que** *to allow*
avoir besoin que *to need*	**préférer que** *to prefer*
demander que *to request, ask*	**recommander que** *to recommend*
désirer que *to desire, want, wish*	**souhaiter que** *to wish*
empêcher que *to prevent, keep*	**suggérer que** *to suggest*
exiger que *to demand*	**vouloir que** *to want*

Note, however, that **espérer** (*to hope*) is followed by the indicative.

The following impersonal expressions signifying imposition of will are followed by the subjunctive.

il est nécessaire/urgent que *it is necessary/urgent*
il est essentiel/important que *it is essential/important*
il est indispensable/utile que *it is indispensable/useful*
il faut que *it is necessary, one has to*

For the subjunctive to be used, the subjects of the main clause and the subordinate clause must be different. If the subjects of the two clauses are the same, the infinitive is usually used.

Je veux que **tu** reviennes.	*I want **you** to come back.*
Je veux revenir.	*I want to come back.*
Ils préfèrent que **nous** restions.	*They prefer that **we** stay.*
Ils préfèrent rester.	*They prefer to stay.*

A   *Moi, je ne veux pas.*   *Un ami vous dit ce que font les autres. Répondez-lui dans chaque cas que vous, vous ne voulez pas que les autres fassent ces choses. Employez le subjonctif dans la proposition subordonnée. Suivez le modèle.*

MODÈLE   Marie étudie huit heures par jour.
      → Moi, je ne veux pas qu'elle étudie huit heures par jour.

1. Serge fait du japonais.

2. Élisabeth laisse les fenêtres ouvertes.

3. Richard sort avec Hélène.

4. Louis boit du vin.

5. Je vois un vieux film.

6. Michel sait ton adresse.

7. Chantal est triste.

8. Robert et Thérèse ont peur.

9. Daniel maigrit.

10. Moi, je grossis.

B   *La fête de samedi soir.*   *C'est à vous d'organiser la fête de samedi. Dites ce que chacun doit faire. Suivez le modèle.*

MODÈLE   je veux / Marie / inviter ses cousins
      → Je veux que Marie invite ses cousins.

1. je préfère / Marc / choisir le gâteau

2. il est nécessaire / Lise et Rachelle / aller chercher les boissons

3. il est important / Roland et Jacqueline / pouvoir venir

4. je veux / Janine / faire les hors-d'œuvre

5. il faut / tu / faire quelques coups de fil

6. il est essentiel / Olivier / venir

7. je préfère / nous / acheter des plats préparés chez le charcutier

8. je veux / tu / venir m'aider samedi après-midi

C *Des étudiants à Paris.* *Un groupe d'étudiants de province vont passer une semaine à Paris. Où aller? Ils ne sont pas d'accord. Construisez des phrases avec les éléments donnés pour savoir ce que chacun souhaite faire. Employez le subjonctif dans les propositions subordonnées. Suivez le modèle.*

MODÈLE   Paul / vouloir / on / aller / d'abord / aux Champs-Élysées
          → Paul veut qu'on aille d'abord aux Champs-Élysées.

1. le professeur / exiger / nous / visiter / tous les monuments de Paris

2. Barbara / souhaiter / nous / commencer / par la visite du Louvre

3. Martin / désirer / le groupe / faire / le tour de Paris en autocar

4. Monique / demander / on / voir / les Tuileries

5. Georges / recommander / nous / aller / à l'Arc de Triomphe

6. Gustave / suggérer / nous / monter / à Montmartre

7. Diane / ordonner / tout le monde / suivre / l'itinéraire

8. Édouard / aimer mieux / on / faire / une promenade à pied dans le Marais

9. Renée / vouloir / nous / prendre / le déjeuner

10. Véronique / ne pas vouloir / nous / passer / toute la journée à discuter

NOTE CULTURELLE

- **Les Champs-Élysées**: Grande et belle avenue qui va de l'Arc de Triomphe à la place de la Concorde. Cette avenue imposante est un grand centre commercial.
- **Le Louvre**: Un des plus célèbres musées d'art du monde. À son origine un palais royal, le Louvre est devenu musée pendant la Révolution. Sa collection comprend plus de 6 000 tableaux et plus de 150 000 pièces de l'antiquité égyptienne, grecque et romaine.
- **Les Tuileries**: Aujourd'hui un jardin public, c'était le site d'un palais construit pour Catherine de Médicis, incendié en 1871 pendant la Guerre civile de la Commune.
- **L'Arc de Triomphe**: La construction de cet arc monumental a été initiée sous les ordres de Napoléon. Il commémore les victoires militaires de l'empereur.
- **Montmartre**: Quartier charmant situé sur la butte Montmartre dans le nord de la ville de Paris. C'est ici qu'on a construit la fameuse église blanche du Sacré-Cœur qui domine le panorama de Paris. Montmartre était pendant longtemps le quartier des artistes et est un des endroits que les touristes ne manquent jamais de visiter.
- **Le Marais**: Ce quartier de la rive droite au nord de l'île de la Cité doit son nom aux inondations dues aux crues de la Seine. Pendant le dix-septième siècle c'était le quartier où habitait la noblesse dans de petits palais splendides appelés **hôtels**. De nos jours, plusieurs des vieux hôtels ont été restaurés pour devenir les résidences des cadres et des hommes d'affaires. La nuit, l'illumination des hôtels rend ce quartier un des plus beaux et des plus intéressants de Paris.

D *Nos souhaits et désirs.* *Joignez les éléments donnés en une seule phrase qui exprime le désir que les actions se réalisent. Employez le subjonctif dans la proposition subordonnée. Suivez le modèle.*

MODÈLE   Tu fais le linge. (j'ai besoin)
→ J'ai besoin que tu fasses le linge.

1. Tout est en règle. (je désire)

2. Les enfants ont peur. (je ne veux pas)

3. Cette famille vit mal. (nous ne voulons pas)

4. Il boit trop de vin. (ses parents empêcheront)

5. Il sait les réponses. (je recommande)

6. Ils conduisent prudemment. (je demande)

7. Elle rejoint son fiancé. (ses parents aiment mieux)

8. Elle sort avec Jean-Philippe. (ses parents ne permettent pas)

E *Une lettre.* *Rozianne, qui habite Québec, écrit à son amie Isabelle, Parisienne. Pour savoir ce que Rozianne écrit dans sa lettre, complétez-en le texte avec la forme correcte des verbes entre parenthèses. Choisissez entre le subjonctif et l'indicatif.*

Ma chère Isabelle,

J'espère que tu _____ (1. aller) bien. Mes parents et moi, nous _____ (2. être)

en bonne santé. J'ai reçu ta lettre hier et je suis vraiment contente que tu puisses venir

me voir pendant les vacances. Je préfère que tu _____ (3. venir) au mois de juillet.

Mes parents demandent que tes parents t'_____ (4. accompagner). Je recommande

que vous _____ (5. prendre) les billets d'avion aussitôt que possible. Je suggère aussi

que vous _____ (6. mettre) quelques pulls dans les valises. À Québec il fait souvent frais

le soir, même en été. Je voudrais que nous _____ (7. aller) tous aux Laurentides et que

nous _____ (8. visiter) ensemble la vieille ville. Mes parents et moi, nous désirons

_____ (9. passer) un mois merveilleux avec vous au Canada.

Amitiés,

Rozianne

F *À vous de vous exprimer sur l'avenir de votre école.* *Quels changements sont nécessaires pour améliorer votre école? Exprimez-les dans des termes de désirs ou souhaits. Utilisez le vocabulaire donné ou ajoutez d'autres idées qui reflètent la réalité de votre école. Exprimez ces changements souhaités comme des désirs à vous ou comme la volonté de vos amis. Suivez les modèles.*

MODÈLES   Je veux (voudrais) qu'il y ait moins d'élèves dans chaque classe.

Les étudiants demandent qu'on améliore la qualité des sandwichs qu'on sert à la cantine.

Mes amis souhaitent qu'on offre des cours d'informatique.

Pour améliorer (*improve*) l'école

acheter des ordinateurs dotés de caméras intégrés *to buy computers with built-in webcams*
aménager le terrain de sports *to fix up the playing field*
donner des bourses d'études à tous les étudiants *to give all students scholarships*
embaucher de nouveaux professeurs *to hire new teachers*
faciliter l'accès à la bibliothèque *to make it easier to use the library*
inaugurer un festival de cinéma *to start a film festival*
offrir des cours du soir *to offer evening classes*
renforcer le programme d'orientation *to strengthen the guidance program*
servir de bons desserts à la cantine *to serve good desserts in the cafeteria*
trouver des stages pour les étudiants *to find internships for students*

Uses of the Subjunctive: Emotion and Opinion

The subjunctive is used in subordinate clauses following verbs and impersonal constructions that express emotion.

Fear

avoir peur que *to be afraid that*
craindre que *to fear that*

Surprise or Curiosity

s'étonner que *to be surprised that*
cela m'étonne que *I'm surprised that*
il est étonnant que *it's surprising that*
il est bizarre/curieux/extraordinaire que *it's strange/strange/extraordinary that*

Happiness and Sadness

être content(e)/heureux(-se)/triste que *to be happy/happy/sad that*
être ravi(e)/satisfait(e)/désolé(e) que *to be delighted/satisfied/sorry that*
regretter que *to be sorry that*
se réjouir que *to rejoice, be glad that*

Annoyance and Negative Reactions

se plaindre que *to complain that*
se fâcher que *to get angry that/because*
être fâché(e)/furieux(-se) que *to be angry/furious that*
avoir honte que *to be ashamed that*
il est ennuyeux/agaçant/énervant que *it's annoying/annoying/irritating that*
cela m'ennuie/m'agace/m'énerve que *it annoys me that*

—Le chef est ravi que vous puissiez l'aider.

The boss is delighted that you can help him.

—Je suis heureux qu'il ait confiance en moi.

I'm happy that he has confidence in me.

—Je m'étonne que le travail ne soit pas fini.

I'm surprised that the work is not finished.

—Cela m'ennuie qu'il nous **fasse** attendre.

I'm annoyed that he's keeping us waiting.

The subjunctive is used after verbs and impersonal expressions that show that the action of the subordinate clause is an opinion, an evaluation, or a possibility.

Evaluation and Opinion

accepter que *to accept that*
approuver que *to approve of (someone's doing something)*
désapprouver que *to disapprove of (someone's doing something)*
il convient que *it is suitable/advisable*
il importe que *it matters that, it is important that*
peu importe que *it matters little that*
il suffit que *it is enough*
il vaut mieux que *it is better that*
il est logique/normal/naturel/juste que *it's logical/normal/natural/right that*
c'est une chance que *it's lucky that*
ce n'est pas la peine que *it's not worth it that*
il est rare que *it is not often that*

Possibility

il se peut que *it's possible that*
il est possible/impossible que *it's possible/impossible that*
il n'y a aucune chance que *there's no chance that*
il n'y a pas de danger que *there's no danger that*

G ***C'est bien.*** *On raconte à Marcelle tout ce qu'il y a de neuf. Dans chaque cas elle exprime sa satisfaction en disant qu'elle est contente de ce qui arrive. Écrivez ce que dit Marcelle en employant le subjonctif dans la proposition subordonnée. Suivez le modèle.*

MODÈLE Pierre ne travaille pas aujourd'hui.
→ Je suis contente qu'il ne travaille pas aujourd'hui.

1. Marianne et Justine sont là.

2. Gérard vend sa bicyclette.

3. Mes parents partent en vacances.

4. Jean-Claude nous attend.

5. Le petit Charles ne désobéit jamais.

6. Christine et moi, nous dînons ensemble.

7. Toi et moi, nous complétons le programme cette année.

8. Frédéric connaît Odile.

H *En une seule phrase, s'il vous plaît.* *Changez l'ordre des deux phrases données pour en faire une seule. Faites les modifications nécessaires. Suivez les modèles.*

MODÈLES   Il n'est pas encore là. C'est étonnant.
→ Il est étonnant qu'il ne soit pas encore là.

Je maigris. Le médecin se réjouit.
→ Le médecin se réjouit que je maigrisse.

1. Tu comprends tout. Je suis ravi.

2. Ils ne veulent pas nous aider. Nous sommes furieux.

3. Le prof ne nous reconnaît pas. Cela m'étonne.

4. Il y a eu un accident. J'ai peur.

5. Tu ne peux pas venir. Elle est désolée.

6. Elle met le foulard que je lui ai offert. Je suis content.

7. Philippe n'apprend pas beaucoup. Son professeur se plaint.

8. Ces enfants se battent tout le temps. Je suis fâché.

9. Un professeur perd son travail. C'est rare.

10. Vous me le dites. Cela suffit.

11. Il ne se rend pas compte du problème. Nous craignons.

12. Elle sait conduire un camion. C'est extraordinaire.

I *Vos réactions, s'il vous plaît!* *Voici une liste de faits et d'événements. Exprimez votre opinion ou votre réaction dans chaque cas. Commencez par un des verbes ou une des expressions de cette section. Suivez le modèle.*

MODÈLE   La bibliothèque est fermée le dimanche.
→ Je désapprouve que la bibliothèque soit fermée le dimanche.
OU Cela m'ennuie que la bibliothèque soit fermée le dimanche.
OU Je suis fâché(e) que la bibliothèque soit fermée le dimanche.

1. On augmente les prix à la cantine.

2. Le latin et le grec sont obligatoires.

3. On ne peut pas passer le permis de conduire à quatorze ans.

4. On interdit l'emploi des gros mots (*vulgar words*) dans les chansons de rock.

5. On abolit la peine de mort.

6. Les professeurs font grève demain.

7. Mon ami Serge perd toujours ses affaires.

8. Le port de la cravate est obligatoire à l'école.

9. Le professeur d'anglais n'écrit jamais rien au tableau.

10. Nous lisons trois cents pages par semaine pour le cours d'histoire.

J **Quel fouillis! Et voilà maman qui arrive!** *Vous habitez un appartement avec trois colocataires. Cette fin de semaine les parents viennent voir leurs enfants à l'université. Vous êtes contents de voir vos parents, mais l'état de l'appartement vous inquiète un peu. L'appartement est une vraie porcherie (pigsty)! Pour décrire la situation, joignez les verbes et les expressions entre parenthèses aux phrases. Suivez le modèle.*

MODÈLE   Nos parents viennent nous rendre visite. (nous sommes contents)
            → Nous sommes contents que nos parents viennent nous rendre visite.

Pour une demeure propre

balayer le parquet *to sweep the floor*	**faire le ménage** *to do the housework*
la bibliothèque *bookcase*	**le fouillis** *mess*
cirer le parquet *to wax the floor*	**ranger** *to put away*
épousseter les meubles (j'époussette)	**récurer les casseroles** *to scour the pots*
to dust the furniture	**la toile d'araignée** *spiderweb, cobweb*

1. Je vis dans le désordre. (ma mère n'acceptera pas)

2. Nous faisons le ménage. (il est essentiel)

3. Nous époussetons les meubles. (il faut que)

4. Bernard et toi, vous récurez les casseroles. (je suis content(e))

5. Toi et moi, nous balayons le parquet. (il convient que)

6. Nous cirons le parquet aussi. (il est possible)

7. Lise et Émile, vous rangez les livres dans les bibliothèques. (il vaut mieux)

8. Philomène enlève les toiles d'araignée. (je me réjouis)

K **La flemme (laziness) de fin de cours.** *C'est le mois de juin et tout le monde a la flemme, sauf vous. Vous essayez de remonter leur morale (buck them up, get them going again) en leur conseillant de travailler avec un peu de diligence. Employez le subjonctif dans l'expression de vos conseils. Suivez le modèle.*

MODÈLE   Charles: Je ne veux pas assister au cours de chimie aujourd'hui.
                      (il est important)
            → Il est important que tu assistes au cours de chimie aujourd'hui.

1. Annette: Je n'étudie pas pour les examens. (il est bizarre)

2. Michel: Je n'ai aucune envie de travailler à la bibliothèque. (ça m'étonne)

3. Françoise: Je n'écris pas la dissertation de philosophie. (il vaut mieux que)

4. André: Je n'écoute pas les enregistrements au laboratoire de langues. (il est utile)

5. Sylvie: Je ne prends plus de notes dans la classe d'histoire. (il est indispensable)

6. Albert: Je ne fais pas mes devoirs. (les profs seront fâchés)

7. Catherine: Je ne lis plus le livre de biologie. (je regrette)

8. Corine: Je m'endors dans la classe d'anglais. (je n'approuve pas)

9. Sébastien: Je fais des dessins dans mon cahier dans la classe de maths.
                (il n'est pas normal)

10. Bruno: Je perds mes cahiers. (il est agaçant)

Uses of the Subjunctive: Negation of Fact and Opinion

The subjunctive is used after verbs that negate the action or idea of the subordinate clause. Such verbs and impersonal expressions include the following.

nier *to deny*
douter *to doubt*
il est douteux que *it is doubtful that*
il est exclu que *it's out of the question that*

—Je doute qu'il **sache** le faire.	*I doubt that he **knows how** to do it.*
—Mais il n'est pas exclu qu'il **puisse** nous aider.	*But it isn't out of the question that he **can** help us.*

NOTE The indicative is usually used after the *negative* of **nier** and **douter**, since when those verbs are used in the negative, they no longer negate facts: **Je ne doute pas qu'il sait le faire.**

When the following verbs and expressions are negative, they are followed by the subjunctive. When they are affirmative, they are followed by the indicative.

il n'est pas certain que *it's not certain that*
il n'est pas sûr que *it's not sure that*
il n'est pas évident que *it's not evident that*
il n'est pas clair que *it's not clear that*
il n'est pas exact que *it's not correct/accurate that*
il n'est pas vrai que *it's not true that*
il est peu probable que *it's not probable that*
il ne paraît pas que *it doesn't seem that*
je ne suis pas sûr(e) que *I'm not sure that*
je ne dis pas que *I'm not saying that*
ça ne veut pas dire que *it doesn't mean that*
ce n'est pas que *it's not that*

—Il n'est pas certain qu'il **vienne.**	*It's not certain that he's coming.*
—Ça ne veut pas dire qu'il ne **veuille** pas nous voir.	*That doesn't mean that he doesn't want to see us.*
—Il n'est pas évident qu'elle **sache** la réponse.	*It is not evident that she **knows** the answer.*
—Moi, **je suis sûr qu'elle** la **sait.**	*I'm sure that she knows it.*

The verbs **penser**, **croire**, and **espérer** are followed by the indicative when affirmative, but by the subjunctive when negative or interrogative.

—Je ne crois pas que cet étranger te **comprenne.**	*I don't think that that foreigner **understands** you.*
—Penses-tu que je **doive** tout répéter?	*Do you think that I **ought to** repeat everything?*
—Oui, **je crois que c'est** nécessaire.	*Yes, I think it's necessary.*

The indicative may be used after the negative and interrogative of **penser** and **croire** instead of the subjunctive to convey that the speaker is certain about the action. Compare the following sentences.

Je ne crois pas que tu as raison.	*I don't think you're right.* (*I think you're wrong.*)
Je ne crois pas que tu aies raison.	*I don't think you're right.* (*But I'm not sure.*)

L   *Conversation.* *Pierrette et Joceline causent ensemble. Pierrette demande à son amie si elle sait ce que leurs amis vont faire. Joceline répond dans chaque cas qu'elle ne croit pas que leurs amis comptent faire tout ça. Reconstruisez leur conversation en employant le subjonctif dans la proposition subordonnée de la réponse de Joceline. Suivez le modèle.*

MODÈLE   Stéphane / arriver aujourd'hui
→ Pierrette: Tu sais si Stéphane arrivera aujourd'hui?
Joceline: Je ne crois pas qu'il arrive aujourd'hui.

1. notre professeur / finir la leçon

2. Ghislaine / rompre avec son petit ami

3. ton cousin / revenir cette semaine

4. Nadine / servir de la pizza à la surboum

5. Philippe / sortir avec Mireille

6. Paul / pouvoir nous rejoindre

7. Alice / être ici ce soir

8. toi et moi / étudier assez

9. Chloë / aller au concert

10. Daniel / prendre un taxi

M   *Exprimez vos doutes.* *Utilisez les expressions données entre parenthèses pour exprimer vos doutes sur les faits suivants. Suivez le modèle.*

MODÈLE   Nous avons un examen aujourd'hui. (je ne crois pas)
→ Je ne crois pas que nous ayons un examen aujourd'hui.

1. Laurence réussit à tous ses examens. (il n'est pas clair)

2. Nous offrons des disques compacts à Renée. (il est douteux)

3. Tu suis un cours d'histoire. (il n'est pas exclu)

4. Il fait des progrès en anglais. (ça ne veut pas dire)

5. Lucette t'écrit. (il est peu probable)

6. Il nous connaît. (je ne suis pas sûr)

7. L'élève apprend tout ça. (je doute)

8. Elle descend faire les courses. (je ne crois pas)

9. Son père vit très mal. (il nie)

10. Ce pays produit des voitures. (il ne paraît pas)

N *Au sujet des amis.* *Deux étudiants parlent de leurs amis au lycée. Ils confirment et nient ce qu'on dit à leur sujet. Écrivez ce qu'ils disent en joignant les deux phrases données en une seule. Choisissez entre l'indicatif et le subjonctif dans les subordonnées. Suivez le modèle.*

MODÈLE   Marcelle suit un cours de maths. (je crois)
          → Je crois que Marcelle suit un cours de maths.

1. La voiture de Jean-François est toujours en panne. (je ne pense pas)

2. Gisèle compte abandonner le lycée. (il est évident)

3. Marc et Luc peuvent s'acheter un ordinateur. (je doute)

4. Michèle sort avec Hervé Duclos. (tout le monde sait)

5. Paul ne fait pas attention en classe. (son frère nie)

6. Chantal se plaint de tout. (il n'est pas exact)

7. Martin étudie beaucoup. (je suis sûr que)

8. Éliane va en France cette année. (il est peu probable)

Uses of the Subjunctive: Special Cases

After expressions of fear, after **empêcher que**, and after the interrogative of **douter**, the word **ne** may be placed before the verb in the subjunctive. This **ne** does not make the verb negative, but rather makes the style more formal. This **ne** is omitted in informal speech and writing.

J'ai peur qu'il **ne** comprenne.	*I'm afraid he understands.*
J'ai empêché qu'il **ne** sorte.	*I kept him from going out.*
Doutez-vous que ce livre **ne** soit utile?	*Do you doubt that this book is useful?*

The subjunctive can be used to express an indirect command for third person subjects. The English equivalent is *have/let him/her/them do something.*

—Suzanne a besoin de nous parler.	*Suzanne needs to speak to us.*
—**Qu'elle vienne** nous voir, alors.	*Let her come see us then.*
—Monsieur, l'avocat est arrivé.	*Sir, the lawyer is here.*
—Je descends tout de suite. **Qu'il attende** dans mon bureau.	*I'm coming right down. Have him wait in my office.*
—Les étudiants ne comprennent pas vos conférences, monsieur.	*The students don't understand your lectures, sir.*
—**Qu'ils fassent** attention.	*Let them pay attention.*

O *Le style soutenu.* *Refaites les phrases suivantes dans le style soutenu en ajoutant le **ne** explétif.*

1. J'ai peur que vous preniez un rhume.

2. Elle craint que nous soyons en colère.

3. Doutez-vous qu'il soit d'accord?

4. Elle empêche que nous finissions notre travail.

P *C'est aux autres de le faire!* *Employez **que** suivi du subjonctif pour donner des ordres à une troisième personne. Remplacez les compléments directs et indirects par les pronoms convenables. Suivez le modèle.*

MODÈLE   Marc veut suivre le cours de philosophie.
→ Qu'il le suive, alors.

1. Marianne et Lisette veulent apprendre le japonais.

2. Serge veut rejoindre ses amis.

3. Simone doit faire son linge.

4. Alexandre doit prendre le train.

5. Les Durand veulent vendre leur voiture.

6. Monique peut nous rendre l'argent.

7. Christian veut traduire le poème.

8. Stéphane doit finir le travail.

Q *En français, s'il vous plaît!* *Traduisez ces phrases en français. Faites attention à l'emploi du subjonctif.*

1. *We want you (tu) to come.*

2. *Let him phone me if he wants to speak to me.*

3. *The mother allows the children to go down(stairs) alone.*

4. *I need you (vous) to help me.*

5. *I'm afraid the child has fever.*

6. *It's surprising that this country produces so many trucks.*

7. *It's improbable that the weather will be nice.*

8. *It's not true that she's a doctor. I'm sure that she's a lawyer.*

R *Activité orale. La vie: impressions et réactions.* *Avec un(e) ami(e), parlez de ce qui vous surprend, de ce qui vous rend heureux(-se) ou triste, de ce qui vous paraît bizarre, des changements que vous voudriez voir. Parlez aussi de vos craintes et doutes. Employez le subjonctif autant que possible.*

The Present Subjunctive

For **-er** verbs, the forms of the present subjunctive and the forms of the present indicative are identical in both speech and writing, except for the **nous** and **vous** forms.

Indicative		Subjunctive	
je parle	nous parl**ons**	que je parle	que nous parl**ions**
tu parles	vous parl**ez**	que tu parles	que vous parl**iez**
il/elle parle	ils/elles parlent	qu'il/qu'elle parle	qu'ils/qu'elles parlent

For **-ir** and **-re** verbs, as well as for most irregular verbs, all forms of the present subjunctive are distinct from the corresponding forms of the present indicative in both speech and writing except for the third person plural (the **ils/elles** form).

Indicative		Subjunctive	
je vends	nous vend**ons**	que je vende	que nous vend**ions**
tu vends	vous vend**ez**	que tu vend**es**	que vous vend**iez**
il/elle vend	ils/elles vendent	qu'il/qu'elle vende	qu'ils/qu'elles vendent

The singular forms of the present indicative end in a vowel in speech (for the verb **vendre**, the nasal vowel /ã/). The singular forms of the present subjunctive end in the pronounced final consonant of the stem: /vãd/. This is indicated in French spelling by the addition of the letter **e** to the verb form.

S   *Activité orale.* *Replace* **je sais que** *by the main clauses indicated. Each substitution will require the verb of the subordinate clause to change to the present subjunctive. Be sure to pronounce the final consonant of the stem clearly. Follow the example.*

MODÈLE   Je sais qu'il finit.
je veux
→ Je veux qu'il finisse.

1. Je sais que tu pars.
je ne veux pas
Je ne veux pas que tu partes.

2. Je sais qu'il boit.
je ne crois pas
Je ne crois pas qu'il boive.

3. Je sais qu'elle le connaît.
je doute
Je doute qu'elle le connaisse.

4. Je sais que tu comprends.
je ne crois pas
Je ne crois pas que tu comprennes.

5. Je sais que l'enfant met ses chaussures.
   je doute
   Je doute que l'enfant mette ses chaussures.

6. Je sais qu'il perd son travail.
   il est triste
   Il est triste qu'il perde son travail.

7. Je sais qu'elle écrit bien.
   je doute
   Je doute qu'elle écrive bien.

8. Je sais que tu lis en allemand.
   je ne crois pas
   Je ne crois pas que tu lises en allemand.

9. Je sais que l'enfant s'endort.
   je veux
   Je veux que l'enfant s'endorme.

10. Je sais que tu attends.
    je ne veux pas
    Je ne veux pas que tu attendes.

The Past Subjunctive; Literary Subjunctives*

Forms and Use of the Past Subjunctive

The past subjunctive is composed of the subjunctive of the auxiliary verb (**avoir** or **être**) plus the past participle. The same rules of agreement apply as in the passé composé.

Verbs Conjugated with **avoir**	Verbs Conjugated with **être**
que j'**aie parlé, fini, perdu**	que je **sois parti(e)**
que tu **aies parlé, fini, perdu**	que tu **sois parti(e)**
qu'il/qu'elle **ait parlé, fini, perdu**	qu'il **soit parti**
	qu'elle **soit partie**
que nous **ayons parlé, fini, perdu**	que nous **soyons parti(e)s**
que vous **ayez parlé, fini, perdu**	que vous **soyez parti(e)(s)**
qu'ils/qu'elles **aient parlé, fini, perdu**	qu'ils **soient partis**
	qu'elles **soient parties**

The past subjunctive is used to indicate that the action of the subordinate clause happened before the action of the main clause. Compare the following pairs of sentences.

Je suis désolé **que tu perdes**.	*I'm sorry **that you're losing**.*
Je suis désolé **que tu aies perdu**.	*I'm sorry **that you lost**.*
Tu crains **qu'elle ne** te **comprenne pas**.	*You fear **that she won't understand** you.*
Tu crains **qu'elle ne** t'**ait pas compris**.	*You fear **that she didn't understand** you.*
Il est content **que nous venions**.	*He's happy **that we're coming**.*
Il est content **que nous soyons venus**.	*He's happy **that we've come**.*

A *Les sentiments. Claudine est en train de vivre un moment difficile. Elle exprime ses sentiments dans cette situation. Écrivez ce qu'elle dit en formant une seule phrase avec les éléments donnés. Employez le passé du subjonctif dans les propositions subordonnées. Suivez le modèle.*

MODÈLE   Mon petit ami Jacques est tombé malade. (je suis désolée)
　　　　→ Je suis désolée que mon petit ami Jacques soit tombé malade.

---

*For recognition only.

1. a. Il a pris une bronchite. (je crains)

    b. Il est allé voir le médecin. (je doute)

2. a. Ma sœur a reçu une mauvaise note en français. (j'ai peur)

    b. Elle a étudié pour l'examen. (je ne crois pas)

    c. Elle a eu des ennuis avec son petit ami. (je soupçonne)

    d. Elle ne nous a pas montré son examen. (je n'approuve pas)

    e. Sylvie ne nous en a pas parlé. (ma mère se plaint)

3. a. Mon père a perdu son emploi. (je suis étonnée)

    b. Il en a trouvé un autre. (il est possible)

    c. Il l'a déjà accepté. (il est peu probable)

4. a. Le prof d'histoire nous a demandé une dissertation de 15 pages. (je suis furieuse)

    b. Il ne nous en a pas demandé deux! (c'est une chance que)

B *Au passé!* *Refaites les échanges suivants en changeant le verbe de la proposition subordonnée au passé du subjonctif. Ensuite, traduisez vos nouvelles phrases en anglais. Suivez le modèle.*

> MODÈLE   —Je suis content que tu reviennes.
> —Et moi, je suis contente que tu m'attendes.
> → —Je suis content que tu sois revenue.
> —Et moi, je suis contente que tu m'aies attendue.
> *I'm happy that you came back (that you've come back).*
> *And I'm happy that you waited for me.*

1. —Le prof est content que Jacquot réponde.
    —Ça ne veut pas dire qu'il comprenne.

2. —Je suis ravi qu'elle puisse venir.
    —Mais il est agaçant que son mari ne vienne pas avec elle.

3. —Colette se réjouit que son chef ait confiance en elle.
    —Il faut qu'elle soit très capable.

4. —Ma mère regrette que ma sœur ne mette pas son nouveau pull.
    —Il est curieux que ce pull ne plaise pas à ta sœur.

5. —Je suis surpris qu'Irène ne m'attende pas.
    —Ça ne veut pas dire qu'elle sorte.

C *Contrastes.* *Traduisez ces paires de phrases en français en faisant attention à l'emploi du présent et du passé du subjonctif.*

1. a. *I'm happy that they're leaving.*

    b. *I'm happy that they left.*

2. a. *It's not that she's going out.*

    b. *It's not that she went out.*

3. a. *I'm not sure that she's taking a course.*

   b. *I'm not sure that she took a course.*

4. a. *I don't think the boy is reading the book.*

   b. *I don't think the boy read the book.*

5. a. *It's improbable that they're on vacation.*

   b. *It's improbable that they were on vacation.*

6. a. *We're surprised that the children don't fight* (se battre).

   b. *We're surprised that the children didn't fight.*

Forms and Use of the Imperfect Subjunctive

The imperfect subjunctive is a literary form, reserved for formal writing. It is formed by adding the following endings to the stem of -**er** verbs: -**asse**, -**asses**, -**ât**, -**assions**, -**assiez**, -**assent**.

For -**ir** and -**re** verbs and for irregular verbs, the endings of the imperfect subjunctive are added to the passé simple form minus the consonants of the ending. The circumflexes of the **nous** and **vous** forms are dropped. The imperfect subjunctive endings for this group of verbs are -**sse**, -**sses**, -ˆ**t**, -**ssions**, -**ssiez**, -**ssent**.

parler	finir	vendre
que je **parlasse**	que je **finisse**	que je **vendisse**
que tu **parlasses**	que tu **finisses**	que tu **vendisses**
qu'il/qu'elle **parlât**	qu'il/qu'elle **finît**	qu'il/qu'elle **vendît**
que nous **parlassions**	que nous **finissions**	que nous **vendissions**
que vous **parlassiez**	que vous **finissiez**	que vous **vendissiez**
qu'ils/qu'elles **parlassent**	qu'ils/qu'elles **finissent**	qu'ils/qu'elles **vendissent**

NOTE Verbs such as **commencer** and **manger** have their spelling changes in all persons of the imperfect subjunctive.

que je commençasse
que je mangeasse

Study the imperfect subjunctive forms of **avoir**, **être**, **faire**, and **venir**.

avoir	être
que j'**eusse**	que je **fusse**
que tu **eusses**	que tu **fusses**
qu'il/qu'elle **eût**	qu'il/qu'elle **fût**
que nous **eussions**	que nous **fussions**
que vous **eussiez**	que vous **fussiez**
qu'ils/qu'elles **eussent**	qu'ils/qu'elles **fussent**

faire	venir
que je **fisse**	que je **vinsse**
que tu **fisses**	que tu **vinsses**
qu'il/qu'elle **fît**	qu'il/qu'elle **vînt**
que nous **fissions**	que nous **vinssions**
que vous **fissiez**	que vous **vinssiez**
qu'ils/qu'elles **fissent**	qu'ils/qu'elles **vinssent**

In formal written French, the imperfect subjunctive is used in a subordinate clause when the subjunctive is required and the main verb is in a past tense. Even in contemporary formal style, the imperfect subjunctive is used almost exclusively in the third person.

EVERYDAY FRENCH	FORMAL FRENCH
Je veux **qu'il vienne**.	Je veux **qu'il vienne**.
Je voulais **qu'il vienne**.	Je voulais **qu'il vînt**.
Je ne crois pas **qu'il puisse** le faire.	Je ne crois pas **qu'il puisse** le faire.
Je ne croyais pas **qu'il puisse** le faire.	Je ne croyais pas **qu'il pût** le faire.
Il faut **qu'il réponde**.	Il faut **qu'il réponde**.
Il a fallu **qu'il réponde**.	Il a fallu **qu'il répondît**.

An inverted third person singular imperfect subjunctive (especially of **être**) often means *even if*. This construction is commonly used for stylistic effect in newspaper writing.

Il ne pourrait pas agir seul, **fût-il** le président.	*He couldn't act alone, **even if he were** the president.*
Elle rêvait d'être à Paris, ne **fût-ce** que pour deux ou trois jours.	*She dreamed of being in Paris, **even if it were** only for two or three days.*

In everyday French, the above sentences would be as follows.

Il ne pourrait pas agir seul, **même s'il était** le président.

Elle rêvait d'être à Paris, **même si ce n'était que** pour deux ou trois jours.

D   ***Dans le style de tous les jours.*** *Refaites ces phrases en français courant en éliminant l'imparfait du subjonctif. Suivez le modèle.*

MODÈLE   Je n'ai pas voulu qu'il vous parlât.
           → Je n'ai pas voulu qu'il vous parle.

1. Je tenais à ce qu'il finît son travail.

2. Il n'y a eu aucune chance qu'elle comprît.

3. J'avais peur que l'enfant ne tombât.

4. Il valait mieux que le chef lût le compte rendu.

5. Il fallait travailler tous les jours, fût-ce un jour de fête.

Forms and Use of the Pluperfect Subjunctive

The pluperfect subjunctive consists of the imperfect subjunctive of the auxiliary verb (**avoir** or **être**) plus the past participle.

Verbs Conjugated with **avoir**	Verbs Conjugated with **être**
que j'**eusse parlé, fini, perdu**	que je **fusse parti(e)**
que tu **eusses parlé, fini, perdu**	que tu **fusses parti(e)**
qu'il/qu'elle **eût parlé, fini, perdu**	qu'il **fût parti**
	qu'elle **fût partie**
que nous **eussions parlé, fini, perdu**	que nous **fussions parti(e)s**
que vous **eussiez parlé, fini, perdu**	que vous **fussiez parti(e)(s)**
qu'ils/qu'elles **eussent parlé, fini, perdu**	qu'ils **fussent partis**
	qu'elles **fussent parties**

The pluperfect subjunctive is used to indicate that the action of the subordinate clause happened before the action of the main clause when the verb of the main clause is in the past. Compare the following pairs of sentences in formal language.

J'étais heureux **qu'il fût** là.	*I was happy **that he was** there.*
J'étais heureux **qu'il eût été** là.	*I was happy **that he had been** there.*
On ne croyait pas **qu'il partît**.	*We didn't think **he was leaving**.*
On ne croyait pas **qu'il fût parti**.	*We didn't think **he had left**.*

Those same sentences in less formal French are as follows.

> J'étais heureux **qu'il soit** là.
> J'étais heureux **qu'il ait été** là.
>
> On ne croyait pas **qu'il parte**.
> On ne croyait pas **qu'il soit parti**.

The pluperfect subjunctive can also replace the pluperfect and the conditional perfect in both parts of a conditional sentence.

S'il me l'**eût dit, j'eusse compris**.	*If **he had told** me, **I would have understood**.*
S'il **fût venu, nous eussions parlé**.	*If **he had come, we would have talked**.*

Those same sentences in less formal French would be as follows.

> S'il me l'**avait dit, j'aurais compris**.
>
> S'il **était venu, nous aurions parlé**.

As in the case of the imperfect subjunctive, you need only recognize the forms of the pluperfect subjunctive.

E   **À *refaire en français moderne.*** *Voici des phrases littéraires, d'un style très surveillé. Refaites-les dans la langue courante. Suivez les modèles.*

MODÈLES   Je ne pensais pas qu'il fût revenu.
→ Je ne pensais pas qu'il soit revenu.

Si vous eussiez vécu en Chine pendant la guerre, vous eussiez beaucoup souffert.
→ Si vous aviez vécu en Chine pendant la guerre, vous auriez beaucoup souffert.

1. Si l'armée française eût vaincu les Allemands en 1940, la France n'eût pas été occupée.

2. Si cet écrivain ne fût pas mort à l'âge de 30 ans, il eût été un des grands romanciers de notre littérature.

3. Si les étrangers eussent parlé en français, nous eussions compris.

4. Si la ligne aérienne n'eût pas fait grève, ils fussent partis en vacances.

5. Si les soldats se fussent approchés de cette maison, ils eussent été tués.

The Subjunctive (Continued)

The Subjunctive After Certain Conjunctions

The subjunctive is used after the following conjunctions.

pour que *so that, in order that*	**en attendant que** *until*
afin que *so that, in order that* (formal)	**de peur que** *for fear that*
de façon que *so that, in order that*	**de crainte que** *for fear that*
bien que *although*	**à moins que** *unless*
quoique *although*	**pourvu que** *provided that, as long as*
encore que *although* (literary)	**à condition que** *on the condition that,*
sans que *without*	*provided that*
avant que *before*	**malgré que** *in spite of the fact that*
jusqu'à ce que *until*	

—Partons **sans que personne ne s'en rende compte**.

*Let's leave **without anyone's realizing**.*

—Alors, parlons tout bas **pour qu'on ne nous entende pas**.

*Then let's speak very softly **so that people don't hear us**.*

—Il faut continuer à travailler **bien qu'il fasse chaud**.

*It's necessary to continue working **although it's hot**.*

—Je vais t'aider **pour que tu puisses** finir.

*I'll help you **so that you can** finish.*

—Allons-nous-en **avant que Paul revienne**.

*Let's go away **before Paul comes back**.*

—Je préfère rester **jusqu'à ce qu'il vienne**.

*I prefer to stay **until he comes**.*

—J'irai **pourvu que vous puissiez** m'accompagner.

*I'll go **as long as you can** accompany me.*

—D'accord. Je vais chercher mon parapluie **de peur qu'il pleuve**.

*OK. I'll go get my umbrella **for fear that it may rain**.*

In formal style, **ne** may precede the subjunctive after **avant que, de peur que, de crainte que**, and **à moins que**.

Allons-nous-en **avant que** Paul **ne** revienne.

*Let's go **before** Paul comes back.*

Je vais chercher mon parapluie **de peur qu'il ne** pleuve.

*I'm going to look for my umbrella **in case** it rains. (lit., **for fear that** it will rain)*

Il viendra **à moins que** son fils **ne**
    soit malade.

*He'll come **unless** his son is sick.*

An infinitive construction replaces the subjunctive if the subject of both clauses is the same.

J'écris l'adresse **pour que tu ne**
    l'oublies pas.

*I'll write down the address **so that you won't**
    forget it.*

J'écris l'adresse **pour ne pas l'oublier.**

*I'll write down the address **so that I won't**
    forget it.*

Il mangera **avant que nous partions.**

*He'll eat **before we leave**.*

Il mangera **avant de partir.**

*He'll eat **before he leaves**.*

A   *Jusqu'à quand?*   *Un groupe de garçons attendent leurs petites amies, mais elles sont en retard. Ils parlent entre eux pour décider combien de temps ils vont attendre. Écrivez ce qu'ils disent en utilisant la conjonction* **jusqu'à ce que**. *Suivez le modèle.*

MODÈLE   Marc: j'attendrai / Cybèle / arriver
         → Marc: J'attendrai jusqu'à ce que Cybèle arrive.

1. Paul: j'attendrai / Marie-Claire / m'appeler

2. Philippe: j'attendrai / Yvette / venir

3. Serge: j'attendrai / l'autobus / arriver pour me ramener

4. Luc: j'attendrai / Robert / faire un coup de fil

5. Baudoin: j'attendrai / vous / s'en aller

6. Maurice: j'attendrai / nous / pouvoir vérifier où elles sont

7. Daniel: j'attendrai / nous / savoir quelque chose

8. Richard: j'attendrai / ma petite amie / apparaître

B   *À ceci près* **(With this exception).** *Un groupe d'amis parlent de ce qu'ils feront, mais posent dans chaque cas une condition qui pourrait les en empêcher avec* **à moins que**. *Écrivez ce qu'ils disent. Suivez le modèle.*

MODÈLE   Marc: J'irai au cinéma.
          Lise: Mais si nous avons une composition à rédiger...
         → Marc: Oui. J'irai au cinéma à moins que nous ayons une composition
              à rédiger.

1. Renée: Hélène sortira avec Nicolas.
   Marie: Mais si elle est occupée...

2. David: Jocelyne partira en Italie.
   Alice: Mais si son père lui défend d'y aller...

3. Paul: Christophe t'expliquera la leçon.
   Luc: Mais s'il ne fait pas attention en classe...

4. Julie: Michel veut inviter tous ses amis chez lui.
   Sara: Mais si ses parents reviennent...

5. Papa: On peut aller chez les Laurentin.
   Maman: Mais s'ils ont des choses à faire...

6. Odile: Il faudra partir sans Jacqueline.
   Diane: Mais si elle peut aller avec nous...

7. Joseph: Nous pouvons faire un pique-nique demain.
   André: Mais s'il fait mauvais...

 C *Des événements qui nous empêchent de faire des choses.* *Lucille rappelle à ses amis toutes les choses qu'il faut faire. Mais dans chaque cas son amie Odile lui rappelle une possibilité qui les empêcherait de faire ces choses. Exprimez ces possibilités posées par les amis de Lucille avec* **à moins que** *suivi du passé du subjonctif. Suivez le modèle.*

   MODÈLE   Nous devons aller voir Agnès. (mais si elle est partie...)
                → À moins qu'elle soit partie.

1. Nous pouvons aller au cinéma. (mais si Gérard a vu le film...)

2. Il nous faut faire les courses. (mais si on a déjà fermé les magasins...)

3. Nous devons attendre Vincent. (mais s'il a oublié notre rendez-vous...)

4. Alain nous emmènera au stade. (mais si sa voiture est tombée en panne...)

5. On peut aller écouter des disques chez Henri. (mais s'il est allé à la bibliothèque...)

6. Christian peut nous prêter son livre d'histoire. (mais s'il l'a perdu...)

7. Je dois téléphoner à Lise. (mais si elle n'est pas encore rentrée...)

D *Pas si vite!* *Jacquot veut sortir, voir ses amis, etc., mais sa mère pose des conditions. Écrivez ce que sa mère lui dit en formant des phrases avec* **pourvu que.** *Suivez le modèle.*

   MODÈLE   Maman, je vais au cinéma avec Albert ce soir. (tu / finir tes devoirs avant)
                → Oui, pourvu que tu finisses tes devoirs avant.

1. Maman, je sors prendre un café avec Éloïse ce soir. (tu / prendre le dessert avec nous)

2. Maman, je vais à la soirée de Victor. (tu / être de retour avant minuit)

3. Maman, je veux aller voir le match de football dimanche. (ton frère / pouvoir t'accompagner)

4. Maman, je dois aller à la bibliothèque. (tu / mettre de l'ordre dans ta chambre)

5. Maman, Guy m'invite à passer l'après-midi chez lui. (tu / faire les courses avant)

6. Maman, je veux inviter Lise à prendre le goûter avec nous. (elle / ne pas venir avant quatre heures)

7. Maman, je peux prendre la voiture ce soir? (ton père / te permettre)

8. Maman, je peux dîner dans un restaurant de luxe? (nous / pouvoir aller avec toi)

E **C'est pour ça.** *Formez des phrases avec* **pour que** *qui expliquent le pourquoi des actions. Suivez le modèle.*

> MODÈLE   L'agent de police parle lentement. (l'étranger / le comprendre)
> → L'agent de police parle lentement pour que l'étranger le comprenne.

François est souffrant.

1. Le médecin lui ordonne des antibiotiques. (il / se remettre (*recover*))

2. Sa mère a baissé les stores (*blinds*). (François / dormir)

3. Elle prépare une bonne soupe. (il / prendre quelque chose de chaud)

4. On lui donne trois couvertures (*blankets*). (il / ne pas avoir froid)

M. et Mme Durand essaient d'orienter un étudiant étranger qui habite chez eux.

5. Nous allons t'acheter un poste de télé. (tu / regarder des émissions en français)

6. On va te dessiner un petit plan du quartier. (tu / ne pas te perdre)

7. On te donne une carte avec notre numéro de téléphone. (tu / pouvoir nous appeler)

8. Nous allons inviter nos neveux et nos nièces. (tu / faire leur connaissance)

F **Courage!** *Vous encouragez votre ami à faire ce qu'il doit faire malgré les ennuis qui se présentent. Employez une proposition avec* **bien que** *pour lui dire qu'il faut surmonter les obstacles. Suivez le modèle.*

> MODÈLE   —Tu ne sors pas?
> —Il pleut.
> → Tu dois sortir bien qu'il pleuve.

1. —Tu ne fais pas tes devoirs?
   —Je suis fatigué.

2. —Tu ne descends pas faire les courses?
   —Il fait mauvais.

3. —Tu ne lis pas le livre de chimie?
   —Je n'en ai pas envie.

4. —Tu ne téléphones pas à Renée?
   —Nous sommes brouillés (*mad at each other*).

5. —Tu ne vas pas au cours?
   —Je ne me sens pas bien.

6. —Tu ne mets pas de cravate?
   —J'ai chaud.

7. —Tu n'écris rien?
   —Je ne sais pas la réponse.

8. —Tu ne finis pas ta rédaction?
   —Il est tard.

Sans ça. *Joignez chaque paire de phrases en une seule avec la conjonction* **sans que** *de façon à ce que la nouvelle phrase exprime la même idée. Suivez les modèles.*

MODÈLES   Elle part. Je ne la vois pas.
          → Elle part sans que je la voie.

          Elle est partie. Je ne l'ai pas vue.
          → Elle est partie sans que je l'aie vue.

1. Il entre doucement. On ne s'en aperçoit pas.

2. Cet étudiant copie. Le professeur ne s'en rend pas compte.

3. Marc a eu des ennuis avec la police. Ses parents ne sont pas au courant.

4. Il parle au téléphone. Je ne peux pas entendre ce qu'il dit.

5. Je te passerai un petit mot (*note*). Le prof ne me verra pas.

6. Il est parti. Nous ne le savions pas.

7. Il est rentré. Nous ne l'avons pas vu.

8. Elle s'est fâchée. Je ne lui ai rien dit.

H **On fait les courses.** *Un groupe d'amis sont en train de faire leurs courses. Décrivez leur activité en formant des phrases avec une proposition adverbiale. Employez les conjonctions indiquées. Suivez le modèle.*

MODÈLE   j'irai à la boucherie / avant / vous / revenir de la charcuterie
         → J'irai à la boucherie avant que vous (ne) reveniez de la charcuterie.

Les boutiques/les commerçants

Les boutiques	*Les commerçants*
la bijouterie *jewelry store*	**le bijoutier/la bijoutière**
la blanchisserie *laundry*	**le blanchisseur/la blanchisseuse**
la boucherie *butcher shop*	**le boucher/la bouchère**
la boulangerie *bakery*	**le boulanger/la boulangère**
la boutique du coiffeur *barbershop*	**le coiffeur/la coiffeuse**
la charcuterie *delicatessen*	**le charcutier/la charcutière**
la crémerie *dairy*	**le crémier/la crémière**
la droguerie *drugstore*	—
l'épicerie *grocery*	**l'épicier/l'épicière**
le kiosque (à journaux) *newsstand*	**le vendeur/la vendeuse de journaux**
la librairie *bookstore*	**le/la libraire**
la pâtisserie *pastry shop*	**le pâtissier/la pâtissière**
la pharmacie *drugstore, pharmacy*	**le pharmacien/la pharmacienne**
le pressing *dry cleaner's*	**le teinturier/la teinturière**
le salon de coiffure *beauty salon*	**le coiffeur/la coiffeuse**
la station-service *gas station*	**le/la pompiste, le mécanicien/la mécanicienne**

1. je ne passerai pas à la blanchisserie / jusqu'à / Louise / descendre au marché

2. Marc ira à la pâtisserie / pour / nous / prendre un bon dessert ce soir

3. Claire ira au kiosque du coin / pourvu / nous / l'accompagner

4. je vais vite au pressing / de peur / ils / fermer pour le déjeuner

5. nous attendrons Chantal à la station-service / jusqu'à / elle / faire le plein

6. Philippe attendra à la station-service / jusqu'à / le mécanicien / changer l'huile

7. nous regarderons l'étalage de la librairie / en attendant / Jean / sortir de chez le coiffeur

8. Odile veut passer à la droguerie / à moins / vous / être pressés pour rentrer

I   *Vos idées.*   *Complétez ces phrases selon vos idées, vos opinions et vos projets. Choisissez une des conjonctions proposées pour former votre phrase.*

1. Le prof continuera à parler (sans que / jusqu'à ce que)

2. Je m'achèterai de nouveaux disques compacts (pourvu que / de façon que)

3. Je sortirai ce week-end (bien que / pour que)

4. Sophie nous attendra devant le bureau (jusqu'à ce que / malgré que)

5. Les étudiants doivent se tenir (*behave*) (de peur que / pour que)

6. Je retrouverai mes amis après les cours (à moins que / quoique)

7. Je finirai de rédiger ce compte rendu (avant que / bien que)

8. Il faut prendre de l'essence (avant que / pour que)

J   *En français, s'il vous plaît.*   *Traduisez ces phrases en français.*

1. *I'll call them before I get to the airport.*

2. *We'll watch the soccer match until it begins to rain.*

3. *Mrs. Dulac set the table an hour before her friends arrived.*

4. *They stood in line in order to buy* (prendre) *tickets.*

5. *You* (vous) *didn't want to go to the department store without our going too.*

6. *Even though it's cold, we should take a walk.*

7. *I'll lend you* (tu) *the book unless you have already bought it.*

8. *You* (tu) *can go as long as your brother goes with you.*

The Subjunctive in Relative Clauses

The subjunctive is used in a relative clause if the antecedent in the main clause does not exist, is sought but not yet found, or is indefinite.

Il n'y a **personne qui** me **comprenne**.	*There's **no one who understands** me.*
Je ne vois **pas d'endroit où nous puissions** nous asseoir.	*I don't see **anyplace where we can** sit down.*
L'entreprise a besoin de **secrétaires qui sachent** trois langues.	*The firm needs **secretaries who know** three languages.*
Je cherche **une voiture qui fasse** du 150 à l'heure.	*I'm looking for **a car that does** 150 kilometers per hour.*
Connaissez-vous **quelqu'un qui puisse** nous aider?	*Do you know **someone who can** help us?*

If the antecedent in the main clause actually exists, the indicative is used in the relative clause.

J'ai besoin **des secrétaires qui savent** trois langues.

*I need **the secretaries who know** three languages.*

J'ai acheté **la voiture qui fait** du 150 à l'heure.

*I bought **the car that does** 150 kilometers per hour.*

Voilà **quelqu'un qui peut** nous aider.

*There's **someone who can** help us.*

K *On cherche un logement.* *Jacquot cherche un appartement avec trois autres étudiants. Il décrit ce que chacun désire dans un logement. À partir des éléments donnés, formez des phrases qui expriment ce qu'il dit. Suivez le modèle.*

MODÈLE   nous / chercher un appartement / avoir quatre chambres à coucher
          → Nous cherchons un appartement qui ait quatre chambres à coucher.

1. toi, tu / vouloir un appartement / avoir deux salles de bains

2. Mathieu / avoir besoin d'un appartement / être climatisé

3. Philippe et moi, nous / préférer un appartement / être près de la faculté

4. nous / vouloir un appartement / ne pas avoir besoin de beaucoup de rénovation

5. moi, je / chercher un appartement / avoir le confort moderne

6. Charles / désirer un appartement / se trouver dans un immeuble neuf

7. Mathieu et Philippe / chercher un appartement / être en face de l'arrêt d'autobus

8. nous / chercher un voisin / ne pas se plaindre du bruit

L *La femme idéale.* *Pour savoir ce que Stéphane raconte à son ami Édouard sur la femme idéale qu'il cherche, complétez les propositions relatives avec le subjonctif du verbe entre parenthèses.*

1. Je cherche une petite amie qui _____ (savoir) être une copine.

2. Je veux trouver une fille avec qui je _____ (pouvoir) parler facilement.

3. J'ai besoin d'une fiancée qui me _____ (comprendre).

4. Je préférerais une petite amie qui _____ (être) très intelligente.

5. Je veux une fille qui _____ (avoir) le sens de l'humour.

6. Je cherche une petite amie qui n'_____ (aimer) que moi.

7. J'ai besoin d'une fille qui me _____ (dire) toujours la vérité.

8. Je cherche une fille qui _____ (faire) des études dans notre faculté.

***Pas de candidates au poste!* (No candidates for the job!)** *Édouard ne peut pas aider son ami Stéphane. Il n'a pas d'amies qui aient toutes les qualités requises pour être la petite amie de Stéphane. Complétez les phrases suivantes avec la forme correcte du verbe entre parenthèses pour savoir ce qu'Édouard dit à son ami.*

1. Je ne connais pas de fille qui _____ (réussir) à te plaire.

2. Il n'y a aucune fille qui _____ (être) si merveilleuse.

3. Tu ne vas pas trouver une fille qui _____ (pouvoir) te comprendre.

4. Il n'y a personne qui ne _____ (mentir) jamais.

5. Je ne connais pas de fille qui _____ (avoir) toutes les qualités que tu cherches.

6. Il n'y a personne avec qui tu _____ (vouloir) sortir.

N ***Au bureau.*** *La compagnie où travaille Chantal cherche des employés. Complétez les phrases suivantes avec le subjonctif ou l'indicatif, selon le cas, pour savoir quels candidats doivent faire une demande d'emploi auprès de son bureau.*

Le bureau moderne
l'infographie [fem.] *computer graphics*
l'interconnexion de réseau [fem.] *networking*
le représentant/la représentante de commerce *traveling salesperson*
le traitement de données *data processing*
le traitement de texte *word processing*

1. Nous avons une représentante de commerce qui _____ (savoir) l'espagnol.

2. Nous cherchons quelqu'un qui _____ (savoir) l'italien.

3. Nous avons besoin d'un secrétaire qui _____ (connaître) bien les programmes pour le traitement de texte.

4. Il faut trouver quelqu'un qui _____ (avoir) des connaissances d'infographie.

5. Nous n'avons personne qui _____ (pouvoir) mettre à jour nos systèmes de traitement de données.

6. Nous n'avons pas encore de collègue qui _____ (être) spécialisé dans l'interconnexion de réseau.

7. Nous avons des employés qui _____ (avoir) une expérience internationale.

8. Mais il n'y a personne qui _____ (être) capable d'ouvrir des bureaux en Asie.

The Subjunctive After Superlatives

The subjunctive is used in clauses after superlatives. These sentences usually express a subjective or personal opinion or evaluation.

—C'est l'entreprise **la plus dynamique que je connaisse**.   *It's **the most dynamic** company **that I am acquainted with**.*

—Et ses produits sont **les plus solides qu'on puisse** trouver.   *And its products are **the most solid ones that you can** find.*

—C'est **le meilleur** livre **que j'aie lu**.   *It's **the best** book **that I have read**.*
—Et la dissertation **la plus difficile**   *And **the hardest** term paper **that we have**
  que nous ayons écrite.   ***written**.*

The subjunctive is also used after **seul**, **unique**, **dernier**, and **premier**.

Vous êtes la **seule** personne **qui**   *You're the **only** person **who can** understand.*
  puisse comprendre.

C'est le **premier** livre **qui soit** utile.   *It's the **first** book **that is** useful.*

O *Un peu d'enthousiasme!* Joignez les deux phrases en une seule. Employez un superlatif
(ou un de ces adjectifs: **seul**, **unique**, **dernier**, **premier**). Utilisez le subjonctif dans la
proposition subordonnée. Suivez les modèles.

MODÈLES   Ce roman est facile. Nous le lisons.
          → C'est le roman le plus facile que nous lisions.

          Vous êtes la seule personne. Vous m'avez téléphoné.
          → Vous êtes la seule personne qui m'ait téléphoné.

1. Cette fille est belle. Je la connais.

2. Ce cours est ennuyeux. Je le suis.

3. Ce compte rendu est intéressant. Marc l'écrit.

4. Ce village est joli. Vous le visitez.

5. Ce patient est le premier. Il vient au cabinet du dentiste.

6. Vous êtes la seule étudiante. Vous faites du chinois.

7. Cette employée est la dernière. Elle s'en va du bureau.

8. Ce repas est mauvais. On l'a servi à la cantine.

9. Ce restaurant est bon. Nous le fréquentons.

10. Ce tableau est beau. Tu l'as peint.

11. Ce loyer est élevé. Je l'ai payé.

12. Tu es le seul ami. Tu me comprends.

P *Et maintenant il s'agit de vous.* Puisez dans (draw on) vos expériences personnelles
pour parler de vos opinions et de vos impressions. Utilisez des superlatifs ou des adjectifs
comme **seul**, **unique**, **dernier**, **premier**. Employez le subjonctif dans les propositions
subordonnées s'il le faut. Suivez le modèle.

MODÈLE   le meilleur livre que vous ayez lu cette année
         → *La peste* de Camus est le meilleur livre que j'aie lu cette année.

1. le cours le plus intéressant que vous ayez suivi

2. l'émission (*TV show*) la plus amusante que vous regardiez

3. la première fois que vous êtes sorti(e) avec votre petit(e) ami(e)

4. l'affiche la plus jolie que vous ayez achetée

5. la personne la plus intéressante que vous connaissiez

6. le garçon le plus charmant ou la fille la plus charmante que vous connaissiez

7. le meilleur film que vous ayez vu cette année

8. l'excursion la plus amusante que vous ayez faite cette année

9. le vêtement le plus élégant que vous ayez acheté cette année

10. la dernière fois que vous êtes allé(e) à la plage

The Subjunctive in Certain Types of Indefinite Clauses

French uses the following construction to express *however* + adjective or *no matter how* + adjective.

$$
\left.\begin{array}{l}
\textbf{tout(e)} \\
\textbf{quelque} \\
\textbf{pour} \\
\textbf{aussi} \\
\textbf{si}
\end{array}\right\} + \text{adjective} + \textbf{que} + \text{subjunctive of } \textbf{être, paraître, etc.}
$$

toute confiante **que** vous soyez   *however confident you may be*
pour petit **qu'**il paraisse   *no matter how small he may seem*
aussi fort **que** ce pays soit   *however strong this country is*
si peu **que** ce soit   *however little it may be*

Quel(le)(s) + **que** + subjunctive of **être** + noun expresses the idea of *whatever*.

quels que soient les problèmes   *whatever the problems may be*
quelles que soient vos craintes   *whatever your fears may be*
quel que soit l'obstacle   *whatever the obstacle may be*

Qui que and **quoi que** followed by the subjunctive mean *whoever* and *whatever*, respectively. **Où que** + subjunctive means *wherever*.

qui que vous soyez   *whoever you may be*
qui que ce soit   *whoever, anyone*
quoi que vous fassiez   *whatever you're doing*
quoi que ce soit   *anything*
où que tu ailles   *wherever you go*

Q   *À traduire. Traduisez les phrases suivantes en anglais.*

1. Qui qu'elle soit, elle n'a pas le droit d'entrer.

2. Si riches qu'ils soient devenus, ils ne peuvent oublier la pauvreté de leur jeunesse.

3. Tout doué que tu sois, il faut que tu étudies.

4. Il comptait nous offrir quoi que ce soit.

5. Je ne lui pardonnerai jamais, quoi qu'il dise.

6. Ce candidat accepte l'argent de qui que ce soit.

7. Quelle que soit la somme offerte, elle ne sera pas suffisante.

8. Où que tu ailles, tu trouveras les mêmes difficultés.

V

Idiomatic Usage

The Passive Voice and Substitutes for the Passive

The Passive Voice (**La voix passive**)

The passive voice in French is similar in formation and function to the passive voice in English. The passive voice serves to remove the focus from the performer of the action (usually the subject of the active sentence) to the action itself. To understand this, it is helpful to see passive sentences as deriving from active ones.

The direct object of the sentence in the active voice becomes the subject of the passive sentence. The subject of the original sentence in the active voice can be added to the corresponding passive sentence in a phrase beginning with **par**. This is called the *agent phrase*.

ACTIVE VOICE	PASSIVE VOICE
Max a réparé la voiture.	La voiture a été réparée par Max.
Max repaired the car.	*The car was repaired by Max.*
Mes parents ont acheté cet appartement.	Cet appartement a été acheté par mes parents.
My parents bought this apartment.	*This apartment was bought by my parents.*

Note that the performer of the action in an agent phrase can be focused on, especially in contrasts.

La voiture a été réparée par Max, pas par moi.	*The car was repaired by Max, not by me.*

In the French passive voice, the past participle agrees in gender and number with the grammatical subject.

Les ordinateurs ont été vendus.	*The computers were sold.*
Les bicyclettes ont été vendu**es**.	*The bicycles were sold.*

The passive voice exists in all tenses.

Les claviers sont réparés par Danielle.	*The keyboards are repaired by Danielle.*
Les claviers ont été réparés par Danielle.	*The keyboards were repaired by Danielle.*
Les claviers vont être réparés par Danielle.	*The keyboards are going to be repaired by Danielle.*

After verbs of mental activity, the agent phrase in a passive sentence may be introduced by **de** instead of **par**.

Ce savant est respecté **de** tous ses collègues.	*This scientist is respected **by** all his colleagues.*
Ma grand-mère était aimée **de** tous ses petits-enfants.	*My grandmother was loved **by** all her grandchildren.*

While the passive voice is relatively frequent in English, the French passive voice belongs more to the written language than to everyday speech. To de-emphasize the performer of the action, spoken French usually uses the pronoun **on** or **ils**. Note that in sentences with passive meaning having **on** or **ils** as the subject, an agent phrase beginning with **par** cannot be added.

Ici on parle français.	*French is spoken here.*
Ils ont réparé la voiture.	*They've repaired the car.*

A   **Au bureau.** *Refaites les phrases suivantes à la voix passive pour raconter ce qui se passe au bureau. Gardez le même temps verbal dans la phrase que vous formez. Suivez le modèle.*

> MODÈLE   La secrétaire ouvre le bureau à huit heures.
> → Le bureau est ouvert à huit heures par la secrétaire.

Les affaires

le chèque *check*	**livrer des marchandises** *to deliver goods*
la demande d'emploi *job application*	**la marchandise** *merchandise, goods*
l'échantillon [masc.] *sample*	**le marché** *market*
expédier *to ship*	**passer une commande** *to place an order*
la facture *bill*	**présenter une demande d'emploi**
faire un versement sur le compte de	*to submit a job application*
to make a deposit	**signer** *to sign*
lancer un produit *to launch a product*	

1. La réceptionniste reçoit les clients.

2. Les employés passent des commandes.

3. La secrétaire a fait un versement sur le compte de l'entreprise.

4. Un camion a livré des marchandises.

5. Le bureau a expédié des échantillons.

6. Le patron a signé des chèques.

7. La secrétaire envoie des factures.

8. Ce jeune homme a présenté une demande d'emploi.

9. L'entreprise va lancer un nouveau produit.

10. Des experts vont étudier le marché.

B | *Le déménagement.* *Décrivez ce qui est arrivé pendant le déménagement des Martel en formant des phrases à la voix passive avec les éléments proposés. Ajoutez* **par** *pour indiquer l'agent. Suivez le modèle.*

MODÈLE   les meubles / mettre dans le fourgon / les déménageurs
→ Les meubles ont été mis dans le fourgon par les déménageurs.

Le déménagement

accrocher *to hang, hang up*	**la machine à laver** *washing machine*
brancher *to plug in*	**la penderie** *closet, walk-in closet*
la caisse *crate*	**le placard** *cupboard*
le déménageur *mover*	**le plombier** *plumber*
le fauteuil *armchair*	**ranger** *to put away*
le fourgon (de déménagement) *moving truck*	**le sous-sol** *basement*

1. les lits / monter / trois hommes

2. les tableaux / accrocher au mur / Pierre et sa sœur

3. la machine à laver / installer / un plombier

4. le fauteuil / placer en face de la télé / M. Martel

5. les vêtements / accrocher dans la penderie / Mme Martel

6. deux grosses caisses en bois / laisser dans le sous-sol / les déménageurs

7. la vaisselle / ranger dans les placards / Mme Martel

8. les lampes / brancher / M. Martel

C | *Oui, c'est lui.* *Monique essaie de vérifier qui va faire les choses nécessaires pour l'organisation de la soirée. Olivier répond à l'affirmatif avec une phrase à la voix passive. Écrivez les réponses d'Olivier. Suivez le modèle.*

MODÈLE   C'est Charles qui va acheter le gâteau?
→ Oui, le gâteau va être acheté par Charles.

1. Ce sont Luc et Catherine qui vont préparer la quiche?

2. C'est Marie qui va inviter les amis du lycée?

3. C'est Bernard qui va apporter le cassettophone?

4. Ce sont Geneviève et Virginie qui vont mettre les couverts?

5. C'est Suzanne qui va acheter le chocolat?

6. C'est Antoine qui va faire le café?

7. C'est Anne et Danielle qui vont choisir les cassettes?

8. C'est Eugène qui va servir les amuse-gueules?

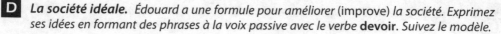

D *La société idéale.* *Édouard a une formule pour améliorer* (improve) *la société. Exprimez ses idées en formant des phrases à la voix passive avec le verbe* **devoir***. Suivez le modèle.*

> MODÈLE   améliorer l'éducation
> → L'éducation doit être améliorée.

1. protéger les enfants

2. respecter les personnes âgées

3. bien payer la police

4. honorer le drapeau

5. obéir à la loi

6. bien former les professionnels

7. subventionner (*subsidize*) les musées

8. moderniser les transports en commun (*public transportation*)

9. encourager les petites entreprises (*small business*)

10. embaucher (*hire*) les jeunes

Substitutes for the Passive Voice

The passive voice is used less in French than in English, and has a slightly formal or literary tone. It is often replaced by the active voice.

> Le conte **a été écrit par Louis**. → **Louis a écrit** le conte.

When a speaker wants to focus on the person who performed an action, the passive can be replaced by a sentence beginning with **c'est** or **ce sont** + **qui** + verb.

> Le conte a été écrit **par Louis**. → **C'est Louis** qui a écrit le conte.

When the performer of the action is not expressed, **on** may be used.

> La chambre **sera nettoyée**. → **On nettoiera** la chambre.
>
> Ici le français **est parlé**. → Ici **on parle** français.

In many cases, but not all, a pronominal construction can be used instead of the passive when the performer of the action is not expressed.

> Cette revue **est** beaucoup **lue**. → Cette revue **se lit** beaucoup.
>
> Ce mot **est** facilement **compris**. → Ce mot **se comprend** facilement.

Here are additional examples.

Ça ne se fait pas.	*That's not done.*
Ça ne se dit plus.	*That's not said anymore.*
Ce produit ne se vend qu'en pharmacie.	*This product is only sold in pharmacies.*
Les œufs ne se mangent pas le matin en France.	*They don't eat eggs in the morning in France.*
Les portes se ferment à 6 heures.	*They close the doors at six o'clock.*

E   ***Comment se tenir à table en France.*** *Les bonnes manières à table ne sont pas les mêmes en France que dans le monde anglo-saxon. Refaites ces indications avec* **on** *pour en faire une liste de conseils utiles au visiteur américain ou canadien. Suivez le modèle.*

> MODÈLE   offrir des fleurs (mais pas des chrysanthèmes) à Madame
> → On offre des fleurs (mais pas des chrysanthèmes) à Madame.

1. ne pas pencher (*tilt*) l'assiette pour finir sa soupe

2. tenir toujours le couteau dans la main droite

3. tenir toujours la fourchette dans la main gauche

4. ne pas essuyer la sauce avec un morceau de pain

5. ne pas poser les coudes sur la table

6. poser les mains sur le bord de la table

7. ne pas couper le pain avec le couteau

8. casser son morceau de pain

9. répondre «Avec plaisir» pour accepter de reprendre (*have a second helping of*) un des plats

10. répondre «Merci» pour ne pas accepter de reprendre un des plats

---

NOTE CULTURELLE

- Il faut remarquer les différences entre la façon française de se tenir à table et les coutumes américaines. N'oubliez pas que pour dire «non» quand on vous offre quelque chose à manger, on dit «Merci». Si vous voulez accepter, vous dites «Avec plaisir, s'il vous plaît».
- Le chrysanthème est la fleur de la mort en France et s'utilise aux enterrements. On ne l'offre donc pas à la famille qui vous invite à dîner.

F   ***Conseils de cuisine.*** *Formulez ces conseils de cuisine de deux façons: avec* **on** *et avec la construction pronominale. Suivez le modèle.*

> MODÈLE   prendre un apéritif avant le repas
> → On prend un apéritif avant le repas.
> Un apéritif se prend avant le repas.

1. offrir des amuses-gueules avec l'apéritif

2. couper un fromage en cubes pour servir avec l'apéritif

3. préparer une bonne soupe la veille (*the day before*)

4. déboucher le vin au moins une heure avant de le servir

5. préparer ce plat une heure avant le repas

6. servir cette viande froide

7. boire ce vin doux après le repas

8. servir des fruits comme dessert

G **_Des renseignements utiles pour un ami étranger._** _Roger reçoit John, un ami américain, à Paris. Il le renseigne sur la France en employant la construction pronominale équivalente à la voix passive. Écrivez ce que Roger dit à son ami. Suivez le modèle._

MODÈLE   en France / les distances / calculer / en kilomètres
          → En France les distances se calculent en kilomètres.

1. le base-ball / ne pas jouer / en France

2. les journaux américains / vendre / partout

3. les bouquinistes / trouver / le long de la Seine

4. les films américains / projeter / dans beaucoup de cinémas

5. les chansons américaines / entendre / à la radio

6. des festivals de théâtre / donner / en été

7. un marché volant / installer / deux fois par semaine dans ce quartier

8. les billets de métro / pouvoir acheter / en carnets de dix

NOTE CULTURELLE

- Les bouquinistes vendent des livres d'occasion. À Paris le long de la Seine il y a des dizaines de bouquinistes dont les étalages sont de grosses boîtes en métal. Beaucoup de ces bouquinistes vendent aussi des cartes postales et des affiches qui attirent le regard du touriste. Le mot **bouquiniste** vient de **bouquin**, un mot familier pour **livre**.
- En été, et surtout en province, il y a des festivals de théâtre, de danse, de musique et de cinéma. Le visiteur peut se renseigner là-dessus dans les offices de tourisme.
- Les marchés volants sont des marchés mobiles qui s'installent dans un quartier urbain deux ou trois fois par semaine. Au marché on peut acheter des fruits et des légumes, des conserves et aussi des articles de ménage (_housewares_).

H **_C'est à vous d'être le professeur de français!_** _Exprimez les aspects suivants de la langue française à une classe d'anglophones. Employez la construction pronominale (**se** + verbe) dans chaque cas pour formuler les règles. Suivez le modèle._

MODÈLE   _exagérer_ / écrire / avec un seul _g_
          → _Exagérer_ s'écrit avec un seul _g_.

1. le verbe _monter_ / conjuguer / avec _être_ au passé composé

2. dans le mot _clef_ / le _f_ final / ne pas prononcer

3. le subjonctif / utiliser / après _jusqu'à ce que_

4. _les rebuts_ (_trash_) est un mot / employer / au Canada

5. _a silent film_ / traduire en français / par _un film muet_

6. les mots _amoral_ et _immoral_ / confondre / souvent

7. le sujet / placer / devant le verbe dans les déclarations

8. le vocabulaire technique / apprendre / sans difficulté

Important Idioms and Proverbs

Idioms with **avoir** and **être**

Expressions with **avoir** (see also Chapter 2)

avoir lieu	*to take place*
avoir qqn dans sa peau	*to have someone under one's skin*
en avoir marre	*to be fed up* (colloquial)
en avoir assez	*to be fed up* (colloquial)
en avoir par-dessus la tête	*to be fed up* (colloquial)
en avoir ras le bol	*to be fed up* (slang)
en avoir plein le dos	*to be fed up* (slang)
en avoir pour son argent	*to get one's money's worth*
avoir maille à partir avec qqn	*to have a bone to pick with someone*
avoir le cafard	*to have the blues, be depressed*
avoir du toupet	*to have a lot of nerve*
avoir horreur de qqch	*to detest something, loathe something*
avoir le cœur sur la main	*to be generous*
avoir toujours le mot pour rire	*to be a real joker, have a good sense of humor*
n'avoir ni queue ni tête	*to make no sense*
avoir bonne/mauvaise mine	*to look good/bad* (usually refers to health)
avoir hâte de faire qqch	*to be impatient/in a rush to do something*
avoir des complexes	*to have hang-ups*
avoir le fou rire	*to have the giggles, laugh uncontrollably*
avoir la langue bien pendue	*to be a good talker, have the gift of gab*
avoir du mal à faire qqch	*to have difficulty doing something*
avoir le mal du pays	*to be homesick*
avoir le mal de mer	*to be seasick*
avoir de l'oreille	*to have an ear for music*
avoir six mètres de haut/long/large	*to be six meters high/long/wide*
en avoir pour cinq minutes	*to take (someone) five minutes (to do something)*
Je t'ai eu!	*I've tricked you! Gotcha!*
Ils m'ont eu!	*I've been had!*
J'ai le cœur qui bat.	*My heart is beating (with excitement/ nervousness).*
J'ai la tête qui tourne.	*I'm dizzy.*
Qu'est-ce qu'il a?	*What's wrong with him?*

Tu n'avais qu'à me demander.	*All you had to do was ask me.*
Il n'a qu'à étudier un peu.	*All he has to do is study a little.*
Il n'y a que toi pour faire ça!	*Only you would do that! It takes you to do that!*
Il n'y a pas de quoi.	*Don't mention it. You're welcome.*
Il doit y avoir une raison.	*There must be a reason.*
Il y a un froid entre eux.	*They're on bad terms. They're angry with each other.*
Ce gosse n'a pas froid aux yeux!	*That kid is plucky/gutsy!*

Expressions with être (see also Chapter 2)

être au courant	*to be informed, be up to date (about a matter)*
être en nage	*to be in a sweat*
être sur la même longueur d'ondes	*to be on the same wavelength*
être dans la lune	*to be off in the clouds somewhere*
être sur le point de faire qqch	*to be on the verge of doing something*
être des nôtres	*to join us (for an activity)*
être de mèche avec	*to be in cahoots with*
être reçu à un examen	*to pass a test*
être reçu au bac	*to pass the baccalaureate exam*
être de retour	*to be back*
être de trop	*to be in the way, be out of place*
être en vue	*to be the object of public attention, be in the public eye*
comme si de rien n'était	*as if nothing had happened*
c'est à moi/toi/lui de…	*it's up to me/you/him/her to . . .*
il est + *singular or plural noun*	*there is, there are* (literary substitute for **il y a**)
J'y suis!	*I've got it! Now I understand!*
Il y est pour beaucoup.	*He's largely responsible.*
Je n'y suis pour rien.	*I'm not at all at fault. I'm not to blame.*
Tout est à refaire.	*Everything has to be redone.*
Il est des gens qui croient cela.	*There are people who believe so.*
On en est là.	*We've come to that.*
Où en sommes-nous?	*Where are we up to?*
Nous sommes quittes.	*We're even.*
J'en suis à ma dernière année au lycée.	*I'm in my last year at school.*
J'en suis à me demander si…	*I'm beginning to wonder if . . .*
J'en suis pour mes frais!	*I've gotten nothing for my money!*
J'en suis pour ma peine!	*I've gotten nothing for my trouble!*

A **Comment le dire?** *Laquelle des deux possibilités exprime l'idée proposée?*

1. Vous voulez dire à un ami que vous serez bientôt prêt.
   a. J'en ai pour cinq minutes.
   b. Tu n'as qu'à attendre.

2. C'est un enfant courageux.
   a. Ce gosse est en nage.
   b. Ce gosse n'a pas froid aux yeux.

3. Vous voulez dire que quelqu'un vous a trompé.
   a. J'en ai par-dessus la tête!
   b. On m'a eu!

4. Vous voulez dire que Marie est généreuse et franche.
   a. Elle a le cœur sur la main.
   b. Elle y est pour beaucoup.

5. Vous entrez tard dans la classe et vous voulez savoir à quelle page on lit. Vous demandez:
   a. Vous y êtes?
   b. Où en sommes-nous?

6. Vous voulez dire que vous ne savez rien au sujet de l'affaire dont on parle.
   a. Il doit y avoir une raison.
   b. Je ne suis pas au courant.

7. Vous voulez nier votre responsabilité. Vous dites:
   a. Je n'y suis pour rien.
   b. Tu as du toupet.

8. Vous voulez exprimer votre émotion. Vous dites:
   a. Je t'ai dans la peau.
   b. J'ai le cœur qui bat.

9. Le travail est tellement mal fait qu'il faut recommencer.
   a. Ça n'a ni queue ni tête.
   b. Tout est à refaire.

10. Vous voulez dire que vos efforts ont été inutiles. Vous dites:
    a. J'en suis pour ma peine.
    b. J'ai maille à partir avec toi.

B **Qu'est-ce que ça veut dire?** *Laquelle des deux possibilités définit l'expression donnée?*

1. J'en suis à me demander si...
   a. Je voudrais vous demander si...
   b. Je commence à penser que...

2. Nous en sommes là.
   a. Nous voilà dans un état lamentable.
   b. Nos efforts ont produit l'effet souhaité.

3. Lui, il ne manque pas de toupet!
   a. Il est audacieux et arrogant.
   b. Il est gentil et généreux.

4. Jacqueline a toujours le mot pour rire.
   a. Elle rit beaucoup.
   b. Elle fait rire les autres.

5. Cet homme d'affaires n'a pas froid aux yeux.
   a. Il est trop prudent.
   b. Il n'a pas peur de prendre des risques.

6. J'ai la tête qui tourne.
   a. J'ai oublié.
   b. J'ai le vertige.

7. Cette histoire n'a ni queue ni tête.
   a. Elle est incohérente.
   b. Elle est difficile.

8. Il y a un froid entre eux.
   a. Ils sont fâchés.
   b. Ils ont froid.

9. Tu n'as qu'à me téléphoner.
   a. Tu ne m'as pas téléphoné.
   b. Il suffit de me téléphoner.

10. Comme si de rien n'était.
    a. Comme si nous n'avions rien à faire.
    b. Comme s'il n'y avait aucun problème.

11. La réunion a eu lieu hier.
    a. On s'est réunis hier.
    b. Il y avait de la place pour la réunion.

12. Il n'a pas bonne mine.
    a. Il n'a pas d'argent.
    b. Il a l'air malade.

Idioms with faire (see also Chapter 2)

faire à sa tête	*to act impulsively, do whatever one wants*
faire acte de présence	*to put in an appearance*
faire de la peine à qqn	*to hurt someone's feelings*
faire de la photographie	*to do photography as a hobby*
faire des bêtises	*to get into mischief*
faire du bricolage	*to do odd jobs, putter around*
faire du sport	*to play sports*
faire du ski	*to ski*
faire de la natation	*to swim*
faire du théâtre	*to be an actor* (professional); *to do some acting* (amateur)
faire du violon	*to study the violin*
faire du piano	*to study the piano*
faire l'école buissonnière	*to play hooky*
faire l'enfant	*to act like a child*
faire l'idiot	*to act the fool*
faire l'Europe	*to travel to Europe, visit Europe*

faire la moue	*to pout*
faire la queue	*to stand in line*
faire le singe	*to play the fool*
faire peau neuve	*to turn over a new leaf*
faire preuve de	*to show, display (a quality or virtue)*
faire savoir	*to let someone know*
faire semblant de faire qqch	*to pretend to do something*
faire ses bagages/valises	*to pack*
faire ses quatre cents coups	*to sow one's wild oats, get into a lot of trouble*
faire son bac	*to study for one's baccalaureate*
faire son droit	*to study for one's law degree*
faire son marché	*to go grocery shopping*
faire toute une histoire de qqch	*to make a federal case out of something*
faire un beau gâchis de qqch	*to make a real mess of something*
faire un clin d'œil à qqn	*to wink at someone*
faire une croix dessus	*to give up on (something), kiss (something) good-bye*
faire un voyage	*to take a trip*
faire une promenade	*to take a walk*
faire une drôle de tête	*to make a strange/funny face*
faire une fugue	*to run away from home*
faire une gaffe	*to blunder, make a mistake* (in conduct)
Si cela ne vous fait rien.	*If you don't mind.*
Ça me fait froid dans le dos.	*That gives me the shivers.*
Ça ne me fait rien.	*That's OK. That doesn't matter.*
Qu'est-ce que cela peut bien te faire?	*What can that possibly matter to you?*
C'est bien fait pour toi!	*It serves you right!*
Que faites-vous dans la vie?	*What do you do for a living?*
Quel métier faites-vous?	*What do you do for a living?*
Qu'est-ce que j'ai fait de mes gants?	*What have I done with my gloves?*
Rien à faire.	*No use insisting.*
Il n'y a rien à faire.	*It's hopeless.*
L'accident a fait huit victimes.	*Eight people were killed in the accident.*

Expressions with se faire

se faire fort de + *infinitive*	*to be confident, claim that one can (do something)*
se faire du mauvais sang	*to worry*
se faire du souci/des soucis	*to worry*
s'en faire	*to worry*
se faire une raison	*to resign oneself (to something)*
se faire tout(e) petit(e)	*to make oneself inconspicuous, try not to be noticed*
se faire à qqch	*to get used to something*
se faire des idées/illusions	*to be fooling oneself*
se faire une montagne de qqch	*to exaggerate the importance of something*
se faire passer pour	*to pass oneself off as*
se faire mal	*to hurt oneself*

C *Même sens.* *Trouvez dans la deuxième colonne des synonymes pour chacune des expressions de la première.*

1. faire une drôle de tête
2. faire son marché
3. se faire du mauvais sang
4. se faire une montagne de qqch
5. C'est bien fait pour toi!
6. se faire à qqch
7. Rien à faire.
8. se faire une raison

a. faire toute une histoire de qqch
b. s'habituer à qqch
c. acheter à manger
d. se résigner
e. s'inquiéter
f. faire une grimace
g. se couper
h. C'est bien mérité.
i. Ça ne vous regarde pas.
j. Inutile d'insister.

D *À compléter.* *Une expression avec **faire** décrit ce que cette personne fait dans chaque cas. Trouvez la bonne expression pour compléter chaque phrase.*

1. Rachelle va en Turquie et en Israël. Elle fait _____.

2. Robert fait une tête de mécontentement. Il fait _____.

3. Samuel veut que personne ne le remarque. Il se fait _____.

4. Michèle se coupe le doigt. Elle se fait _____.

5. Charles étudie pour devenir avocat. Il fait _____.

6. Mon père cherche toujours quelque chose à réparer à la maison. Il fait _____.

7. Mon frère fait des actes dangereux. Il fait _____.

8. Chantal est sûre qu'elle va gagner à la loterie. C'est impossible. Elle se fait _____.

Idioms with **prendre** (see also Chapter 2)

passer prendre qqn	to go pick someone up
prendre à gauche/droite	to turn left/right
prendre au pied de la lettre	to take literally
prendre au sérieux	to take seriously
prendre des risques	to take chances
prendre du poids	to gain weight
prendre feu	to catch fire
prendre fin	to come to an end
prendre froid	to catch cold
prendre un rhume	to catch cold
prendre garde	to be careful, watch out
prendre goût à qqch	to take a liking to something, begin to like something
prendre l'air	to get a breath of fresh air
prendre le frais	to get a breath of fresh air
prendre qqn en grippe	to take a dislike to someone

prendre qqn la main dans le sac	*to catch someone red-handed*
prendre qqn par son point faible	*to take advantage of someone's weak spot*
prendre rendez-vous avec	*to make an appointment with*
prendre sa retraite	*to retire (from one's career)*
prendre ses jambes à son cou	*to run off, flee*
prendre son courage à deux mains	*to get up one's courage*
être pris	*to have previous engagements, be tied up*
être pris de vertige	*to get dizzy*
être pris de remords	*to be stricken by remorse*
être pris de panique	*to be panic-stricken*
un parti pris	*prejudice, preconceived notion*
Pourriez-vous me prendre un journal?	*Could you buy/get a newspaper for me?*
Je t'y prends!	*I've got you! I've caught you!*
On m'a pris pour un Allemand.	*I was taken for a German.*
Que je t'y prenne…!	*Just let me catch you doing that (again)!*
Si je t'y prends encore!	*Just let me catch you doing that (again)!*
Il a bien/mal pris la chose.	*He took it well/badly.*
Qu'est-ce qui t'a pris?	*What's gotten into you?*
On ne sait jamais par quel bout le prendre.	*You never know how to take him.*

Expressions with **se prendre**

s'en prendre à qqn	*to attack someone, pick on someone*
s'y prendre	*to go about doing something*
s'y prendre bien/mal	*to do a good/bad job*
se faire prendre	*to get caught*
Pour qui te prends-tu?	*Who do you think you are?*
Ils se prennent pour des intellectuels.	*They think they're intellectuals.*

E   *De nouvelles phrases. Refaites les phrases suivantes avec une des expressions avec **prendre**.*

1. Il s'est retiré des affaires.

2. Il s'attaque à ses critiques.

3. C'est un préjugé.

4. Fais attention!

5. Tu peux me procurer un journal?

6. Le petit garçon m'a compris littéralement.

7. Je me suis enrhumé(e).

8. L'enfant a grossi.

9. On a attrapé le voleur en train de fouiller dans les tiroirs.

10. J'ai été frappé(e) par un sentiment de panique.

11. Il ne sait pas faire ce travail.

12. Il sort respirer un peu dehors.

Idioms with **mettre**

mettre à jour	*to bring up to date*
mettre qqn au courant	*to inform someone, bring someone up to date*
mettre le feu à qqch	*to set fire to something*
mettre qqn à la porte	*to throw someone out; to fire someone*
mettre le couvert	*to set the table*
mettre la table	*to set the table*
mettre du soin à faire qqch	*to take care in doing something*
mettre les bouts	*to leave, scram* (slang)
mettre les voiles	*to leave, scram* (slang)
mettre en cause	*to call into question, implicate*
mettre en contact	*to put in touch*
mettre en garde contre	*to warn (someone) against*
mettre qqch en lumière	*to bring something to light, bring something out in the open*
mettre en marche	*to get (something) going, start (something) up*
mettre en œuvre	*to implement, make use of*
mettre qqn en quarantaine	*to give someone the silent treatment*
mettre au point	*to fine-tune, adjust, perfect*
mettre en relief	*to emphasize*
mettre en service	*to bring into service, put into operation*
mettre en train	*to get something under way*
mettre en valeur	*to develop (property)*
mettre fin à qqch	*to put an end to something*
mettre sens dessus dessous	*to turn things upside down*
mettre qqn sur la voie	*to put someone on the right track*
J'ai mis une heure à le faire.	*I took an hour to do it.*
J'en mettrais ma main au feu!	*I'd swear to it!*
Mettons que...	*Let's say that . . .*

Expressions with **se mettre**

se mettre en quatre pour qqn	*to go all out for someone, make a superhuman effort for someone*
se mettre en colère	*to get angry*
se mettre d'accord	*to agree, come to an agreement*
se mettre à genoux	*to kneel, get on one's knees*
se mettre au lit	*to go to bed*
se mettre au travail	*to get to work*
se mettre en route	*to set out on a trip*
se mettre au français	*to begin the study of French, get down to the business of studying French*
se mettre à faire qqch	*to begin to do something*
se mettre à l'abri	*to take shelter*
se mettre à table	*to sit down to eat*
n'avoir rien à se mettre	*to have nothing to wear*
Je ne savais plus où me mettre.	*I didn't know where to hide. (out of embarrassment, etc.)*
Le temps se met au beau.	*It's clearing up.*

F   *Savez-vous une expression avec **mettre**?* *Écrivez l'expression avec **mettre** qui est l'équivalent de chacune des locutions données.*

1. congédier qqn
2. se coucher
3. s'agenouiller
4. brûler qqch
5. faire savoir

6. commencer à faire qqch
7. s'asseoir pour manger
8. partir
9. faire un grand effort pour qqn
10. mettre qqn à l'écart, ne pas lui parler

G   *Comment est-ce qu'on pourrait dire ça?* *Choisissez une des expressions avec **mettre** de la liste suivante pour compléter ces phrases. Modifiez la forme de l'expression pour l'intégrer correctement s'il le faut.*

Le temps se met au beau.	mettre sur la voie
mettre en relief	n'avoir rien à se mettre
mettre en service	se mettre à l'abri
mettre en valeur	se mettre aux maths
mettre les bouts	se mettre en colère

1. Il commence à pleuvoir. On va _____ pour ne pas se mouiller.

2. Beaucoup de touristes viennent dans cette région et toi, tu as un terrain près du lac. Tu dois le _____.

3. Viens, ma belle. Il est tard. On doit y aller. Excuse-nous, Marguerite. Véronique et moi, on _____.

4. On a _____ un TGV entre Paris et Rennes.

5. L'examen de maths est dans un mois. La dernière fois tu n'as pas réussi. Il te faut _____ dès aujourd'hui.

6. Toutes mes robes sont vieilles et démodées. Je n'ai _____.

7. Il m'a donné de très bons conseils. Je dirais même qu'il m'a _____.

8. Je répète cette idée pour la _____.

9. Si tu arrives en retard encore une fois, le prof va _____.

10. Regardez! Il ne pleut plus et le soleil se montre. _____!

Idioms with **voir**

voir trente-six chandelles	*to see stars*
voir la vie en rose	*to see life through rose-colored glasses*
se voir en cachette	*to meet secretly*
n'y voir goutte	*not to be able to see a thing* (because of the dark, etc.)
n'y voir que du feu	*to be completely fooled/taken in*
en faire voir de dures	*to give (someone) a hard time*
en faire voir de toutes les couleurs	*to give (someone) a hard time*

en faire voir des vertes et des pas mûres	*to give (someone) a hard time*
ne voir aucun mal à qqch	*not to see any harm in something*
faire voir trente-six chandelles à qqn	*to knock the living daylights out of someone*
Fais voir!	*Show me!*
Vous voyez d'ici le tableau!	*Just picture it!*
On aura tout vu!	*That would be the limit. That would be too much.*
Cela n'a rien à voir avec...	*That has nothing to do with . . .*
Je n'ai rien à voir dans cette affaire.	*I have nothing to do with that. I'm not responsible for that.*
Je ne peux pas les voir (en peinture)!	*I can't stand them!*
Ils ne peuvent pas se voir.	*They can't stand each other.*
C'est quelque chose qui ne se voit pas tous les jours.	*It's a rare thing.*
Je te vois venir!	*I know what you're up to!*
Je l'ai vu de mes propres yeux.	*I saw it with my own eyes.*
On verra bien!	*We'll see!*
Je voudrais vous y voir!	*I'd like to see how well you'd do (in that situation)!*
Voyons!	*Come on, now!*
On n'en voit pas la fin.	*The end is nowhere in sight.*
Je n'y vois pas d'inconvénient.	*I don't see any problem. I have no objection.*
Essaie un peu pour voir!	*Just you try it!* (colloquial)
C'est mal vu.	*People don't like that. People don't look favorably on that.*

H *Comment le dire? Laquelle des deux possibilités exprime l'idée proposée?*

1. Tu n'oserais pas faire ça!
   a. Tu n'y vois aucun mal.
   b. Essaie un peu pour voir.

2. Tu ne ferais pas mieux que moi.
   a. Je te vois venir!
   b. Je voudrais vous y voir.

3. J'ai eu très, très mal.
   a. J'ai vu trente-six chandelles.
   b. Je n'y ai vu que du feu.

4. Je n'ai pas eu la vie facile.
   a. C'est quelque chose qui ne se voit pas tous les jours.
   b. J'en ai vu des vertes et des pas mûres.

5. Les gens n'aiment pas les choses comme ça.
   a. Ils se voient en cachette.
   b. C'est mal vu.

6. Ça c'est le comble.
   a. On aura tout vu!
   b. On verra bien!

7. Jean a été dupe.
   a. Il n'y voit que du feu.
   b. Il ne peut pas le voir.

8. Je me rends compte de vos intentions.
   a. Je l'ai vu de mes propres yeux.
   b. Je vous vois venir.

I *Les expressions avec voir.* *Utilisez une des expressions avec* **voir** *pour exprimer les idées suivantes.*

1. Vous voulez que quelqu'un vous montre quelque chose. Vous dites:

2. Vous voulez dire que votre ami Pierre est toujours optimiste, confiant. Vous dites:

3. Vous voulez dire que l'obscurité vous empêche de distinguer quoi que ce soit. Vous dites:

4. Vous voulez menacer quelqu'un en lui disant que vous le battrez très fort. Vous dites:

5. Vous demandez à une amie d'imaginer une scène amusante. Vous dites:

6. Vous voulez dire que pour vous le plan ne présente pas de problèmes. Vous dites:

7. Vous voulez dire qu'à votre avis la situation va continuer pour longtemps. Vous dites:

8. Vous voulez dire que Marc et sa petite amie ne se rencontrent que secrètement. Vous dites:

9. Vous voulez dire que deux personnes ne se supportent pas. Vous dites:

10. Vous voulez dire que quelque chose n'arrive que très rarement. Vous dites:

Idioms with **dire**

dire à qqn ses quatre vérités	*to tell someone off*
dire à qqn son fait	*to tell someone off*
dire que...	*to think that . . .*
dire ce qu'on a sur le cœur	*to get something off one's chest*
dire des sottises	*to talk nonsense*
dire toujours amen	*to be a yes-man*
ne pas se le faire dire deux fois	*not to have to be told twice*
vouloir dire	*to mean*
à vrai dire	*to tell the truth*
à ce qu'il dit	*according to him, according to what he says*
ou pour mieux dire	*to put it another way*
c'est-à-dire	*that is to say, in other words*
pour ainsi dire	*so to speak*
comme on dit	*so to speak*
on dirait que...	*you'd think that . . .*
autrement dit	*in other words*
À qui le dites-vous (le dis-tu)?	*You're telling me?*
C'est moi qui vous le dis.	*Just take my word for it.*

C'est vous qui le dites.	*That's what you say.*
Cela va sans dire.	*It goes without saying.*
Ça te dit?	*Does that appeal to you? Do you feel like doing that?*
Ça ne me dit rien.	*That doesn't appeal to me at all. I don't feel like doing that.*
Ça ne me dit pas grand-chose.	*I don't think much of that.*
Ça me dit quelque chose.	*That rings a bell.*
C'est peu dire.	*That's an understatement.*
C'est beaucoup dire.	*That's saying a lot.*
C'est trop dire.	*That's saying too much.*
C'est plus facile à dire qu'à faire.	*That's easier said than done.*
Je ne dis pas non.	*I won't say no.*
Je ne vous le fais pas dire!	*I'm not putting words into your mouth.*
Il n'y a pas à dire.	*There's no doubt about it.*
Je vous l'avais dit.	*I told you so.*
Vous dites?	*I beg your pardon.*
On se dirait en France.	*You'd think you were in France.*

J **Qu'est-ce que cela veut dire?** *Trouvez dans la deuxième colonne des équivalents pour chacune des expressions avec **dire** de la première.*

1. Ça te dit?	a. C'est évident.
2. Ça me dit quelque chose.	b. C'est une façon de parler.
3. Je ne dis pas non.	c. Je ne suis pas de votre avis.
4. comme on dit	d. Il n'y a pas de doute.
5. C'est beaucoup dire.	e. J'accepte.
6. Vous dites?	f. Je crois que je m'en souviens.
7. C'est vous qui le dites.	g. en d'autres termes
8. Cela va sans dire.	h. Vous exagérez l'importance de l'affaire.
9. Je vous l'avais dit.	i. Je le fais avec empressement, sans attendre.
10. Je ne me le fais pas dire deux fois.	j. Je l'avais prévu.
11. autrement dit	k. Répétez, s'il vous plaît.
12. Il n'y a pas à dire.	l. Tu en as envie?

Expressions with Other Common Verbs

Expressions with casser

se casser la jambe/le bras	*to break one's leg/arm*
se casser la figure	*to fall flat on one's face*
se casser la tête	*to rack one's brains*
Ça ne casse rien.	*That's no great shakes.*
Tu me casses les pieds!	*You're a pain in the neck! You're annoying me!*

Expressions with **chercher**

chercher midi à 14 heures	*to look for problems where there are none, complicate things*
chercher querelle/noise à qqn	*to pick a fight with someone*
chercher des histoires à qqn	*to try to make trouble for someone*
chercher la petite bête	*to split hairs*
aller/venir chercher qqn	*to go/come get someone, go/come pick someone up*

Expressions with **demander**

se demander	*to wonder*
On vous demande au téléphone.	*You're wanted on the phone.*
Je ne demande qu'à vous voir.	*All I ask for is to see you.*
Je ne demande pas mieux que rester ici.	*I ask for nothing better than to stay here.*

Expressions with **donner**

donner la chair de poule à qqn	*to give someone goosebumps*
donner du fil à retordre à qqn	*to give someone a load of work, give someone a lot of trouble*
donner le feu vert à	*to give the go-ahead to*
donner le la	*to set the tone*
donner l'exemple	*to set an example*
donner rendez-vous à	*to make an appointment with*
donner un coup de fil à qqn	*to give someone a ring, call someone up*
donner un coup de main à qqn	*to help someone out*
donner une fête	*to throw a party*

Expressions with **entrer**

entrer dans les mœurs	*to become a way of life*
entrer en vigueur	*to take effect* (of laws, regulations, etc.)
faire entrer qqch dans	*to fit something into, make something fit into*
faire entrer qqn	*to show someone in*
Entrez sans frapper.	*Walk right in. Enter without knocking.*

Expressions with **payer**

être payé pour le savoir	*to have learned something the hard way, know through bitter experience*
se payer la tête de qqn	*to make fun of someone*
payer les pots cassés	*to pay for the damage*
payer ses dettes	*to pay one's debts*
payer ses impôts	*to pay one's taxes*
payer comptant	*to pay cash*
les congés payés	*paid vacation*
Je te paie un café.	*I invite you to have a cup of coffee.*

Expressions with **perdre**

perdre connaissance	*to lose consciousness, black out*
perdre courage	*to lose courage*
perdre le nord	*to lose one's bearings*
perdre patience	*to lose patience*
perdre du poids	*to lose weight*
perdre qqn de vue	*to lose sight of someone*
perdre son temps	*to waste one's time*
perdre du terrain	*to lose ground*
se perdre	*to get lost*
Tu n'y perds rien!	*It's no loss.*

Expressions with **rouler**

rouler sur l'or	*to be loaded, be very rich*
se faire rouler	*to get taken, get swindled*
se rouler par terre de rire	*to be rolling on the ground with laughter*
Sur l'autoroute on roule à 90 à l'heure.	*On the superhighway, we go 90 kilometers an hour.*
C'est à se rouler (par terre)!	*It's a scream! It's a riot!*

Expressions with **sonner**

Il est trois heures sonnées.	*It's already past three.*
Minuit sonne.	*The clock strikes midnight.*

Expressions with **tenir**

tenir bon	*to hold one's ground*
tenir compte de	*to keep in mind, take into account*
tenir le coup	*to hold out, make it through, weather the storm*
se tenir au courant de qqch	*to keep informed about something*
se tenir les côtes	*to split one's sides laughing*
Ce raisonnement ne tient pas debout.	*That reasoning doesn't hold water.*
Tenez votre droite/gauche.	*Keep to the right/left. (driving)*
Qu'à cela ne tienne.	*That's no problem.*

Expressions with **tirer**

se tirer d'affaire	*to manage, get along*
s'en tirer	*to manage, get along*
s'en tirer à bon compte	*to get off cheaply/easy*
tirer au sort	*to draw lots*
tirer la langue	*to stick out one's tongue*
tiré à quatre épingles	*dressed to kill*
tiré par les cheveux	*far-fetched*

K   *Exprimez-vous comme il faut.* *Choisissez dans la liste ci-dessous l'expression convenable pour les situations proposées.*

Tu me casses les pieds.	Il roule sur l'or.
Donne-moi un coup de main.	Tu me tiens au courant.
tient bon	cherchent la bagarre
Il a perdu le nord.	Ce raisonnement ne tient pas debout.
On va tirer au sort.	Il a payé ses dettes.
entrent dans les mœurs	Il cherche midi a 14 h.
Ils me donnent du fil à retordre.	On vous demande au téléphone.

1. Quand quelque chose manque de logique, on dit:

2. Quand une armée ne cède pas devant l'attaque de l'ennemi, on dit qu'elle...

3. Quand quelqu'un vous ennuie avec ses questions et ses objections, vous lui dites:

4. Quand vous voulez appeler quelqu'un parce qu'il y a un coup de fil pour lui, vous dites:

5. Pour exprimer l'idée que quelqu'un est très, très riche, vous dites (d'une façon familière):

6. Vous êtes professeur. Pour dire que vos étudiants vous font travailler trop, vous dites:

7. Pour dire à quelqu'un que Charles a remboursé l'argent qu'il devait, vous dites:

8. Vous notez que Serge est désorienté. Vous dites:

9. Vous proposez une méthode impartielle pour choisir la personne qui va demander au prof de remettre l'examen à la semaine prochaine. Vous dites:

10. Vous voulez que votre ami vous aide. Vous lui dites:

L   *Répondez.* *Choisissez la réponse ou la réaction correcte.*

1. L'enfant a fait un geste de mépris?
   a. Oui, il a tiré la langue.
   b. Oui, il m'a donné la chair de poule.

2. Cette fille sert de modèle aux autres?
   a. Oui, elle donne l'exemple.
   b. Oui, elle se roule par terre.

3. La solution va être difficile à trouver.
   a. Oui, il faudra se casser la figure.
   b. Oui, il faudra se casser la tête.

4. Tu vas te faire avoir!
   a. Non, je ne me fais jamais rouler.
   b. Non, je ne me fais jamais entrer.

5. Est-ce que Jeanne a résisté jusqu'à la fin?
   a. Oui, elle a donné du fil à retordre.
   b. Oui, elle a tenu le coup.

6. Vous avez déjà commencé?
   a. Oui, on nous a donné le la.
   b. Oui, on nous a donné le feu vert.

7. Il a maigri?
   a. Oui, il a perdu du poids.
   b. Oui, il nous a perdu de vue.

8. On dit que ces idées sont moins importantes qu'avant.
   a. C'est vrai. Elles sont entrées en vigueur.
   b. C'est vrai. Elles ont perdu du terrain.

9. Il se moque de nous?
   a. Oui, il se paie notre tête.
   b. Oui, il cherche la petite bête.

10. Pourquoi est-ce que tu dis que je cherche midi à 14 heures?
    a. Parce que tu cherches des complications inutiles.
    b. Parce que tu paies les pots cassés.

Idioms from Rural Life: The Farm, Cats, Dogs, and Cabbages

Rural Images

aller comme un tablier (*apron*) à une vache	*to look terrible on someone* (of an item of clothing)
avoir un bœuf sur la langue	*to be hesitant to speak up*
être sur la paille	*to be destitute*
faire l'âne pour avoir du son	*to play dumb* (with the idea of getting something)
ménager la chèvre et le chou	*to sit on the fence, not take sides*
mettre la charrue devant les bœufs	*to put the cart before the horse*
mourir sur le fumier	*to die in poverty, die destitute*
la brebis galeuse	*black sheep*
connu comme le loup blanc	*well-known, easily recognized*
doux comme un agneau	*gentle as a lamb*
entre chien et loup	*at twilight*
fauché comme les blés	*flat broke*
têtu comme une mule	*stubborn as a mule*
un nid de poule	*a pothole*
C'est une pierre dans mon jardin.	*It's an insult to me. It's a dig at me.*
Le champ est libre.	*The coast is clear.*
On n'a pas gardé les cochons ensemble!	*Why are you getting so familiar with me?*
Quand les poules auront des dents.	*That'll be the day.*

Les chats

ne pas réveiller le chat qui dort	*to let sleeping dogs lie*
avoir un chat dans la gorge	*to have a frog in one's throat*
acheter chat en poche	*to buy a pig in a poke*
appeler un chat un chat	*to call a spade a spade*
avoir d'autres chats à fouetter	*to have other fish to fry*
s'entendre comme chien et chat	*not to get along at all*
À bon chat, bon rat.	*Tit for tat.*

Chat échaudé craint le feu.	*He won't make the same mistake twice.*
Il n'y avait pas un chat!	*There wasn't a soul!*
Je donne ma langue au chat.	*I give up (trying to answer a riddle, etc.).*

Les chiens

arriver comme un chien dans un jeu de quilles (*bowling*)	*to turn up when least needed or wanted*
avoir du chien	*to have style*
dormir en chien de fusil	*to sleep all curled up*
être d'une humeur de chien	*to be in a lousy mood*
s'entendre comme chien et chat	*not to get along at all*
se donner un mal de chien	*to work like a dog*
se regarder en chiens de faïence	*to glare at each other*
traiter qqn comme un chien	*to treat someone like a dog*
malade comme un chien	*sick as a dog*
Ce n'est pas fait pour les chiens.	*It's meant to be used.*
Chien méchant.	*Beware of the dog.* (sign)
Il fait un temps de chien.	*The weather is terrible.*

Les choux

ménager la chèvre et le chou	*to play both ends against the middle*
être dans les choux	*to be in difficulty, be out of the running, have done badly on one's tests*
C'est bête comme chou.	*It's as easy as pie.*
C'est chou vert et vert chou.	*It's six of one and half dozen of the other. It's all the same.*
Ta chambre est très chou.	*Your room is lovely.*
Cette enfant est très chou dans sa nouvelle jupe.	*This little girl is adorable in her new skirt.*

 Les expressions à l'œuvre. *Utilisez une des expressions de cette section pour exprimer les idées suivantes.*

1. Le patron a l'air très irrité aujourd'hui.

2. Tu fais toujours d'abord ce qui doit être fait ensuite.

3. Cette chaussée est pleine de trous.

4. Marc a raté ses examens.

5. C'est un type qui n'aime pas prendre parti.

6. Les rues étaient désertes.

7. On l'a fait pour être utilisé.

8. Ils se regardent avec beaucoup d'hostilité.

9. Il n'y a vraiment pas de différence.

10. Ce couple est toujours en train de disputer.

11. Il arrive toujours à un moment inopportun et il dérange tout le monde.

12. Il est trop prudent à cause de l'accident qu'il a eu.

13. C'est un homme trop décidé, incapable de changer d'avis.

14. Me voici absolument sans argent.

15. Pourquoi me tutoyez-vous?

16. Qu'est-ce que tu as? Tu as la voix enrouée (*hoarse*).

17. Il faut appeler les choses par leur nom.

18. Le professeur m'a traité très, très mal.

19. Lucie fait semblant de ne pas comprendre pour gagner quelque chose.

20. C'est très facile à faire.

NOTE CULTURELLE

Il y a des expressions françaises qui sont difficiles à comprendre sans avoir des connaissances de la culture française.

- **Une fenêtre à guillotine** (*sash window*): La fenêtre française (la porte-fenêtre) typique s'ouvre au milieu, comme deux portes. La fenêtre américaine qui s'ouvre de haut en bas s'appelle **fenêtre à guillotine** parce qu'elle rappelle la machine à exécution française dont l'adoption en 1791 a été proposée par le docteur Joseph Guillotin.
- **Traverser entre les clous** (*to cross in the crosswalk*): En France la traversée des piétons dans les villes est marquée non pas par des lignes peintes sur la chaussée mais par deux lignes de clous enfoncés dans la rue.
- **Être Gros-Jean comme devant** (*to be back at square one, back where one started from*): Gros-Jean est une figure traditionnelle qui représente un homme simple et ignorant.
- **Un violon d'Ingres** (*a hobby*): Le fameux peintre français du dix-neuvième siècle, Jean Auguste Ingres, jouait du violon à ses heures libres.
- **Se porter comme le Pont Neuf** (*to be in the best of health, feel fit as a fiddle*): Le Pont Neuf est le plus vieux pont de Paris, un pont de pierre très solide, utilisable même aujourd'hui pour les piétons et les voitures.

Idioms Relating to Time, Weather, the Life Cycle, and Eating

Le passage du temps

remettre qqch à la Saint-Glinglin	*to postpone something forever/till the cows come home*
renvoyer aux calendes grecques	*to put off till the cows come home*
à la dernière minute	*at the last minute, under the wire*
en ce moment	*at this time*
pour le moment	*for the time being*
à une heure avancée	*late*
les heures d'affluence	*rush hour*

les heures de pointe	*rush hour*
à ses heures	*when one is free, when one feels like doing something*
du jour au lendemain	*overnight*
La semaine des quatre jeudis.	*Never in a month of Sundays.*
Tous les trente-six du mois.	*Once in a blue moon.*
Il est grand temps.	*It's high time.*

Le temps qu'il fait

parler de la pluie et du beau temps	*to make small talk*
rapide comme l'éclair	*fast as lightning*
Il pleut à seaux.	*It's pouring.*
Il pleut des cordes.	*It's raining cats and dogs.*
Je ne suis pas tombé(e) de la dernière pluie.	*I wasn't born yesterday.*
Il fait lourd.	*It's humid out.*

La vie humaine

être né(e) coiffé(e)	*to be born with a silver spoon in one's mouth*
faire les quatre cents coups	*to sow one's wild oats, have a wild youth*
avoir le coup de foudre	*to fall head over heels in love*
avoir quarante ans bien sonnés	*to be well past forty*
friser la cinquantaine	*to be pushing fifty*
se faire vieux	*to be getting on in years*
faire de vieux os	*to live to a ripe old age*
mourir de sa belle mort	*to die of old age*
casser sa pipe	*to kick the bucket*
trouver la mort	*to lose one's life*
en bas âge	*little, young*
d'un certain âge	*middle-aged*
Quel âge me donnez-vous?	*How old do you think I am?*
Sa vie ne tient qu'à un fil.	*His life hangs by a thread. He's deathly ill.*

À table

aimer la table	*to like good food*
avoir/vendre qqch pour une bouchée de pain	*to get/sell something for a song*
casser la croûte	*to have a bite*
avoir l'estomac dans les talons	*to be famished*
manger à sa faim	*to eat one's fill*
manger son pain blanc le premier	*to eat one's cake first, not save the best for last*
manger comme quatre	*to eat like a horse, eat for four*
marcher sur des œufs	*to walk on eggs, tread lightly*
mourir de faim	*to be dying of hunger*
faire venir l'eau à la bouche à qqn	*to make someone's mouth water*
avoir un appétit d'oiseau	*to eat like a bird*
n'avoir rien à se mettre sous la dent	*to have nothing to eat*

avoir un bon fromage	to have a cushy/soft job
une bonne fourchette	a hearty eater
long comme une journée sans pain	endless
entre la poire et le fromage	at the end of a meal

N *Vous comprenez?* *Laquelle des deux possibilités est une réponse logique?*

1. Pierre mange beaucoup.
   a. Oui, il a l'estomac dans les talons.
   b. Oui, c'est une bonne fourchette.

2. Le vieux monsieur Jospin a cassé sa pipe.
   a. Oui, je sais qu'il est mort.
   b. Oui, il faut le remettre à la Saint-Glinglin.

3. Tu es amoureux?
   a. Oui, c'était le coup de foudre.
   b. Oui, je suis né coiffé.

4. C'est un type qui connaît tout, n'est-ce pas?
   a. Oui, il a un bon fromage.
   b. Oui, il n'est pas tombé de la dernière pluie, lui.

5. Je crois qu'elle a presque quarante ans.
   a. Moi aussi, je crois qu'elle frise la quarantaine.
   b. Moi aussi, je crois qu'elle a quarante ans bien sonnés.

6. C'est un jeune homme trop prudent.
   a. Oui, il fait de vieux os.
   b. Oui, il marche sur des œufs.

7. Tu le vois très peu, n'est-ce pas?
   a. Tous les trente-six du mois.
   b. À la petite semaine.

8. Ce film est interminable.
   a. Oui, long comme une journée sans pain.
   b. Oui, rapide comme l'éclair.

9. Il m'ennuie. Il ne dit que des banalités, des choses sans importance.
   a. Je sais. Il fait ses quatre cents coups.
   b. Je sais. Il parle de la pluie et du beau temps.

10. Quel beau manteau! Il t'a coûté cher?
    a. Non, j'ai mangé mon pain blanc le premier.
    b. Non, je l'ai eu pour une bouchée de pain.

Other Idioms

Prepositions and Prepositional Phrases

à base de	composed of, made of
à deux pas de	just a stone's throw from
à part	aside from

d'après	*according to*
à raison de	*at the rate of*
à titre de	*in the capacity of*
au lieu de	*instead of*
en dépit de	*in spite of*
en qualité de	*in one's capacity as*
en raison de	*on account of*
y compris	*including*

Conversation Fillers, Reactions, Interjections, and Transition Words

d'abord	*first*
à mon avis	*in my opinion*
à propos	*by the way*
au fait	*by the way*
au fond	*actually, basically*
au reste	*moreover*
du reste	*moreover*
avant tout	*above all*
dans l'ensemble	*on the whole*
de toute façon	*anyway*
en fait	*as a matter of fact*
par contre	*on the other hand*
selon le cas	*as the case may be*
somme toute	*all in all*
À d'autres!	*What a ridiculous story!*
À quoi bon?	*What's the good of it? What's the use?*
C'est dommage.	*It's a shame/pity.*
Bien entendu!	*Of course!*
C'est de la blague!	*It's not serious! It's ridiculous!*
Bon débarras!	*Good riddance!*
Ça alors!	*Well, I'll be darned!*
Ça va de soi.	*It goes without saying.*
C'est entendu.	*Agreed.*
Et comment!	*And how!*
Et pour cause!	*And for good reason!*
Et après?	*So what?*
Je m'en fiche!	*I don't give a darn!* (slang)
Fiche-moi la paix!	*Leave me alone!*
Mon œil!	*My eye!*
Motus!	*Keep it quiet! Don't breathe a word of it!*
Pas question!	*Nothing doing!*
Sans blague!	*No kidding!*
Ta gueule!	*Shut up!* (somewhat vulgar slang)
Tant mieux!	*Great! So much the better!*
Tant pis!	*Too bad! Tough luck!*
Vous voulez rire.	*You're joking.*

Expressions of Time

donner le temps de	*to give enough time to (do something)*
à plusieurs reprises	*several times*
à tour de rôle	*in turn*
d'avance	*in advance*
dans huit jours	*in a week*
d'ici là	*until then, in the meantime*
encore une fois	*again*
une fois pour toutes	*once and for all*
il y a belle lurette	*it's been a long time, it happened a long time ago*
jusqu'ici	*so far, thus far*
sous peu	*shortly*
tour à tour	*in turn*

Descriptions

être collant	*to be a real leech, be hard to shake, be hard to get rid of*
à bout	*exhausted*
à plat	*exhausted*
à la page	*in the know, up to date*
à la perfection	*just right, perfectly done, to a T*
à perte de vue	*as far as the eye can see*
à point	*well-done* (of meat)
à quatre pattes	*on all fours*
à souhait	*perfectly, to perfection, as well, as much as you could want*
au bout du monde	*in the middle of nowhere*
au-dessous de tout	*hopeless, disgracefully bad, incompetent*
bel et bien	*altogether*
cousu d'or	*filthy rich*
dans le vent	*in the swing of things*
de mal en pis	*from bad to worse*
en cachette	*on the sly*
en douceur	*gently, softly*
en bon/mauvais état	*in good/bad condition*
en panne	*out of order, broken*
en panne sèche	*out of gas*
en un clin d'œil	*in a jiffy, in a flash*
une femme de tête	*a capable woman*
fort en anglais	*good at English*
hors de soi	*beside oneself*
de la peine perdue	*wasted effort*
C'est du gâteau!	*It's easy as pie. It's a piece of cake!*
C'est son pere tout craché.	*He's the spitting image of his father.*
C'est le dernier cri.	*It's the latest thing. It's the latest fashion.*
C'est tout un.	*It's really the same thing.*

Expressions of Manner and Degree

à bout portant	*point-blank*
à contrecœur	*reluctantly*
à fond	*thoroughly*
à moitié	*halfway*
à mi-chemin	*halfway*
à peine	*hardly*
à peu près	*almost, just about*
à tout prix	*at all costs*
de bon gré	*willingly*
peu s'en faut	*almost, very nearly*
raison de plus pour	*all the more reason to*

Other Idioms

arriver à faire qqch	*to manage to do something*
se débrouiller	*to get along, manage*
l'échapper belle	*to have a narrow escape*
faire l'appel	*to take attendance*
ficher le camp	*to scram, get out of here* (slang)
à la une	*on the front page*
au besoin	*if you need it, if need be*
au loin	*in the distance*
un coup de tête	*an impulse*
un coup monté	*a setup*
coûte que coûte	*at any cost, come what may*
de loin	*from afar, far and away*
entre l'enclume et le marteau	*between a rock and a hard place* (the anvil and the hammer)
et ainsi de suite	*and so on*
faute de mieux	*for want of anything better (to do, etc.)*
une mauvaise langue	*a gossip, a viper* (evil-tongued)
Monsieur un Tel	*Mr. So-and-so, Mr. What's-his-name*
le petit coin	*the bathroom, the john*
pile ou face	*heads or tails*
un pot de vin	*a bribe*
pour rire	*as a joke, just for fun*
pour une fois	*for a change*
sauf avis contraire	*unless you hear something to the contrary*
sauf erreur	*unless there is a mistake*
Au secours!	*Help!*
Ça fait mon affaire.	*That's just what I wanted. That's what I was looking for.*
Ça m'arrange.	*That suits me just fine.*
Ça revient à la même chose.	*That amounts to the same thing.*
C'est bonnet blanc et blanc bonnet.	*It's six of one and half a dozen of the other.*
Défense de fumer!	*No smoking.*
Défense d'entrer!	*No admittance. Keep out.*

En avant!	Let's move along! Let's go ahead!
	Let's get going!
On n'en est pas trop avancé.	A lot of good that did us.
Pour l'amour de Dieu!	For God's sake!

O **Traduction.** *Écrivez l'équivalent français de ces locutions anglaises.*

1. *on the other hand*
2. *wasted effort*
3. *as the case may be*
4. *in turn*
5. *Don't breathe a word of it!*
6. *to be hard to get rid of*
7. *And for good reason!*
8. *once and for all*
9. *a setup*
10. *thus far*

11. *a gossip*
12. *point-blank*
13. *What's the use?*
14. *No kidding.*
15. *thoroughly*
16. *instead of*
17. *No admittance.*
18. *beside oneself*
19. *My eye!*
20. *broken, out of order*

P **Synonymes.** *Trouvez dans la deuxième colonne des synonymes pour chacune des expressions de la première.*

1. Vous voulez rire.
2. au fait
3. à tout prix
4. en ce moment
5. au besoin
6. Ça fait mon affaire.
7. à peine
8. à bout
9. du reste
10. en dépit de
11. en un clin d'œil
12. C'est tout un.
13. Ta gueule!
14. ficher le camp
15. à titre de
16. peu s'en faut

a. au reste
b. ne... guère
c. faute de mieux
d. filer
e. C'est bonnet blanc et blanc bonnet.
f. malgré
g. maintenant
h. Tant mieux!
i. presque
j. à plat
k. C'est dommage.
l. Tais-toi.
m. s'il le faut
n. coûte que coûte
o. Vous blaguez.
p. à propos
q. en qualité de
r. tout de suite
s. entre l'enclume et le marteau
t. Ça m'arrange.

Proverbs

À bon vin, point d'enseigne.	*The reputation of a good thing precedes it.*
Après la pluie, le beau temps.	*Every cloud has a silver lining.*
Aux grands maux, les grands remèdes.	*Big problems require big solutions.*
Les beaux esprits se rencontrent.	*Great minds think alike.*
Les bons comptes font les bons amis.	*Don't let money squabbles ruin a friendship.*
Charbonnier est maître chez soi.	*Every man's home is his castle.*
Le chat parti, les souris dansent.	*When the cat's away, the mice will play.*
Comme on fait son lit, on se couche.	*As you make your bed, so you shall lie in it.*
Deux avis valent mieux qu'un.	*Two heads are better than one.*
L'enfer est pavé de bonnes intentions.	*The road to hell is paved with good intentions.*
C'est en forgeant qu'on devient forgeron.	*Practice makes perfect.*
Des goûts et des couleurs il ne faut pas discuter.	*There's no accounting for taste.*
La goutte d'eau qui fait déborder le vase.	*The straw that breaks the camel's back.*
L'habit ne fait pas le moine.	*Clothes don't make the man.*
Une hirondelle ne fait pas le printemps.	*One swallow doesn't make a summer.*
Il faut battre le fer pendant qu'il est chaud.	*Strike while the iron is hot.*
Il n'est pire eau que l'eau qui dort.	*Still water runs deep.*
Il n'y a pas de fumée sans feu.	*Where there's smoke, there's fire.*
Il y a loin de la coupe aux lèvres.	*There's many a slip twixt the cup and the lip.*
Loin des yeux, loin du cœur.	*Out of sight, out of mind.*
Ce n'est pas la mer à boire.	*It's not very difficult to do.*
Mieux vaut tard que jamais.	*Better late than never.*
Paris ne s'est pas fait en un jour.	*Rome wasn't built in a day.*
Petit à petit, l'oiseau fait son nid.	*Slow and steady wins the race.*
Pierre qui roule n'amasse pas mousse.	*A rolling stone gathers no moss.*
Plus on est de fous, plus on rit.	*The more, the merrier.*
Point de nouvelles, bonnes nouvelles.	*No news is good news.*
Qui se ressemble, s'assemble.	*Birds of a feather flock together.*
Santé passe richesse.	*Health is better than riches.*
Tel père, tel fils.	*Like father, like son.*
Un(e) de perdu(e), dix de retrouvé(e)s.	*There are plenty more like him/her out there.*
Vouloir, c'est pouvoir.	*Where there's a will, there's a way.*

Q **Quel proverbe?** *Écrivez le proverbe que vous utiliseriez dans chaque cas.*

1. *You want to tell a friend that clothes are not as important as he or she thinks.*

2. *You try to warn a friend not to be too encouraged by one positive sign.*

3. *You want to console a friend who has just broken up with his girlfriend.*

4. *You want to say that every person can make the rules in his or her own house.*

5. *You and your friend come up with the same brilliant idea at the same time.*

6. *You want to advise a friend who is trying to decide whether to take a job in a different city that it would be a good option for him.*

7. *You encourage people to invite more friends to the party.*

8. *You want to warn a friend that she shouldn't overwork and ruin her health.*

9. *You want to say that great things take a long time to accomplish.*

10. *You warn a friend that something drastic may have to be done because the situation is so serious.*

11. *You claim that the children were mischievous because their parents weren't around.*

12. *You tell your friend to take advantage of the opportunities that have presented themselves or they may disappear.*

Appendices

Verb Charts

Auxiliary Verbs

avoir *to have*

INDICATIVE MOOD

PRESENT	ai, as, a · avons, avez, ont
IMPERFECT	avais, avais, avait · avions, aviez, avaient
PASSÉ COMPOSÉ	ai eu, as eu, a eu · avons eu, avez eu, ont eu
PLUPERFECT	avais eu, avais eu, avait eu · avions eu, aviez eu, avaient eu
FUTURE	aurai, auras, aura · aurons, aurez, auront
CONDITIONAL	aurais, aurais, aurait · aurions, auriez, auraient
PASSÉ SIMPLE	eus, eus, eut · eûmes, eûtes, eurent
FUTURE PERFECT	aurai eu, auras eu, aura eu · aurons eu, aurez eu, auront eu
CONDITIONAL PERFECT	aurais eu, aurais eu, aurait eu · aurions eu, auriez eu, auraient eu

SUBJUNCTIVE MOOD

PRESENT	aie, aies, ait · ayons, ayez, aient
PAST	aie eu, aies eu, ait eu · ayons eu, ayez eu, aient eu
IMPERFECT	eusse, eusses, eût · eussions, eussiez, eussent

IMPERATIVE MOOD

aie (BUT aies-en), ayons, ayez

PRESENT PARTICIPLE

ayant

être *to be*

INDICATIVE MOOD

PRESENT	suis, es, est · sommes, êtes, sont
IMPERFECT	étais, étais, était · étions, étiez, étaient
FUTURE	serai, seras, sera · serons, serez, seront
CONDITIONAL	serais, serais, serait · serions, seriez, seraient
PASSÉ COMPOSÉ	ai été, as été, a été · avons été, avez été, ont été
PASSÉ SIMPLE	fus, fus, fut · fûmes, fûtes, furent
PLUPERFECT	avais été, avais été, avait été · avions été, aviez été, avaient été
FUTURE PERFECT	aurai été, auras été, aura été · aurons été, aurez été, auront été
CONDITIONAL PERFECT	aurais été, aurais été, aurait été · aurions été, auriez été, auraient été

SUBJUNCTIVE MOOD

PRESENT	sois, sois, soit · soyons, soyez, soient
PAST	aie été, aies été, ait été · ayons été, ayez été, aient été
IMPERFECT	fusse, fusses, fût · fussions, fussiez, fussent

IMPERATIVE MOOD

sois, soyons, soyez

PRESENT PARTICIPLE

étant

Regular Verbs

-er Verbs

parler *to speak*

INDICATIVE MOOD

PRESENT	parle, parles, parle · parlons, parlez, parlent
IMPERFECT	parlais, parlais, parlait · parlions, parliez, parlaient
FUTURE	parlerai, parleras, parlera · parlerons, parlerez, parleront
CONDITIONAL	parlerais, parlerais, parlerait · parlerions, parleriez, parleraient
PASSÉ COMPOSÉ	ai parlé, as parlé, a parlé · avons parlé, avez parlé, ont parlé
PASSÉ SIMPLE	parlai, parlas, parla · parlâmes, parlâtes, parlèrent
PLUPERFECT	avais parlé, avais parlé, avait parlé · avions parlé, aviez parlé, avaient parlé
FUTURE PERFECT	aurai parlé, auras parlé, aura parlé · aurons parlé, aurez parlé, auront parlé
CONDITIONAL PERFECT	aurais parlé, aurais parlé, aurait parlé · aurions parlé, auriez parlé, auraient parlé

SUBJUNCTIVE MOOD

PRESENT	parle, parles, parle · parlions, parliez, parlent
PAST	aie parlé, aies parlé, ait parlé · ayons parlé, ayez parlé, aient parlé
IMPERFECT	parlasse, parlasses, parlât · parlassions, parlassiez, parlassent

IMPERATIVE MOOD

parle (BUT parles-en), parlons, parlez

PRESENT PARTICIPLE

parlant

The compound tenses of **arriver**, a verb conjugated with **être**, follow.

arriver *to arrive*

INDICATIVE MOOD

PASSÉ COMPOSÉ	suis arrivé(e), es arrivé(e), est arrivé(e) · sommes arrivé(e)s, êtes arrivé(e)(s), sont arrivé(e)s
PLUPERFECT	étais arrivé(e), étais arrivé(e), était arrivé(e) · étions arrivé(e)s, étiez arrivé(e)(s), étaient arrivé(e)s
FUTURE PERFECT	serai arrivé(e), seras arrivé(e), sera arrivé(e) · serons arrivé(e)s, serez arrivé(e)(s), seront arrivé(e)s
CONDITIONAL PERFECT	serais arrivé(e), serais arrivé(e), serait arrivé(e) · serions arrivé(e)s, seriez arrivé(e)(s), seraient arrivé(e)s

SUBJUNCTIVE MOOD

PAST	sois arrivé(e), sois arrivé(e), soit arrivé(e) · soyons arrivé(e)s, soyez arrivé(e)(s), soient arrivé(e)s

-ir Verbs

finir *to finish*

INDICATIVE MOOD

PRESENT	finis, finis, finit · finissons, finissez, finissent
IMPERFECT	finissais, finissais, finissait · finissions, finissiez, finissaient
FUTURE	finirai, finiras, finira · finirons, finirez, finiront
CONDITIONAL	finirais, finirais, finirait · finirions, finiriez, finiraient
PASSÉ COMPOSÉ	ai fini, as fini, a fini · avons fini, avez fini, ont fini
PASSÉ SIMPLE	finis, finis, finit · finîmes, finîtes, finirent
PLUPERFECT	avais fini, avais fini, avait fini · avions fini, aviez fini, avaient fini
FUTURE PERFECT	aurai fini, auras fini, aura fini · aurons fini, aurez fini, auront fini
CONDITIONAL PERFECT	aurais fini, aurais fini, aurait fini · aurions fini, auriez fini, auraient fini

SUBJUNCTIVE MOOD

PRESENT	finisse, finisses, finisse · finissions, finissiez, finissent
PAST	aie fini, aies fini, ait fini · ayons fini, ayez fini, aient fini
IMPERFECT	finisse, finisses, finît · finissions, finissiez, finissent

IMPERATIVE MOOD

finis, finissons, finissez

PRESENT PARTICIPLE

finissant

-re Verbs

vendre *to sell*

INDICATIVE MOOD

PRESENT	vends, vends, vend · vendons, vendez, vendent
IMPERFECT	vendais, vendais, vendait · vendions, vendiez, vendaient
FUTURE	vendrai, vendras, vendra · vendrons, vendrez, vendront
CONDITIONAL	vendrais, vendrais, vendrait · vendrions, vendriez, vendraient
PASSÉ COMPOSÉ	ai vendu, as vendu, a vendu · avons vendu, avez vendu, ont vendu
PASSÉ SIMPLE	vendis, vendis, vendit · vendîmes, vendîtes, vendirent
PLUPERFECT	avais vendu, avais vendu, avait vendu · avions vendu, aviez vendu, avaient vendu
FUTURE PERFECT	aurai vendu, auras vendu, aura vendu · aurons vendu, aurez vendu, auront vendu
CONDITIONAL PERFECT	aurais vendu, aurais vendu, aurait vendu · aurions vendu, auriez vendu, auraient vendu

SUBJUNCTIVE MOOD

PRESENT	vende, vendes, vende · vendions, vendiez, vendent
PAST	aie vendu, aies vendu, ait vendu · ayons vendu, ayez vendu, aient vendu
IMPERFECT	vendisse, vendisses, vendît · vendissions, vendissiez, vendissent

IMPERATIVE MOOD

vends, vendons, vendez

PRESENT PARTICIPLE

vendant

Verbs with Spelling Changes

Verbs whose stems end in **-c**, such as **commencer**, add a cedilla under the **c** (**ç**) before the letters **a** and **o**.

commencer *to begin*

PRESENT	commence, commences, commence · commençons, commencez, commencent
IMPERFECT	commençais, commençais, commençait · commencions, commenciez, commençaient
PASSÉ SIMPLE	commençai, commenças, commença · commençâmes, commençâtes, commencèrent
PRESENT PARTICIPLE	commençant

Verbs whose stems end in **-g**, such as **manger**, add an **e** after the **g** before the letters **a** and **o**.

manger *to eat*

PRESENT	mange, manges, mange · mangeons, mangez, mangent
IMPERFECT	mangeais, mangeais, mangeait · mangions, mangiez, mangeaient
PASSÉ SIMPLE	mangeai, mangeas, mangea · mangeâmes, mangeâtes, mangèrent
PRESENT PARTICIPLE	mangeant

Verbs whose stems end in **-y**, such as **nettoyer**, change the **y** to **i** before a silent **e**.

nettoyer *to clean*

PRESENT	nettoie, nettoies, nettoie · nettoyons, nettoyez, nettoient
PRESENT SUBJUNCTIVE	nettoie, nettoies, nettoie · nettoyions, nettoyiez, nettoient
FUTURE	nettoierai, nettoieras, nettoiera · nettoierons, nettoierez, nettoieront
CONDITIONAL	nettoierais, nettoierais, nettoierait · nettoierions, nettoieriez, nettoieraient
IMPERATIVE	nettoie, nettoyons, nettoyez

NOTE Verbs ending in **-ayer** may either change **y** to **i** before a silent **e** or keep the **y** in all forms: **je paie** or **je paye**. Verbs in **-oyer** and **-uyer** must change the **y** to **i** before a silent **e**.

In **-er** verbs that have mute **e** as their stem vowel (**acheter**, **appeler**, **jeter**, **mener**, etc.), the mute **e** is pronounced **è** in those forms where the ending has a mute **e**. In the present tense, this means all singular forms and the third person plural. This change in sound may be spelled in one of two ways.

- Verbs such as **lever** change the **e** to **è** to show the change in pronunciation.

lever *to raise*

PRESENT	lève, lèves, lève · levons, levez, lèvent
PRESENT SUBJUNCTIVE	lève, lèves, lève · levions, leviez, lèvent
FUTURE	lèverai, lèveras, lèvera · lèverons, lèverez, lèveront
CONDITIONAL	lèverais, lèverais, lèverait · lèverions, lèveriez, lèveraient
IMPERATIVE	lève, levons, levez

- Verbs like **appeler** and **jeter** double the consonant after the mute **e** to show the sound change of mute **e** to **è**.

appeler *to call*

PRESENT	appelle, appelles, appelle · appelons, appelez, appellent
PRESENT SUBJUNCTIVE	appelle, appelles, appelle · appelions, appeliez, appellent
FUTURE	appellerai, appelleras, appellera · appellerons, appellerez, appelleront
CONDITIONAL	appellerais, appellerais, appellerait · appellerions, appelleriez, appelleraient
IMPERATIVE	appelle, appelons, appelez

jeter *to throw*

PRESENT	jette, jettes, jette · jetons, jetez, jettent
PRESENT SUBJUNCTIVE	jette, jettes, jette · jetions, jetiez, jettent
FUTURE	jetterai, jetteras, jettera · jetterons, jetterez, jetteront
CONDITIONAL	jetterais, jetterais, jetterait · jetterions, jetteriez, jetteraient
IMPERATIVE	jette, jetons, jetez

- First-conjugation verbs such as **espérer**, which have **é** as the stem vowel, change **é** to **è** when the ending has a mute **e**. However, unlike verbs like **lever**, verbs like **espérer** keep the acute accent in the future and conditional.

espérer *to hope*

PRESENT	espère, espères, espère · espérons, espérez, espèrent
PRESENT SUBJUNCTIVE	espère, espères, espère · espérions, espériez, espèrent
FUTURE	espérerai, espéreras, espérera · espérerons, espérerez, espéreront
CONDITIONAL	espérerais, espérerais, espérerait · espérerions, espéreriez, espéreraient
IMPERATIVE	espère, espérons, espérez

Irregular Verbs

For the conjugation of the following irregular verbs, consult the listing under the infinitive indicated in parentheses.

accueillir *to welcome* (LIKE **cueillir**)
admettre *to admit* (LIKE **mettre**)
apercevoir *to perceive* (LIKE **recevoir**)
apparaître *to appear* (LIKE **connaître**)
appartenir *to belong* (LIKE **tenir**)
apprendre *to learn* (LIKE **prendre**)
atteindre *to reach, attain* (LIKE **peindre**)
combattre *to fight, combat* (LIKE **battre**)
comprendre *to understand* (LIKE **prendre**)
construire *to build* (LIKE **conduire**)
contenir *to contain* (LIKE **tenir**)
contredire *to contradict* (LIKE **dire**, BUT **vous contredisez** (PRESENT))
couvrir *to cover* (LIKE **ouvrir**)
décevoir *to disappoint* (LIKE **recevoir**)
découvrir *to discover* (LIKE **ouvrir**)
décrire *to describe* (LIKE **écrire**)
défaire *to undo* (LIKE **faire**)
détruire *to destroy* (LIKE **conduire**)
devenir *to become* (LIKE **venir**)
disparaître *to disappear* (LIKE **connaître**)
dormir *to sleep* (LIKE **partir**)
éteindre *to put out, extinguish* (LIKE **peindre**)
interdire *to forbid* (LIKE **dire**, BUT **vous interdisez** (PRESENT))
maintenir *to maintain* (LIKE **tenir**)
mentir *to lie* (LIKE **partir**)
obtenir *to get, obtain* (LIKE **tenir**)
offrir *to offer* (LIKE **ouvrir**)
paraître *to seem, appear* (LIKE **connaître**)
permettre *to permit* (LIKE **mettre**)
plaindre *to pity* (LIKE **craindre**)
poursuivre *to pursue, continue* (LIKE **suivre**)
prévoir *to foresee* (LIKE **voir**)
produire *to produce* (LIKE **conduire**)
promettre *to promise* (LIKE **mettre**)
reconnaître *to recognize* (LIKE **connaître**)
réduire *to reduce* (LIKE **conduire**)
refaire *to redo* (LIKE **faire**)
remettre *to delay, postpone* (LIKE **mettre**)
reprendre *to take again, begin again* (LIKE **prendre**)
retenir *to retain* (LIKE **tenir**)
revenir *to come back* (LIKE **venir**)
revoir *to see again* (LIKE **voir**)
sentir *to feel* (LIKE **partir**)
servir *to serve* (LIKE **partir**)

sortir *to go out* (LIKE **partir**)
souffrir *to suffer* (LIKE **ouvrir**)
sourire *to smile* (LIKE **rire**)
soutenir *to sustain, support* (LIKE **tenir**)
se souvenir *to remember* (LIKE **venir**)
surprendre *to surprise* (LIKE **prendre**)
se taire *to keep quiet* (LIKE **plaire**)
traduire *to translate* (LIKE **conduire**)

aller *to go, be going (to)*

PRESENT	vais, vas, va · allons, allez, vont
IMPERFECT	allais, allais, allait · allions, alliez, allaient
PASSÉ COMPOSÉ	suis allé(e), *etc.*
FUTURE	irai, iras, ira · irons, irez, iront
CONDITIONAL	irais, irais, irait · irions, iriez, iraient
PASSÉ SIMPLE	allai, allas, alla · allâmes, allâtes, allèrent
PRESENT SUBJUNCTIVE	aille, ailles, aille · allions, alliez, aillent
IMPERATIVE	va, allons, allez
PRESENT PARTICIPLE	allant

s'asseoir *to sit down*

PRESENT	m'assieds, t'assieds, s'assied · nous asseyons, vous asseyez, s'asseyent (m'assois, t'assois, s'assoit · nous assoyons, vous assoyez, s'assoient)
IMPERFECT	m'asseyais, t'asseyais, s'asseyait · nous asseyions, vous asseyiez, s'asseyaient (m'assoyais, t'assoyais, s'assoyait · nous assoyions, vous assoyiez, s'assoyaient)
PASSÉ COMPOSÉ	me suis assis(e), *etc.*
FUTURE	m'assiérai, t'assiéras, s'assiéra · nous assiérons, vous assiérez, s'assiéront (m'assoirai, t'assoiras, s'assoira · nous assoirons, vous assoirez, s'assoiront)
CONDITIONAL	m'assiérais, t'assiérais, s'assiérait · nous assiérions, vous assiériez, s'assiéraient (m'assoirais, t'assoirais, s'assoirait · nous assoirions, vous assoiriez, s'assoiraient)
PASSÉ SIMPLE	m'assis, t'assis, s'assit · nous assîmes, vous assîtes, s'assirent
PRESENT SUBJUNCTIVE	m'asseye, t'asseyes, s'asseye · nous asseyions, vous asseyiez, s'asseyent (m'assoie, t'assoies, s'assoie · nous assoyions, vous assoyiez, s'assoient)
IMPERATIVE	assieds-toi, asseyons-nous, asseyez-vous (assois-toi, assoyons-nous, assoyez-vous)
PRESENT PARTICIPLE	s'asseyant (s'assoyant)

battre *to beat, strike, hit*

PRESENT	bats, bats, bat · battons, battez, battent
IMPERFECT	battais, battais, battait · battions, battiez, battaient
PASSÉ COMPOSÉ	ai battu, *etc.*
FUTURE	battrai, battras, battra · battrons, battrez, battront
CONDITIONAL	battrais, battrais, battrait · battrions, battriez, battraient
PASSÉ SIMPLE	battis, battis, battit · battîmes, battîtes, battirent
PRESENT SUBJUNCTIVE	batte, battes, batte · battions, battiez, battent
IMPERATIVE	bats, battons, battez
PRESENT PARTICIPLE	battant

boire *to drink*

PRESENT	bois, bois, boit · buvons, buvez, boivent
IMPERFECT	buvais, buvais, buvait · buvions, buviez, buvaient
PASSÉ COMPOSÉ	ai bu, *etc.*
FUTURE	boirai, boiras, boira · boirons, boirez, boiront
PASSÉ SIMPLE	bus, bus, but · bûmes, bûtes, burent
PRESENT SUBJUNCTIVE	boive, boives, boive · buvions, buviez, boivent
IMPERATIVE	bois, buvons, buvez
PRESENT PARTICIPLE	buvant

conduire *to drive*

PRESENT	conduis, conduis, conduit · conduisons, conduisez, conduisent
IMPERFECT	conduisais, conduisais, conduisait · conduisions, conduisiez, conduisaient
PASSÉ COMPOSÉ	ai conduit, *etc.*
FUTURE	conduirai, conduiras, conduira · conduirons, conduirez, conduiront
CONDITIONAL	conduirais, conduirais, conduirait · conduirions, conduiriez, conduiraient
PASSÉ SIMPLE	conduisis, conduisis, conduisit · conduisîmes, conduisîtes, conduisirent
PRESENT SUBJUNCTIVE	conduise, conduises, conduise · conduisions, conduisiez, conduisent
IMPERATIVE	conduis, conduisons, conduisez
PRESENT PARTICIPLE	conduisant

connaître *to know (a person, place, etc.)*

PRESENT	connais, connais, connaît · connaissons, connaissez, connaissent
IMPERFECT	connaissais, connaissais, connaissait · connaissions, connaissiez, connaissaient
PASSÉ COMPOSÉ	ai connu, *etc.*
FUTURE	connaîtrai, connaîtras, connaîtra · connaîtrons, connaîtrez, connaîtront
CONDITIONAL	connaîtrais, connaîtrais, connaîtrait · connaîtrions, connaîtriez, connaîtraient
PASSÉ SIMPLE	connus, connus, connut · connûmes, connûtes, connurent
PRESENT SUBJUNCTIVE	connaisse, connaisses, connaisse · connaissions, connaissiez, connaissent
IMPERATIVE	connais, connaissons, connaissez
PRESENT PARTICIPLE	connaissant

courir *to run*

PRESENT	cours, cours, court · courons, courez, courent
IMPERFECT	courais, courais, courait · courions, couriez, couraient
PASSÉ COMPOSÉ	ai couru, *etc.*
FUTURE	courrai, courras, courra · courrons, courrez, courront
CONDITIONAL	courrais, courrais, courrait · courrions, courriez, courraient
PASSÉ SIMPLE	courus, courus, courut · courûmes, courûtes, coururent
PRESENT SUBJUNCTIVE	coure, coures, coure · courions, couriez, courent
IMPERATIVE	cours, courons, courez
PRESENT PARTICIPLE	courant

craindre *to fear*

PRESENT	crains, crains, craint · craignons, craignez, craignent
IMPERFECT	craignais, craignais, craignait · craignions, craigniez, craignaient
PASSÉ COMPOSÉ	ai craint, *etc.*
FUTURE	craindrai, craindras, craindra · craindrons, craindrez, craindront
CONDITIONAL	craindrais, craindrais, craindrait · craindrions, craindriez, craindraient
PASSÉ SIMPLE	craignis, craignis, craignit · craignîmes, craignîtes, craignirent
PRESENT SUBJUNCTIVE	craigne, craignes, craigne · craignions, craigniez, craignent
IMPERATIVE	crains, craignons, craignez
PRESENT PARTICIPLE	craignant

croire *to believe, think*

PRESENT	crois, crois, croit · croyons, croyez, croient
IMPERFECT	croyais, croyais, croyait · croyions, croyiez, croyaient
PASSÉ COMPOSÉ	ai cru, *etc.*
FUTURE	croirai, croiras, croira · croirons, croirez, croiront
CONDITIONAL	croirais, croirais, croirait · croirions, croiriez, croiraient
PASSÉ SIMPLE	crus, crus, crut · crûmes, crûtes, crurent
PRESENT SUBJUNCTIVE	croie, croies, croie · croyions, croyiez, croient
IMPERATIVE	crois, croyons, croyez
PRESENT PARTICIPLE	croyant

cueillir *to gather, pick (flowers, etc.)*

PRESENT	cueille, cueilles, cueille · cueillons, cueillez, cueillent
IMPERFECT	cueillais, cueillais, cueillait · cueillions, cueilliez, cueillaient
PASSÉ COMPOSÉ	ai cueilli, *etc.*
FUTURE	cueillerai, cueilleras, cueillera · cueillerons, cueillerez, cueilleront
CONDITIONAL	cueillerais, cueillerais, cueillerait · cueillerions, cueilleriez, cueilleraient
PASSÉ SIMPLE	cueillis, cueillis, cueillit · cueillîmes, cueillîtes, cueillirent
PRESENT SUBJUNCTIVE	cueille, cueilles, cueille · cueillions, cueilliez, cueillent
IMPERATIVE	cueille, cueillons, cueillez
PRESENT PARTICIPLE	cueillant

devoir *to owe; must, should, ought to*

PRESENT	dois, dois, doit · devons, devez, doivent
IMPERFECT	devais, devais, devait · devions, deviez, devaient
PASSÉ COMPOSÉ	ai dû, *etc.*
FUTURE	devrai, devras, devra · devrons, devrez, devront
CONDITIONAL	devrais, devrais, devrait · devrions, devriez, devraient
PASSÉ SIMPLE	dus, dus, dut · dûmes, dûtes, durent
PRESENT SUBJUNCTIVE	doive, doives, doive · devions, deviez, doivent
IMPERATIVE	dois, devons, devez
PRESENT PARTICIPLE	devant

dire *to say, tell*

PRESENT	dis, dis, dit · disons, dites, disent
IMPERFECT	disais, disais, disait · disions, disiez, disaient
PASSÉ COMPOSÉ	ai dit, *etc.*
FUTURE	dirai, diras, dira · dirons, direz, diront
CONDITIONAL	dirais, dirais, dirait · dirions, diriez, diraient
PASSÉ SIMPLE	dis, dis, dit · dîmes, dîtes, dirent
PRESENT SUBJUNCTIVE	dise, dises, dise · disions, disiez, disent
IMPERATIVE	dis, disons, dites
PRESENT PARTICIPLE	disant

écrire *to write*

PRESENT	écris, écris, écrit · écrivons, écrivez, écrivent
IMPERFECT	écrivais, écrivais, écrivait · écrivions, écriviez, écrivaient
PASSÉ COMPOSÉ	ai écrit, *etc.*
FUTURE	écrirai, écriras, écrira · écrirons, écrirez, écriront
CONDITIONAL	écrirais, écrirais, écrirait · écririons, écririez, écriraient
PASSÉ SIMPLE	écrivis, écrivis, écrivit · écrivîmes, écrivîtes, écrivirent
PRESENT SUBJUNCTIVE	écrive, écrives, écrive · écrivions, écriviez, écrivent
IMPERATIVE	écris, écrivons, écrivez
PRESENT PARTICIPLE	écrivant

envoyer *to send*

PRESENT	envoie, envoies, envoie · envoyons, envoyez, envoient
IMPERFECT	envoyais, envoyais, envoyait · envoyions, envoyiez, envoyaient
PASSÉ COMPOSÉ	ai envoyé, *etc.*
FUTURE	enverrai, enverras, enverra · enverrons, enverrez, enverront
CONDITIONAL	enverrais, enverrais, enverrait · enverrions, enverriez, enverraient
PASSÉ SIMPLE	envoyai, envoyas, envoya · envoyâmes, envoyâtes, envoyèrent
PRESENT SUBJUNCTIVE	envoie, envoies, envoie · envoyions, envoyiez, envoient
IMPERATIVE	envoie, envoyons, envoyez
PRESENT PARTICIPLE	envoyant

faire *to do, make*

PRESENT	fais, fais, fait · faisons, faites, font
IMPERFECT	faisais, faisais, faisait · faisions, faisiez, faisaient
PASSÉ COMPOSÉ	ai fait, *etc.*
FUTURE	ferai, feras, fera · ferons, ferez, feront
CONDITIONAL	ferais, ferais, ferait · ferions, feriez, feraient
PASSÉ SIMPLE	fis, fis, fit · fîmes, fîtes, firent
PRESENT SUBJUNCTIVE	fasse, fasses, fasse · fassions, fassiez, fassent
IMPERATIVE	fais, faisons, faites
PRESENT PARTICIPLE	faisant

falloir *to be necessary*

PRESENT	il faut
IMPERFECT	il fallait
PASSÉ COMPOSÉ	il a fallu
FUTURE	il faudra
CONDITIONAL	il faudrait
PASSÉ SIMPLE	il fallut
PRESENT SUBJUNCTIVE	il faille

joindre *to join*

PRESENT	joins, joins, joint · joignons, joignez, joignent
IMPERFECT	joignais, joignais, joignait · joignions, joigniez, joignent
PASSÉ COMPOSÉ	ai joint, *etc.*
FUTURE	joindrai, joindras, joindra · joindrons, joindrez, joindront
CONDITIONAL	joindrais, joindrais, joindrait · joindrions, joindriez, joindraient
PASSÉ SIMPLE	joignis, joignis, joignit · joignîmes, joignîtes, joignirent
PRESENT SUBJUNCTIVE	joigne, joignes, joigne · joignions, joigniez, joignent
IMPERATIVE	joins, joignons, joignez
PRESENT PARTICIPLE	joignant

lire *to read*

PRESENT	lis, lis, lit · lisons, lisez, lisent
IMPERFECT	lisais, lisais, lisait · lisions, lisiez, lisaient
PASSÉ COMPOSÉ	ai lu, *etc.*
FUTURE	lirai, liras, lira · lirons, lirez, liront
CONDITIONAL	lirais, lirais, lirait · lirions, liriez, liraient
PASSÉ SIMPLE	lus, lus, lut · lûmes, lûtes, lurent
PRESENT SUBJUNCTIVE	lise, lises, lise · lisions, lisiez, lisent
IMPERATIVE	lis, lisons, lisez
PRESENT PARTICIPLE	lisant

mettre *to put*

PRESENT	mets, mets, met · mettons, mettez, mettent
IMPERFECT	mettais, mettais, mettait · mettions, mettiez, mettaient
PASSÉ COMPOSÉ	ai mis, *etc.*
FUTURE	mettrai, mettras, mettra · mettrons, mettrez, mettront
CONDITIONAL	mettrais, mettrais, mettrait · mettrions, mettriez, mettraient
PASSÉ SIMPLE	mis, mis, mit · mîmes, mîtes, mirent
PRESENT SUBJUNCTIVE	mette, mettes, mette · mettions, mettiez, mettent
IMPERATIVE	mets, mettons, mettez
PRESENT PARTICIPLE	mettant

mourir *to die*

PRESENT	meurs, meurs, meurt · mourons, mourez, meurent
IMPERFECT	mourais, mourais, mourait · mourions, mouriez, mouraient
PASSÉ COMPOSÉ	suis mort(e), *etc.*
FUTURE	mourrai, mourras, mourra · mourrons, mourrez, mourront
CONDITIONAL	mourrais, mourrais, mourrait · mourrions, mourriez, mourraient
PASSÉ SIMPLE	mourus, mourus, mourut · mourûmes, mourûtes, moururent
PRESENT SUBJUNCTIVE	meure, meures, meure · mourions, mouriez, meurent
IMPERATIVE	meurs, mourons, mourez
PRESENT PARTICIPLE	mourant

naître *to be born*

PRESENT	nais, nais, naît · naissons, naissez, naissent
IMPERFECT	naissais, naissais, naissait · naissions, naissiez, naissaient
PASSÉ COMPOSÉ	suis né(e), *etc.*
FUTURE	naîtrai, naîtras, naîtra · naîtrons, naîtrez, naîtront
CONDITIONAL	naîtrais, naîtrais, naîtrait · naîtrions, naîtriez, naîtraient
PASSÉ SIMPLE	naquis, naquis, naquit · naquîmes, naquîtes, naquirent
PRESENT SUBJUNCTIVE	naisse, naisses, naisse · naissions, naissiez, naissent
IMPERATIVE	nais, naissons, naissez
PRESENT PARTICIPLE	naissant

ouvrir *to open*

PRESENT	ouvre, ouvres, ouvre · ouvrons, ouvrez, ouvrent
IMPERFECT	ouvrais, ouvrais, ouvrait · ouvrions, ouvriez, ouvraient
PASSÉ COMPOSÉ	ai ouvert, *etc.*
FUTURE	ouvrirai, ouvriras, ouvrira · ouvrirons, ouvrirez, ouvriront
CONDITIONAL	ouvrirais, ouvrirais, ouvrirait · ouvririons, ouvririez, ouvriraient
PASSÉ SIMPLE	ouvris, ouvris, ouvrit · ouvrîmes, ouvrîtes, ouvrirent
PRESENT SUBJUNCTIVE	ouvre, ouvres, ouvre · ouvrions, ouvriez, ouvrent
IMPERATIVE	ouvre, ouvrons, ouvrez
PRESENT PARTICIPLE	ouvrant

partir *to leave*

PRESENT	pars, pars, part · partons, partez, partent
IMPERFECT	partais, partais, partait · partions, partiez, partaient
PASSÉ COMPOSÉ	suis parti(e), *etc.*
FUTURE	partirai, partiras, partira · partirons, partirez, partiront
CONDITIONAL	partirais, partirais, partirait · partirions, partiriez, partiraient
PASSÉ SIMPLE	partis, partis, partit · partîmes, partîtes, partirent
PRESENT SUBJUNCTIVE	parte, partes, parte · partions, partiez, partent
IMPERATIVE	pars, partons, partez
PRESENT PARTICIPLE	partant

peindre *to paint*

PRESENT	peins, peins, peint · peignons, peignez, peignent
IMPERFECT	peignais, peignais, peignait · peignions, peigniez, peignaient
PASSÉ COMPOSÉ	ai peint, *etc.*
FUTURE	peindrai, peindras, peindra · peindrons, peindrez, peindront
CONDITIONAL	peindrais, peindrais, peindrait · peindrions, peindriez, peindraient
PASSÉ SIMPLE	peignis, peignis, peignit · peignîmes, peignîtes, peignirent
PRESENT SUBJUNCTIVE	peigne, peignes, peigne · peignions, peigniez, peignent
IMPERATIVE	peins, peignons, peignez
PRESENT PARTICIPLE	peignant

plaire *to please*

PRESENT	plais, plais, plaît · plaisons, plaisez, plaisent
IMPERFECT	plaisais, plaisais, plaisait · plaisions, plaisiez, plaisaient
PASSÉ COMPOSÉ	ai plu, *etc.*
FUTURE	plairai, plairas, plaira · plairons, plairez, plairont
CONDITIONAL	plairais, plairais, plairait · plairions, plairiez, plairaient
PASSÉ SIMPLE	plus, plus, plut · plûmes, plûtes, plurent
PRESENT SUBJUNCTIVE	plaise, plaises, plaise · plaisions, plaisiez, plaisent
IMPERATIVE	plais, plaisons, plaisez
PRESENT PARTICIPLE	plaisant

pleuvoir *to rain*

PRESENT	il pleut
IMPERFECT	il pleuvait
PASSÉ COMPOSÉ	il a plu
FUTURE	il pleuvra
CONDITIONAL	il pleuvrait
PASSÉ SIMPLE	il plut
PRESENT SUBJUNCTIVE	il pleuve
PRESENT PARTICIPLE	pleuvant

pouvoir *can, to be able to*

PRESENT	peux, peux, peut · pouvons, pouvez, peuvent
IMPERFECT	pouvais, pouvais, pouvait · pouvions, pouviez, pouvaient
PASSÉ COMPOSÉ	ai pu, *etc.*
FUTURE	pourrai, pourras, pourra · pourrons, pourrez, pourront
CONDITIONAL	pourrais, pourrais, pourrait · pourrions, pourriez, pourraient
PASSÉ SIMPLE	pus, pus, put · pûmes, pûtes, purent
PRESENT SUBJUNCTIVE	puisse, puisses, puisse · puissions, puissiez, puissent
IMPERATIVE	NOT USED
PRESENT PARTICIPLE	pouvant

prendre *to take*

PRESENT	prends, prends, prend · prenons, prenez, prennent
IMPERFECT	prenais, prenais, prenait · prenions, preniez, prenaient
PASSÉ COMPOSÉ	ai pris, *etc.*
FUTURE	prendrai, prendras, prendra · prendrons, prendrez, prendront
CONDITIONAL	prendrais, prendrais, prendrait · prendrions, prendriez, prendraient
PASSÉ SIMPLE	pris, pris, prit · prîmes, prîtes, prirent
PRESENT SUBJUNCTIVE	prenne, prennes, prenne · prenions, preniez, prennent
IMPERATIVE	prends, prenons, prenez
PRESENT PARTICIPLE	prenant

recevoir *to receive*

PRESENT	reçois, reçois, reçoit · recevons, recevez, reçoivent
IMPERFECT	recevais, recevais, recevait · recevions, receviez, recevaient
PASSÉ COMPOSÉ	ai reçu, *etc.*
FUTURE	recevrai, recevras, recevra · recevrons, recevrez, recevront
CONDITIONAL	recevrais, recevrais, recevrait · recevrions, recevriez, recevraient
PASSÉ SIMPLE	reçus, reçus, reçut · reçûmes, reçûtes, reçurent
PRESENT SUBJUNCTIVE	reçoive, reçoives, reçoive · recevions, receviez, reçoivent
IMPERATIVE	reçois, recevons, recevez
PRESENT PARTICIPLE	recevant

rire *to laugh*

PRESENT	ris, ris, rit · rions, riez, rient
IMPERFECT	riais, riais, riait · riions, riiez, riaient
PASSÉ COMPOSÉ	ai ri, *etc.*
FUTURE	rirai, riras, rira · rirons, rirez, riront
CONDITIONAL	rirais, rirais, rirait · ririons, ririez, riraient
PASSÉ SIMPLE	ris, ris, rit · rîmes, rîtes, rirent
PRESENT SUBJUNCTIVE	rie, ries, rie · riions, riiez, rient
IMPERATIVE	ris, rions, riez
PRESENT PARTICIPLE	riant

savoir *to know*

PRESENT	sais, sais, sait · savons, savez, savent
IMPERFECT	savais, savais, savait · savions, saviez, savaient
PASSÉ COMPOSÉ	ai su, *etc.*
FUTURE	saurai, sauras, saura · saurons, saurez, sauront
CONDITIONAL	saurais, saurais, saurait · saurions, sauriez, sauraient
PASSÉ SIMPLE	sus, sus, sut · sûmes, sûtes, surent
PRESENT SUBJUNCTIVE	sache, saches, sache · sachions, sachiez, sachent
IMPERATIVE	sache, sachons, sachez
PRESENT PARTICIPLE	sachant

suivre *to follow*

PRESENT	suis, suis, suit · suivons, suivez, suivent
IMPERFECT	suivais, suivais, suivait · suivions, suiviez, suivaient
PASSÉ COMPOSÉ	ai suivi, *etc.*
FUTURE	suivrai, suivras, suivra · suivrons, suivrez, suivront
CONDITIONAL	suivrais, suivrais, suivrait · suivrions, suivriez, suivraient
PASSÉ SIMPLE	suivis, suivis, suivit · suivîmes, suivîtes, suivirent
PRESENT SUBJUNCTIVE	suive, suives, suive · suivions, suiviez, suivent
IMPERATIVE	suis, suivons, suivez
PRESENT PARTICIPLE	suivant

tenir *to hold*

PRESENT	tiens, tiens, tient · tenons, tenez, tiennent
IMPERFECT	tenais, tenais, tenait · tenions, teniez, tenaient
PASSÉ COMPOSÉ	ai tenu, *etc.*
FUTURE	tiendrai, tiendras, tiendra · tiendrons, tiendrez, tiendront
CONDITIONAL	tiendrais, tiendrais, tiendrait · tiendrions, tiendriez, tiendraient
PASSÉ SIMPLE	tins, tins, tint · tînmes, tîntes, tinrent
PRESENT SUBJUNCTIVE	tienne, tiennes, tienne · tenions, teniez, tiennent
IMPERATIVE	tiens, tenons, tenez
PRESENT PARTICIPLE	tenant

valoir *to be worth*

PRESENT	vaux, vaux, vaut · valons, valez, valent
IMPERFECT	valais, valais, valait · valions, valiez, valaient
PASSÉ COMPOSÉ	ai valu, *etc.*
FUTURE	vaudrai, vaudras, vaudra · vaudrons, vaudrez, vaudront
CONDITIONAL	vaudrais, vaudrais, vaudrait · vaudrions, vaudriez, vaudraient
PASSÉ SIMPLE	valus, valus, valut · valûmes, valûtes, valurent
PRESENT SUBJUNCTIVE	vaille, vailles, vaille · valions, valiez, vaillent
IMPERATIVE	vaux, valons, valez
PRESENT PARTICIPLE	valant

venir *to come*

PRESENT	viens, viens, vient · venons, venez, viennent
IMPERFECT	venais, venais, venait · venions, veniez, venaient
PASSÉ COMPOSÉ	suis venu(e), *etc.*
FUTURE	viendrai, viendras, viendra · viendrons, viendrez, viendront
CONDITIONAL	viendrais, viendrais, viendrait · viendrions, viendriez, viendraient
PASSÉ SIMPLE	vins, vins, vint · vînmes, vîntes, vinrent
PRESENT SUBJUNCTIVE	vienne, viennes, vienne · venions, veniez, viennent
IMPERATIVE	viens, venons, venez
PRESENT PARTICIPLE	venant

vivre *to live*

PRESENT	vis, vis, vit · vivons, vivez, vivent
IMPERFECT	vivais, vivais, vivait · vivions, viviez, vivaient
PASSÉ COMPOSÉ	ai vécu, *etc.*
FUTURE	vivrai, vivras, vivra · vivrons, vivrez, vivront
CONDITIONAL	vivrais, vivrais, vivrait · vivrions, vivriez, vivraient
PASSÉ SIMPLE	vécus, vécus, vécut · vécûmes, vécûtes, vécurent
PRESENT SUBJUNCTIVE	vive, vives, vive · vivions, viviez, vivent
IMPERATIVE	vis, vivons, vivez
PRESENT PARTICIPLE	vivant

voir *to see*

PRESENT	vois, vois, voit · voyons, voyez, voient
IMPERFECT	voyais, voyais, voyait · voyions, voyiez, voyaient
PASSÉ COMPOSÉ	ai vu, *etc.*
FUTURE	verrai, verras, verra · verrons, verrez, verront
CONDITIONAL	verrais, verrais, verrait · verrions, verriez, verraient
PASSÉ SIMPLE	vis, vis, vit · vîmes, vîtes, virent
PRESENT SUBJUNCTIVE	voie, voies, voie · voyions, voyiez, voient
IMPERATIVE	vois, voyons, voyez
PRESENT PARTICIPLE	voyant

vouloir *to want*

PRESENT	veux, veux, veut · voulons, voulez, veulent
IMPERFECT	voulais, voulais, voulait · voulions, vouliez, voulaient
PASSÉ COMPOSÉ	ai voulu, *etc.*
FUTURE	voudrai, voudras, voudra · voudrons, voudrez, voudront
CONDITIONAL	voudrais, voudrais, voudrait · voudrions, voudriez, voudraient
PASSÉ SIMPLE	voulus, voulus, voulut · voulûmes, voulûtes, voulurent
PRESENT SUBJUNCTIVE	veuille, veuilles, veuille · voulions, vouliez, veuillent
IMPERATIVE	veuille, veuillons, veuillez
PRESENT PARTICIPLE	voulant

Written Conventions

The French language is written in the same alphabet as English, but conventions of writing are different. French makes use of a series of diacritical marks called accent marks, which appear over vowels and are part of French spelling.

There are four accent marks in French. All may occur over the letter **e**.

- é   **e accent aigu** (*acute accent*)
- è   **e accent grave** (*grave accent*)
- ê   **e accent circonflexe** (*circumflex accent*)
- ë   **e tréma** (*diaeresis*)

L'accent aigu

The acute accent appears only on the letter **e** in French. The original function of **accent aigu** was to indicate that the **e** was pronounced as a closed vowel. The closest English sound to **é** is the first part of the diphthong *ai* in *wait*. The acute accent is written on the past participle of all **-er** verbs: **allé**, **parlé**, **remboursé**, **gagné**, etc. The letter **é** corresponds to the English *y* in the suffix **-té**: **liberté**, **hostilité**, **qualité**, **quantité**, etc. It appears in the prefixes **é-**, corresponding to the English *ex-*, and **dé-**, corresponding to the English *dis-, de-, un-*: **échange**, **découvrir**, **déduire**, **défaire**. The initial **é** often corresponds to *s-* in English: **étrange**, **école**, **écriture**, **épice**.

L'accent grave

The grave accent in French may appear over the vowels **a**, **e**, and **u**. **Accent grave** appears over the vowel **a** in the preposition **à** and in the adverb **là**. The accent mark distinguishes those words from other very common words.

à	*to, at*	**a**	*has*
là	*there*	**la**	*the* [fem.]

Aside from this use, **accent grave** appears over the vowel **u** in the adverb **où** (*where*). The accent mark distinguishes it from **ou** (*or*).

Accent grave is used almost exclusively over the letter **e**. Its original function was to indicate that the **e** was pronounced as an open vowel. The closest English sound to **è** is the *e* in *bet*.

The vowels **é** and **è** often contrast in verbs: **nous préférons** vs. **je préfère**. The vowel **è** is used before **s** in several common words: **après**, **dès**, **près**, **très**.

L'accent circonflexe

The circumflex accent may appear over any vowel. The original purpose of **accent circonflexe** was to indicate a long vowel resulting from the dropping of a consonant, usually **s**. It can be useful to think of cognate English words with **s** to remember which French words have the circumflex accent. Compare the following examples.

> **la bête** *beast*
> **la fête** *holiday, party, festival*
> **Pâques** *Easter, paschal*
> **la pâte** *dough, paste*
> **râper** *to grate, rasp*

The circumflex accent is used to distinguish pairs of words in writing.

je crois *I believe*	**je croîs** *I grow*
cru past participle of **croire**	**crû** past participle of **croître**
du *of the; some*	**dû** past participle of **devoir**

Le tréma

The **tréma** may appear over **e** and **i**. It indicates that the vowel has its full sound and is not part of a diphthong. It can also indicate that a preceding **u** should be pronounced (that the **u** is not merely showing the pronunciation of the preceding **g**).

> **Noël** *Christmas*
> **aiguë** feminine form of **aigu**

Cédille

French also uses a diacritical mark called a *cedilla* (**cédille**) under the letter **c** to indicate that the **c** is pronounced /s/ before the vowels **a**, **o**, and **u**. Compare the following pairs of words.

ça	**cas**
commençons	**flocon**
reçu	**recul**

Answer Key

I Verbs—Basic Forms and Uses

1 Present Tense

A

1. Maman prépare un bon dîner.
2. Papa finit son livre.
3. Ma sœur Lise attend un coup de téléphone.
4. Moi, j'écoute mon nouveau cédé.
5. Maman invite nos cousins à prendre le dessert avec nous.
6. Ils acceptent.
7. Mon cousin Philippe joue de la guitare.
8. Nous chantons ensemble.
9. Nous applaudissons.
10. Après, nous bavardons jusqu'à une heure du matin.

B

1. attendons
2. dînent
3. arrivent
4. salue
5. apporte
6. remercie
7. passe
8. remplit

C

1. entre
2. choisissons
3. regardent
4. cherche
5. écoute
6. réussis
7. répond
8. finit
9. fermons
10. descendent

D

1. rangeons
2. balaie (balaye)
3. nettoie
4. commençons
5. essuient
6. essaie (essaye)

E

1. Oui, nous commençons (Non, nous ne commençons pas) à lire des livres en français.
2. Oui, nous corrigeons (Non, nous ne corrigeons pas) nos copies en classe.
3. Oui, nous effaçons (Non, nous n'effaçons pas) les mots mal écrits.
4. Oui, nous employons (Non, nous n'employons pas) le français dans nos conversations.
5. Oui, nous dérangeons (Non, nous ne dérangeons pas) les autres étudiants.
6. Oui, nous tutoyons (Non, nous ne tutoyons pas) le professeur.
7. Oui, nous prononçons (Non, nous ne prononçons pas) correctement.
8. Oui, nous téléchargeons (Non, nous ne téléchargeons pas) des documents en français.

F

1. Est-ce que tu préfères travailler en été?
2. Qu'est-ce que tu espères faire après l'université?
3. Combien est-ce que tu pèses?
4. Comment est-ce que tu épelles ton nom?
5. Est-ce que tu rejettes les idées extrémistes?
6. Où est-ce que tu achètes les livres pour les cours?

G

1. Jean-Claude espère devenir interprète.
2. Il préfère les langues.
3. Il projette un voyage aux États-Unis.
4. Il feuillette des brochures de l'agence de voyages.
5. Il renouvelle son passeport.
6. Il complète un cours intensif d'anglais.
7. Ses idées reflètent l'influence de sa mère.
8. Elle lui répète toujours l'importance d'une orientation internationale.

H

1. change; Tomorrow I'm changing jobs.
2. travaille; I've been working in the same office for two years.
3. gagne; I've been earning the same salary for eighteen months.
4. demande; I've been asking for a raise for ten months.

5. répète; And for ten months my boss has been repeating the same answer: No.

6. cherchent; All of my co-workers are looking for new jobs.

7. désirent; They've been wanting to quit their jobs here for a long time.

8. annoncent; Next week they'll announce their decision to the boss.

I

1. Voilà (Il y a) dix ans que Madame Ferron enseigne dans notre lycée. (Madame Ferron enseigne dans notre lycée depuis dix ans.)

2. Il y a (Voilà) huit ans qu'elle encourage les étudiants à étudier à l'étranger. (Elle encourage les étudiants à étudier à l'étranger depuis huit ans.)

3. Voilà (Il y a) sept ans qu'elle organise des voyages pour les étudiants. (Elle organise des voyages pour les étudiants depuis sept ans.)

4. Il y a (Voilà) quatre ans que trois étudiants passent un semestre au Québec chaque année. (Trois étudiants passent un semestre au Québec chaque année depuis trois ans.)

5. Voilà (Il y a) trois ans que mon ami Charles étudie l'allemand. (Mon ami Charles étudie l'allemand depuis trois ans.)

6. Il y a (Voilà) deux mois qu'il projette un voyage d'études en Allemagne. (Il projette un voyage d'études en Allemagne depuis deux mois.)

7. Voilà (Il y a) six semaines que Charles feuillette des brochures. (Charles feuillette des brochures depuis six semaines.)

8. Il y a (Voilà) un mois que Madame Ferron cherche le programme idéal pour Charles. (Madame Ferron cherche le programme idéal pour Charles depuis un mois.)

J

1. Il enlève ses chaussures et il met ses pantoufles.

2. Au bureau, nous rédigeons et corrigeons des articles.

3. Je nettoie la cuisine. J'essuie la table et je balaie le plancher.

4. Il feuillette la revue, mais il achète le journal.

5. Est-ce que tu complètes le travail aujourd'hui? Ou est-ce que tu préfères finir demain?

6. Nous envoyons des textos à nos amis.

L

1. to reabsorb
2. to readmit
3. to replace
4. to renovate
5. to represent
6. to reproduce

M

1. repartir
2. reverser
3. remettre
4. revoir
5. reformuler
6. ravoir
7. redonner
8. regrimper

N

1. to take a patient back to the hospital
2. to call someone back tomorrow
3. to bring the documents back
4. to tie the dog back up
5. to learn to speak again after one's accident
6. to fall in love again
7. to touch up a painting
8. to start negotiations again

2 Present Tense of Irregular Verbs

A

1. Je dois passer la journée à la bibliothèque, mais je ne veux pas.

2. Elle doit rester à la maison, mais elle ne veut pas.

3. Ils doivent aller chez le médecin, mais ils ne veulent pas.

4. Nous devons rentrer tôt, mais nous ne voulons pas.

5. Tu dois préparer le dîner, mais tu ne veux pas. (Vous devez préparer le dîner, mais vous ne voulez pas.)

6. Vous devez prendre un taxi, mais vous ne voulez pas.

B

1. Moi, je fais la vaisselle.
2. Mon grand-père fait du bricolage.
3. Mes frères font le jardin.
4. Ma sœur et moi, nous faisons les courses.
5. Ma grand-mère fait le linge.
6. Mon père fait les carreaux.
7. Moi, je fais les lits.
8. Ma mère, ma grand-mère et moi, nous faisons la cuisine.

C

1. Il a sommeil.
2. J'ai faim.
3. Nous avons soif.
4. Elles ont chaud.
5. Tu as froid.
6. Il a peur.
7. Vous avez raison.
8. On a honte.
9. Tu as tort.
10. Elle a de la chance.

D

1. Pierre et Michèle ont mal aux jambes.
2. Frédéric a mal au(x) bras.
3. Rachelle a mal au dos.
4. Toi, tu as mal à l'épaule droite.
5. Moi, j'ai mal aux genoux.
6. Alfred et moi, nous avons mal aux pieds.

E

1. sont
2. ont
3. fait
4. fait
5. ont
6. prennent
7. fait
8. font
9. fait
10. prennent

F

1. Toi aussi, tu prends un café?
2. Toi aussi, tu as faim?
3. Toi aussi, tu fais les courses maintenant?
4. Toi aussi, tu as vingt ans?
5. Toi aussi, tu es en vacances?
6. Toi aussi, tu as mal à la tête?
7. Toi aussi, tu comprends l'italien?
8. Toi aussi, tu es sur le point de sortir?

G

1. Le journal est sous le banc.
2. Moi, je suis à côté du banc.
3. Mes amis sont assis sur le banc.
4. Les arbres sont derrière le banc.
5. Toi et moi, nous sommes près du lac.
6. Nous sommes en face du café.
7. Le lac est entre la forêt et le pré.
8. Vous êtes devant le café.

H

1. fait
2. fait
3. suis
4. ai
5. fais
6. prends
7. fais
8. faisons
9. faisons
10. prenons

I

1. Non, je ne crains rien.
2. Non, je ne reçois rien.
3. Non, je ne dois rien.
4. Non, je ne construis rien.
5. Non, je ne reconnais rien.
6. Non, je ne peins rien.
7. Non, je ne traduis rien.
8. Non, je ne découvre rien.

J

1. Nicole peint tous les jours.
2. La nature apparaît dans ses tableaux.
3. Nous apercevons son talent.
4. Nous découvrons de nouveaux thèmes.
5. Maintenant, Nicole introduit la vie de la ville dans son art.
6. Ses nouveaux tableaux ne déçoivent pas.
7. Le public accueille son art avec enthousiasme.

K

1. Nous aussi, nous ouvrons toutes les fenêtres (en été).
2. Nous aussi, nous accueillons souvent des étudiants étrangers (à la maison).
3. Nous aussi, nous recevons beaucoup de lettres des étudiants étrangers.
4. Nous aussi, nous conduisons avec prudence.
5. Nous aussi, nous connaissons beaucoup de monde dans le quartier.
6. Nous aussi, nous partons en vacances au mois de juillet.
7. Nous aussi, nous cueillons des fleurs dans notre jardin.
8. Nous aussi, nous peignons en été.

L

1. Josette part en vacances.
2. Elle rejoint des amis.
3. Elle conduit une vieille voiture.
4. Elle dort dans des hôtels très modestes.
5. Elle arrive dans le désert.
6. Elle sent la chaleur.
7. Elle souffre d'allergies.
8. Elle repart à la maison.

M

1. Josette veut aller au bord de la mer.
2. Elle croit que ça va être amusant.
3. Elle écrit aux copains pour les inviter.
4. Elle sait arriver à la plage.
5. Elle boit de l'eau parce qu'il fait chaud.
6. Elle meurt de soif.
7. Elle court sur la plage pour faire de l'exercice.
8. Elle voit le coucher du soleil sur la mer.
9. Elle dit que c'est très joli.
10. Le soir, elle lit des romans.
11. Elle suit l'actualité en écoutant la radio.
12. Elle vit des jours heureux au bord de la mer.

N

1. —J'apprends à danser.
   —Moi aussi, je veux danser.
2. —J'apprends à jouer aux échecs.
   —Moi aussi, je veux jouer aux échecs.
3. —J'apprends à chanter.
   —Moi aussi, je veux chanter.
4. —J'apprends à conduire.
   —Moi aussi, je veux conduire.
5. —J'apprends à faire la cuisine.
   —Moi aussi, je veux faire la cuisine.
6. —J'apprends à programmer l'ordinateur.
   —Moi aussi, je veux programmer l'ordinateur.

O

1. —Est-ce que tu vas faire le linge?
   —Mais je viens de faire le linge.
2. —Est-ce que les étudiants vont déjeuner?
   —Mais ils viennent de déjeuner.
3. —Est-ce que vous allez faire les courses?
   —Mais nous venons de faire les courses.
4. —Est-ce que Christine va messager?
   —Mais elle vient de messager.
5. —Est-ce que nous allons visiter les monuments?
   —Mais vous venez de visiter les monuments.
6. —Est-ce que je vais voir un film?
   —Mais vous venez (tu viens) de voir un film.

P

1. Ils savent qu'ils doivent marcher tous les jours, mais ils disent qu'ils ne peuvent pas et qu'ils ne veulent pas.
2. Nous savons que nous devons faire de l'exercice, mais nous disons que nous ne pouvons pas et que nous ne voulons pas.
3. Tu sais que tu dois nager une heure tous les jours mais tu dis que tu ne peux pas et que tu ne veux pas.
4. Je sais que je dois faire du sport, mais je dis que je ne peux pas et que je ne veux pas.
5. Elle sait qu'elle doit suivre un régime pour maigrir, mais elle dit qu'elle ne peut pas et qu'elle ne veut pas.
6. Vous savez que vous devez faire du vélo, mais vous dites que vous ne pouvez pas et que vous ne voulez pas.

Q

1. Quand est-ce que vous partez?
2. Nous partons demain.
3. Et quand est-ce que vous revenez?

4. Moi, je reviens vendredi. Ma femme et les enfants reviennent la semaine prochaine.
5. Qu'est-ce que tu fais aujourd'hui?
6. Ma femme et moi, nous peignons la maison.
7. Vous savez peindre la maison?
8. Mon frère va nous aider. Lui, il sait peindre.
9. Moi, je viens regarder.
10. Si tu viens, tu vas peindre.

S

1. il casse / ils cassent
2. il coupe / ils coupent
3. il pousse / ils poussent
4. il recommande / ils recommandent
5. il travaille / ils travaillent
6. il visite / ils visitent
7. il aide / ils_aident
8. il allume / ils_allument
9. il apporte / ils_apportent
10. il écoute / ils_écoutent
11. il imite / ils_imitent
12. il ose / ils_osent

T

1.	/s/	ss	il connaît	ils connaissent
2.	/m/	m	il dort	ils dorment
3.	/s/	ss	il réfléchit	ils réfléchissent
4.	/d/	d	il vend	ils vendent
5.	/t/	t	il part	ils partent
6.	/t/	tt	il met	ils mettent
7.	/s/	ss	il réussit	ils réussissent
8.	/z/	s	il construit	ils construisent
9.	/p/	p	il rompt	ils rompent
10.	/d/	d	il entend	ils entendent
11.	/v/	v	il doit	ils doivent
12.	/v/	v	il reçoit	ils reçoivent
13.	/v/	v	il vit	ils vivent
14.	/z/	s	il dit	ils disent

3 Negative Sentences

A

1. Non, elle ne téléphone jamais.
2. Non, je ne mange avec personne.
3. Non, je ne regarde jamais la télé.
4. Non, je ne travaille plus.
5. Non, personne n'organise d'activités pour les nouveaux étudiants.
6. Non, je n'aime rien ici.

B

1. Non, je ne suis plus seul.
2. Non, je ne suis jamais triste.

3. Non, je ne désire plus rentrer chez moi.
4. Non, personne ne dérange les étudiants quand ils travaillent.
5. Non, je ne trouve rien à critiquer.
6. Non, rien ne m'effraie maintenant.

C

1. Nous n'arrivons jamais en retard.
2. Nous n'interrompons jamais le professeur.
3. Nous n'oublions jamais nos devoirs.
4. Nous ne perdons jamais nos livres.
5. Nous n'applaudissons jamais après la classe.
6. Nous ne jetons jamais nos stylos en l'air.
7. Nous ne confondons jamais les rois de France dans la classe d'histoire.
8. Nous ne textons jamais nos amis pendant le cours.

D

1. Les Dulac n'habitent plus l'immeuble en face.
2. M. Beauchamp ne vend plus sa poterie aux voisins.
3. Nous n'achetons plus le journal au kiosque du coin.
4. Ma mère ne descend plus faire les courses tous les jours.
5. Moi, je ne joue plus du piano.
6. Mme Duverger n'enseigne plus au lycée du quartier.
7. Nos amis ne passent plus beaucoup de temps dans le quartier.

E

1. Personne n'avertit les étudiants.
2. Personne ne parle avec les étudiants.
3. Personne n'écoute les étudiants.
4. Personne ne salue les étudiants.
5. Personne n'encourage les étudiants.
6. Personne ne donne de conseils aux étudiants.

F

Answers will vary.

G

1. Il n'aime ni la physique ni la littérature.
2. Il ne finit ni ses devoirs ni ses compositions.
3. Il n'étudie ni à la bibliothèque ni à la maison.
4. Il ne réfléchit ni à son travail ni à son avenir.
5. Il ne demande de conseils ni à ses amis ni à ses professeurs.
6. Il n'écoute ni les conférences ni les discussions.

H

1. Il n'explique aucun texte.
2. Il ne corrige aucune composition.
3. Il ne recommande aucun livre.
4. Il ne propose aucun thème de discussion.
5. Il ne présente aucune idée.
6. Il n'analyse aucun problème.

I

1. Je ne respecte que Philippe ici.
2. Je ne nettoie que ma chambre.
3. Je n'invite qu'Alice.
4. Elle n'apprécie que la littérature française.
5. Ils ne réfléchissent qu'à l'avenir.
6. Je ne téléphone qu'à Odile.
7. Je ne joue qu'au football.
8. Elle ne prépare que le dîner à la maison.

J

1. Nous ne faisons pas de projets parce que nous ne faisons pas de voyage.
2. Personne ne veut partir en vacances.
3. Donc, nous n'allons nulle part.
4. Nous n'allons ni à la plage ni à la montagne. Ni à Paris non plus.
5. Et nous ne voulons plus aller à l'étranger.

L

1. They didn't serve us any wine. Just water.
2. What did he say? Just nonsense.
3. Since his divorce, all he does is drink.
4. If you want to make an appointment with her, all you have to do is send her an e-mail.
5. Merely by listening to him, you suspect he isn't quite normal.
6. Why criticize me? All I'm doing is repeating your words.
7. He says he earns money just by surfing the Web.
8. She's writing a book just on this little village.

4 Interrogative Sentences

A

1. Invitez-vous souvent vos amis à dîner? / Est-ce que tu invites souvent tes amis à dîner?
2. Appréciez-vous la musique classique? / Est-ce que tu apprécies la musique classique?
3. Habitez-vous un beau quartier? / Est-ce que tu habites un beau quartier?

4. Cherchez-vous une maison à la campagne? /
   Est-ce que tu cherches une maison à la
   campagne?
5. Travaillez-vous près de votre appartement? /
   Est-ce que tu travailles près de ton
   appartement?
6. Dînez-vous généralement au restaurant? /
   Est-ce que tu dînes généralement au
   restaurant?

B

1. Aime-t-elle les maths comme moi?
2. Étudie-t-elle les mêmes matières que moi?
3. Habite-t-elle près du lycée?
4. Pense-t-elle à moi de temps en temps?
5. Travaille-t-elle à la bibliothèque?
6. Déjeune-t-elle à la cantine du lycée?

C

1. Est-ce que Chantal habite près de chez toi?
2. Est-ce que tu arrives au lycée à la même
   heure que Chantal?
3. Est-ce que tu salues Chantal?
4. Est-ce que Chantal aime les mêmes activités
   que toi?
5. Est-ce que tu déjeunes avec elle?
6. Est-ce que Chantal bavarde avec toi
   de temps en temps?

D

1. Mme Savignac prononce-t-elle parfaitement
   l'anglais?
2. M. Paul enseigne-t-il l'espagnol aussi?
3. Mlle Moreau répond-elle toujours aux
   questions des étudiants?
4. M. Michelet arrive-t-il au lycée à 7 heures
   du matin?
5. M. et Mme Lamoureux enseignent-ils dans
   le même lycée?
6. Mme Leboucher choisit-elle des textes
   intéressants pour sa classe?
7. Les professeurs organisent-ils des activités
   pour les étudiants?
8. Les étudiants aiment-ils les cours de
   français?

E

1. Ne dérangent-ils pas tout le monde?
2. Ne désobéissent-ils pas au professeur?
3. Ne perdent-ils pas souvent leurs cahiers?
4. Ne bavardent-ils pas trop en classe?
5. Ne confondent-ils pas les dates?
6. Ne travaillent-ils pas sans intérêt?

F

1. Ne lançons-nous pas une bonne affaire?
2. Ne dirigeons-nous pas la compagnie d'une
   façon intelligente?
3. N'engageons-nous pas de bons travailleurs?
4. N'aménageons-nous pas les bureaux?
5. Ne changeons-nous pas nos stratégies selon
   chaque situation?
6. Ne commençons-nous pas à gagner de
   l'argent?

G

1. Ne lance-t-on pas une bonne affaire? /
   On ne lance pas une bonne affaire?
2. Ne dirige-t-on pas la compagnie d'une façon
   intelligente? / On ne dirige pas la compagnie
   d'une façon intelligente?
3. N'engage-t-on pas de bons travailleurs? /
   On n'engage pas de bons travailleurs?
4. N'aménage-t-on pas les bureaux? /
   On n'aménage pas les bureaux?
5. Ne change-t-on pas nos (les) stratégies selon
   chaque situation? / On ne change pas nos
   (les) stratégies selon chaque situation?
6. Ne commence-t-on pas à gagner de
   l'argent? / On ne commence pas à gagner
   de l'argent?

H

1. —Claire n'arrive pas ce matin?
   —Non, elle arrive ce soir.
2. —Marc et Geneviève ne sont pas au bureau?
   —Non, ils sont malades.
3. —Tu n'as pas sommeil?
   —Non, j'ai envie de sortir.
4. —Je n'ai pas raison?
   —Non, tu as tort. (Non, vous avez tort.)
5. —Ton frère et toi, vous ne prenez pas le petit
   déjeuner à la maison?
   —Non, nous prenons un café au bureau.
6. —Lise ne suit pas un régime?
   —Non, elle prend du poids.
7. —Vous et vos parents, vous n'êtes pas en
   colère?
   —Non, nous sommes de bonne humeur.
8. —Tu ne sors pas?
   —Non, je reste à la maison.

I

1. —Il n'a pas mal au dos?
   —Si, et il a mal aux jambes aussi.
2. —Il ne fait pas de vent?
   —Si, et il fait froid aussi.

3. —Tu ne fais pas les lits chez toi?
   —Si, et je fais le linge aussi.
4. —Marianne ne joue pas du violon?
   —Si, et elle chante aussi.
5. —Ta sœur et toi, vous n'apprenez pas
   à parler chinois?
   —Si, et nous apprenons à écrire aussi.
6. —Je ne peux pas assister à la conférence?
   —Si, et tu peux aller au concert aussi.

J

1. L'écologie est-elle importante?
2. Les animaux jouent-ils un rôle important
   dans notre vie?
3. Les gens souffrent-ils à cause de la pollution?
4. Les légumes sont-ils bons pour la santé?
5. Les cigarettes font-elles mal?

5 Imperative

A

1. Ne déchirez pas vos copies.
2. Ne laissez pas vos crayons sur la table.
3. Ne mangez pas dans la salle de classe.
4. Ne mâchez pas de chewing-gum en classe.
5. Ne salissez pas la salle de classe.
6. Ne faites pas de bruit.
7. Ne jetez pas de papiers par terre.
8. N'interrompez pas le professeur.
9. Ne lisez pas de bandes dessinées en classe.
10. N'oubliez pas vos calculettes.

B

1. Non, ne partons pas la semaine prochaine.
   Attendons la fin du mois.
2. Non, ne prenons pas l'avion. Prenons le
   train.
3. Non, ne descendons pas dans un hôtel
   de luxe. Choisissons une auberge.
4. Non, ne visitons pas les monuments en taxi.
   Louons une voiture.
5. Non, n'assistons pas aux concerts. Allons
   voir les pièces de théâtre.
6. Non, ne mangeons pas dans le restaurant
   de l'hôtel. Dînons dans les restaurants de
   la ville.

C

1. D'abord, descends dans la rue.
2. Ensuite, cherche une librairie.
3. Là-bas, demande un livre sur la Suisse.
4. Rentre tout de suite à ton appartement.
5. Après, lis le livre.

6. Choisis ton itinéraire.
7. Après, téléphone à l'agent de voyages.
8. Finalement, fais les valises.

D

1. Lis les annonces.
2. Regarde les rabais.
3. Va aux grands magasins.
4. Essaie (Essaye) les vêtements qui te plaisent.
5. Choisis une robe.
6. Paie (Paye) avec la carte de crédit.
7. Reviens à la maison.
8. Mets ta nouvelle robe.

E

1. Allons en ville.
2. Prenons le train de 9 heures.
3. Descendons à la gare centrale.
4. Faisons une promenade.
5. Regardons les vitrines des magasins.
6. Déjeunons dans un bon restaurant.
7. Cherchons un bon film.
8. Après le film, flânons dans le jardin public.
9. Achetons des livres dans une librairie.
10. Rentrons par le train de 5 heures.

F

1. Non, ne mens pas. Dis la vérité.
2. Non, ne descends pas. Reste en haut.
3. Non, ne lis pas le texte. Écris la composition.
4. Non, ne suis pas ce régime. Fais du sport.
5. Non, ne mincis pas. Prends du corps.
6. Non, ne prépare pas le déjeuner. Fais la
   vaisselle.
7. Non, ne nettoie pas la cuisine. Balaie
   (Balaye) l'escalier.
8. Non, ne jette pas cette robe. Offre les vieux
   vêtements aux voisins.

G

1. Ne renverse pas la bouteille!
2. N'écris pas sur les murs!
3. Ne débranche pas l'ordinateur!
4. Ne jette pas mon portefeuille à la poubelle!
5. Ne dessine pas sur mon cahier!
6. Ne grimpe pas sur la table!
7. Ne laisse pas le frigo ouvert!
8. Ne cache pas les clés de la voiture!

H

1. Descendez à 7 heures et demie.
2. Allez à la boulangerie.
3. Achetez du pain.
4. Traversez la rue.

5. Entrez chez le marchand de légumes.
6. Prenez un kilo d'asperges et de la salade.
7. Passez à la boucherie.
8. Cherchez le poulet que j'ai commandé hier.
9. Rentrez tout de suite.
10. Commencez à préparer le dîner.

I

1. Arrive à l'heure. / Arrivez à l'heure.
2. Écoute le patron. / Écoutez le patron.
3. Ne dors pas au bureau. / Ne dormez pas au bureau.
4. N'oublie jamais les documents. / N'oubliez jamais les documents.
5. Réponds à tes e-mails. / Répondez à vos e-mails.
6. Sois gentil(le) avec tout le monde. / Soyez gentil(le)s avec tout le monde.
7. Essaie (Essaye) de comprendre tes collègues. / Essayez de comprendre vos collègues.
8. Ne dérange pas les autres employés. / Ne dérangez pas les autres employés.

6 Passé Composé

A

1. Non. Mais il a nagé hier.
2. Non. Mais nous avons déjeuné en ville hier.
3. Non. Mais il a pris de l'essence hier.
4. Non. Mais nous avons nettoyé notre chambre hier.
5. Non. Mais ils ont rédigé un compte rendu hier.
6. Non. Mais j'ai appris le vocabulaire hier.
7. Non. Mais il a fait le linge hier.
8. Non. Mais nous avons fini hier.
9. Non. Mais j'ai attendu mes amis hier.
10. Non. Mais elle a répondu en classe hier.
11. Non. Mais ils ont obtenu les résultats de l'examen hier.
12. Non. Mais le film a repris hier.
13. Non. Mais j'ai eu mal à l'estomac hier.
14. Non. Mais tu as été (vous avez été) en avance hier.
15. Non. Mais il a fait beau hier.

B

1. J'ai invité mon copain Serge à faire une promenade en voiture avec moi.
2. Nous avons décidé d'aller à la campagne.
3. Nous avons fait le plein avant de partir.

4. Tout d'un coup, nous avons entendu un bruit.
5. Nous avons eu un pneu crevé.
6. Nous avons poussé la voiture au bord du boulevard.
7. Nous avons acheté un nouveau pneu à la station-service.
8. Nous avons dépensé tout notre argent.
9. Nous n'avons pas pu aller à la campagne.
10. J'ai remonté le boulevard.
11. J'ai garé la voiture devant mon immeuble.
12. Serge et moi, nous avons passé la journée devant la télé.

C

1. J'ai décidé d'acheter un nouvel ordinateur.
2. Mon père et moi, nous avons lu une brochure ensemble.
3. Nous avons demandé d'autres brochures.
4. Mon père a trouvé un revendeur bien informé.
5. Nous avons posé beaucoup de questions au revendeur.
6. Il a répondu patiemment à nos questions.
7. Nous avons choisi un ordinateur multimédia.
8. J'ai acheté des logiciels.
9. Mon père a trouvé des CD-ROM intéressants.
10. J'ai mis mon nouvel ordinateur dans ma chambre.

D

1. Marie a reçu une lettre.
2. Elle a ouvert l'enveloppe.
3. Elle a lu la lettre.
4. Son cousin François a écrit la lettre.
5. Il a été malade.
6. Il a passé deux semaines à l'hôpital.
7. Marie a montré la lettre à ses parents.
8. Ils ont dit à Marie de téléphoner à François.
9. Elle a invité François à passer les vacances chez elle.
10. François a accepté.
11. Il a été très content.
12. Il a promis d'arriver au début du mois de juillet.

E

1. Je suis arrivée chez moi vers 5 heures et demie.
2. J'ai posé mes affaires sur le lit.
3. Je suis redescendue.

4. Je suis allée au supermarché pour acheter quelque chose à manger.
5. Je suis rentrée tout de suite.
6. J'ai préparé mon dîner.
7. Lise et Solange sont passées vers 7 heures.
8. Elles sont restées une heure.
9. Elles sont parties à 8 heures.
10. J'ai fait mes devoirs.
11. J'ai regardé les informations à la télé.
12. J'ai fermé le poste vers 11 heures pour me coucher.

F

1. Cette fois ils ne sont pas arrivés en retard.
2. Cette fois ils n'ont pas parlé de football.
3. Cette fois ils n'ont pas commandé de sandwich.
4. Cette fois ils n'ont pas bu beaucoup de Coca avec le repas.
5. Cette fois ils n'ont pas sorti la calculette pour vérifier l'addition.
6. Cette fois ils ont payé.
7. Cette fois ils ont laissé un pourboire.
8. Cette fois ils ne sont pas rentrés tout de suite après le repas.

G

1. Trois de mes amis et moi, nous avons voulu coucher à la belle étoile.
2. Nous sommes allés à la campagne.
3. Nous avons campé à côté du fleuve.
4. Claude et moi, nous avons fait un feu.
5. Marc et Philippe ont dressé les tentes.
6. Nous avons mangé autour du feu.
7. Vers 9 heures, nous sommes entrés sous nos tentes.
8. Chacun est entré dans son sac de couchage.
9. Soudain, j'ai entendu un cri affreux.
10. Marc a remarqué un serpent sous la tente.
11. Philippe et lui sont sortis de la tente en courant.
12. Nous avons été pris de panique.
13. Le serpent est parti en rampant.
14. Je crois que le pauvre serpent a eu peur.
15. Nous avons arrêté de hurler.
16. Chacun est rentré sous sa tente.
17. Personne n'a fermé l'œil de la nuit.
18. Le matin nous avons plié les tentes.
19. Nous sommes retournés chez nous.
20. Tout le monde a été épuisé.

H

1. a sorti
2. est parti
3. a monté
4. a vu
5. a dû
6. est arrivé
7. a demandé
8. est sortie
9. a fait
10. a étendu
11. sont descendues
12. ont descendu
13. sont rentrées
14. ont monté
15. sont entrées
16. a commencé
17. a dit
18. ont rentré

I

1. quitté
2. offert
3. accepté
4. fait
5. pris
6. arrivée
7. commencé
8. lues
9. vus
10. donné
11. cherchée
12. entrée
13. demandé
14. montrés
15. choisi
16. trouvée
17. commencé
18. présentée
19. accueillie

J

1. Les devoirs que j'ai faits hier?
2. La lettre que j'ai reçue hier?
3. La composition que j'ai rédigée hier?
4. Le sac à dos que j'ai acheté hier?
5. L'appareil photo que j'ai employé hier?
6. Le DVD que j'ai regardé hier?
7. Les disques compacts que j'ai écoutés hier?
8. Les chaussures que j'ai mises hier?
9. Les lunettes de soleil que j'ai portées hier?
10. Les revues que j'ai lues hier?

K

1. Hier j'ai téléphoné à Berthe.
2. Je lui ai demandé, «Tu veux aller au cinéma?»
3. Elle a répondu, «Oui».
4. Je suis passé la prendre à 7 heures.
5. Elle est descendue et nous avons pris l'autobus.
6. Nous sommes arrivés au cinéma à 7 heures et demie.
7. J'ai tout de suite pris (acheté) les billets.
8. Berthe et moi, nous avons cherché un café.
9. Nous avons pris un café et une pâtisserie.
10. J'ai regardé ma montre.
11. J'ai dit, «Il est 8 heures moins 5».
12. Nous sommes vite rentrés (retournés) au cinéma et nous sommes entrés.

7   Imperfect; Imperfect Versus Passé Composé

A

1. Vous ne croyez plus à cette histoire. Avant vous croyiez à cette histoire.
2. Il ne lit plus en allemand. Avant il lisait en allemand.
3. Elles ne font plus les carreaux. Avant elles faisaient les carreaux.
4. Tu n'habites plus en ville. Avant tu habitais en ville.
5. Ils ne vivent plus bien. Avant ils vivaient bien.
6. Mon chien n'obéit plus. Avant il obéissait.
7. Elle ne rougit plus. Avant elle rougissait.
8. Je ne réponds plus en classe. Avant je répondais en classe.
9. Tu ne voyages plus. Avant tu voyageais.
10. Elle ne prononce plus correctement. Avant elle prononçait correctement.
11. Vous n'appréciez plus la musique classique. Avant vous appréciiez la musique classique.
12. Ils ne rangent plus leurs affaires. Avant ils rangeaient leurs affaires.

B

1. Nous avions une maison dans un quartier tranquille.
2. Elle était grande.
3. La maison avait dix pièces.
4. Mes parents travaillaient en ville.
5. Ils allaient au bureau en autobus.
6. L'arrêt était au coin de la rue.
7. Beaucoup d'autres jeunes filles habitaient dans notre rue.
8. Je jouais avec elles.
9. Nous allions à l'école ensemble.
10. Je gardais souvent ma petite sœur Marguerite.
11. Je l'emmenais au parc.
12. Nous étions tous très contents.

C

1. Nous vivions à la campagne.
2. Je partageais une chambre avec ma sœur.
3. Nous n'avions pas beaucoup d'argent.
4. Mais on était heureux.
5. Je nageais dans le lac.
6. Les enfants couraient dans les champs.
7. Mes parents élevaient des vaches.
8. Nous vendions le lait.
9. Ton grand-père commençait à venir me voir.
10. J'avais 18 ans.

D

1. Je passais souvent les vacances chez ma tante.
2. Je voulais toujours aller au bord de la mer.
3. Ma famille et moi, nous visitions chaque été une région de France.
4. Mes cousins m'invitaient tous les ans chez eux.
5. Nous, on prenait le plus souvent les vacances en hiver.
6. Ma cousine Élisabeth venait en général chez nous à Paris.
7. Nous partions d'habitude en Suisse.
8. Mon père louait tous les étés un appartement à Nice.

E

1. Il faisait du vent quand je suis arrivée à l'arrêt.
2. Il bruinait quand l'autobus est venu.
3. Il pleuvait quand je suis montée dans l'autobus.
4. Il faisait froid quand je suis arrivée à la faculté.
5. Il gelait quand j'ai retrouvé mon amie Hélène.
6. Il neigeait quand nous sommes entré(e)s dans l'amphithéâtre.
7. Il tonnait quand le professeur a commencé sa conférence.
8. Il grêlait quand nous sommes sorti(e)s de l'amphithéâtre.

F

1. Il était 8 heures et demie quand mon train est venu.
2. Il était 9 heures pile quand je suis arrivé en ville.
3. Il était un peu tard quand je suis entré dans le bureau.
4. Il était midi quand mon collègue m'a invité à déjeuner.
5. Il était une heure et demie quand nous avons fini de manger.
6. Il était tard dans l'après-midi quand j'ai quitté le bureau.
7. Il était déjà 7 heures quand j'ai retrouvé ma fiancée pour dîner.
8. Il était presque minuit quand je suis rentré chez moi.

G

1. Il a nettoyé la cuisine pendant que les enfants jouaient dans le jardin.
2. Il a fait le linge pendant que sa mère promenait le chien.
3. Il a préparé le dîner pendant que sa sœur faisait les courses.
4. Il a mis la table pendant que son fils aîné réparait la voiture.
5. Il a rangé les livres pendant que son père bricolait dans le sous-sol.
6. Il a ciré les meubles pendant que son frère lisait le journal.

H

1. Je ne suis pas allé(e) au restaurant parce que je n'avais pas envie de sortir.
2. Nous n'avons pas fait une promenade parce que nous n'avions pas le temps.
3. Je n'ai pas lu le chapitre parce que j'avais mal à la tête.
4. Albert n'a pas pris le petit déjeuner parce qu'il était trop occupé.
5. Chantal n'est pas venue à la réunion parce qu'elle travaillait.
6. Nos copains ne sont pas allés au concert parce qu'ils n'avaient pas d'argent.
7. Les voisins ne sont pas sortis parce que leur voiture était en panne.
8. Tu n'as pas répondu au professeur parce que tu ne faisais pas attention à sa question.

I

1. Quand j'ai connu Josette, elle était étudiante.
2. Quand j'ai connu Josette, elle travaillait déjà.
3. Quand j'ai connu Josette, elle était institutrice.
4. Quand j'ai connu Josette, elle sortait avec Frédéric.
5. Quand j'ai connu Josette, elle était mariée.
6. Quand j'ai connu Josette, elle avait deux enfants.

J

1. Le ciel était couvert pendant qu'ils cherchaient un endroit pour camper.
2. Il bruinait pendant que les deux garçons dressaient leur tente.
3. Il pleuvait pendant que Guy faisait un feu.
4. Il faisait du vent pendant qu'Alain cuisinait.
5. La température baissait pendant qu'ils mangeaient.

6. Des éclairs illuminaient le ciel pendant qu'ils ouvraient les sacs de couchage.
7. Il tonnait pendant que les deux garçons essayaient de dormir.
8. Mais le matin, il faisait beau pendant qu'ils pliaient leur tente.

K

1. Vous attendiez le bus depuis vingt minutes quand Jean-Claude est venu vous prendre avec sa voiture. (Il y avait (Ça faisait) vingt minutes que vous attendiez le bus quand Jean-Claude est venu vous prendre avec sa voiture.) / You had been waiting for the bus for twenty minutes when Jean-Claude came by to get you in his car.
2. Nous étudiions à la bibliothèque depuis six heures quand Christine nous a invités à dîner chez elle. (Il y avait (Ça faisait) six heures que nous étudiions à la bibliothèque quand Christine nous a invités à dîner chez elle.) / We had been studying in the library for six hours when Christine invited us to have dinner at her house.
3. Odile dormait depuis dix minutes quand le téléphone a sonné. (Il y avait (Ça faisait) dix minutes qu'Odile dormait quand le téléphone a sonné.) / Odile had been sleeping for ten minutes when the telephone rang.
4. Sylvain entrait des données depuis deux heures quand il y a eu une panne d'électricité. (Il y avait (Ça faisait) deux heures que Sylvain entrait des données quand il y a eu une panne d'électricité.) / Sylvain had been inputting data for two hours when there was a power failure.
5. Brigitte faisait du jogging depuis une heure quand il a commencé à pleuvoir. (Il y avait (Ça faisait) une heure que Brigitte faisait du jogging quand il a commencé à pleuvoir.) / Brigitte had been jogging for an hour when it began to rain.
6. Alain rangeait ses affaires depuis dix minutes quand ses amis l'ont appelé pour jouer au football. (Il y avait (Ça faisait) dix minutes qu'Alain rangeait ses affaires quand ses amis l'ont appelé pour jouer au football.) / Alain had been straightening up his things for ten minutes when his friends called him to play soccer.

L

1. Si nous jouions aux cartes? /
   Si on jouait aux cartes?
2. Si nous achetions le journal? /
   Si on achetait le journal?
3. Si nous passions chez Françoise? /
   Si on passait chez Françoise?
4. Si nous regardions un film à la télé? /
   Si on regardait un film à la télé?
5. Si nous mangions au restaurant? /
   Si on mangeait au restaurant?
6. Si nous commencions nos devoirs? /
   Si on commençait nos devoirs?

M

1. —Saviez-vous le nom de la rue où elle
   habite?
   —Non, mais je l'ai su ce matin.
2. —Est-ce qu'ils voulaient passer la journée
   en ville?
   —Oui, mais ils n'ont pas pu.
3. Je pouvais travailler hier, mais je n'ai pas
   voulu quitter la maison.
4. —Est-ce que tu as eu la lettre hier?
   —Non, j'avais la lettre depuis une semaine.
5. —Est-ce que vous avez connu le professeur?
   —Je le connaissais déjà.

N

1. voulais
2. suis entré(e)
3. étaient
4. avait
5. ai vu
6. suis passé(e)
7. suis monté(e)
8. ai trouvé
9. suis descendu(e)
10. voulais
11. ai remarqué
12. intéressaient
13. avais
14. ai acheté
15. ai décidé

O

1. a quitté
2. a pris
3. est arrivé
4. avait
5. connaissait
6. a trouvé
7. fallait
8. recevait
9. vivait
10. a renoncé
11. a invité
12. a mis
13. ont ouvert
14. étaient
15. sont devenus

Q

1. c
2. a
3. a
4. d
5. a
6. b

8 Reflexive Verbs

A

1. Je me lève tout de suite. Jérôme se lève tout
   de suite aussi.
2. Je me brosse les dents. Jérôme se brosse
   les dents aussi.
3. Je me peigne. Jérôme se peigne aussi.
4. Je me rase. Jérôme se rase aussi.
5. Je m'habille. Jérôme s'habille aussi.
6. Je me lave les mains. Jérôme se lave les mains
   aussi.
7. Je me lave la figure. Jérôme se lave la figure
   aussi.
8. Je me repose. Jérôme se repose aussi.
9. Je me couche à 11 heures. Jérôme se couche
   à 11 heures aussi.
10. Je m'endors tout de suite. Jérôme s'endort
    tout de suite aussi.

B

1. Ils se lèvent tout de suite.
2. Ils se brossent les dents.
3. Ils se peignent.
4. Ils se rasent.
5. Ils s'habillent.
6. Ils se lavent les mains.
7. Ils se lavent la figure.
8. Ils se reposent.
9. Ils se couchent à 11 heures.
10. Ils s'endorment tout de suite.

C

1. Nous nous levons immédiatement.
2. Nous nous lavons les mains et la figure.
3. Nous nous brossons les dents.
4. Nous nous lavons la tête.
5. Nous nous séchons les cheveux.
6. Nous nous maquillons.
7. Nous nous peignons.
8. Nous nous brossons les cheveux.
9. Nous nous limons les ongles.
10. Nous nous habillons avec soin.

D

1. Je me réunis avec mes amis.
2. Ils se trouvent dans un café du centre.
3. Je m'approche du café.
4. Mes amis se lèvent.
5. Nous nous éloignons du café.
6. Nous nous dirigeons vers le cinéma.
7. Nous nous dépêchons.

8. Nous nous arrêtons au guichet pour prendre les billets.
9. Nous entrons dans le cinéma et nous nous asseyons.

E

1. Je ne veux pas m'inquiéter.
2. Vous devez vous calmer.
3. Il ne peut pas se sentir triste.
4. Elles ne veulent pas s'ennuyer.
5. Tu ne dois pas te mettre en colère.
6. Nous n'allons pas nous offenser.
7. Le professeur va s'impatienter.
8. Tu dois t'animer.

F

1. En général, je ne me fâche pas, mais cette fois je vais me fâcher.
2. En général, elles ne s'énervent pas, mais cette fois elles vont s'énerver.
3. En général, tu ne t'impatientes pas, mais cette fois tu vas t'impatienter.
4. En général, il ne s'offense pas, mais cette fois il va s'offenser.
5. En général, nous ne nous inquiétons pas, mais cette fois nous allons nous inquiéter.
6. En général, vous ne vous embêtez pas, mais cette fois vous allez vous embêter.
7. En général, je ne me sens pas de trop, mais cette fois je vais me sentir de trop.
8. En général, tu ne te passionnes pas, mais cette fois tu vas te passionner.

G

1. Vous devez vous calmer.
2. Elle doit s'amuser un peu.
3. Je dois me sentir heureux (heureuse).
4. Nous ne devons pas nous mettre en colère.
5. Ils doivent s'enthousiasmer.
6. Tu ne dois pas t'impatienter.
7. Je dois m'animer un peu.
8. Vous ne devez pas vous offenser.

H

1. —Quand est-ce que tu vas te mettre à préparer le dîner?
   —Je me suis déjà mise à préparer le dîner.
2. —Quand est-ce que les enfants vont se coucher?
   —Ils se sont déjà couchés.
3. —Quand est-ce que vous allez vous occuper du linge, Josette et toi?
   —Nous nous sommes déjà occupées du linge.

4. —Quand est-ce que tu vas te reposer?
   —Je me suis déjà reposée.
5. —Quand est-ce qu'Elvire va se laver la tête?
   —Elle s'est déjà lavé la tête.
6. —Quand est-ce que tu vas te limer les ongles?
   —Je me suis déjà limé les ongles.
7. —Quand est-ce que Carole et Paulette vont se calmer?
   —Elles se sont déjà calmées.
8. —Quand est-ce que je vais me brosser les cheveux?
   —Tu t'es déjà brossé les cheveux.

I

1. Non, je ne me suis pas encore levée.
2. Non, je ne me suis pas encore rasé.
3. Non, nous ne nous sommes pas encore brossé les dents.
4. Non, je ne me suis pas encore lavé la tête.
5. Non, je ne me suis pas encore habillé.
6. Non, nous ne nous sommes pas encore peignés.

J

1. Olivier et Jean se sont réveillés de bonne heure.
2. Christine s'est lavé la tête.
3. Monique et Véronique se sont préparées pour le départ.
4. Mireille s'est dépêchée comme une folle.
5. Christian et Pierre se sont chargés de la nourriture.
6. Tous les étudiants se sont réunis devant le lycée.
7. Ils se sont assis dans les autocars.
8. Les autocars se sont éloignés de l'établissement.

K

1. Le petit Claude s'est mouillé la chemise en buvant un Coca.
2. Marlise s'est salie dans le garage.
3. Les jumeaux se sont moqués du voisin.
4. Les parents de Philippe se sont mis en panique.
5. Leur fils s'est échappé de la maison.
6. Caroline s'est plainte de tout.
7. Le petit Baudoin s'est caché au sous-sol.
8. Odile s'est coupé le doigt avec un couteau.
9. Moi, je me suis fatiguée.
10. Je me suis couchée de bonne heure.

L

1. Oui, mais hier nous ne nous sommes pas vus.
2. Oui, mais hier nous ne nous sommes pas écrit.
3. Oui, mais hier nous ne nous sommes pas parlé.
4. Oui, mais hier nous ne nous sommes pas téléphoné.
5. Oui, mais hier nous ne nous sommes pas donné rendez-vous.
6. Oui, mais hier nous ne nous sommes pas aidés.
7. Oui, mais hier nous ne nous sommes pas accompagnés.
8. Oui, mais hier nous ne nous sommes pas invités.

M

1. Ils se sont connus.
2. Ils se sont parlé.
3. Ils se sont compris.
4. Ils sont tombés amoureux.
5. Ils se sont acheté des petits cadeaux.
6. Ils se sont fiancés.
7. Après un temps, ils se sont disputés.
8. Ils se sont menti.
9. Ils ont rompu.
10. Ils ne se sont pas mariés.

N

1. Lève-toi. / Levez-vous.
2. Habille-toi. / Habillez-vous.
3. Dépêche-toi. / Dépêchez-vous.
4. Lave-toi les mains. / Lavez-vous les mains.
5. Ne t'énerve pas. / Ne vous énervez pas.
6. Ne te repose plus. / Ne vous reposez plus.
7. Ne te fâche pas. / Ne vous fâchez pas.
8. Ne te recouche pas. / Ne vous recouchez pas.
9. Dirige-toi vers la porte. / Dirigez-vous vers la porte.
10. Prépare-toi pour partir. / Préparez-vous pour partir.

O

1. Rasons-nous.
2. Habillons-nous.
3. Dépêchons-nous.
4. Lavons-nous les mains.
5. Ne nous énervons pas.
6. Ne nous reposons plus.
7. Ne nous fâchons pas.

8. Aidons-nous.
9. Dirigeons-nous vers la porte.
10. Préparons-nous pour partir.

P

1. Ce produit se vend-il bien?
2. Les étudiants s'amusent-ils au bal?
3. Ne vous dirigez-vous pas vers la sortie?
4. Ne se sont-ils pas approchés du guichet?
5. Ne nous éloignons-nous pas du centre de la ville?
6. Pourquoi vos amis ne se sont-ils plus réunis?
7. Pourquoi ne t'intéresses-tu plus au cinéma?
8. À quelle heure se sont-elles mises en route?
9. Ne se sont-ils pas offensés?
10. S'est-elle souvenue de moi?
11. Pourquoi ne s'est-elle pas habituée à la vie française?
12. Vous attendez-vous à le voir?

Q

1. Ils s'en sont allés. Moi aussi, je compte m'en aller.
2. Nous nous sommes trompés de train.
3. Ce parc s'appelle le jardin du Luxembourg.
4. Ça (Cela) ne se dit pas.
5. Je me méfie des chiens que je ne connais pas.
6. Il ne se souciait jamais de son travail.
7. Nous nous sommes fiés (Nous nous fiions) à nos amis.
8. Est-ce que vous vous souvenez du professeur Gauthier?
9. Ils ne se sont pas donné la peine de chercher un bon hôtel.
10. Je me demande s'ils se sont perdus.

9 Future and Conditional; Conditional Sentences (1)

A

1. Non, je ferai le ménage demain.
2. Non, ils reviendront demain.
3. Non, il ira au bureau demain.
4. Non, vous travaillerez demain.
5. Non, tu répondras demain.
6. Non, je saurai la réponse demain.
7. Non, tu enverras le courriel demain.
8. Non, vous emmènerez les enfants au zoo demain.
9. Non, nous projetterons le film demain.
10. Non, ils compléteront leur travail demain.

B

1. Je crois que tu réussiras.
2. Je crois qu'ils descendront.
3. Je crois qu'il ira.
4. Je crois qu'il neigera.
5. Je crois que je sortirai.
6. Je crois que vous arriverez à l'heure.
7. Je crois qu'ils nous prêteront la voiture.
8. Je crois que je compléterai mes devoirs.

C

1. Je ne sais pas s'ils partiront.
2. Je ne sais pas si je travaillerai.
3. Je ne sais pas si tu passeras (vous passerez) l'examen.
4. Je ne sais pas s'il reviendra.
5. Je ne sais pas s'ils iront à l'école.
6. Je ne sais pas si je conduirai.
7. Je ne sais pas s'ils liront.
8. Je ne sais pas si on projettera un film.
9. Je ne sais pas si je voudrai venir.
10. Je ne sais pas s'il pourra rentrer.

D

1. Maman fera les valises.
2. La fille aînée s'occupera des petits.
3. Papa se chargera de la voiture.
4. Tout le monde se réveillera à 7 heures du matin.
5. Tous les membres de la famille se dépêcheront.
6. Personne ne se mettra en colère.
7. Les enfants s'entraideront.
8. Les grands-parents prépareront le petit déjeuner.
9. La tante Marie fermera les fenêtres.
10. Les Ramonet se mettront en route vers 10 heures du matin.

E

1. Je ferai ma valise dès que le linge sera sec.
2. Les enfants s'habilleront quand ils rentreront de l'école.
3. Nous mangerons quand maman reviendra du marché.
4. Mon frère mettra les valises dans la voiture aussitôt que papa reviendra de la station-service.
5. Nous choisirons la route quand je trouverai la carte.
6. Nous partirons quand il fera beau.
7. Nous chercherons un hôtel lorsque nous arriverons à Aurillac.

8. Je me coucherai aussitôt que nous serons dans l'hôtel.

F

1. Sortez dès que la cloche sonnera.
2. Téléphone aussitôt qu'Albert arrivera.
3. Mettez-vous à prendre des notes quand le professeur commencera sa conférence.
4. Descends à la cuisine quand je t'appellerai.
5. Venez me voir quand vous pourrez.
6. Ferme la porte à clé quand tu t'en iras.
7. Dites bonjour de ma part à votre fils quand vous le verrez.
8. Lisez mon courriel dès que vous la recevrez.

G

1. Oui, tu rentrerais si tu pouvais. (Oui, vous rentreriez si vous pouviez.)
2. Oui, elles feraient du ski si elles pouvaient.
3. Oui, je deviendrais poète si je pouvais.
4. Oui, vous vous verriez tous les jours si vous pouviez.
5. Oui, tu te mettrais en route si tu pouvais. (Oui, vous vous mettriez en route si vous pouviez.)
6. Oui, il se promènerait s'il pouvait.
7. Oui, nous achèterions du pain si nous pouvions.
8. Oui, vous seriez de retour si vous pouviez.

H

1. Moi non plus, je ne prendrais pas la voiture.
2. Moi non plus, je ne ferais pas la vaisselle.
3. Moi non plus, je ne m'assoirais (m'assiérais) pas dans le jardin.
4. Moi non plus, je ne regarderais pas la télé.
5. Moi non plus, je n'enlèverais pas mon pull.
6. Moi non plus, je ne projetterais pas ce film.
7. Moi non plus, je ne répéterais pas ces slogans.
8. Moi non plus, je ne courrais pas.

I

1. Impossible! Je ne renoncerais pas à mon travail.
2. Impossible! Elle ne rejetterait pas notre offre.
3. Impossible! Il ne se lèverait pas pendant la classe.
4. Impossible! Ils ne feraient pas grève.
5. Impossible! Je n'exagérerais pas.
6. Impossible! Tu ne perdrais pas les billets.
7. Impossible! Il ne tomberait pas en skiant.
8. Impossible! Il ne jetterait pas son dîner à la poubelle.

J

1. Si Jean-Pierre s'habillait bien, les autres étudiants ne se moqueraient pas de lui.
2. Si Jean-Pierre faisait du sport, il connaîtrait beaucoup de monde.
3. Si Jean-Pierre s'intéressait à ses études, il serait préparé en classe.
4. Si Jean-Pierre ne s'absentait pas souvent, les professeurs ne se fâcheraient pas contre lui.
5. Si Jean-Pierre ne lisait pas de bandes dessinées en classe, les profs ne seraient pas furieux.
6. Si Jean-Pierre ne mangeait pas toujours seul, il parlerait avec les autres étudiants.

K

1. Si maman installe la machine à laver au sous-sol, nous aurons plus de place dans la cuisine.
2. Si je mets la lampe à côté du fauteuil, je pourrai lire.
3. Si nous nettoyons le tapis, nous le mettrons dans le salon.
4. Si tu trouves la table en plastique, tu pourras la mettre sur la terrasse.
5. Si on laisse l'ordinateur dans ma chambre, je ferai mes devoirs sans embêter les autres.
6. Si les déménageurs montent une étagère dans ma chambre, je rangerai tous mes livres.

L

1. Si on avait deux postes de télé, on pourrait regarder la télé dans le séjour.
2. Si cette maison avait un grenier, il y aurait de la place pour les boîtes.
3. Si la cheminée fonctionnait, nous pourrions faire un feu.
4. Si on avait des tableaux dans le salon, il serait accueillant.
5. Si j'avais une chaîne stéréo dans ma chambre, je n'écouterais pas mes disques dans le séjour.
6. Si le frigo n'était pas tellement petit, maman ne devrait pas faire les courses plusieurs fois par semaine.
7. Si tu décrochais les rideaux, je pourrais les laver.
8. Si cette fenêtre se fermait bien, il ne ferait pas froid dans ma chambre.

M

1. Si je me sentais mal, j'irais chez le médecin.
2. S'il me fallait maigrir, je ne mangerais que des légumes et des fruits.
3. S'il sortait sous la pluie, il attraperait un rhume.
4. Si elle tombait malade, elle se reposerait.
5. Si nous allions pieds nus, nous nous ferions mal au pied.
6. Si tu avais mal à la tête, tu prendrais des comprimés d'aspirine.
7. Si le médecin m'ordonnait des antibiotiques, je ne les prendrais pas.
8. Si j'étais en forme, je ne me fatiguerais pas tellement.

10 Pluperfect, Future Perfect, and Past Conditional; Conditional Sentences (2)

A

1. Les étudiants avaient pris leur place quand le professeur Jourdain est entré.
2. Le professeur avait déjà commencé à parler quand Marc a sorti son cahier.
3. Rachelle s'était endormie quand le professeur a commencé à poser des questions.
4. Le professeur avait fini sa conférence quand la cloche a sonné.
5. Nous nous étions assis dans la cantine quand Jacques est arrivé.
6. Il nous a demandé si nous avions assisté à la classe du professeur Jourdain.
7. Hélène lui a répondu que nous avions tous été présents.
8. Je lui ai prêté les notes que j'avais prises.

B

1. C'est qu'elle m'avait déjà téléphoné avant-hier.
2. C'est qu'elle était déjà venue me voir avant-hier.
3. C'est qu'ils avaient déjà demandé le nom du médecin avant-hier.
4. C'est que j'avais déjà passé mon permis de conduire avant-hier.
5. C'est qu'elles avaient déjà fait leur travail avant-hier.
6. C'est que j'avais déjà posté la lettre avant-hier.
7. C'est qu'il avait déjà fait le plein avant-hier.
8. C'est qu'elle avait déjà balayé la cuisine avant-hier.

C

1. ... ma sœur avait pris une douche.
2. ... ma mère avait préparé le petit déjeuner.
3. ... je m'étais levé(e).
4. ... mon amie Ghislaine avait téléphoné deux fois.
5. ... mon père n'était pas parti pour le bureau.
6. ... j'avais relu mes notes de biologie.
7. ... mes frères avaient mis leurs dossiers dans leurs serviettes.
8. ... je ne m'étais pas habillé(e).

D

1. Elle m'a demandé si nous avions invité Suzanne.
2. Elle m'a demandé si Marc avait fini le projet.
3. Elle m'a demandé si tu avais trouvé un emploi.
4. Elle m'a demandé si elles avaient choisi une spécialisation.
5. Elle m'a demandé s'ils s'étaient réunis hier.
6. Elle m'a demandé si M. Jourdain s'était fâché.
7. Elle m'a demandé si Paul et Christine s'étaient fiancés.
8. Elle m'a demandé si nous nous étions trompés de train.

E

1. Marie-France aura préparé les hors-d'œuvre.
2. Claude et Alain seront allés chercher les boissons.
3. Sylvie aura mis les couverts.
4. Jean-Paul aura choisi la musique.
5. Sophie et Odile auront invité tout le monde.
6. Hervé et Nathalie auront décoré la salle.
7. Marguerite aura acheté les gobelets.
8. Robert aura organisé les attractions.

F

1. Il m'offrira un coup de main quand j'aurai fini.
2. Elle sonnera à la porte quand nous nous serons couché(e)s.
3. Tu viendras quand tout le monde sera parti.
4. Ils trouveront la carte quand nous nous serons perdu(e)s.
5. Nous arriverons quand ils auront fermé le restaurant.
6. Il nous renseignera quand nous aurons trouvé la solution.
7. Elle apportera le pain quand nous aurons fini de manger.
8. Tu viendras nous prendre en voiture quand nous serons parti(e)s en autocar.

G

1. Tu recevras une bonne note parce que tu auras étudié sérieusement.
2. On donnera un prix à Marc parce qu'il aura rédigé la meilleure composition.
3. On récompensera les étudiants parce qu'ils se seront conduits comme il faut.
4. Les journaux loueront cet agent de police parce qu'il aura agi héroïquement.
5. Le petit Pierrot recevra une bonne correction parce qu'il n'aura pas rangé ses affaires.
6. Ses parents gronderont Michèle parce qu'elle aura séché ses cours.
7. Je répondrai à toutes les questions de l'examen parce que j'aurai compris la matière.
8. Tout le monde sera déçu parce que nos cousins ne seront pas arrivés.

H

1. Nous mangerons un dîner magnifique que nous aurons cuisiné.
2. J'écouterai le disque compact que j'aurai acheté.
3. Maman servira un dessert formidable avec la pâtisserie qu'elle aura achetée.
4. Ma sœur nous racontera l'histoire du roman qu'elle aura lu.
5. Mon père lira des articles dans la revue qu'il aura achetée.
6. Nous regarderons tous le film que nous aurons loué.
7. Mon père et moi, nous parlerons des articles qu'il aura lus.
8. Ma sœur chantera les nouvelles chansons qu'elle aura apprises à l'école.

I

1. Moi, je ne me serais pas couché(e) à 5 heures du matin.
2. Moi, je n'aurais pas pris rendez-vous avec le directeur.
3. Moi, je ne me serais pas mis(e) en route sous la pluie.
4. Moi, je n'aurais pas fait dix kilomètres à pied.
5. Moi, je n'aurais pas cueilli des fleurs dans le jardin public.
6. Moi, je n'aurais pas cru à l'histoire que Marc a racontée.

7. Moi, je n'aurais pas dépensé tout mon argent.
8. Moi, je n'aurais pas oublié la date de la réception.

J

1. Vraiment? Guillaume aurait conduit la voiture d'André.
2. Vraiment? Jacqueline et Martin seraient descendus.
3. Vraiment? Vincent et moi, nous aurions interrompu.
4. Vraiment? Moi, j'aurais répondu.
5. Vraiment? Albert aurait employé ce mot.
6. Vraiment? Simone et moi, nous aurions plongé.
7. Vraiment? Ségolène aurait dérangé Georges.
8. Vraiment? Solange et Marie se seraient disputées avec lui.

K

1. Mais si elle était allée en ville hier, moi aussi, je serais allé(e) en ville.
2. Mais si elle avait acheté des livres hier, moi aussi, j'aurais acheté des livres.
3. Mais si elle s'était promenée hier, moi aussi, je me serais promené(e).
4. Mais si elle avait envoyé ses paquets hier, moi aussi, j'aurais envoyé mes paquets.
5. Mais si elle avait pris son billet hier, moi aussi, j'aurais pris mon billet.
6. Mais si elle s'était préparée pour partir hier, moi aussi, je me serais préparé(e) pour partir.
7. Mais si elle avait écouté le cédé hier, moi aussi, j'aurais écouté le cédé.
8. Mais si elle avait travaillé hier, moi aussi, j'aurais travaillé.

L

1. Si Rachelle avait rédigé sa composition, elle se serait réunie avec ses amis.
2. Si Philippe avait relu ses leçons de chimie, il aurait pu jouer au football.
3. Si Louise et Danielle avaient préparé le compte rendu, elles seraient allées aux grands magasins.
4. Si Olivier et Jean-Luc étaient allés au laboratoire, ils auraient regardé la télé.
5. Si Françoise et Guy avaient étudié l'histoire du dix-septième siècle, ils seraient allés danser.

6. Si Mireille avait fait les problèmes de maths, elle serait sortie avec Charles.
7. Si Monique et Édouard avaient révisé leurs notes de littérature française, ils auraient dîné en ville.
8. Si Jean-François avait appris le poème par cœur, il aurait joué aux jeux vidéo.

M

1. Michèle aurait salué Yves si elle l'avait vu.
2. Sylvie aurait téléphoné à Roger si elle n'avait pas passé toute la journée à la bibliothèque.
3. Damien aurait dit à Judith qu'il y avait une réunion aujourd'hui s'il s'en était souvenu.
4. Ariane aurait suivi son régime si elle n'avait pas eu envie de manger du chocolat.
5. Nicolas aurait fait le ménage s'il avait eu le temps.
6. Patrick aurait pris sa bicyclette s'il ne s'était pas foulé la cheville.
7. Paul et Virginie seraient sortis s'ils n'avaient pas dû étudier.
8. Louis serait venu au bureau s'il n'était pas allé chez le médecin.

N

Answers will vary.

11 Passé Simple

A

1. je gagnai
2. tu commenças
3. elle choisit
4. elles t'attendirent
5. vous espérâtes
6. tu nageas
7. il m'encouragea
8. nous déménageâmes
9. je descendis
10. tu annonças
11. ils rangèrent
12. elles défendirent
13. vous obéîtes
14. nous entendîmes
15. je remplaçai
16. on rédigea
17. nous réfléchîmes
18. vous essayâtes
19. tu allas
20. nous partageâmes

B

1. La nuit tomba.
2. La ville devint silencieuse.
3. Les habitants rentrèrent chez eux.
4. On ferma les magasins.
5. J'entrai dans un bistrot.
6. Je m'assis à une petite table.
7. J'attendis Michèle.
8. Elle voulut me voir.

9. Elle me rejoignit à 7 heures.
10. Nous prîmes un café ensemble.
11. Nous sortîmes.
12. Nous nous promenâmes dans la ville endormie.
13. Michèle me dit:
14. «Je décidai de te quitter».
15. Elle rompit avec moi.
16. Je ne pus rien faire.
17. Je rentrai chez moi.
18. Je pleurai.

C

1. Marthe sortit de sa maison.
2. Elle marcha à travers champ.
3. Elle s'approcha du fleuve.
4. Elle y vit trois amis.
5. Ils la saluèrent.
6. Ils l'invitèrent à manger avec eux.
7. Elle accepta.
8. Elle s'assit avec eux.
9. Ils partagèrent leur déjeuner avec elle.
10. Soudain, le temps changea.
11. Il commença à pleuvoir.
12. Les quatre amis revinrent en ville.
13. Ils se mouillèrent un peu.
14. Ils cherchèrent un café.
15. Ils commandèrent un chocolat.
16. Ils burent leur chocolat ensemble.

12 Present Participles; Uses of the Infinitive

A

1. Tu auras une bonne note en faisant tes devoirs de maths tous les jours.
2. Tu arriveras à l'heure en quittant la maison à 7 heures et demie.
3. En apprenant toutes les dates par cœur, on évite les problèmes dans le cours d'histoire.
4. En écoutant des programmes en anglais à la radio, tu te prépareras pour l'examen oral.
5. On évite la fatigue en organisant son travail.
6. En regardant très peu la télé, on peut toujours finir son travail.

B

1. Les voyageurs partant pour le Nord sont priés de passer au quai numéro 3.
2. Nous annonçons un retard pour tous les avions provenant d'Afrique.

3. Le docteur Gobert verra les malades souffrant d'un problème gastrique.
4. Les étudiants passant leurs examens demain doivent arriver au lycée à 8 heures.
5. C'est un manuel d'anglais contenant tout le vocabulaire essentiel.
6. Voici une carte montrant le site des centrales nucléaires.

C

1. Les Maurois aiment faire un grand réveillon pour la Saint-Sylvestre.
2. Ils vont s'offrir des étrennes le jour de l'An.
3. Le 6 janvier ils espèrent inviter des amis pour manger la galette des Rois.
4. La grand-mère veut passer le dimanche de Pâques avec eux.
5. Le 8 mai ils comptent aller en Normandie pour commémorer la victoire des Alliés en 1945.
6. Leurs amis les Dufau doivent les inviter pour la Pentecôte.
7. Eux, ils pensent inviter les Dufau à Paris pour le 14 juillet.
8. Pour l'Assomption ils désirent être dans leur maison à la campagne.
9. Ils doivent aller fleurir les tombes de leurs parents décédés le 2 novembre.
10. Ils vont aller à la messe de minuit le 24 décembre.

D

1. Philippe voulait nager tous les jours.
2. Alice et Géraldine ont pu faire du tourisme.
3. Georges ne savait pas nager très bien.
4. Il n'osait pas s'éloigner de la plage.
5. Claudette et Brigitte préféraient jouer au tennis.
6. Louis aimait visiter les petits villages des alentours.
7. Solange n'a pas pu acheter des souvenirs.
8. Richard a dû écrire beaucoup de lettres.

E

1. à
2. à
3. X
4. X
5. à
6. à
7. à
8. X
9. à

F

1. Le professeur nous encourage à lire un livre par semaine.
2. J'aime mieux rédiger mes comptes rendus à l'ordinateur.
3. Jacques réussira à finir son compte rendu demain.
4. Son chef engage Philomène à faire de l'allemand.
5. L'administration de l'école vous autorise à chercher du travail.
6. Henri et Jules se résignent à recevoir une mauvaise note en maths.
7. Chantal continue à réviser ses notes d'histoire.
8. Odile passe son temps à recopier ses notes.

G

1. d'	7. de
2. à	8. de
3. X	9. à
4. X	10. à
5. d'	11. X
6. à	12. de

H

1. Loïc et Charles tiennent à voir un match de football.
2. Marie-Noëlle s'empresse de s'acheter des livres.
3. Richard descend tous les jours acheter des journaux.
4. Albert se flatte de connaître parfaitement toutes les lignes du métro.
5. Berthe et Christine entreprennent d'organiser un pique-nique au Bois de Boulogne.
6. Philippe compte visiter le marché aux timbres.
7. Chantal passe son temps à regarder les robes aux grands magasins.
8. Tous les étudiants brûlent de visiter le Louvre.
9. Martin essaie d'organiser une journée à la campagne.
10. Paulette et Mireille espèrent avoir le temps de voir Montmartre.

I

1. Je viens de parler avec Jean-Pierre.
2. Je lui ai expliqué qu'il risque de perdre l'année scolaire.
3. Je l'ai encouragé à commencer à étudier sérieusement.

4. Il doit s'empêcher de sortir tous les jours.
5. Il a promis de faire attention en classe.
6. Il s'est excusé d'avoir eu de mauvaises notes.
7. Il ne perdra plus de temps à regarder la télé.
8. Il s'est décidé à être un bon étudiant.
9. J'ai l'intention de parler avec Jean-Pierre la semaine prochaine.
10. Nous tâcherons de (tenterons de OR essaierons de OR chercherons à) parler toutes les semaines jusqu'à la fin de l'année scolaire.

J

1. Il faut l'encourager à apprendre les mots.
2. Il faut le commander de faire attention.
3. Il faut lui déconseiller de sortir tous les jours.
4. Il faut lui persuader de répondre.
5. Il faut leur dire de se taire.
6. Il faut leur conseiller de se concentrer sur leurs études.
7. Il faut l'aider à résoudre les problèmes.
8. Il faut les dissuader de le faire.

K

1. Le grand-père a convaincu son gendre Guillaume de ne pas quitter son travail.
2. Les enfants de Guillaume et Sylvie se sont empressés d'apporter des fleurs à la tante Émilie.
3. Le petit Bertrand a demandé à sa mère de lui acheter une bicyclette.
4. La grand-mère a pardonné à sa petite-fille Giselle d'avoir oublié son anniversaire.
5. Guillaume et Sylvie ont félicité leur fille Christine d'avoir eu 18 à l'examen de philo.
6. L'oncle François a enseigné à sa nièce à se servir de l'ordinateur.
7. Anne-Marie a interdit à sa fille Mireille de sortir avec Frédéric.
8. Nadine a prié ses parents de l'emmener au bord de la mer.
9. Sylvie a invité ses beaux-parents à dîner.
10. Guillaume a proposé à ses parents de passer leurs vacances avec sa famille.

L

Answers will vary.

M

1. à	6. pour
2. de	7. de
3. à	8. de
4. de	9. à
5. à	10. pour

N

1. Il faut le faire retapisser.
2. Il faut la faire réparer.
3. Il faut le faire nettoyer.
4. Il faut la faire remplacer.
5. Il faut le faire paver.
6. Il faut les faire plâtrer.
7. Il faut le faire débarrasser.

O

1. Mlle Arnaud lui fait réciter des poèmes.
2. Mlle Arnaud lui fait présenter son travail devant un petit groupe.
3. Mlle Arnaud leur fait écrire une composition.
4. Mlle Arnaud lui fait relire l'explication dans son livre.
5. Mlle Arnaud leur fait regarder un film.
6. Mlle Arnaud leur fait aider leurs camarades.
7. Mlle Arnaud lui fait observer une leçon de français.
8. Mlle Arnaud nous fait écouter la chanson que les élèves ont apprise.

P

1. Son petit ami l'a fait pleurer.
2. Le vent les a fait trembler.
3. Mon voisin les a fait pousser.
4. Leur institutrice les a fait lire.
5. Le clown les a fait rire.
6. Le mécanicien l'a fait démarrer.
7. Ses enfants l'ont fait sourire.
8. La chaleur l'a fait soupirer.
9. Le froid l'a fait grelotter.
10. La vendeuse l'a fait rager.

II   Nouns and Their Modifiers; Pronouns

---

13 Nouns: Gender, Number, and Articles; Uses of Articles

A

1. le cahier / les cahiers
2. la calculette / les calculettes
3. l'étudiant / les étudiants
4. la serviette / les serviettes
5. le papier / les papiers
6. le stylo / les stylos
7. la leçon / les leçons

8. le calendrier / les calendriers
9. la bibliothèque / les bibliothèques
10. le dictionnaire / les dictionnaires
11. l'histoire / les histoires
12. la cloche / les cloches
13. l'exposé / les exposés
14. la cantine / les cantines
15. le magnétoscope / les magnétoscopes

B

1. un pull / des pulls
2. une chemise / des chemises
3. un pantalon / des pantalons
4. une cravate / des cravates
5. un rayon / des rayons
6. un vendeur / des vendeurs
7. une vendeuse / des vendeuses
8. une robe / des robes
9. un maillot de bain / des maillots de bain
10. une veste / des vestes
11. un costume / des costumes
12. un chemisier / des chemisiers
13. un solde / des soldes
14. un blouson / des blousons
15. un anorak / des anoraks

C

1. Je veux deux chapeaux.
2. J'assiste à deux festivals.
3. J'ai deux neveux.
4. Mon nom s'écrit avec deux *l*.
5. Je cherche deux messieurs.
6. J'étudie deux vitraux.
7. Je prononce deux discours.
8. Je cherche deux métaux.
9. Je prends deux morceaux.
10. Je visite deux pays.
11. J'ai deux choix.
12. Je prépare deux repas.
13. Je lis deux journaux.
14. Je change deux pneus.
15. J'ai deux rivaux.

D

1. épicière
2. pharmacienne
3. une
4. une
5. le
6. la
7. une
8. le

E

1. Marguerite est musicienne aussi.
2. Émilie? Elle est épicière aussi.
3. Ma nièce est une élève de cette école primaire aussi.
4. Éloïse? C'est une Bretonne aussi.
5. Simone de Beauvoir est un écrivain célèbre aussi.
6. Hélène a été victime de son imprudence aussi.
7. Lise est une institutrice formidable aussi.
8. Mme Chauvin est la propriétaire de l'établissement aussi.
9. Sa femme est l'avocate de la défense aussi.
10. Chantal est un médecin respecté aussi.
11. Cette femme est aviatrice aussi.
12. Mireille est une nageuse formidable aussi.
13. Caroline est notre championne aussi.
14. Je connais Mme Mercier, la commerçante, aussi.

F

1. une	10. le
2. un	11. une
3. une	12. mon
4. Une	13. la
5. Le	14. la
6. Quelle	15. le
7. le	16. une
8. une	17. Un
9. la	18. le

G

1. C'est	6. C'est
2. Elle est	7. C'est
3. Ils sont	8. Elle est
4. Ce sont	9. Il est
5. C'est	10. Ils sont

H

1. —Vous avez du jambon?
   —Non, monsieur. Il n'y a plus de jambon.
2. —Vous avez de la salade niçoise?
   —Non, monsieur. Il n'y a plus de salade niçoise.
3. —Vous avez du fromage?
   —Non, monsieur. Il n'y a plus de fromage.
4. —Vous avez des carottes râpées?
   —Non, monsieur. Il n'y a plus de carottes râpées.
5. —Vous avez du saucisson?
   —Non, monsieur. Il n'y a plus de saucisson.
6. —Vous avez du saumon fumé?
   —Non, monsieur. Il n'y a plus de saumon fumé.
7. —Vous avez des quiches?
   —Non, monsieur. Il n'y a plus de quiches.
8. —Vous avez des sandwichs?
   —Non, monsieur. Il n'y a plus de sandwichs.

I

1. Suzanne a cherché de la farine, mais elle n'a pas cherché d'œufs.
2. Moi, j'ai rapporté du pain, mais je n'ai pas rapporté de beurre.
3. Laurent a trouvé des champignons, mais il n'a pas trouvé de salade.
4. Élisabeth a pris des pommes, mais elle n'a pas pris d'oranges.
5. Toi et moi, nous avons acheté des petits pois, mais nous n'avons pas acheté de haricots verts.
6. Vous avez rapporté du fromage, mais vous n'avez pas rapporté de yaourt.
7. Toi, tu as cherché de la viande, mais tu n'as pas cherché de poulet.
8. Les garçons ont pris du lait, mais ils n'ont pas pris de Coca.

J

1. —C'est du bœuf, ça?
   —Non, ce n'est pas du bœuf. C'est du porc.
2. —C'est du poulet, ça?
   —Non, ce n'est pas du poulet. C'est du dindon.
3. —Ce sont des haricots verts, ça?
   —Non, ce ne sont pas des haricots verts. Ce sont des endives.
4. —C'est du riz, ça?
   —Non, ce n'est pas du riz. C'est du couscous.
5. —C'est du vin, ça?
   —Non, ce n'est pas du vin. C'est du champagne.
6. —C'est du thon, ça?
   —Non, ce n'est pas du thon. C'est du saumon.
7. —C'est de la bouillabaisse, ça?
   —Non, ce n'est pas de la bouillabaisse. C'est de la soupe à l'oignon.
8. —C'est de la crème caramel, ça?
   —Non, ce n'est pas de la crème caramel. C'est de la glace.

K

1. du	8. de
2. de	9. de
3. des	10. de
4. de	11. des
5. des	12. de
6. des	13. d'
7. du	14. des

L

1. —Nous avons besoin de café.
   —J'ai acheté du café.
   —Combien de café as-tu acheté?
   —Assez de café. Et j'ai acheté trois cents grammes de thé aussi.
2. —La plupart des livres que j'ai lus étaient intéressants.
   —Trop des livres que j'ai lus étaient ennuyeux.

M

1. le / les	10. le
2. de	11. des / les
3. de / le	12. de (des)
4. une / un	13. de / du
5. de	14. L' / les
6. un	15. d' / de l'
7. la	16. L'
8. X	17. des
9. les / X	18. Les / les

N

1. Il a parlé avec intelligence.
2. Elle a agi avec courage.
3. Nous nous sommes mis en route sans peur.
4. Il a répondu avec haine.
5. Il a joué sans joie.
6. Il a rédigé sa composition sans soin.
7. Elle lui a parlé avec tendresse.
8. Il a écouté avec attention.

14 Stressed Pronouns; Subject-Verb Agreement

A

1. Nous, nous partons en Italie. Elles, elles partent en Grèce.
2. Moi, je prends le train. Eux, ils partent en voiture.
3. Toi, tu fais de l'alpinisme. Lui, il fait de la natation.
4. Mes cousins vont à la campagne. Nous, on va leur rendre visite.
5. Moi, j'ai trois semaines de vacances. Vous, vous avez un mois.
6. Moi, je préfère voyager seul. Toi, tu préfères voyager en groupe.
7. Nous, on compte faire du cyclisme. Lui, il veut faire du tourisme.
8. Elle, elle fait un stage linguistique en Allemagne. Toi, tu te détends.

B

1. Tu as tort! Je ne sors pas avec Émilie, moi.
2. Tu as tort! Je ne me lève pas à 8 heures, moi.
3. Tu as tort! Je ne dors pas en classe, moi.
4. Tu as tort! Je ne joue pas de la clarinette, moi.
5. Tu as tort! Je ne cherche pas de travail, moi.
6. Tu as tort! Je ne vais pas chez Olivier après les cours, moi.

C

1. Qu'est-ce que tu dis? Il n'a jamais dormi en classe, lui.
2. Qu'est-ce que tu dis? Il n'a jamais été en retard, lui.
3. Qu'est-ce que tu dis? Il n'a jamais interrompu le professeur, lui.
4. Qu'est-ce que tu dis? Il ne s'est jamais disputé avec Serge, lui.
5. Qu'est-ce que tu dis? Il ne s'est jamais moqué des cours, lui.
6. Qu'est-ce que tu dis? Il n'a jamais dérangé les autres étudiants, lui.

D

1. Non, il n'est pas pour toi.
2. Non, je ne compte pas dîner avec eux.
3. Non, je n'ai pas l'intention de passer chez elle.
4. Non, tu ne peux pas compter sur moi.
5. Non, elle n'a pas été invitée par lui.
6. Non, il n'est pas fâché contre nous.
7. Non, je ne m'assieds pas derrière elle.
8. Non, je n'ai pas d'attitude hostile envers eux.

E

1. —C'est toi dans la photo?
   —Non, ce n'est pas moi. C'est ma sœur Barbara.
2. —C'est moi le suivant?
   —Non, ce n'est pas toi (vous). C'est lui.
3. —C'est M. Charpentier assis sur le banc?
   —Non, ce n'est pas lui. C'est notre voisin M. Beauchamp.

4. —C'est Adèle Malmaison dans la boutique?
   —Non, ce n'est pas elle. C'est Mlle Lachaux.
5. —Ce sont nos amis là, à l'entrée du lycée?
   —Non, ce n'est pas (ce ne sont pas) eux.
   Ce sont d'autres étudiants.
6. —Ce sont Gisèle et Marie-Claire à l'arrêt
   d'autobus?
   —Non, ce n'est pas (ce ne sont pas) elles.
   Ce sont Christine et Yvette.

F

1. Oui. Je n'aime que toi.
2. Oui. On ne respecte que lui.
3. Oui. Ils n'admirent que lui.
4. Oui. Ils n'estiment qu'elle.
5. Oui. Nous n'aidons que vous.
6. Oui. Il n'apprécie qu'eux.
7. Oui. Ils n'encouragent qu'elles.
8. Oui. Il n'amène qu'elle.

G

1. je	9. toi
2. elle	10. elles
3. Elle	11. elles
4. moi	12. nous
5. lui	13. vous
6. eux	14. toi
7. elle	15. toi
8. moi	

H

1. sont	6. vivent
2. l'ont	7. sont
3. sont	8. viennent
4. fais	9. pouvez
5. t'attendent	10. viendra

I

1. Lui, il achète du pain. Nous, on achète du
   vin.
2. Nous avons vu Julien et Colette. Nous nous
   sommes approchés d'eux.
3. Gérard ne pense qu'à lui.
4. C'est vous qui enseignez l'histoire?
5. Nous sommes entrés après lui mais avant toi.
6. Beaucoup ont reçu nos invitations, mais
   seulement la moitié ont accepté.
7. Et je croyais que vous n'invitiez que moi!
8. Voilà Marc et Serge. L'un ou l'autre sait la
   réponse.

15 Possessive and Demonstrative Adjectives and Pronouns

A

1. Oui. Voilà sa voiture.
2. Oui. Voilà notre calculatrice.
3. Oui. Voilà leurs disques.
4. Oui. Voilà mes cartes.
5. Oui. Voilà tes lettres.
6. Oui. Voilà son chien.
7. Oui. Voilà leurs billets.
8. Oui. Voilà leur salle de réunion.
9. Oui. Voilà son sac à dos.
10. Oui. Voilà son ordinateur.

B

1. Non. Ce n'est pas leur moto.
2. Non. Ce ne sont pas ses voitures de sport.
3. Non. Ce n'est pas notre caravane.
4. Non. Ce n'est pas sa mobylette.
5. Non. Ce n'est pas son autobus.
6. Non. Ce n'est pas notre camion.
7. Non. Ce n'est pas mon bateau.
8. Non. Ce n'est pas sa bicyclette.

C

1. Sa mère à lui ou sa mère à elle?
2. Ses enfants à lui ou ses enfants à elle?
3. Leur voiture à eux ou leur voiture à elles?
4. Son cousin à lui ou son cousin à elle?
5. Son chien à elle ou mon chien à moi?
6. Son départ à lui ou son départ à elle?

D

1. Roger a donné son affiche.
2. Louise et Simone ont donné leur répondeur.
3. Charles a donné ses feutres.
4. Hélène a donné son imprimante.
5. Le professeur de biologie a donné son papier
   à lettres.
6. Albert et vous, vous avez donné votre
   calendrier.
7. Moi, j'ai donné mon annuaire.
8. Toi, tu as donné ton dictionnaire
   scientifique.

E

1. Moi, j'ai mon portable, mais Françoise
   a laissé le sien au bureau.
2. Nous, nous avons nos téléphones mobiles,
   mais nos collègues ont laissé les leurs au
   bureau.
3. Toi, tu as ta serviette, mais le directeur
   a laissé la sienne au bureau.

4. David a ses dossiers, mais Christine a laissé les siens au bureau.
5. Odile a ses disquettes, mais moi, j'ai laissé les miennes au bureau.
6. Vous, vous avez votre carte mémoire, mais nous, nous avons laissé la nôtre au bureau.
7. Mes amis ont leurs agendas, mais vous, vous avez laissé les vôtres au bureau.
8. La secrétaire a son carnet d'adresses, mais toi, tu as laissé le tien au bureau.

F
1. Les tiennes sont ici, les leurs sont en bas.
2. La nôtre (La mienne) est ici, la sienne est en bas.
3. Le vôtre est ici, le sien est en bas.
4. Les miennes sont ici, les siens sont en bas.
5. Les tiennes sont ici, les leurs sont en bas.
6. Le tien est ici, le sien est en bas.

G
1. Aux miens.
2. Dans le leur.
3. De la nôtre. (Des nôtres.)
4. À la sienne.
5. Des siennes.
6. Contre les siens.
7. Du mien.

H
1. Pierre et moi, nous employons des calculatrices. La sienne est vieille, la mienne est neuve.
2. Mon professeur d'anglais est sympathique, le tien est antipathique.
3. Le sac à dos de Christine est rouge, le mien est vert.
4. Mes amis sont plus calés en maths que les tiens.
5. Vos examens sont difficiles. Les nôtres sont plus difficiles.
6. Le compte rendu de Solange est longue. Le mien est plus long.
7. Ma journée est plus courte que la leur.
8. Les ordinateurs de l'école sont plus puissants que les siens.

J
1. Vous pouvez me dire le prix de cet ordinateur, s'il vous plaît?
2. Vous pouvez me dire le prix de cette unité de disque, s'il vous plaît?
3. Vous pouvez me dire le prix de ces disquettes, s'il vous plaît?

4. Vous pouvez me dire le prix de ce logiciel, s'il vous plaît?
5. Vous pouvez me dire le prix de ce lecteur de CD-ROM, s'il vous plaît?
6. Vous pouvez me dire le prix de ce disque dur, s'il vous plaît?
7. Vous pouvez me dire le prix de ce clavier, s'il vous plaît?
8. Vous pouvez me dire le prix de cette souris, s'il vous plaît?

K
1. Oui, mais ils préfèrent ces livres-là.
2. Oui, mais je préfère cet anorak-là.
3. Oui, mais elle préfère ce chapeau-là.
4. Oui, mais nous préférons ces bijoux-là.
5. Oui, mais ils préfèrent cet appartement-là.
6. Oui, mais je préfère ces quartiers-là.
7. Oui, mais je préfère cet immeuble-là.

L
1. Ce pantalon-ci ou ce pantalon-là?
2. Cet imperméable-ci ou cet imperméable-là?
3. Ces chaussettes-ci ou ces chaussettes-là?
4. Cette robe bleue-ci ou cette robe bleue-là?
5. Cet anorak-ci ou cet anorak-là?
6. Ce tee-shirt-ci ou ce tee-shirt-là?
7. Ces sandales-ci ou ces sandales-là?
8. Cette veste jaune-ci ou cette veste jaune-là?

M
1. Non, pas celle-là.
2. Non, pas celui-là.
3. Non, pas celui-là.
4. Non, pas ceux-là.
5. Non, pas celle-là.
6. Non, pas celle-là.
7. Non, pas celles-là.
8. Non, pas celui-là.

N
1. —Qui a oublié ce Walkman? Gisèle?
   —Non, je crois que c'est celui de Josette.
2. —Qui a oublié ce stylo? Colin?
   —Non, je crois que c'est celui de Luc.
3. —Qui a oublié ces chaussures? Fabien?
   —Non, je crois que ce sont celles de Martin.
4. —Qui a oublié ces gants? Julie?
   —Non, je crois que ce sont ceux d'Hélène.
5. —Qui a oublié ces cahiers? Eugénie et Colette?
   —Non, je crois que ce sont ceux d'Élisabeth et Monique.
6. —Qui a oublié cette calculatrice? Gérard?
   —Non, je crois que c'est celle de Paul.
7. —Qui a oublié ces lunettes? Loïc?
   —Non, je crois que ce sont celles de Thomas.

O

1. Pas tellement. Mais j'aime ceux que tu prépares.
2. Pas tellement. Mais j'aime celle que tu joues.
3. Pas tellement. Mais j'aime celle que tu conduis.
4. Pas tellement. Mais j'aime celle que tu sers.
5. Pas tellement. Mais j'aime celles que tu portes.
6. Pas tellement. Mais j'aime ceux que tu fais.
7. Pas tellement. Mais j'aime celles que tu achètes.

P

1. Cet exercice n'est pas bien fait. Ceci (Cela) est (C'est) inacceptable.
2. Ce livre est plus difficile que celui-là.
3. Ils arrivent toujours en retard. Je n'aime pas cela (ça).
4. Le port de Marseille et le port de Cherbourg sont importants. Celui-ci est moins grand que celui-là.
5. —À qui sont ces valises?
   —Celle-là est à moi.
6. Je n'ai pas dit cela (ça). Je ne pense pas comme cela (ça).

16 Interrogative Adjectives and Pronouns, and Other Question Words

A

1. Quel vélo?
2. Quels CD?
3. Avec quelle raquette?
4. Quelle voiture?
5. Quelle carte?
6. Sur quelle moto?
7. Quelle chambre?
8. Quelles jumelles?
9. De quelle caméra?
10. De quel appareil-photo?

B

1. Quels billets a-t-elle pris?
2. Dans quel magasin sont-ils entrés?
3. De quelle disquette a-t-elle besoin?
4. Avec quel professeur ont-ils parlé?
5. À quel examen difficile a-t-il réussi?
6. Dans quelle classe a-t-il reçu une mauvaise note?
7. Quels médicaments ont-ils achetés?
8. Quelles émissions ont-ils regardées à la télé?

C

1. a. Quelle
2. b. Quelle
3. a. Quel
4. a. Quelle
5. b. Quelle
6. a. Quelle
7. a. Quelle

D

1. Lequel? Celui-là?
2. Lesquelles? Celles-là?
3. Lequel? Celui-là?
4. Lesquelles? Celles-là?
5. Laquelle? Celle-là?
6. Lesquels? Ceux-là?
7. Lequel? Celui-là?

E

1. Lequel veux-tu (voulez-vous) exactement?
2. Lesquelles met-elle exactement?
3. Lesquels lavez-vous exactement?
4. Desquelles as-tu (avez-vous) besoin exactement?
5. Lesquels cherche-t-elle exactement?
6. Auxquels pensent-ils exactement?
7. Lequel prends-tu (prenez-vous) exactement?

F

1. Laquelle? Ah, non. Celle-là n'est pas la mienne.
2. Lesquels? Ah, non. Ceux-là ne sont pas les miens.
3. Lequel? Ah, non. Celui-là n'est pas le sien.
4. Lesquels? Ah, non. Ceux-là ne sont pas les nôtres.
5. Lesquelles? Ah, non. Celles-là ne sont pas les leurs.
6. Laquelle? Ah, non. Celle-là n'est pas la mienne.
7. Lesquelles? Ah, non. Celles-là ne sont pas les nôtres.
8. Lesquelles? Ah, non. Celles-là ne sont pas les miennes.
9. Lequel? Ah, non. Celui-là n'est pas le mien.
10. Laquelle? Ah, non. Celle-là n'est pas la sienne.

G

1. Qui	4. Qu'est-ce qui
2. Qu'est-ce que	5. qui
3. Qu'est-ce que	6. quoi

H

1. c
2. a
3. d
4. b
5. d
6. c
7. a
8. b

I

1. Qu'ont-ils préparé?
2. Qui Marie a-t-elle vu?
3. Quand vos amis ont-ils loué cet appartement?
4. Quel logiciel recommandes-tu?
5. Dans quel hôtel Céline va-t-elle rester?
6. Pourquoi cet enfant pleure-t-il?
7. Combien ont-elles payé?

J

1. Elle habite où?
2. Elle arrive quand?
3. Jacqueline voyage avec qui?
4. Elle va rester combien de temps avec vous?
5. Jacqueline s'intéresse à quoi?
6. Elle aime quoi? (Elle aime quelle cuisine?)
7. Elle aime faire quoi?
8. Jacqueline a besoin de quoi?

17 Adjectives, Comparatives, and Superlatives

A

1. Elle est fraîche aussi.
2. Elle est amère aussi.
3. Elle est très sotte aussi.
4. Elle est complète aussi.
5. Elle est ancienne aussi.
6. Elle est brune aussi.
7. Elle est merveilleuse aussi.
8. Elle est très discrète aussi.
9. Elle est rousse aussi.
10. Elle est sensationnelle aussi.
11. Elle est sportive aussi.
12. Elle est mignonne aussi.

B

1. l'administration actuelle
2. un récit drôle
3. une écharpe chic
4. un résultat logique
5. la langue grecque
6. l'opinion publique
7. une mère nerveuse
8. un paquet léger
9. un film favori
10. une viande exquise
11. une tranquillité trompeuse
12. une nourriture délicate

C

1. Je vais passer deux examens oraux.
2. J'ai vu deux films affreux.
3. Il y a deux gros immeubles dans cette rue.
4. J'ai deux examens finals aujourd'hui.
5. Il a deux cousins roux.
6. Il a écrit deux livres banals.
7. Il étudie deux cas spéciaux.
8. Ils ont fait deux voyages dangereux.
9. J'ai appris deux mots nouveaux.
10. Il y a deux œufs frais dans le frigo.
11. Nous allons visiter deux monuments nationaux.
12. J'ai acheté deux produits locaux.

D

1. Voici les parfums français.
2. Voici les légumes frais.
3. Voici les journaux espagnols.
4. Voici les fromages crémeux.
5. Voici les fromages gras.
6. Voici les pantalons gris.
7. Voici les foulards bleus.
8. Voici les romans québécois.

E

1. a. actuelles
   b. actuelle
   c. actuels
2. a. internationaux
   b. internationales
   c. internationale
3. a. grecque
   b. grecques
   c. grecs
4. a. classique
   b. classiques
   c. classiques
5. a. religieuse
   b. religieux
   c. religieuses
6. a. européenne
   b. européens
   c. européennes
7. a. concrets
   b. concrète
   c. concrètes
8. a. étrangères
   b. étrangère
   c. étrangers

9. a. fictifs
   b. fictive
   c. fictives
10. a. navale
    b. navals
    c. navales

F

1. mon ancien professeur
2. le mois dernier
3. une famille pauvre
4. la seule étudiante
5. une vraie amie
6. un appartement sale
7. une histoire vraie
8. ma propre bicyclette

G

1. une belle terrasse
2. de vieilles églises
3. un vieil objet
4. un nouvel ordinateur
5. une nouvelle industrie
6. de vieux instruments
7. de belles îles
8. un bel accent
9. de nouvelles usines
10. de beaux animaux
11. une vieille assiette
12. de nouveaux avions

H

1. Nous assistons aux conférences dans une grande salle ancienne.
2. Pour la classe d'anglais nous préparons de petits exposés intéressants.
3. Dans la classe de maths nous subissons de longues épreuves difficiles.
4. Derrière le lycée il y a un petit et joli jardin.
5. J'y vais souvent avec mon ami Philippe. C'est un beau et gentil garçon.
6. Nous parlons des nouveaux poèmes français qu'il faut préparer.
7. Il y a plusieurs professeurs excellents au lycée.
8. Ils font des cours passionnants et utiles.

I

Answers will vary.

J

1. Le stade est plus grand que la salle de concert.
2. Les cinémas sont plus nombreux que les théâtres.

3. La faculté de médecine est aussi importante que la faculté de droit.
4. Le jardin zoologique reçoit autant de visiteurs que la bibliothèque municipale.
5. Le musée scientifique est moins grand que le musée d'art.
6. Les restaurants ici sont aussi chers que les restaurants parisiens.
7. Les rues de la vieille ville sont plus étroites que les rues des quartiers modernes.
8. Le quartier des affaires est moins animé que le quartier des étudiants.
9. La piscine municipale est meilleure que la plage au bord du fleuve.
10. La maison de la culture offre autant d'activités que le centre communautaire.

K

1. Frédéric suit plus de cours que Marc.
2. Sylvie écrit plus de thèmes que Robert.
3. Monique subit moins d'examens que Marcelle.
4. Maurice résout autant de problèmes de maths que Philippe.
5. Marie-Laure étudie autant de langues étrangères qu'Alfred.
6. Claudine apprend moins de poèmes que Chantal.
7. Hervé analyse plus d'œuvres que Charles.
8. Julie fait autant d'expériences de chimie que Serge.

L

1. Ce n'est pas vrai. Il dort moins que moi.
2. Ce n'est pas vrai. Elle étudie plus qu'Éliane.
3. Ce n'est pas vrai. Il parle moins que le professeur de Justine.
4. Ce n'est pas vrai. Il mange autant que les autres chiens.
5. Ce n'est pas vrai. Je lis plus que toi.
6. Ce n'est pas vrai. Il comprend autant que les autres étudiants.

M

1. Monique répond moins intelligemment que Christine.
2. Édouard rédige plus soigneusement que Louis.
3. Nicole travaille aussi rapidement que Lucien.
4. Anne-Marie écoute aussi attentivement que Guillaume.
5. Gérard oublie moins souvent que Paulette.
6. François se comporte mieux que Georges.

N

Possible answers:

1. Nos manuels sont plus/moins/aussi intéressants que ceux de l'année dernière.
2. Mes camarades de classe sont plus/moins/aussi sympathiques que ceux de l'année dernière.
3. Les professeurs sont plus/moins/aussi exigeants que ceux de l'année dernière.
4. Les devoirs sont plus/moins/aussi faciles que ceux de l'année dernière.
5. La nourriture qu'on sert à la cantine est meilleure/pire/aussi bonne que celle de l'année dernière.
6. Mon horaire est plus/moins/aussi commode que celui de l'année dernière.
7. La classe de français est plus/moins/aussi passionnante que celle de l'année dernière.
8. Les bals qu'on organise sont plus/moins/aussi amusants que ceux de l'année dernière.

O

Answers will vary.

P

1. Le voyage en train était plus long que celui de l'année dernière.
2. L'hôtel en Auvergne était plus luxueux que celui où on est descendu en Bretagne.
3. Le paysage auvergnat était plus montagneux que celui de Bretagne.
4. Le poisson en Bretagne était meilleur que celui qu'on a servi en Auvergne.
5. Les grandes randonnées qu'on a faites en Auvergne étaient plus intéressantes que celles qu'on a faites en Bretagne.
6. Les restaurants en Auvergne étaient moins chers que ceux de Bretagne.
7. Les nuits en Auvergne étaient plus fraîches que celles de Bretagne.

Q

1. Marylène est la plus diligente.
2. Jacques et Pierre sont les moins obéissants.
3. Solange est la plus sympathique.
4. Irène et Marie sont les moins travailleuses.
5. Olivier est le plus intelligent.
6. Anne-Marie est la plus bavarde.
7. Jean-Paul est le plus charmant.
8. Colette et Brigitte sont les moins préparées.

R

1. Voilà la place la plus imposante de la ville.
2. Ici vous voyez la cathédrale la plus ancienne de la région.
3. En face il y a l'université la plus connue du pays.
4. C'est la rue la plus longue de la ville.
5. Dans cette rue il y a les plus beaux magasins de la région.
6. Voilà la charcuterie la plus appréciée du quartier.
7. Devant nous il y a l'hôtel le plus international du pays.
8. Dans cette rue se trouvent les cafés les plus fréquentés de la ville.
9. Ici vous voyez la plus vieille maison de la ville.
10. Voilà le plus grand stade de la région.

S

1. C'est le poème le plus connu de la littérature européenne.
2. C'est la pièce de théâtre la plus représentée de l'année.
3. C'est la comédie la plus applaudie du théâtre national.
4. C'est le roman le plus vendu de la littérature moderne.
5. C'est la tragédie la plus estimée de notre théâtre.
6. C'est le poète le plus merveilleux de son siècle.
7. C'est le romancier le plus lu du monde.
8. C'est le dramaturge le plus apprécié de notre époque.

T

1. C'est Lucie qui parle le plus poliment.
2. C'est Olivier qui travaille le moins efficacement.
3. C'est Albert qui étudie le moins sérieusement.
4. C'est Suzanne qui chante le mieux.
5. C'est Hélène qui arrive en retard le plus souvent.
6. C'est Roger qui répond le plus calmement.

U

Answers will vary.

18 Object Pronouns

A

1. Elle les regarde.
2. Elle l'essaie.
3. Elle ne la prend pas.
4. Elle l'achète.
5. Elle les cherche.
6. Elle le prend.
7. Elle les regarde.
8. Elle les essaie.
9. Elle ne les achète pas.
10. Elle le paie.

B

1. Vous pouvez le mettre dans le salon.
2. Vous pouvez le monter à la chambre de mon fils.
3. Vous pouvez la descendre au sous-sol.
4. Vous pouvez la laisser dans le salon.
5. Vous pouvez la placer dans la salle à manger.
6. Vous pouvez les mettre dans la penderie.
7. Vous pouvez le monter à la chambre de ma fille.
8. Vous pouvez les laisser dans le salon.

C

1. Non, je ne peux pas te déposer en ville.
2. Non, je ne peux pas t'emmener à la poste.
3. Non, je ne peux pas te raccompagner.
4. Non, je ne peux pas t'attendre.
5. Non, je ne peux pas vous rejoindre.
6. Non, je ne peux pas vous appeler.
7. Non, je ne peux pas vous inviter.
8. Non, je ne peux pas vous présenter.

D

1. Sabine va la balayer.
2. Marc et David vont les laver.
3. Élisabeth et Stéphanie vont les nettoyer.
4. Moi, je vais les faire.
5. Édouard va les sortir.
6. Barbara va le passer.
7. Charles et Michèle vont les épousseter.
8. Odile et François vont les faire.
9. Louis et Denise vont les récurer.
10. Toi, tu vas les laver!

E

1. Je l'ai déjà écrite.
2. Ils l'ont déjà rédigé.
3. Nous les avons déjà faits.
4. Elle les a déjà écrits.
5. Je l'ai déjà étudiée.
6. Elle l'a déjà faite.

7. Il les a déjà révisées.
8. Ils les ont déjà téléchargées.
9. Je les ai déjà écoutées.
10. Je les ai déjà relus.

F

1. Nous ne leur donnons pas d'argent.
2. Elle ne me montre pas ses logiciels.
3. Je ne leur ai pas écrit de courriel.
4. Ils ne leur vendent pas leur voiture.
5. Je ne vais pas lui offrir un collier.
6. Vous ne lui envoyez pas d'affiches.
7. Il ne m'apporte pas mes pantoufles.
8. Il ne lui a pas dit son numéro de téléphone.
9. Il ne leur a pas expliqué la méthode.
10. Je ne vais pas lui demander d'argent pour l'essence.

G

1. Il faut lui écrire une lettre.
2. Il faut leur payer la dernière cargaison de marchandises.
3. Il faut leur envoyer la note encore une fois.
4. Il faut lui prêter trois cent mille francs.
5. Il faut leur louer trois voitures et un camion.
6. Il faut lui emprunter un million de francs.
7. Il faut lui montrer les nouvelles annonces.
8. Il faut leur présenter la nouvelle gamme de produits.

H

1. Son père lui a prêté la voiture.
2. Nous lui avons offert une montre pour son anniversaire.
3. Moi, je lui ai expliqué les idées du livre.
4. Nous leur avons demandé de jouer avec nous.
5. Vous lui avez apporté des revues et des journaux.
6. Nous leur avons rendu les livres que nous leur avions empruntés.
7. Nous lui avons montré nos notes.
8. Moi, je leur ai envoyé une lettre.
9. Nous lui avons répondu.
10. Nous leur avons téléphoné.

I

1. Non, elle n'y travaille jamais.
2. Non, ils n'y étudient jamais.
3. Non, il n'y attend jamais.
4. Non, ils n'y passent jamais leurs vacances.
5. Non, je n'y achète (Non, nous n'y achetons) jamais à manger.
6. Non, ils n'y jouent jamais.

7. Non, ils ne s'y réunissent jamais.
8. Non, je n'y laisse jamais mes livres.
9. Non, je n'y mange jamais.
10. Non, ils n'y viennent jamais.

J

1. Il faut y penser.
2. Il faut y réfléchir.
3. Il faut y prendre garde.
4. Il faut y renoncer.
5. Il faut s'y intéresser.
6. Il faut y rêver.
7. Il faut y croire.
8. Il faut y aller.

K

1. Oui, elle s'en vante. (Non, elle ne s'en vante pas.)
2. Oui, ils en regorgent. (Non, ils n'en regorgent pas.)
3. Oui, elles en sont pleines. (Non, elles n'en sont pas pleines.)
4. Oui, il faut s'en soucier. (Non, il ne faut pas s'en soucier.)
5. Oui, je m'en méfie. (Non, je ne m'en méfie pas.)
6. Oui, ils en sont bordés. (Non, ils n'en sont pas bordés.)
7. Oui, elles en sont encombrées. (Non, elles n'en sont pas encombrées.)
8. Oui, elle en manque. (Non, elle n'en manque pas.)

L

1. Non, il y en a trente-deux.
2. Non, il en gagne deux mille cent.
3. Non, j'en ai deux cent cinquante.
4. Non, nous en avons parcouru trois cents.
5. Non, j'en ai eu quatre-vingt-dix.
6. Non, elle en a cinq.
7. Non, nous allons en acheter quinze.
8. Non, j'en veux deux douzaines.

M

1. Elles en ont déjà suivi.
2. Il s'en est déjà plaint.
3. Il en a déjà été accablé.
4. Il s'en est déjà chargé.
5. Elle en a déjà joué.
6. Il s'en est déjà mêlé.
7. Il en a déjà fait.
8. Elle en a déjà demandé.
9. Il en est déjà revenu.
10. Il en a déjà donné.

N

1. Nous devons lui en écrire.
2. Je vais les lui prêter.
3. Nous devons le lui rendre.
4. Tu peux l'y retrouver.
5. J'ai l'intention de les leur montrer.
6. Il faut leur en donner.
7. Je vais te les (vous les) expliquer.
8. Marguerite peut vous en rapporter.
9. Vous pouvez les y amener.
10. Nous devons nous y habituer.

O

1. Mais si! Il leur en a déjà servi.
2. Mais si! Je lui en ai déjà donné.
3. Mais si! Ils s'y sont déjà opposés.
4. Mais si! Ils s'en sont déjà servis.
5. Mais si! Nous nous en sommes déjà rendu compte.
6. Mais si! Il nous les a déjà rendues.
7. Mais si! Elle leur en a déjà lu.
8. Mais si! Ils le leur ont déjà enseigné.
9. Mais si! Il leur en a déjà proposé.
10. Mais si! Je t'en ai déjà envoyé.

P

1. Si on les leur prêtait?
2. Si on l'y retrouvait?
3. Si on les y amenait?
4. Si on lui en apportait une demi-douzaine?
5. Si on allait l'y attendre?
6. Si on s'en éloignait?
7. Si on s'en servait pour la rédiger?
8. Si on le leur donnait?
9. Si on les lui demandait?
10. Si on le leur vendait?

Q

1. Oui, je me fie à eux.
2. Oui, elle s'y intéresse.
3. Oui, il s'intéresse à elle.
4. Oui, il en a honte.
5. Oui, il a honte de lui.
6. Oui, je m'en souviens.
7. Oui, je me souviens d'eux.
8. Oui, il en doute.
9. Oui, il se doute de lui.
10. Oui, j'en ai peur. (Oui, nous en avons peur.)

R

1. Va t'en.
2. Dépose-moi là(-bas).
3. Donne-m'en.
4. Opposez-vous-y.
5. Éloigne-toi d'eux.
6. Habille-toi là(-bas).
7. Arrêtez-vous-y.
8. Charge-t'en.
9. Rendez-la-moi.

S

1. Je lui ai demandé son livre de littérature, mais il ne me l'a pas donné.
2. Il n'a plus sa voiture parce que quelqu'un la lui a volée.
3. Ces gens s'intéressent à votre maison. Vendez-la-leur.
4. Nous avons posé des questions sur la leçon au professeur, mais il n'y a pas répondu.
5. J'ai cherché des journaux français et j'en ai trouvé deux. Je te les montrerai.
6. Elle est au troisième étage. Montes-y et tu la verras.
7. Les enfants jouaient sur le toit, mais ils en sont descendus.
8. Tu as fait de la soupe. Apporte-m'en et je l'essaierai.

III Other Elements of the Sentence

19 Numbers; Time; Dates

A

1. Non. Nous avons besoin de soixante et onze livres.
2. Non. Ça coûte soixante-dix-neuf dollars.
3. Non. Elle est à cinquante-huit kilomètres d'ici.
4. Non. Il a soixante-six ans.
5. Non. Ils ont passé quatre-vingt-trois jours en Suisse.
6. Non. J'ai reçu un chèque pour quatre-vingt-dix francs.
7. Non. Tu dois téléphoner à quatre-vingt-onze personnes.
8. Non. Ils arrivent le vingt-six avril.

B

1. Non. Son numéro de téléphone est le zéro-trois, quatre-vingt-sept, trente-quatre, quarante-quatre, cinquante-sept.
2. Non. Il a payé quatre-vingt-dix-neuf francs.
3. Non. Elle a soixante-seize ans.
4. Non. Ils ont invité quatre-vingt-deux personnes.
5. Non. Il y a quatre-vingt-quinze appartements.
6. Non. Nous avons fait soixante-quatorze kilomètres.
7. Non. La charcuterie a coûté quatre-vingts francs.
8. Non. Des représentants de quatre-vingt-dix-huit pays sont venus au congrès international.

C

1. L'Espagne a quarante-six millions trente mille habitants.
2. Le Danemark a cinq millions cinq cent mille habitants.
3. Le Japon a cent vingt-sept millions trois cent mille habitants.
4. La Chine a un milliard trois cent cinquante millions d'habitants.
5. L'Argentine a quarante millions cent mille habitants.
6. La Suisse a sept millions huit cent mille habitants.
7. Le Nigeria a cent cinquante-quatre millions huit cent mille habitants.
8. Le Viêt-nam a quatre-vingt-cinq millions huit cent mille habitants.

D

1. L'agglomération urbaine de Paris a dix millions cent quarante-deux mille neuf cent quatre-vingt-trois habitants dont deux millions deux cent un mille cinq cent soixante-dix-huit habitent dans la ville même.
2. L'agglomération urbaine de Marseille a un million quatre cent dix-huit mille quatre cent quatre-vingt-un habitants dont huit cent quarante-sept mille quatre-vingt-quatre habitent dans la ville même.
3. L'agglomération urbaine de Lyon a un million quatre cent dix-sept mille quatre cent soixante-trois habitants dont quatre cent quatre-vingts mille sept cent soixante-dix-huit habitent dans la ville même.

4. L'agglomération urbaine de Lille a un million seize mille deux cent cinq habitants dont deux cent trente-deux mille quatre cent trente-deux habitent dans la ville même.

5. L'agglomération urbaine de Nice a neuf cent quarante mille dix-huit habitants dont trois cent cinquante mille sept cent trente-cinq habitent dans la ville même.

6. L'agglomération urbaine de Toulouse a huit cent cinquante mille huit cent soixante-seize habitants dont quatre cent quarante-quatre mille trois cent quatre-vingt-douze habitent dans la ville même.

7. L'agglomération urbaine de Bordeaux a huit cent mille cent dix-sept habitants dont deux cent trente-cinq mille huit cent soixante-dix-huit habitent dans la ville même.

8. L'agglomération urbaine de Nantes a cinq cent soixante-huit mille sept cent quarante-trois habitants dont deux cent quatre-vingt-dix mille huit cent soixante et onze habitent dans la ville même.

9. L'agglomération urbaine de Strasbourg a quatre cent quarante mille deux cent soixante-quatre habitants dont deux cent soixante-seize mille huit cent soixante-sept habitent dans la ville même.

10. L'agglomération urbaine de Montpellier a trois cent dix-huit mille deux cent vingt-trois habitants dont deux cent cinquante-quatre mille neuf cent soixante-quatorze habitent dans la ville même.

E

Answers will vary.

F

1. Je travaille au soixante-treizième étage.
2. Gilles travaille au vingt et unième étage.
3. Dorothée travaille au quatre-vingt-quinzième étage.
4. Richard et Maurice travaillent au trente-neuvième étage.
5. Paulette travaille au dix-huitième étage.
6. Suzanne et Émilie travaillent au quatre-vingt-quatrième étage.
7. Marc travaille au quarante-cinquième étage.
8. Josette travaille au soixante-dix-neuvième étage.

G

1. le quarante-cinquième jour
2. le tiers des enfants
3. la cinquante-neuvième leçon
4. la centième lettre
5. les trois huitièmes des étudiants
6. une trentaine de livres
7. le trois millième numéro
8. Louis neuf

H

1. Il est sept heures. Mme Raynaud met les dernières choses dans les valises.
2. Il est sept heures et demie. Les Raynaud prennent le petit déjeuner à l'hôtel.
3. Il est huit heures vingt. Le chasseur descend leurs bagages.
4. Il est huit heures trente-cinq. (Il est neuf heures moins vingt-cinq.) M. Raynaud appelle un taxi.
5. Il est neuf heures cinq. Les Raynaud arrivent à la gare.
6. Il est neuf heures et quart. Le petit Charles tombe et se fait mal au genou.
7. Il est neuf heures et demie. Le pharmacien de la gare met un pansement sur le genou de Charles.
8. Il est dix heures moins le quart. Les Raynaud prennent leurs places dans le train pour Paris.
9. Il est dix heures moins cinq. Le train part.
10. Il est trois heures vingt. Ils arrivent à Paris.

I

1. Je suis arrivé à la boutique à six heures et quart.
2. La livraison du lait et des œufs est venue à six heures trente-cinq.
3. Mes commis sont arrivés à sept heures moins dix.
4. Nous avons ouvert l'épicerie à sept heures pile.
5. La première cliente a franchi le seuil à sept heures dix.
6. Ma sœur est passée me voir à onze heures moins le quart.
7. Nous avons fermé pour le déjeuner à deux heures moins vingt.
8. J'ai rouvert ma boutique à trois heures et demie.

J

1. Il y a un train à seize heures cinquante et un deuxième train à dix-neuf heures dix.
2. Il y a un train pour La Plaine à quatorze heures six.
3. Le train pour Zurich part à cinq heures cinquante-huit et à dix-neuf heures vingt-cinq.
4. Il y a un train à quinze heures trente-cinq pour Milan et un train à vingt heures vingt-cinq pour Naples.
5. On peut prendre le train pour Bern à vingt et une heures cinquante-huit.
6. Il y a un train pour Lyon à dix heures vingt-deux et un train pour Nice à vingt-trois heures douze.
7. Il faut prendre le train à neuf heures cinq.
8. Il y a un train pour Dortmund à treize heures huit et un train pour Barcelone à vingt-deux heures cinquante.
9. Je prendrai le train de dix-neuf heures vingt-cinq.
10. Il y a un train pour Lausanne à dix-sept heures vingt-deux.

K

1. le deux janvier
2. le vingt-quatre janvier
3. le quatorze février
4. le dix mars
5. le premier avril
6. le vingt-huit mai
7. le vingt-quatre juin
8. le quatre juillet
9. le seize juillet
10. le trente août
11. le six septembre
12. le vingt-cinq novembre

L

1. le premier juillet neuf cent quatre-vingt-sept
2. le quinze août mil quatre-vingt-seize
3. le vingt-sept juillet douze cent quatorze
4. le trente mai quatorze cent trente et un
5. le quinze avril quinze cent quatre-vingt-dix-huit
6. le sept juin seize cent cinquante-quatre
7. le quatorze juillet dix-sept cent quatre-vingt-neuf
8. le dix-huit mai dix-huit cent quatre
9. le quatre septembre dix-huit cent soixante-dix

M

1. dix-neuf cent quatorze
2. dix-neuf cent dix-huit
3. dix-neuf cent vingt-neuf
4. dix-neuf cent trente-neuf
5. dix-neuf cent quarante
6. dix-neuf cent quarante-cinq
7. dix-neuf cent cinquante-huit
8. dix-neuf cent soixante-deux

N

Answers will vary.

O

1. —Quelle est la date aujourd'hui?
   (—Le combien sommes-nous?)
   —C'est (Nous sommes) le vingt et un mars.
2. Il viendra nous voir la semaine des quatre jeudis.
3. Je ne suis qu'un peintre du dimanche.
4. —Quel jour sommes-nous?
   (—C'est quel jour aujourd'hui?)
   —Nous sommes (C'est) samedi.
5. Vous êtes tous endimanchés.
6. Je vais en Italie au printemps.
7. —Quelle heure est-il?
   —Il est huit heures pile.
   —Bon. Je suis en avance.
8. —Est-ce que Jean s'est déjà levé?
   —Non, il n'est pas matinal, tu sais.
   —Je sais qu'il aime faire la grasse matinée.

20 Adverbs

A

1. affreusement
2. intelligemment
3. correctement
4. possiblement
5. gentiment
6. tristement
7. massivement
8. gaiment
9. confusément
10. fréquemment
11. moralement
12. pratiquement
13. généreusement
14. actuellement
15. évidemment
16. légèrement
17. longuement
18. précisément
19. exactement
20. complètement

B

1. Oui, il lui parle nerveusement.
2. Oui, elle lui parle confusément.
3. Oui, il lui parle honnêtement.
4. Oui, elles lui parlent tristement.
5. Oui, ils lui parlent furieusement.

6. Oui, elle lui parle patiemment.
7. Oui, ils lui parlent poliment.
8. Oui, elle lui parle discrètement.
9. Oui, ils lui parlent intensément.
10. Oui, il lui parle gentiment.

C

1. Oui, elle travaille diligemment.
2. Oui, il réagit violemment.
3. Oui, elle dessine bien.
4. Oui, elle sort fréquemment.
5. Oui, ils prononcent mal.
6. Oui, il l'aime aveuglément.
7. Oui, elle punit uniformément.
8. Oui, il réfléchit profondément.

D

1. Tu prononces mal le vocabulaire.
2. Elle nettoie soigneusement la cuisine.
3. Nous trouvons ce projet complètement ridicule.
4. Les membres de cette famille sont étroitement unis.
5. Il marche sans empressement.
6. Les enfants se sont conduits d'une façon déplaisante.
7. Marcelle travaille dur à la bibliothèque.
8. C'est une idée largement acceptée.
9. Ils ont vite compris le texte.
10. Elle m'a répondu brusquement.

E

1. insultingly
2. doubtlessly
3. kindly
4. indignantly
5. drily
6. extravagantly
7. decisively
8. intelligently

F

1. sans effort
2. avec goût
3. sans imagination
4. avec indifférence
5. avec colère
6. avec tolérance
7. sans cérémonie
8. sans tact

G

1. f
2. a
3. d
4. e
5. c
6. b

H

Answers will vary.

I

1. e
2. d
3. g
4. a
5. b
6. c
7. f

J

Answers will vary.

1. C'est une jolie maison. Il y a des arbres autour.
2. Il y a un jardin derrière.
3. Je regarde le salon en bas.
4. Je voudrais voir les chambres en haut.
5. Je cherche les propriétaires partout.
6. Je ne les vois nulle part.
7. Travaillent-ils dehors?
8. Je les entends quelque part.
9. Il y a deux voix tout près.
10. Les voilà devant.

K

1. —Hier, j'ai cherché ma montre partout.
   —Je l'ai vue quelque part. Est-ce que tu l'as cherchée en haut?
2. —Il pleut ici toutes les semaines.
   —Je sais. Je voudrais vivre ailleurs.
3. —Mercredi je ne suis allé nulle part.
   —Moi non plus. Je sors rarement en semaine.
4. —Auparavant je faisais le marché tous les jours.
   —Actuellement tu fais le marché une fois par semaine, n'est-ce pas?
5. —J'irais la voir n'importe quand, n'importe où.
   —Tu ne devras pas aller loin. La voilà, là-bas.

L

1. en
2. sur
3. en
4. à
5. par
6. en
7. Par
8. à
9. d'
10. à
11. par
12. en
13. en
14. à

M

1. J'ai fait un effort pour organiser la classe dès le début.
2. J'ai dit aux étudiants qu'il est défendu de venir en classe sans chaussures.

3. Je leur ai dit que je ne veux pas qu'ils laissent la salle de classe en désordre (en pagaille).

4. Ils ne doivent laisser ni leurs livres ni leurs papiers par terre.

5. Jean-Claude Mercier vient au cours un jour sur deux.

6. Noëlle Chenu se promène sans but dans les couloirs.

7. Elle travaille un peu par intervalles.

8. Elle prépare ses devoirs à la hâte.

9. Lise Monnet est sans doute la meilleure étudiante de la classe.

10. Elle travaille à merveille.

11. D'habitude (D'ordinaire), les autres étudiants l'admirent.

12. À partir de demain, nous avons une semaine de congé.

13. Je vais faire un effort pour améliorer cette classe dès notre retour.

14. Nous allons faire des excursions de temps en temps.

15. Nous irons à Versailles en groupe.

16. Les vieilles méthodes ne sont pas toujours bonnes à l'époque où nous sommes.

17. Je jugerai cette expérience sur quatre mois.

21 Negatives and Indefinites

A

1. Ne dis pas d'idioties! Personne ne te donnera un million de francs.

2. Ne dis pas d'idioties! Aucune fille ne te croit le plus beau garçon du lycée.

3. Ne dis pas d'idioties! Tu n'as jamais vingt à l'examen de philo.

4. Ne dis pas d'idioties! La femme du Président de la République ne t'a rien envoyé.

5. Ne dis pas d'idioties! Ton père ne va t'offrir ni une Ferrari ni une Jaguar.

6. Ne dis pas d'idioties! Il ne te reste plus rien de l'argent que tu as reçu pour ton anniversaire.

7. Ne dis pas d'idioties! Tu ne connais personne à Istamboul.

8. Ne dis pas d'idioties! Tu ne connais personne à Singapour non plus.

9. Ne dis pas d'idioties! Tu n'iras nulle part avec Solange.

10. Ne dis pas d'idioties! On ne t'offrira rien d'autre.

B

1. Personne n'apportera rien à manger.

2. Nous ne boirons rien.

3. Nous n'écouterons ni des cassettes ni des disques compacts.

4. Jeanine n'a pas encore acheté de jus de fruits.

5. Olivier n'a aucune nouvelle cassette.

6. Odile n'amène jamais personne d'intéressant.

7. Ces soirées ne sont jamais amusantes.

8. Après la soirée, nous n'irons nous promener nulle part.

C

1. —N'avez-vous plus de paquets?
   —Non. Je n'ai plus rien.

2. —Ce pâtissier fait les gâteaux mieux que personne.
   —Oui. C'est pour ça qu'il a plus de clients que jamais.

3. —Il n'apporte jamais rien quand on l'invite à dîner.
   —Ne l'invitez jamais plus.

4. —Est-ce que tu as déjà parlé avec Alfred?
   —Non. Il ne comprend ni l'anglais ni le français. Je préfère ne pas lui parler.

D

Answers will vary.

E

Answers will vary.

F

Answers will vary.

G

1. N'importe quoi.
2. N'importe où.
3. N'importe lequel.
4. N'importe quand.
5. À n'importe lequel.
6. N'importe combien.
7. N'importe comment.
8. À n'importe qui.

H

1. Marc a donné le message à je ne sais qui.

2. Elle va parler avec je ne sais quel professeur.

3. Elles se sont mises en colère je ne sais pourquoi.

4. Le malade avait pris je ne sais combien de pilules.

5. Il a réussi je ne sais comment aux examens.

6. Nos cousins arriveront je ne sais quand.

I

1. a. Tu peux trouver ce pain dans n'importe quelle boulangerie.
   b. Il n'y a pas de boulangerie par ici.
   c. Il travaille dans je ne sais quelle boulangerie.
   d. Il y a quelques boulangeries dans ce quartier. Certaines sont très bonnes. (Il y en a qui sont très bonnes.)
2. a. Ils achètent quelque chose.
   b. Achètent-ils quelque chose?
   c. Ils n'achètent rien.
   d. Ils achètent je ne sais quoi.
   e. Ils n'achètent pas n'importe quoi (quoi que ce soit).
3. a. Nous adorons ces chansons et nous en apprenons quelques-unes.
   b. Nous apprenons quelques chansons.
   c. Nous pouvons apprendre n'importe quelles chansons.
   d. Nous pouvons apprendre n'importe laquelle.
   e. Nous n'avons appris aucune chanson.
4. a. Nous pouvons partir n'importe quand.
   b. Ils vont partir je ne sais quand.
5. a. N'importe qui peut faire ça.
   b. Personne ne peut faire ça.
   c. Certains peuvent faire ça, d'autres ne peuvent pas. (Il y en a qui peuvent faire ça, il y a d'autres qui ne peuvent pas.)

J

1. de
2. d'autre
3. Chaque
4. ailleurs
5. toutes

K

1. Tout le monde est content maintenant. (Tous sont contents maintenant.)
2. Il fait un voyage d'affaires toutes les trois semaines.
3. Donne-nous quelque chose de bon à manger, maman!
4. Tu devrais contacter quelqu'un d'autre.
5. J'ai trois petites cousines et je veux acheter une poupée pour chacune.
6. Tout café sert des croissants.
7. Il a quelque chose d'effrayant.

L

1. b	6. a
2. a	7. a
3. b	8. a
4. a	9. b
5. b	10. b

M

1. b	5. b
2. a	6. a
3. a	7. b
4. b	8. b

22 Prepositions; Prepositions with Geographical Names

A

1. à la une: on the front page; à la page: up-to-date, in the know
2. à plusieurs reprises: several times; à la fois: at the same time
3. à l'étroit: crowded, short of space; à la hauteur: up to a task, capable of doing
4. une bouteille à lait: a milk bottle; une bouteille de lait: a bottle of milk
5. au suivant: Who's next?; à suivre: to be continued

B

1. antonymes
2. antonymes
3. synonymes
4. antonymes
5. synonymes
6. antonymes
7. synonymes

C

1. la glace au chocolat
2. l'homme au costume bleu
3. à notre grande tristesse
4. vendre à la livre
5. reconnaître quelqu'un à la voix
6. à titre confidentiel
7. à ses heures (libres)
8. lire à haute voix
9. à deux cents mètres du cinéma
10. la fille aux cheveux blonds
11. à tour de rôle
12. tout au plus

D

1. a. à la une
   b. à main armée
2. a. à la folie
   b. à titre de père
3. a. à bon compte
   b. à prix d'or
4. a. à la perfection
   b. à moitié

E

1. de	6. À
2. de	7. de
3. à	8. du
4. à	9. de / de
5. de	

F

1. de suite: in a row;
   à suivre: to be continued
2. de hauteur: in height;
   à la hauteur: up to the task
3. à côté: next door, close by;
   de côté: aside
4. Il est au Japon.: He's in Japan.;
   Il est du Japon.: He's from Japan.
5. une corbeille à papier: a wastepaper basket;
   une corbeille de papier: a basket (full) of paper
6. travailler de jour: to work days;
   travailler à la journée: to work by the day (be paid by the day)

G

1. d'une tête
2. drôle d'idée
3. changer d'avis
4. faculté de médecine
5. de bonne matin
6. à fond
7. à deux pas
8. de
9. de
10. de toute sa vie

H

1. a	6. a
2. b	7. b
3. a	8. b
4. a	9. b
5. b	10. a

I

1. sans	6. Avec
2. avec	7. avec
3. sans	8. sans
4. Sans	9. avec
5. Sans	10. sans

J

1. sans doute
2. sans ça
3. se lever avec le jour
4. sans cœur
5. les sans-emploi
6. avec amour
7. avec gentillesse
8. sans le sou
9. Et avec ça (cela)?
10. sans hésiter, sans hésitation

K

1. dans	11. en
2. dans	12. en
3. en	13. dans
4. en	14. en
5. en	15. en
6. en	16. en
7. dans	17. dans
8. en	18. en
9. en	19. Dans
10. dans	20. dans

L

1. dans l'escalier
2. être en nage
3. son père en plus grand
4. dans les coulisses
5. en haut
6. en pleine nuit
7. dans le sens de la longueur
8. être dans le pétrin
9. être dans les affaires
10. être en pyjama
11. en guerre
12. C'est en quoi?

M

1. J'en ai par-dessus la tête.
2. Jacques et Marie marchent bras dessus, bras dessous.
3. Ces étudiants sont en dessous de la moyenne.
4. Le détective est sur la bonne piste.
5. Nous avons acheté des pommes sur le marché.

6. J'aime me promener sous la pluie.
7. Je suis libre un samedi sur deux.
8. Il travaille sous une identité d'emprunt.
9. Elle pense que le travail est au-dessous d'elle.
10. Les enfants au-dessous de dix ans ne paient pas.
11. C'est au-dessus de mes forces.
12. Il a écrit un article sur la Tunisie.

N

1. Pour	8. Par
2. pour	9. Entre
3. d'entre	10. par
4. par	11. entre
5. pour	12. par
6. pour	13. pour
7. pour	14. par

O

1. We'll see each other around six o'clock.
2. According to the doctor, he is not out of danger.
3. You live better outside the city.
4. He was very generous to his children.
5. She looks out the window.
6. The teacher spoke about the test.
7. I have to go see my lawyer (at his office).
8. I'll give you these stamps for that coin.

P

1. selon les journaux
2. pendant la classe
3. malgré la difficulté
4. près de la gare
5. quant à moi
6. trois voix contre deux
7. environ dix étudiants
8. hors jeu
9. à travers champs
10. chez les Français
11. avant de descendre
12. après être descendu(e)(s)

Q

1. Monique travaille aux Canada, à Québec.
2. Olivier travaille aux États-Unis, à La Nouvelle-Orléans.
3. Mariek travaille au Japon, à Tokyo.
4. Fernand travaille au Brésil, à Sao Paolo.
5. Gérard travaille au Mexique, à Mexico.
6. Stella travaille à Haïti, à Port-au-Prince.
7. Luc travaille au Sénégal, à Dakar.
8. Brigitte travaille aux Pays-Bas, à Amsterdam.
9. Sylvie travaille en Égypte, au Caire.
10. Béatrice travaille au Portugal, à Lisbonne.
11. Jan travaille au Viêt-nam, à Saïgon.
12. Raymond travaille en Israël, à Jérusalem.

R

1. Fatima est d'Irak.
2. Lise est de Bruxelles.
3. Martin et Santos sont du Chili.
4. Sven est du Danemark.
5. Rosa et Laura sont de Naples.
6. Mei-Li est de Chine.
7. Amalia est de Mexico.
8. Fred et Jane sont de Californie.
9. Kimberly est du Vermont.
10. Odile est du Luxembourg.
11. Corazon est des Philippines.
12. Mies est des Pays-Bas.
13. Hanako et Hiro sont du Japon.
14. Bill est des États-Unis.
15. Olivier est du Havre.

IV Verbs in Two-Clause Sentences

23 Relative Clauses

A

1. qui	9. que
2. que	10. qui
3. qui	11. que
4. que	12. qui
5. qui	13. qu'
6. qui	14. qui
7. que	15. que
8. qui	16. qu'

B

1. Le médecin qui a son cabinet dans ce bâtiment.
2. Les comprimés que mon médecin m'a ordonnés.
3. Le régime que j'ai trouvé au centre diététique.
4. Le sirop que j'ai laissé sur la table.
5. La piqûre que l'infirmière m'a faite hier.
6. Les pilules que j'ai prises hier.
7. La crème que le pharmacien m'a conseillée.
8. Les vitamines qui sont bonnes pour le cœur.

C

1. a. Le professeur que tous les étudiants adorent.
   b. Le professeur qui enseigne le français et l'espagnol.
   c. Le professeur qui vient de se marier.
   d. Le professeur que mes parents connaissent (que connaissent mes parents).
2. a. La maison que Jeanne et Richard ont achetée.
   b. La maison qui a un jardin et une piscine.
   c. La maison qu'on a construite en 1975.
   d. La maison qui est en briques.
3. a. Les cadeaux que mon frère et moi, nous avons reçus il y a une semaine.
   b. Les cadeaux que mon oncle et ma tante nous ont envoyés.
   c. Les cadeaux que je t'ai montrés hier.
   d. Les cadeaux qui t'ont beaucoup plu.
4. a. Le restaurant que nos amis ont ouvert l'année dernière.
   b. Le restaurant qui a une ambiance alsacienne.
   c. Le restaurant qui a des nappes rouges.
   d. Le restaurant que beaucoup d'artistes fréquentent (que fréquentent beaucoup d'artistes).
5. a. Le sénateur que le peuple a élu l'année dernière.
   b. Le sénateur qui a promis de combattre l'inflation.
   c. Le sénateur qui est marié avec une journaliste.
   d. Le sénateur que les ouvriers appuient (qu'appuient les ouvriers).

D

1. Avec la fille à qui il pense tout le temps.
2. La lettre à laquelle j'ai répondu.
3. Le débat auquel nos copains ont pris part.
4. Des habitudes auxquelles il faut renoncer.
5. Avec l'homme à qui elle se fiait.
6. Les clients à qui nous avons téléphoné.
7. Les détails auxquels vous avez veillé.
8. Les méthodes auxquelles je crois.

E

1. à laquelle
2. à qui
3. auquel
4. à qui
5. qu'
6. auxquels
7. auxquelles
8. à laquelle
9. à laquelle
10. qui

F

1. La fille dont la mère est médecin.
2. L'ami dont l'oncle travaille au ministère.
3. Le sénateur dont le pays entier a écouté le discours.
4. Les ouvriers dont le syndicat compte entreprendre une grève.
5. Les étudiants dont on a publié le rapport.
6. Le professeur dont le cours est toujours plein.
7. L'infirmière dont tout le monde admire le travail.
8. La programmeuse dont les logiciels se vendent très bien.
9. Les voisins dont les enfants assistent à cette école.
10. Le groupe de rock dont tous les jeunes écoutent les chansons.

G

1. Notre guide nous a montré un paysage dont nous nous sommes émerveillés.
2. Nous avons visité les murailles dont la vieille ville est entourée.
3. Une amie nous a invités au festival de danse auquel elle prenait part.
4. Nous sommes allés voir une rue qu'on transformait en rue piétonne.
5. On est allés voir une comédie dont on a beaucoup ri.
6. Nous avons essayé la cuisine régionale dont la ville se vante.
7. On nous a signalé l'absence d'une université dont nous nous sommes aperçus.
8. C'est la vie universitaire dont la ville manquait.
9. Nous avions des amis dans la région à qui nous avons téléphoné.
10. Nous avons passé une belle journée avec eux dont nous nous souvenons encore.
11. La crise dont tout le monde avait peur est arrivée.
12. Un ministre faisait mal les fonctions dont il était responsable.
13. C'était un homme respecté dont personne ne se doutait.
14. Ce ministre est un homme bien en vue à qui la nation entière se fiait.
15. On dit qu'il a donné des emplois à des gens non qualifiés, dont plusieurs parents et amis (dont plusieurs étaient ses parents et ses amis).

16. Ils faisaient un travail dont on commençait à se plaindre.
17. Il y avait cent employés au ministère dont on a congédié une trentaine.
18. C'est la confiance de la nation dont le ministre a abusé.

H

1. The government took a step the consequences of which are regrettable.
2. The policemen made an effort the importance of which our team recognizes.
3. It's an economic crisis in consequence of which unemployment has increased.
4. People are waiting for a statement from the general under whose orders the army was fighting.
5. Our country is participating in an international effort whose success is predicted.
6. She had an illness following which she had to resign from her job.
7. They made a study of the conditions in which the underprivileged of our city are living.
8. We were attending the press conference during which the new plans for road construction were announced.

I

1. laquelle
2. avec lequel
3. auxquels
4. sur laquelle
5. avec lequel
6. sur lesquelles
7. lequel
8. dont (desquelles)

J

1. laquelle
2. laquelle
3. auxquels
4. lesquels
5. laquelle
6. laquelle
7. laquelle
8. duquel
9. lequel
10. qui
11. dont
12. desquelles

K

1. celui que
2. ce que
3. Ce qui
4. tout ce qu'
5. celle qu'
6. ce dont
7. ce qu'
8. ce dont
9. ce qui
10. ce que
11. ce qui
12. ce que

L

1. ce qu'
2. Ce qui
3. ce que
4. ce que
5. Ce qui
6. Ce dont
7. ce qui
8. ce que
9. ce dont
10. ce qui
11. ce que
12. ce dont

M

1. Élisabeth a un poste dont elle veut démissionner.
2. Il y a d'autres emplois sur lesquels elle essaie de se renseigner.
3. Elle manque de qualifications dont nous ne pouvons pas nous passer dans mon bureau.
4. Elle a téléphoné à d'autres entreprises dont je lui ai donné le nom.
5. Il y a des cours d'orientation auxquels elle assiste.
6. Il y a de nouveaux logiciels pour le bureau avec lesquels Élisabeth se familiarise.
7. Elle a déjà trouvé une entreprise pour laquelle elle voudrait travailler.
8. Je vais te montrer les choses dont j'ai besoin pour préparer mon petit déjeuner.
9. Voilà le réchaud sur lequel je fais mon café.
10. Voilà le bol dans lequel je bois mon café du matin.
11. Voilà la boulangerie dans laquelle (où) j'achète mes croissants et mon pain.
12. Voilà la porte de la boutique au-dessus de laquelle il y a une enseigne.

N

1. J'ai compris tout ce qu'ils ont dit.
2. Ceux qui sont venus en avance ont trouvé des places.
3. Voilà la gare près de laquelle elle travaille.
4. Voici le café devant lequel je l'ai vu.
5. C'est un livre sans lequel je ne peux pas finir mon travail.
6. Je ne vois pas le parc vers lequel nous allons.
7. Nous sommes allés à la ville où (dans laquelle) elle travaille.
8. Nous avons fait la connaissance du professeur dont notre ami avait parlé.
9. Ce dont il se souvient est un secret.
10. Ce à quoi il participe est intéressant.

24 The Present Subjunctive

A

1. Moi, je ne veux pas qu'il fasse du japonais.
2. Moi, je ne veux pas qu'elle laisse les fenêtres ouvertes.
3. Moi, je ne veux pas qu'il sorte avec Hélène.
4. Moi, je ne veux pas qu'il boive du vin.
5. Moi, je ne veux pas que tu voies un vieux film.
6. Moi, je ne veux pas qu'il sache mon adresse.
7. Moi, je ne veux pas qu'elle soit triste.
8. Moi, je ne veux pas qu'ils aient peur.
9. Moi, je ne veux pas qu'il maigrisse.
10. Moi, je ne veux pas que tu grossisses.

B

1. Je préfère que Marc choisisse le gâteau.
2. Il est nécessaire que Lise et Rachelle aillent chercher les boissons.
3. Il est important que Roland et Jacqueline puissent venir.
4. Je veux que Janine fasse les hors-d'œuvre.
5. Il faut que tu fasses quelques coups de fil.
6. Il est essentiel qu'Olivier vienne.
7. Je préfère que nous achetions des plats préparés chez le charcutier.
8. Je veux que tu viennes m'aider samedi après-midi.

C

1. Le professeur exige que nous visitions tous les monuments de Paris.
2. Barbara souhaite que nous commencions par la visite du Louvre.
3. Martin désire que le groupe fasse le tour de Paris en autocar.
4. Monique demande qu'on voie les Tuileries.
5. Georges recommande que nous allions à l'Arc de Triomphe.
6. Gustave suggère que nous montions à Montmartre.
7. Diane ordonne que tout le monde suive l'itinéraire.
8. Édouard aime mieux qu'on fasse une promenade à pied dans le Marais.
9. Renée veut que nous prenions le déjeuner.
10. Véronique ne veut pas que nous passions toute la journée à discuter.

D

1. Je désire que tout soit en règle.
2. Je ne veux pas que les enfants aient peur.
3. Nous ne voulons pas que cette famille vive mal.
4. Ses parents empêcheront qu'il boive trop de vin.
5. Je recommande qu'il sache les réponses.
6. Je demande qu'ils conduisent prudemment.
7. Ses parents aiment mieux qu'elle rejoigne son fiancé.
8. Ses parents ne permettent pas qu'elle sorte avec Jean-Philippe.

E

1. vas	6. mettiez
2. sommes	7. allions
3. viennes	8. visitions
4. accompagnent	9. passer
5. preniez	

F

Answers will vary.

G

1. Je suis contente qu'elles soient là.
2. Je suis contente qu'il vende sa bicyclette.
3. Je suis contente qu'ils partent en vacances.
4. Je suis contente qu'il nous attende.
5. Je suis contente qu'il ne désobéisse jamais.
6. Je suis contente que vous dîniez ensemble.
7. Je suis contente que nous complétions le programme cette année.
8. Je suis contente qu'il connaisse Odile.

H

1. Je suis ravi que tu comprennes tout.
2. Nous sommes furieux qu'ils ne veuillent pas nous aider.
3. Il m'étonne que le prof ne nous reconnaisse pas.
4. J'ai peur qu'il y ait eu un accident.
5. Elle est désolée que tu ne puisses pas venir.
6. Je suis content qu'elle mette le foulard que je lui ai offert.
7. Son professeur se plaint que Philippe n'apprenne pas beaucoup.
8. Je suis fâché que ces enfants se battent tout le temps.
9. Il est rare qu'un professeur perde son travail.
10. Il suffit que vous me le disiez.
11. Nous craignons qu'il ne se rende pas compte du problème.
12. Il est extraordinaire qu'elle sache conduire un camion.

I

Answers will vary. The subjunctive forms of the verbs are as follows.

1. augmente
2. soient
3. puisse
4. interdise
5. abolisse
6. fassent
7. perde
8. soit
9. écrive
10. lisions

J

1. Ma mère n'acceptera pas que je vive dans le désordre.
2. Il est essentiel que nous fassions le ménage.
3. Il faut que nous époussetions les meubles.
4. Je suis content(e) que Bernard et toi, vous récuriez les casseroles.
5. Il convient que toi et moi, nous balayions le parquet.
6. Il est possible que nous cirions le parquet aussi.
7. Lise et Émile, il vaut mieux que vous rangiez les livres dans les bibliothèques.
8. Je me réjouis que Philomène enlève les toiles d'araignée.

K

1. Il est bizarre que tu n'étudies pas pour les examens.
2. Ça m'étonne que tu n'aies aucune envie de travailler à la bibliothèque.
3. Il vaut mieux que tu écrives la dissertation de philosophie.
4. Il est utile que tu écoutes les enregistrements au laboratoire de langues.
5. Il est indispensable que tu prennes des notes dans la classe d'histoire.
6. Les profs seront fâchés que tu ne fasses pas tes devoirs.
7. Je regrette que tu ne lises plus le livre de biologie.
8. Je n'approuve pas que tu t'endormes dans la classe d'anglais.
9. Il n'est pas normal que tu fasses des dessins dans ton cahier dans la classe de maths.
10. Il est agaçant que tu perdes tes cahiers.

L

1. —Tu sais si notre professeur finira la leçon?
   —Je ne crois pas qu'il finisse la leçon.
2. —Tu sais si Ghislaine rompra avec son petit ami?
   —Je ne crois pas qu'elle rompe avec son petit ami.

3. —Tu sais si ton cousin reviendra cette semaine?
   —Je ne crois pas qu'il revienne (cette semaine).
4. —Tu sais si Nadine servira du pizza à la surboum?
   —Je ne crois pas qu'elle serve du pizza (à la surboum).
5. —Tu sais si Philippe sortira avec Mireille?
   —Je ne crois pas qu'il sorte avec Mireille.
6. —Tu sais si Paul pourra nous rejoindre?
   —Je ne crois pas qu'il puisse nous rejoindre.
7. —Tu sais si Alice sera ici ce soir?
   —Je ne crois pas qu'elle soit ici ce soir.
8. —Tu sais si toi et moi, nous étudierons assez?
   —Je ne crois pas que nous étudiions assez.
9. —Tu sais si Chloë ira au concert?
   —Je ne crois pas qu'elle aille au concert.
10. —Tu sais si Daniel prendra un taxi?
    —Je ne crois pas qu'il prenne un taxi.

M

1. Il n'est pas clair que Laurence réussisse à tous ses examens.
2. Il est douteux que nous offrions des disques compacts à Renée.
3. Il n'est pas exclu que tu suives un cours d'histoire.
4. Ça ne veut pas dire qu'il fasse des progrès en anglais.
5. Il est peu probable que Lucette t'écrive.
6. Je ne suis pas sûr qu'il nous connaisse.
7. Je doute que l'élève apprenne tout ça.
8. Je ne crois pas qu'elle descende faire des courses.
9. Il nie que son père vive très mal.
10. Il ne paraît pas que ce pays produise des voitures.

N

1. Je ne pense pas que la voiture de Jean-François soit toujours en panne.
2. Il est évident que Gisèle compte abandonner le lycée.
3. Je doute que Marc et Luc puissent s'acheter un ordinateur.
4. Tout le monde sait que Michèle sort avec Hervé Duclos.
5. Son frère nie que Paul ne fasse pas attention en classe.
6. Il n'est pas exact que Chantal se plaigne de tout.

7. Je suis sûr que Martin étudie beaucoup.
8. Il est peu probable qu'Éliane aille en France cette année.

O

1. J'ai peur que vous ne preniez un rhume.
2. Elle craint que nous ne soyons en colère.
3. Doutez-vous qu'il ne soit d'accord?
4. Elle empêche que nous ne finissions notre travail.

P

1. Qu'elles l'apprennent, alors.
2. Qu'il les rejoigne, alors.
3. Qu'elle le fasse, alors.
4. Qu'il le prenne, alors.
5. Qu'ils la vendent, alors.
6. Qu'elle nous le rende, alors.
7. Qu'il le traduise, alors.
8. Qu'il le finisse, alors.

Q

1. Nous voulons que tu viennes.
2. Qu'il me téléphone s'il veut me parler.
3. La mère permet que les enfants descendent seuls.
4. J'ai besoin que vous m'aidiez.
5. J'ai peur que l'enfant (n')ait de la fièvre.
6. Il est étonnant que ce pays produise tant de camions.
7. Il est peu probable qu'il fasse beau.
8. Il n'est pas vrai qu'elle soit médecin. Je suis sûr qu'elle est avocate.

25 The Past Subjunctive; Literary Subjunctives

A

1. a. Je crains qu'il ait pris une bronchite.
   b. Je doute qu'il soit allé voir le médecin.
2. a. J'ai peur que ma sœur (n')ait reçu une mauvaise note en français.
   b. Je ne crois pas qu'elle ait étudié pour l'examen.
   c. Je soupçonne qu'elle ait eu des ennuis avec son petit ami.
   d. Je n'approuve pas qu'elle ne nous ait pas montré son examen.
   e. Ma mère se plaint que Sylvie ne nous en ait pas parlé.
3. a. Je suis étonnée que mon père ait perdu son emploi.
   b. Il est possible qu'il en ait trouvé un autre.
   c. Il est peu probable qu'il l'ait déjà accepté.

4. a. Je suis furieuse que le prof d'histoire nous ait demandé (de rédiger) une dissertation de 15 pages.
   b. C'est une chance qu'il ne nous en ait pas demandé deux!

B

1. —Le prof est content que Jacquot ait répondu.
   —Ça ne veut pas dire qu'il ait compris.
   The teacher is happy that Jacquot answered.
   That doesn't mean that he understood.
2. —Je suis ravi qu'elle ait pu venir.
   —Mais il est agaçant que son mari ne soit pas venu avec elle.
   I'm delighted that she was able to come.
   But it's irritating that her husband didn't come with her.
3. —Colette se réjouit que son chef ait eu confiance en elle.
   —Il faut qu'elle ait été très capable.
   Colette is glad that her boss had confidence in her.
   She must have been very capable.
4. —Ma mère regrette que ma sœur n'ait pas mis son nouveau pull.
   —Il est curieux que ce pull n'ait pas plu à ta sœur.
   My mother is sorry that my sister didn't wear (put on) her new sweater.
   It's strange that your sister didn't like that sweater.
5. —Je suis surpris qu'Irène ne m'ait pas attendu.
   —Ça ne veut pas dire qu'elle soit sortie.
   I'm surprised that Irène didn't wait for me.
   That doesn't mean that she went out.

C

1. a. Je suis content(e)/heureux(-se) qu'ils partent.
   b. Je suis content(e)/heureux(-se) qu'ils soient partis.
2. a. Ce n'est pas qu'elle sorte.
   b. Ce n'est pas qu'elle soit sortie.
3. a. Je ne suis pas sûr(e) qu'elle suive un cours.
   b. Je ne suis pas sûr(e) qu'elle ait suivi un cours.
4. a. Je ne crois pas que le garçon lise le livre.
   b. Je ne crois pas que le garçon ait lu le livre.

5. a. Il est peu probable qu'ils soient en vacances.

b. Il est peu probable qu'ils aient été en vacances.

6. a. Nous sommes surpris (étonnés) que les enfants ne se battent pas.

b. Nous sommes surpris (étonnés) que les enfants ne se soient pas battus.

D

1. Je tenais à ce qu'il finisse son travail.
2. Il n'y a eu aucune chance qu'elle comprenne.
3. J'avais peur que l'enfant ne tombe.
4. Il valait mieux que le chef lise le compte rendu.
5. Il fallait travailler tous les jours, même si c'était un jour de fête.

E

1. Si l'armée française avait vaincu les Allemands en 1940, la France n'aurait pas été occupée.
2. Si cet écrivain n'était pas mort à l'âge de 30 ans, il aurait été un des grands romanciers de notre littérature.
3. Si les étrangers avaient parlé en français, nous aurions compris.
4. Si la ligne aérienne n'avait pas fait grève, ils seraient partis en vacances.
5. Si les soldats s'étaient approchés de cette maison, ils auraient été tués.

26 The Subjunctive (Continued)

A

1. Paul: J'attendrai jusqu'à ce que Marie-Claire m'appelle.
2. Philippe: J'attendrai jusqu'à ce qu'Yvette vienne.
3. Serge: J'attendrai jusqu'à ce que l'autobus arrive pour me ramener.
4. Luc: J'attendrai jusqu'à ce que Robert fasse un coup de fil.
5. Baudoin: J'attendrai jusqu'à ce que vous vous en alliez.
6. Maurice: J'attendrai jusqu'à ce que nous puissions vérifier où elles sont.
7. Daniel: J'attendrai jusqu'à ce que nous sachions quelque chose.
8. Richard: J'attendrai jusqu'à ce que ma petite amie apparaisse.

B

1. Oui. Hélène sortira avec Nicolas à moins qu'elle soit occupée.
2. Oui. Jocelyne partira en Italie à moins que son père lui défende d'y aller.
3. Oui. Christophe t'expliquera la leçon à moins qu'il ne fasse pas attention en classe.
4. Oui. Michel veut inviter tous ses amis chez lui à moins que ses parents reviennent.
5. Oui. On peut aller chez les Laurentin à moins qu'ils aient des choses à faire.
6. Oui. Il faudra partir sans Jacqueline à moins qu'elle puisse aller avec nous.
7. Oui. Nous pouvons faire un pique-nique demain à moins qu'il fasse mauvais.

C

1. À moins que Gérard ait vu le film.
2. À moins qu'on ait déjà fermé les magasins.
3. À moins qu'il ait oublié notre rendez-vous.
4. À moins que sa voiture soit tombée en panne.
5. A moins qu'il soit allé à la bibliothèque.
6. À moins qu'il l'ait perdu.
7. À moins qu'elle ne soit pas encore rentrée.

D

1. Oui, pourvu que tu prennes le dessert avec nous.
2. Oui, pourvu que tu sois de retour avant minuit.
3. Oui, pourvu que ton frère puisse t'accompagner.
4. Oui, pourvu que tu mettes de l'ordre dans ta chambre.
5. Oui, pourvu que tu fasses les courses avant.
6. Oui, pourvu qu'elle ne vienne pas avant quatre heures.
7. Oui, pourvu que ton père te permette.
8. Oui, pourvu que nous puissions aller avec toi.

E

1. Le médecin lui ordonne des antibiotiques pour qu'il se remette.
2. Sa mère a baissé les stores pour que François dorme.
3. Elle prépare une bonne soupe pour qu'il prenne quelque chose de chaud.
4. On lui donne trois couvertures pour qu'il n'ait pas froid.
5. Nous allons t'acheter un poste de télé pour que tu regardes des émissions en français.

6. On va te dessiner un petit plan du quartier pour que tu ne te perdes pas.

7. On te donne une carte avec notre numéro de téléphone pour que tu puisses nous appeler.

8. Nous allons inviter nos neveux et nos nièces pour que tu fasses leur connaissance.

F

1. Tu dois faire tes devoirs bien que tu sois fatigué.

2. Tu dois descendre faire les courses bien qu'il fasse mauvais.

3. Tu dois lire le livre de chimie bien que tu n'en aies pas envie.

4. Tu dois téléphoner à Renée bien que vous soyez brouillés.

5. Tu dois aller au cours bien que tu ne te sentes pas bien.

6. Tu dois mettre une cravate bien que tu aies chaud.

7. Tu dois écrire quelque chose bien que tu ne saches pas la réponse.

8. Tu dois finir ta rédaction bien qu'il soit tard.

G

1. Il entre doucement sans qu'on s'en aperçoive.

2. Cet étudiant copie sans que le professeur s'en rende compte.

3. Marc a eu des ennuis avec la police sans que ses parents soient au courant.

4. Il parle au téléphone sans que je puisse entendre ce qu'il dit.

5. Je te passerai un petit mot sans que le prof me voie.

6. Il est parti sans que nous le sachions.

7. Il est rentré sans que nous l'ayons vu.

8. Elle s'est fâchée sans que je lui aie rien dit.

H

1. Je ne passerai pas à la blanchisserie jusqu'à ce que Louise descende au marché.

2. Marc ira à la pâtisserie pour que nous prenions un bon dessert ce soir.

3. Claire ira au kiosque du coin pourvu que nous l'accompagnions.

4. Je vais vite au pressing de peur qu'ils (ne) ferment pour le déjeuner.

5. Nous attendrons Chantal à la station-service jusqu'à ce qu'elle fasse le plein.

6. Philippe attendra à la station-service jusqu'à ce que le mécanicien change l'huile.

7. Nous regarderons l'étalage de la librairie en attendant que Jean sorte de chez le coiffeur.

8. Odile veut passer à la droguerie à moins que vous (ne) soyez pressés pour rentrer.

I

Answers will vary.

J

1. Je leur téléphonerai (Je les appellerai) avant d'arriver à l'aéroport.

2. Nous regarderons le match de football jusqu'à ce qu'il commence à pleuvoir.

3. Mme Dulac a mis la table une heure avant que ses amis soient arrivés.

4. Ils ont fait la queue pour prendre des billets.

5. Vous ne vouliez pas aller au grand magasin sans que nous y allions aussi.

6. Bien qu'il fasse froid, nous devons faire une promenade.

7. Je te prêterai le livre à moins que tu l'aies déjà acheté.

8. Tu peux aller au cinéma pourvu que ton frère aille avec toi.

K

1. Toi, tu veux un appartement qui ait deux salles de bains.

2. Mathieu a besoin d'un appartement qui soit climatisé.

3. Philippe et moi, nous préférons un appartement qui soit près de la faculté.

4. Nous voulons un appartement qui n'ait pas besoin de beaucoup de rénovation.

5. Moi, je cherche un appartement qui ait le confort moderne.

6. Charles désire un appartement qui se trouve dans un immeuble neuf.

7. Mathieu et Philippe cherchent un appartement qui soit en face de l'arrêt d'autobus.

8. Nous cherchons un voisin qui ne se plaigne pas du bruit.

L

1. sache	5. ait
2. puisse	6. aime
3. comprenne	7. dise
4. soit	8. fasse

M

1. réussisse
2. soit
3. puisse
4. mente
5. ait
6. veuilles

N

1. sait
2. sache
3. connaisse
4. ait
5. puisse
6. soit
7. ont
8. soit

O

1. C'est la plus belle fille que je connaisse.
2. C'est le cours le plus ennuyeux que je suive.
3. C'est le compte rendu le plus intéressant que Marc écrive.
4. C'est le village le plus joli que vous visitiez.
5. C'est le premier patient qui vienne au cabinet du dentiste.
6. Vous êtes la seule étudiante qui fasse du chinois.
7. C'est la dernière employée qui s'en aille du bureau.
8. C'est le pire repas qu'on ait servi à la cantine.
9. C'est le meilleur restaurant que nous fréquentions.
10. C'est le plus beau tableau que tu aies peint.
11. C'est le loyer le plus élevé que j'aie payé.
12. Tu es le seul ami qui me comprenne.

P

Answers will vary.

Q

1. Whoever she may be, she doesn't have the right to go in.
2. However rich they may have become, they cannot forget the poverty of their youth.
3. However gifted you may be, you must study.
4. He expected to offer us anything (any old thing, anything at all).
5. I will never forgive him, no matter what he says.
6. This candidate accepts money from anyone.
7. Whatever the sum offered may be, it won't be enough.
8. Wherever you may go, you'll find the same difficulties.

V   **Idiomatic Usage**

27   The Passive Voice and Substitutes for the Passive

A

1. Les clients sont reçus par la réceptionniste.
2. Les commandes sont passées par les employés.
3. Un versement sur le compte de l'entreprise a été fait par la secrétaire.
4. Des marchandises ont été livrées par un camion.
5. Des échantillons ont été expédiés par le bureau.
6. Des chèques ont été signés par le patron.
7. Des factures ont été envoyées par la secrétaire.
8. Une demande d'emploi a été présentée par ce jeune homme.
9. Un nouveau produit va être lancé par l'entreprise.
10. Le marché va être étudié par des experts.

B

1. Les lits ont été montés par trois hommes.
2. Les tableaux ont été accrochés au mur par Pierre et sa sœur.
3. La machine à laver a été installée par un plombier.
4. Le fauteuil a été placé en face de la télé par M. Martel.
5. Les vêtements ont été accrochés dans la penderie par Mme Martel.
6. Deux grosses caisses en bois ont été laissées dans le sous-sol par les déménageurs.
7. La vaisselle a été rangée dans les placards par Mme Martel.
8. Les lampes ont été branchées par M. Martel.

C

1. Oui, la quiche va être préparée par Luc et Catherine.
2. Oui, les amis du lycée vont être invités par Marie.
3. Oui, le cassettophone va être apporté par Bernard.
4. Oui, les couverts vont être mis par Geneviève et Virginie.
5. Oui, le chocolat va être acheté par Suzanne.
6. Oui, le café va être fait par Antoine.

7. Oui, les cassettes vont être choisies par Anne et Danielle.

8. Oui, les amuse-gueules vont être servis par Eugène.

D

1. Les enfants doivent être protégés.
2. Les personnes âgées doivent être respectées.
3. La police doit être bien payée.
4. Le drapeau doit être honoré.
5. La loi doit être obéie.
6. Les professionnels doivent être bien formés.
7. Les musées doivent être subventionnés.
8. Les transports en commun doivent être modernisés.
9. Les petites entreprises doivent être encouragées.
10. Les jeunes doivent être embauchés.

E

1. On ne penche pas l'assiette pour finir sa soupe.
2. On tient toujours le couteau dans la main droite.
3. On tient toujours la fourchette dans la main gauche.
4. On n'essuie pas la sauce avec un morceau de pain.
5. On ne pose pas les coudes sur la table.
6. On pose les mains sur le bord de la table.
7. On ne coupe pas le pain avec le couteau.
8. On casse son morceau de pain.
9. On répond «Avec plaisir» pour accepter de reprendre un des plats.
10. On répond «Merci» pour ne pas accepter de reprendre un des plats.

F

1. On offre des amuses-gueules avec l'apéritif. / Des amuses-gueules s'offrent avec l'apéritif.
2. On coupe un fromage en cubes pour servir avec l'apéritif. / Un fromage se coupe en cubes pour servir avec l'apéritif.
3. On prépare une bonne soupe la veille. / Une bonne soupe se prépare la veille.
4. On débouche le vin au moins une heure avant de le servir. / Le vin se débouche au moins une heure avant de le servir.
5. On prépare ce plat une heure avant le repas. / Ce plat se prépare une heure avant le repas.
6. On sert cette viande froide. / Cette viande se sert froide.

7. On boit ce vin doux après le repas. / Ce vin doux se boit après le repas.
8. On sert des fruits comme dessert. / Des fruits se servent comme dessert.

G

1. Le base-ball ne se joue pas en France.
2. Les journaux américains se vendent partout.
3. Les bouquinistes se trouvent le long de la Seine.
4. Les films américains se projettent dans beaucoup de cinémas.
5. Les chansons américaines s'entendent à la radio.
6. Des festivals de théâtre se donnent en été.
7. Un marché volant s'installe deux fois par semaine dans ce quartier.
8. Les billets de métro peuvent s'acheter en carnets de dix.

H

1. Le verbe *monter* se conjugue avec *être* au passé composé.
2. Dans le mot *clef* le *f* final ne se prononce pas.
3. Le subjonctif s'utilise après *jusqu'à ce que*.
4. *Les rebuts* est un mot qui s'emploie au Canada.
5. *A silent film* se traduit en français par *un film muet*.
6. Les mots *amoral* et *immoral* se confondent souvent.
7. Le sujet se place devant le verbe dans les déclarations.
8. Le vocabulaire technique s'apprend sans difficulté.

28 Important Idioms and Proverbs

A

1. a	6. b
2. b	7. a
3. b	8. b
4. a	9. b
5. b	10. a

B

1. b	7. a
2. a	8. a
3. a	9. b
4. b	10. b
5. b	11. a
6. b	12. b

C

1. f
2. c
3. e
4. a
5. h
6. b
7. j
8. d

D

1. un voyage
2. la moue
3. tout petit
4. mal
5. son droit
6. du bricolage
7. les quatre cents coups
8. des idées (des illusions)

E

1. Il a pris sa retraite.
2. Il s'en prend à ses critiques.
3. C'est un parti pris.
4. Prends garde!
5. Tu peux me prendre un journal?
6. Le petit garçon m'a pris au pied de la lettre.
7. J'ai pris froid. (J'ai pris un rhume.)
8. L'enfant a pris du corps.
9. On a attrapé le voleur la main dans le sac.
10. J'ai été pris(e) de panique.
11. Il ne sait pas s'y prendre.
12. Il sort prendre le frais (prendre l'air).

F

1. mettre qqn à la porte
2. se mettre au lit
3. se mettre à genoux
4. mettre le feu à qqch
5. mettre au courant
6. se mettre à faire qqch
7. se mettre à table
8. se mettre en route
9. se mettre en quatre pour qqn
10. mettre qqn en quarantaine

G

1. se mettre à l'abri
2. mettre en valeur
3. met les bouts (met les voiles)
4. mis en service
5. te mettre aux maths
6. rien à me mettre
7. mis sur la voie
8. mettre en relief
9. se mettre en colère
10. Le temps se met au beau

H

1. b
2. b
3. a
4. b
5. b
6. a
7. a
8. b

I

1. Fais voir. (Faites voir.)
2. Il voit la vie en rose.
3. Je n'y vois goutte.
4. Je vous ferais voir trente-six chandelles.
5. Vous voyez d'ici le tableau!
6. Je n'y vois pas d'inconvénient.
7. On n'en voit pas la fin.
8. Il se voient en cachette.
9. Ils ne peuvent pas se voir (en peinture).
10. C'est quelque chose qui ne se voit pas tous les jours.

J

1. l
2. f
3. e
4. b
5. h
6. k
7. c
8. a
9. j
10. i
11. g
12. d

K

1. Ce raisonnement ne tient pas debout.
2. tient bon.
3. Tu me casses les pieds.
4. On vous demande au téléphone.
5. Il roule sur l'or.
6. Ils me donnent du fil à retordre.
7. Il a payé ses dettes.
8. Il a perdu le nord.
9. On va tirer au sort.
10. Donne-moi un coup de main.

L

1. a
2. a
3. b
4. a
5. b
6. b
7. a
8. b
9. a
10. a

M

1. Il est d'une humeur de chien.
2. Tu mets la charrue devant les bœufs.
3. Elle a des nids de poule.
4. Marc est dans les choux.
5. C'est un type qui ménage la chèvre et le chou.
6. Il n'y avait pas un chat.

7. Ce n'est pas fait pour les chiens.
8. Ils se regardent en chiens de faïence.
9. C'est chou vert et vert chou.
10. Ils s'entendent comme chien et chat.
11. Il arrive comme un chien dans un jeu de quilles.
12. Chat échaudé craint le feu.
13. Il est têtu comme une mule.
14. Je suis fauché(e) comme les blés.
15. On n'a pas gardé les cochons ensemble!
16. Tu as un chat dans la gorge.
17. Il faut appeler un chat un chat.
18. Il m'a traité comme un chien.
19. Elle fait l'âne pour avoir du son.
20. C'est bête comme chou.

N

1. b	6. b
2. a	7. a
3. a	8. a
4. b	9. b
5. a	10. b

O

1. par contre
2. de la peine perdue
3. selon le cas
4. tour à tour (à tour de rôle)
5. Motus!
6. être collant
7. Et pour cause!
8. une fois pour toutes
9. un coup monté
10. jusqu'ici

11. une mauvaise langue
12. à bout portant
13. À quoi bon?
14. Sans blague.
15. à fond
16. au lieu de
17. Défense d'entrer.
18. hors de soi
19. Mon œil!
20. en panne

P

1. o	9. a
2. p	10. f
3. n	11. r
4. g	12. e
5. m	13. l
6. t	14. d
7. b	15. q
8. j	16. i

Q

1. L'habit ne fait pas le moine.
2. Une hirondelle ne fait pas le printemps.
3. Une de perdue, dix de retrouvées.
4. Charbonnier est maître chez soi.
5. Les beaux esprits se rencontrent.
6. Pierre qui roule n'amasse pas mousse.
7. Plus on est de fous, plus on rit.
8. Santé passe richesse.
9. Paris ne s'est pas fait en un jour.
10. Aux grand maux, les grands remèdes.
11. Le chat parti, les souris dansent.
12. Il faut battre le fer pendant qu'il est chaud.

Index

About the Authors

David M. Stillman, Ph.D., is a well-known writer of foreign language textbooks, reference books, and instructional multimedia programs. He is president of Mediatheque Publishers Services, a leader in the development of foreign language instructional materials. He holds a Ph.D. in Spanish linguistics from the University of Illinois, and has taught and coordinated foreign language programs at Boston University, Harvard, and Cornell. He teaches languages and linguistics and coordinates an innovative program of student-led conversation practice at The College of New Jersey. He is a frequent presenter at national and regional conventions of language educators, has consulted on states' K-12 academic standards for world languages, and has been appointed to national committees devoted to the improvement of teacher training.

Ronni L. Gordon, Ph.D., is a prominent author of foreign language textbooks, reference books, and instructional multimedia programs. She is vice president of Mediatheque Publishers Services, a leader in the development of foreign language instructional materials. She holds a Ph.D. in Spanish language and Spanish and Spanish American literature from Rutgers University, and has taught and coordinated Spanish language programs and taught Spanish American literature at Harvard University and Boston University. An education consultant, she has read in foreign languages for the National Endowment for the Humanities, presented at the United States Department of Education, and consulted on states' K-12 academic standards for world languages. She is an associate scholar of a Philadelphia-based think tank and is chairman of the board of directors of the Dolce Suono Ensemble.